Ubiquitous Commerce for Creating the Personalized Marketplace:
Concepts for Next Generation Adoption

Humphry Hung
Hong Kong Polytechnic University, Hong Kong

Y. H. Wong
Hong Kong Polytechnic University, Hong Kong

Vincent Cho
Hong Kong Polytechnic University, Hong Kong

INFORMATION SCIENCE REFERENCE

Hershey • New York

Director of Editorial Content:	Kristin Klinger
Senior Managing Editor:	Jamie Snavely
Managing Editor:	Jeff Ash
Assistant Managing Editor:	Carole Coulson
Typesetter:	Sean Woznicki
Cover Design:	Lisa Tosheff
Printed at:	Yurchak Printing Inc.

Published in the United States of America by
Information Science Reference (an imprint of IGI Global)
701 E. Chocolate Avenue,
Hershey PA 17033
Tel: 717-533-8845
Fax: 717-533-8661
E-mail: cust@igi-global.com
Web site: http://www.igi-global.com/reference

and in the United Kingdom by
Information Science Reference (an imprint of IGI Global)
3 Henrietta Street
Covent Garden
London WC2E 8LU
Tel: 44 20 7240 0856
Fax: 44 20 7379 0609
Web site: http://www.eurospanbookstore.com

Library of Congress Cataloging-in-Publication Data

Ubiquitous commerce for creating the personalized marketplace : concepts for next generation adoption / Humphry Hung, Y.H. Wong, and Vincent Cho, editors.

   p. cm.

 Includes bibliographical references and index.

 Summary: "This book is a compendium of definitions and explanations of concepts and processes within u-commerce"--Provided by publisher.

 ISBN 978-1-60566-378-4 (hardcover) -- ISBN 978-1-60566-379-1 (ebook) 1. Electronic commerce. 2. Ubiquitous computing. I. Hung, Humphry, 1955- II. Wong, Y. H., 1953- III. Cho, Vincent, 1963-

 HF5548.32.U25 2009

 658.8'72--dc22

                        2008052198

British Cataloguing in Publication Data
A Cataloguing in Publication record for this book is available from the British Library.

All work contributed to this book is new, previously-unpublished material. The views expressed in this book are those of the authors, but not necessarily of the publisher.

Table of Contents

Detailed Table of Contents

Chapter I

Humphry Hung, Hong Kong Polytechnic University, Hong Kong
Vincent Cho, Hong Kong Polytechnic University, Hong Kong
Y. H. Wong, Hong Kong Polytechnic University, Hong Kong

The rapid growth of u-commerce, the new generation of e-commerce, together with the need for the adoption of new technologies, has necessitated the need for effective organizational changes to this challenging and eminent trend. The authors posit that firms should explore the consumers' perception of u-commerce and further exploit the strategic advantages of u-commerce with reference to their adoption of new u-commerce technologies. They propose a conceptual reference framework for helping organizations deal with this dynamic situation.

Chapter II

Giovanni Frattini, Atos Origin Italia S.p.A., Italy
Ivano De Furio, Atos Origin Italia S.p.A., Italy
Roberto Russo, Atos Origin Italia S.p.A., Italy
Luigi Romano, Atos Origin Italia S.p.A., Italy
Federico Ceccarini, Atos Origin Italia S.p.A., Italy

The authors will discuss on new methods and tools for building high personalized, virtual e-business services. A new service provisioning architecture based on Web services has been conceived, taking into account issues related to end-user mobility. The following pages deal with a proposal for creating real localized, personalized virtual environments using Web services and domain ontologies. In particular, to overcome interoperability issues that could arise from a lack of uniformity in service descriptions, they propose a way for controlling and enforcing annotation policies based on a Service Registration Authority. It allows services to be advertised according to guidelines and domain rules. Furthermore, this solution enables enhanced service/component discovery and validation, helping software engineers to build services by composing building blocks and provision/deliver a set of personalized services.

Chapter III
Planning for the Introduction of Mobile Applications to Support the Sales Force:
A Value-Based Approach 36
Chihab BenMoussa, Åbo Akademi University, Finland

Performance gains from SFA investments have often been obstructed by the sales force's unwillingness to accept and use available systems. Studies show that a strong reason for resistance by the sales force to the technology is the failure to convince salespeople of the advantages and benefits of the new technology. Consequently firms face the challenge of selecting SFA technologies that their sales force will perceive as valuable and accept to use to enhance its performance. This issue becomes more challenging when it comes to introducing emerging technologies such as mobile technologies, where there is a risk of falling into the trap of overestimating/underestimating their potential value. The present study proposes a value-based approach for planning the introduction of mobile applications to support the sales force. The approach suggested provides guidelines on how to determine whether or not mobile technologies would add value to the sales force before those technologies actually get selected and implemented. Good planning of SFA investment would help firms avoid resistance of the sales force towards the implemented systems, rather than having to treat it at the post-implementation stage.

Chapter IV
Virtual Economy and Consumer: How do Consumers Perceive and use Virtual Currency
in Web 2.0 Communities? 55
Dong Hee Shin, Towson University, USA & Sung Kyun Kwan University, South Korea

By expanding the technology acceptance model, this study analyzes the consumer purchasing behaviors with virtual currency in Web2.0 drawing data from 311 users. This study focuses on which variables influence the intention to transact with virtual currency in Web2.0. Individuals' responses to questions about attitude and intention to transact in Web2.0 were collected and combined with various factors modified from the technology acceptance model. The results of the proposed model show that subjective norm is a key behavioral antecedent to use virtual currency. In the extended model, subjective norm's moderating effects on the relations among the variables are found significant. The new set of variables can be virtual environment-specific factors, playing as enhancing factors to attitudes and behavioral intention in Web2.0 transactions. This study provides a more intensive view of Web2.0 system users and is an important step towards a better understanding of the consumer behavior in Web2.0.

Chapter V
U-Commerce in the Financial Marketspace 75
Alexander Y. Yap, Elon University, USA

The mission of this chapter is to investigate (1) how u-commerce is made available by online brokerage agents and the different interfaces they provide via mobile phone transactions, computer transactions, and/or land-line telephone transactions (either thru broker assisted transactions or interactive voice-response phone systems), (2) how the anytime anywhere demand and supply of financial knowledge and availability or non-availability of ubiquitous trading tools and systems affect the behavior of traders and investors in the financial market, and (3) to what extent ubiquity of information and systems tools are regulated in relation to stock trading, stock manipulation, and global volatility of financial markets.

The advancements in information and communication technology (ICT) have resulted in the new concepts being developed in this discipline. Ubiquitous and pervasive computing is among the number of other concepts provided by the ICT. Especially these concepts are providing scope for radical changes in business processes of organizations. It would become a necessity for integrating business with these concepts to face the new realities in business process in organizations. This chapter describes the historical background of commerce in electronic environment, the concepts related to context computing, ubiquitous computing and pervasive computing, and Grid computing. Further it explains the recent trends and also talks about the three business models with these concepts incorporated in three different contexts.

Group-buying (or volume discount) is a promising field in electronic commerce for applying software agent technologies. In a traditional group-buying mechanism, either a customer or the supplier calls up a sufficient number of buyers for a target item, and then coordinates the actions of all participants during the whole process. Most participants involved in a group-buying project are passive. Studies in this field were therefore focused on developing an effective mechanism so as to enhance the utility of every participant in a fair way. However, the utility of a customer can only be maximized if the customer can buy the item he/she personally needs at a possibly lowest price, not just an item recommended by another customer or the supplier that he/she is supposed to like. In other words, it would be more flexible if every customer can initiate a group-buying project of his/her own for the item he/she personally needs in a convenient way. As a result, there will be multiple group-buying projects for multiple target items at the same time. To this end, a software agent is developed in this study to make every customer easily reach the web page he/she browses for a target item for group-buying. The data of the item will be automatically extracted and uploaded onto a website which then informs every registered user of the group-buying project of this item. Requests for the same item will be combined, and there are always multiple target items on the website for group-buying at the same time. As a result, cross group-buying becomes possible. An experimental system is constructed in this study to demonstrate the applicability of the software agent. Its advantages and/or disadvantages are also discussed.

Ubiquitous computing will change the way people live with technology. At the same time it will also affect the way people access and use services. It is obvious that these new ubiquitous services have a lot of business potential. However, before this potential can be fully exploited, people need to understand the crucial factors behind creating commercially successful ubiquitous services. To do so, research is needed in three important areas. Firstly, the authors need to understand the basic nature of ubiquitous services, that is, their unique characteristics. Secondly, people need to know the needs of the customers in order to create value to them so that they will accept and use ubiquitous services. This can be done by involving users into the innovation process of ubiquitous services. And thirdly, people need to understand the value creating networks developing and commercializing the ubiquitous services as well as to find an appropriate business model for describing them. Value creation is impossible without a successful network business model which is yet to be found. Thus, the aim of this chapter is to describe, examine and give proposals for further research in these three important research fields which can be seen as the prerequisites for developing commercially successful ubiquitous services.

Chapter IX

Jon T.S. Quah, Nanyang Technological University, Singapore
V. Jain, Nanyang Technological University, Singapore

This chapter discusses a service oriented framework to realize proximity aware services for mobile devices. It describes the architecture at both client and server ends. Using the proposed framework we develop a prototype to realize a real world application. The chapter ends with a discussion on the framework and possible future enhancements.

Chapter X

Vincent Cho, Hong Kong Polytechnic University, Hong Kong
Humphry Hung, Hong Kong Polytechnic University, Hong Kong

In models to study technology acceptance, the empirically validated path from perceived ease of use (PEOU) to perceived usefulness (PU) is usually rationalized by the argument that the less effort it is required to use a technology, the more useful the technology is. This argument is rather generic to fully account for the relationship between PEOU and PU. In this study the authors examine the effects of the common antecedents of PEOU and PU on their relationship. The authors first extensively reviewed the literature to identify the common antecedents of PEOU and PU. We then conducted a survey of users' acceptance of some common e-learning forums such as ICQ, WebCT, and MSN. Based on variance analysis we found that user-interface design (UID) explains 43% of the relationship between PEOU and PU, and that learners consider UID very important in deciding whether to accept an e-learning forum for their learning and communication. This paper contributes to research by identifying the factors that account for the relationship between PEOU and PU, and provides e-learning developers with managerial insights on how to leverage UID for business success.

This chapter will review the studies on the data quality on the Internet and will propose some suggestions to improve existing Internet resources. The layout of this chapter is as follows. First, the definitions of data quality will be visited. Next, the author would like to review the reasons of poor data quality. Framework and assessment based on the past literature will be reviewed and finally some recommendations are highlighted.

Over the past decade, electronic commerce has expanded and has provided new ways of conducting businesses in a brand new environment. Lately u-commerce seems to be pioneering the field of electronic transactions. Where "u" stands for ubiquitous, unison, unique and universal, u-commerce offers the opportunity to users to conduct business everywhere and at any given moment in time. The simplicity of u-commerce transactions makes the issue of domain names more relevant than ever before. This chapter examines the procedural unfairness of the Uniform Domain Name Dispute Resolution Policy (UDRP) in an effort to demonstrate that the "regulatory" framework surrounding domain names does not respect their technological necessity.

Chapter XIII

Koreans envision a world in which anyone can access information and the tools to explore it anytime, anywhere. Korea has been one of the leaders in mobile industry and this chapter explores the past, the present, and the future of mobile technology and markets in Korea. Starting with background and a brief overview of the current situation, this chapter uses the CLIP framework to describe mobile services in Korea. The chapter concludes with a brief discussion of challenges and future strategies.

Chapter XIV

The growth and convergence of wireless telecommunications and ubiquitous networks has created a tremendous potential platform for providing business services. In consumer markets, mobile marketing is likely to be a key growth area. The immediacy, interactivity and mobility of wireless devices provide a novel platform for marketing. The personal and ubiquitous nature of devices means that interactivity can, ideally, be provided anytime and anywhere. However, as experience has shown, it is important to keep the consumer in mind. Mobile marketing permission and acceptance are core issues that marketers have yet to fully explain or resolve. This chapter provides direction in this area. After briefly discussing some background on mobile marketing, the chapter conceptualizes key characteristics for mobile marketing permission and acceptance. The chapter concludes with predictions on the future of mobile marketing and some core areas of further research.

Chapter XV

This chapter has the aim to point out an important functionality of a ubiquitous mobile system and more specifically its application in the learning domain. This functionality is the possibility to access the learning material from mobile devices, like PDAs (Personal Digital Assistants) during their offline periods and the technique to approach it, called hoarding. The chapter starts with the overview of a concrete mobile learning system – Mobile ELDIT, thus that to give a clear idea of when and how this problem appears and why it is important to pay attention to it. Later, a description of the development approaches for both general and concrete solutions are discussed, followed by more detailed description of the important hoarding steps.

Chapter XVI

The advancement of technologies to connect people and objects anywhere has provided many opportunities for enterprises. This chapter will review the different wireless networking technologies and mobile devices that have been developed, and discuss how they can help organizations better bridge the gap between their employees or customers and the information they need. The chapter will also discuss the promising application areas and human-computer interactions modes in the pervasive computing world, and propose a service-oriented architecture to better support such applications and interactions.

Chapter XVII

This chapter introduces the notion of trust as a means to establish security in mobile ubiquitous applications. It argues that trust is an essential requirement to enable security in open network environments. In particular in wireless ad hoc environments where there is no network topology. In such environments communication can only be achieved via routes that have to be trusted. In general it may be hard, or even impossible, to establish, recall and maintain trust relationships. It is therefore important to understand the limitations of such environments and to find mechanisms that may support trust either explicitly or implicitly. The author considers several models that can be used to enable trust in such environments, based on economic, insurance, information flow and evolutionary paradigms.

Chapter XVIII

Hanne Westh Nicolajsen, Technical University of Denmark, Denmark
Jørgen P. Bansler, Technical University of Denmark, Denmark

This chapter examines how people in organizations appropriate new computer-based media, that is, how they adopt, reconfigure and integrate advanced communication technologies such as groupware or desktop conferencing systems into their work practice. The chapter presents and analyses findings from an in-depth field study of the adoption and use of a Web-based groupware application – a "virtual workspace" – in a large multinational firm. The analysis focuses, in particular, on the fact that people in modern organizations have plenty of media at their disposal and often combines old and new media to accomplish their work tasks. Furthermore, it highlights the crucial role of organizational communication genres in shaping how people adopt and use new media. The authors argue that understanding and facilitating the process of appropriation is the key to the successful introduction of new media in organizations.

Preface

AN OVERVIEW OF THE UBIQUITOUS WORLD OF MARKETPLACE

The Internet has undoubtedly introduced a significant wave of changes. The increased electronic transmission capacity and technology is further paving a super-highway towards unrestricted communication networks. Another wave of change, heading towards a world of ubiquitous networks and universal devices, which will present a new perspective to time and space, is on its way. It is expected that the next-generation commerce will emerge from traditional commerce, e-commerce, m-commerce (mobile commerce), and eventually to ubiquitous commerce. This gives an excellent opportunity to empirically examine the issue of the marketplace of u-commerce as the focus of our book.

U-commerce (ubiquitous commerce) is the use of ubiquitous networks, including Internet, mobile phone and digital TV, to support personalized and uninterrupted communications and transactions between various types of users. It is a fusion of e-commerce, m-commerce (mobile commerce), and traditional over-the-counter retail business. U-commerce is a dynamic convergence of the physical and the digital, the interface of brick-and-mortar commerce with Web-based wireless and other next-generation technologies in ways that will create new levels of convenience and value for buyers and sellers, and it is considered to be substantially more advanced than PC-based e-commerce. In short, u-commerce is the creation of a marketplace that reaches individuals where they are, at using the devices that they want to use, with the networks doing the work without the user needing to modify or intervene.

One of the most interesting and challenging issues in u-commerce is that this is a world-wide phenomenon. Because of the need to standardize the application, inter-phase, and inter-connectivity of all hardware and software relevant to the adoption and usage of u-commerce, the study of the adoption of u-commerce can have extended and universal implications for the practice of u-commerce in other places of the world.

This book is one of the first of its kind to set out to reveal the factors contributing to the supply, adoption and prospect of u-commerce. We have contributions from academics and professionals from all over the world. The book is designed to be an accessible document incorporating the elements of business decisions of firms and individuals involved in u-commerce. Our book will be of interest to marketers currently involved in e-commerce and m-commerce, and also to academics in the fields of marketing and IT. Both are keen to determine how they can perform further relevant research and position themselves well in the next generation of u-commerce. Last but not least, it is also a useful resource to guide students, scholars and researchers in relevant studies in this approaching ubiquitous business world.

The first chapter by Hung et al sets the path for a study of u-commerce by constructing a model of its related new technologies. This important introductory chapter argues that firms should explore the consumers' perception of u-commerce and further exploit the strategic advantages of u-commerce with reference to their adoption of new u-commerce technologies and proposes a conceptual reference framework for helping organizations deal with this dynamic situation. The practical aspect of the first chapter is further extended in second chapter by Frattini et al., which discusses the concept of new virtual home environment with reference to service-level roaming. They present a proposal for creating real localized, personalized virtual environments using web services and domain ontologies and in order to overcome interoperability issues that could arise from a lack of uniformity in service descriptions, they also identify a way for controlling and enforcing annotation policies based on the Service Registration Authority which allows services to be advertised according to guidelines and domain rules.

The introduction of mobile applications to support the sales force is discussed in great depth in Ben-Moussa's chapter. Many managers have observed that the resistance by the sales force to the technology may be attributable to the failure to convince salespeople of the advantages and benefits of the new technology. The chapter thus proposes a value-based approach for planning the introduction of mobile applications to support the sales force and good planning can help firms avoid resistance of the sales force towards the implemented systems, rather than having to treat it with much more difficulties at the post-implementation stage. Dong's chapter on purchasing behaviors in virtual economy focuses on the antecedent factors that will influence the intention to transact with virtual currency in Web2.0. The author observes that a new set of virtual environment-specific factors are playing as enhancing factors to attitudes and behavioral intention in Web2.0 transactions. A more intensive view of Web2.0 system users, as an important step towards a better understanding of the consumer behavior in Web2.0, can thus be developed.

In Yap's chapter on U-commerce in the financial marketplace, the author presents how u-commerce is made available by online brokerage agents and the different interfaces they provide via various types of transactions, and how the ubiquitous demand and supply of financial knowledge and availability of trading tools and systems affect the behavior of traders and investors in the financial market. Last but not least, the author also explores how information and systems tools are regulated in relation to stock trading, stock manipulation, and global volatility of financial markets. In his chapter on related software for u-commerce, Rao presents the history of commerce in electronic environment, the concepts related to context computing, ubiquitous computing and pervasive computing, and grid computing. The recent trends and discussion about business models in relation to these concepts incorporated in various different contexts are also discussed.

The issue of multiple group-buying projects for multiple target items at the same time is analyzed in the chapter on the development of a software agent by Chen et al. It is suggested that it will be more flexible if every customer can initiate a group-buying project of his/her own for the item he/she personally needs in a convenient way and as such, a software agent is developed in this study to make every customer easily reach the Web page he/she browses for a target item for group-buying. An experimental system is constructed in this study to demonstrate the applicability of the software agent. Its advantages and/or disadvantages are also discussed. How research can help to create successful ubiquitous services is discussed in the chapter written by Palo et al. The authors examine and suggest proposals for further research in three important research fields, which are the basic nature of ubiquitous services, the needs of the customers, and the value creating networks developing and commercializing the ubiquitous services. These fields can be seen as the prerequisites for developing commercially successful ubiquitous services.

A framework for proximity aware mobile services is developed in the chapter by Quah and Jain. It describes the architecture at both client and server ends. Using the proposed framework, the authors develop a prototype to realize a real world application. The chapter by Cho and Hung examines the effects of the common antecedents of perceived ease of use (PEOU) and perceived usefulness (PU) on their mutual relationship. They conducted a survey of users' acceptance of some common e-learning forums such as ICQ, WebCT, and MSN and observe that user-interface design (UID) explains 43% of the relationship between PEOU and PU, and that learners consider UID very important in deciding whether to accept an e-learning forum for their learning and communication.

Data quality on the Internet is getting more important as it is key resource for planning, producing, and communicating in the new millennium. The chapter by Cho provides an overall assessment and monitoring of data quality on the Internet, which would help individuals or organizations utilize high quality Internet resources for the decision making. From a legal perspective, Komaitis's chapter on procedural fairness on the Internet discusses the disputes concerning the conflicting rights of trade mark owners and domain name holders are regulated under the umbrella of the Internet Corporation's for Assigned Names and Numbers (ICANN) Uniform Domain Name Dispute Resolution Policy (UDRP). The last few chapters by Bang and Choi, Baarnes et al., Fronova, Zhang, Burmester, and Little et al., all provide some excellent illustrations of the exciting and growing world of ubiquitous commerce.

To conclude, in a rapidly changing world, the implications of the creation of personalized marketplace of ubiquitous commerce are important concerns for both the academic and business worlds. This book contains the latest thinking garnered from some of the most thoughtful scholars and researchers in many different countries. I have personally learned much from the authors featured in this book, much about the ubiquitous marketplace which is up to date and of direct relevance to my research in u-commerce. I hope this book can benefit all readers in the same way as it benefits me.

Humphry Hung
Hong Kong Polytechnic University, Hong Kong

Y. H. Wong
Hong Kong Polytechnic University, Hong Kong

Vincent Cho
Hong Kong Polytechnic University, Hong Kong

Chapter I
Constructing a Model of the Adoption of New Technologies of U–Commerce

Humphry Hung
Hong Kong Polytechnic University, Hong Kong

Vincent Cho
Hong Kong Polytechnic University, Hong Kong

Y. H. Wong
Hong Kong Polytechnic University, Hong Kong

ABSTRACT

The rapid growth of u-commerce, the new generation of e-commerce, together with the need for the adoption of new technologies, has necessitated the need for effective organizational changes to this challenging and eminent trend. The authors posit that firms should explore the consumers' perception of u-commerce and further exploit the strategic advantages of u-commerce with reference to their adoption of new u-commerce technologies. They propose a conceptual reference framework for helping organizations deal with this dynamic situation.

INTRODUCTION

The emergence of ubiquitous commerce, or u-commerce, is considered to be a major revolutionary paradigm shift in the next-generation mode of e-business, which will be of significant interests to both academics and managers.

U-commerce (ubiquitous commerce, or sometimes known as ultimate commerce) is the use of ubiquitous networks to support personalized and uninterrupted communications and transactions between various types of users (Viswanathan, 2000; Fram, 2002; Watson et al, 2002). U-commerce is considered to be substantially more advanced than PC-based e-commerce (Watson et al, 2002). As such, u-commerce is believed to have more competitive advantages and growth potential than e-commerce and is expected to replace completely e-commerce eventually (Gallaugher, 2002; Galanxhi-Janaqi & Nah, 2004).

In this chapter, we intend to analyze the implications and acceptability of new technologies in relation to u-commerce based primarily on the dimensions of six U's, namely, ubiquity, universality, ultra-yield, ultimacy, usefulness, and uniformity (Davis et al., 1989; Junglas & Watson, 2003; Galanxhi-Janaqi & Nah, 2004). We plan to investigate the implications of the users' perception of u-commerce and we further exploit the strategic advantages of u-commerce with reference to the adoption of new technologies by organizations.

We intend to provide a conceptual framework for exploring the following:

1. The adoption of new technologies related to u-commerce by potential buyers in u-commerce.
2. The adoption of new technologies related to u-commerce by organizations.
3. The possible competitive advantages and potential benefits of the adoption of new technologies by organizations in relation to their company performance.

Because of the ubiquitous nature of u-commerce, the study of the adoption of new technologies of u-commerce can have extended and universal implications to practically most of places of the world. Our proposed framework can make significant contributions to a more in-depth understanding in the spread and acceptability of u-commerce through knowing how relevant new technologies are adopted.

PRIMARY TARGET OF ANALYSIS

Our proposed conceptual framework is about the adoption of new technologies in relation to u-commerce, the new generation of e-commerce, based on ubiquitous networks. We incorporate the approach of ambidexterity by combining the perspectives of both exploration and exploitation. Exploration is about the experimentation with new, distant and sometimes uncertain alternatives, while exploitation is about the refinement and extension of existing competencies, approaches, methodologies and paradigms exhibiting potentially attractive, positive, predictable and proximate returns (March, 1991: Lumpkin & Dess, 1996; O'Reilly & Tushman, 2004; Birkinshaw & Gibson, 2004; Gibson & Birkinshaw, 2004).

In the proposed framework, we are exploring new concepts, new insights and new buying behavior in the ubiquitous world of u-commerce with reference to both the demand and supply sides of u-commerce, which we believe, are still not fully understood by most marketers and scholars (cf.: Stevens & McElhill, 2000; Struss et al., 2003,). The implications of our model will be of interest to practitioners in u-commerce and also academics in organizational theories, marketing and IT fields, who are keen to know how they can perform further relevant research and position well themselves in the next generation u-commerce.

TERMINOLOGY

Since we intend to explore new ground, we need to introduce and explain some new terms. U-commerce, or ubiquitous commerce, is defined as the use of ubiquitous networks to support personalized and uninterrupted communications and transactions between a firm and its various stakeholders, including customers, to provide a level of value over and above other types of traditional commerce (Viswanathan, 2000; Fram,

2002; Watson et al, 2002). Ubiquitous networks are connections that allow users to link up to networks at any time from anywhere to acquire and exchange information freely (Gallaugher, 2002). M-commerce or mobile commerce is the second generation e-commerce by making use of the wireless communication technology. Customers who purchase through e-commerce and u-commerce are called e-shoppers and u-shoppers respectively. All devices, including hardware, software, web sites and telecommunication technologies, that will be used for as well as facilitate the operations of u-commerce, will be called u-devices.

KEY ISSUE AND POSSIBLE OUTCOME: RELEVANCE, SIGNIFICANCE AND VALUE

One of the most interesting and challenging issues in u-commerce is that: this is not just a potential trend in any particular cities, countries or continents, but a world-wide phenomenon. Because of the need of the standardization of the application, inter-phase and inter-connectivity of all hardware and software relevant to the adoption and usage of u-commerce, the study of the adoption of new technologies of u-commerce can have extended and universal implications to the practices of u-commerce in most places of the world. Our study on the adoption of new technologies of u-commerce, being a world-wide phenomenon, therefore, can have some important, universal and global applicability.

In this proposed framework, we intend to use technology acceptance models (both TAM and TAM2) and options model as our basic framework of studying u-commerce. We contribute to literature by exploring and identifying the various options, or independent variables, which will affect the decision of buyers to adopt new technologies related to u-commerce. We propose six constructs: ubiquity, universality, ultra-yield, ultimacy,

usefulness and uniformity, for incorporating into the dimensions of potential participation in u-commerce (Watsons et al, 2002). We consider these constructs are relevant to the decision of u-shoppers in adopting new u-commerce technologies and we plan to investigate the extent of influence each of these constructs and dimensions can have on the adoption decision.

Furthermore, we intend to look into the relationship between adoption of new technologies and company performance of suppliers of devices related to u-commerce. We also design a reference structure to further investigate whether a company with above average (or below average) performance in the IT industry will be more (or less) inclined to adopt new u-commerce technology. We also explore and look into the possible impact of some moderating factors such as peer group pressure, demographics, and price in the adoption of new u-commerce technologies.

THEORETICAL MODELS FOR THE ADOPTION OF NEW TECHNOLOGY

The emergence of u-commerce requires relevant new technologies. Empirical observation suggests that there is typically a substantial lag between the discovery of a new technology and its adoption (Doraszelski, 2004). Earlier literature on delayed technology adoption has stressed the role of sunk costs in existing technology (Salter, 1966) or in complementary technologies (Frankel, 1955). More recent models associate diffusion lags of new technologies with the reduction of complementary costs such as specific human capital (Chari and Hopenhayn, 1990), learning-by-doing (Parente, 1994; Jovanovic & Lach, 1989), and search costs (Jovanovic & MacDonald, 1994). Other behaviour-based models, such as information cascades theory of new technology adoption, suggests that an individual who adopts new technologies may be contrary to his or her private preference based on the actions of others (Bikhchandi et al. 1992). This isomorphic behaviour is closely related to group pressure.

Two models about the adoption of new technology are of interest to our study: options model and technology acceptance model. Options model demonstrates that a new technology with moderate expected improvement in performance can experience substantial adoption delays and price distortions even in a competitive market (Bessen, 1999; Sheasley, 2000). Rather than adopting a new technology that demonstrates only marginal improvement, consumers have the options of not adopting until the new technology, in terms of performance, is substantially better than the old technology. Consumers contemplating the adoption of a new technology are, of course, aware of the possibility of sequential improvement. They consider not only the current technical level of the new technology, but also their expectations of possible upgrading and changes in future of the new technology (Gort & Klepper, 1982; Sheasley, 2000).

Technology acceptance model (TAM) is an information systems theory that models how users come to accept and use a new technology, with reference to two major considerations, perceived usefulness and perceived ease of use (Bagozzi et al., 1992; Davis et al., 1989). The former is about the degree to which a person believes that using a particular system would make his or her life easier e.g. enhance his or her job performance or reduce the workload, while the latter is the degree to which a person believes that it is not difficult to actually use a particular system (Davis et al., 1989). Later an extended version of the TAM model, referred to as TAM2, has been developed to explain perceived usefulness and usage intentions in terms of social influence and cognitive instrumental processes (Venkatesh and Davis, 2000).

SIX U'S OF THE ADOPTION OF NEW TECHNOLOGIES FOR U-COMMERCE

Based on literature review, we identify six dimensions or constructs relevant to consumers' preference for the adoption of new technologies related to u-commerce. These constructs are ubiquity, universality, ultra-yield, ultimacy, usefulness and uniformity.

First, we refer to the observations of Watsons and his colleagues (2002) and Galanxhi-Janaqi and Nah (2004) who identified four constructs which form the fundamental dimensions of the preference of u-commerce by consumers: ubiquity, uniqueness, universality, and unison. Ubiquity is the possibility of allowing users to access networks from anywhere and at any time. Uniqueness allows users to be uniquely identified, in terms of their identity and preferences. Universality means mobile devices are universally usable and multifunctional. Unison covers the idea of integrated data across multiple applications so that users have a consistent view on their information, irrespective of the devices to be used. However, these 4 U's are relevant to the general nature of u-commerce but not to the specific issue of adoption of new technology in the unique context of ubiquitous networks in relation to the acceptance and applications of u-commerce by consumers. We feel that we need some more relevant measures of the acceptability of new technologies to the potential users.

Out of the four U's identified by Watsons et al (2002), we think that ubiquity and universality are more applicable to the adoption of new technologies because they describe the major features of u-commerce in terms of the extent of the new technologies in helping the enhancement of embeddedness of networks. However, uniqueness and unison are considered to be more related to the identification of users and consistency of information in the process of u-commerce, which are somehow relevant to the data privacy rather than the network embeddedness and the extent of the adoption of new technologies. Since these two constructs are more relevant to the general characteristics of u-commerce but not to specific issues such as the adoption of new technology in u-commerce, we need some more applicable constructs.

With regards to the options model, we identify two U's, ultra-yield and ultimacy. Ultra-yield is about the degree to which a buyer believes that the new technology can provide significant improvement. Ultimacy is the perception of users that the current new technology will be the ultimate one and it is unlikely that there will be significant subsequent improvement. With reference to TAM, we add two more U's, usefulness and uniformity, for relating the acceptability of new u-commerce technologies to users. Usefulness is related to the perceived value in the adoption of new technologies and uniformity is the degree to which a person can make the best use of the new technologies with appropriate recognition by his/her peer groups (Bessen, 1999; Venkatesh & Davis, 2000). Figure 1 is a graphical representation of our model of six U's.

COMPETITIVE ADVANTAGES OF U-COMMERCE

U-commerce is an inevitable trend that can enable as well as enhance the following competitive advantages for suppliers of u-devices in u-commerce. Based on the suggestions of Galanxhi-Janaqi and Nah (2004), we identify four possible competitive advantages of organizations involved in u-commerce:

1. U-commerce will increase employee productivity and operating efficiency by providing real-time information sharing and giving remote workers the ability to remain in continuous contact with central databases.
2. U-commerce can extend the reach of low-cost electronic channels beyond the PC, to the telephone, television and other personal devices, which can effectively enhance customer services.
3. By allowing services to be tailored to the individual user's needs and location, u-commerce will increase the personalization of services.
4. U-commerce can enable continuous supply chain connectivity between suppliers, vendors and customers in making operating processes more efficient, improving productivity and enhancing security.

Figure 1. The six U's of the adoption of new u-commerce technologies

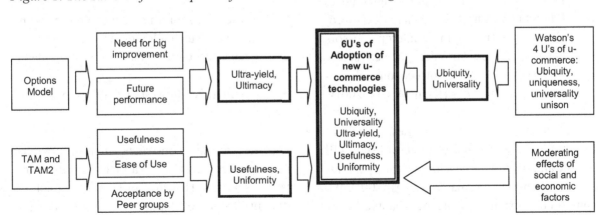

NEW TECHNOLOGIES FOR U-COMMERCE

PC-based e-commerce is now often referred to as traditional e-commerce (Zwass, 1996). New forms of data processing and communication technologies and devices are emerging and can form the basis for next-generation u-commerce (Junglas & Watson, 2003). We identify four possible new technologies that are considered to be closely related to u-commerce (Junglas & Watson, 2003). They are:

1. Wireless technology can combine effectively with mobile phones, personal computers and other hand-held devices.
2. New voice recognition and radio frequency technology, including automated speech-recognition, radio frequency identification (RFID), text-to-speech and voice-identification technologies, can provide a low-cost interface to electronic channels for efficient identification and recognition of information.
3. New digital TV technology can cater for interactivity and can allow the penetration of e-commerce, and later u-commerce, into general households.
4. Microprocessor technology can have the ability to track and monitor products and pieces of equipment, as well as to increase the level of automation in the manufacturing processes. The major breakthrough is not in the technology itself, but rather in the affordability of attaching these microprocessors and tags to everyday objects, which rapidly increases the number of economically attractive applications (Kiang & Chi, 2001).

Based on these new technologies, we believe that the new business environment so created will initiate and sustain the development and penetration of u-commerce (Jallat, & Capek, 2001). We consider the current computer merchants are very likely to be the potential suppliers of these new u-devices by adopting these new technologies. We also link the preference of adoption of new technologies to the company performance of u-devices suppliers.

THEORETICAL MODEL

We plan to explore the underlying principles of the adoption of new u-commerce technologies by identifying the primary factors of considerations by consumers (B2C) and organizations (B2B). We also exploit the possible competitive advantages and potential benefits of the adoption of new technologies of organizations in relation to their company performance. We further posit that for organizations, perceived competitive advantages should have a positive effect on the adoption of new u-commerce technologies, which is considered to have an enhancing effect on company performance. As for u-shoppers, both dimensions and perceived competitive advantages should have a positive effect on the adoption of new u-commerce technologies.

Based on the review and analysis in the previous section, we develop a model which indicates the key relationships among the variables that may affect the adoption of new technologies of u-commerce.

In our proposed model, we identify three sets of constructs as independent variables:

1. Dimensions of the adoption of new u-commerce technologies (U)
2. Choices of new technologies for u-commerce (C)
3. Competitive advantages of u-commerce (A)

There are six constructs, namely ubiquity (U1), universality (U2), ultra-yield (U3), ultimacy (U4), usefulness (U5) and uniformity (U6) of the dimensions of the adoption of new u-commerce

Figure 2. A model of the adoption of new technologies of u-commerce by organizations

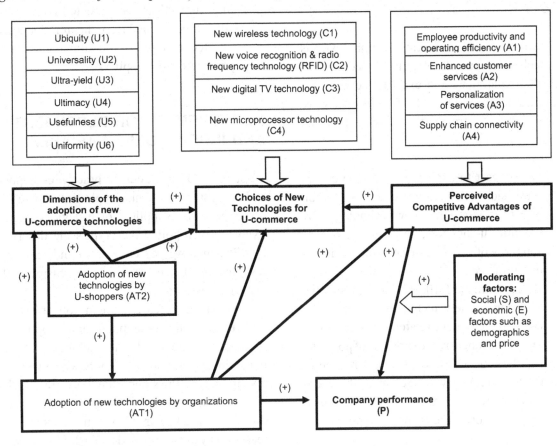

technologies, which we posit, will have a positive relationship with the four constructs of the types of new technologies (i.e. technologies related to new wireless (C1), new voice recognition and radio frequency (C2), new digital TV (C3) and new microprocessor (C4)). These constructs of new technologies will also have a positive relationship with the competitive advantages of u-commerce to organizations (employee productivity and operating efficiency (A1), enhanced customer service (A2), personalization of services (A3) and supply chain connectivity (A4)), which are independent variables.

We also relate these various types of constructs to company performance and we further suggest that the relationship is moderated by some social and economic factors such as demographics and

market prices. We further identify the following dependent variables:

1. Adoption of new technologies by organizations (AT1)
2. Adoption of new technologies by u-shoppers (AT2)

In our model, we relate the first dependent variable (AT1) to all the three independent variables (U1 to U6, C1 to C4, A1 to A4) and we posit that there will be some positive relationship among them. We also relate the second dependent variable (AT2) to two sets of independent variables (U1 to U6, C1 to C4) and again we posit that there will be positive relationships.

IMPLICATIONS FOR FURTHER RESEARCH

Since we recommend adopting an ambidextrous approach of research development by combining both the exploratory and exploitative perspectives (Lumpkin & Dess, 1996; Birkinshaw & Gibson, 2004), we propose the following research framework:

1. We suggest to explore how the perceived dimensions of u-commerce, the six U's, can affect the adoption of new technologies by potential u-shoppers, as well as those by suppliers of u-devices (the demand side of u-commerce).
2. We recommend further exploiting how the adoption of new technologies related to u-commerce can be related to the enhancement of competitive advantages of potential suppliers of u-devices (the supply side of u-commerce) and we also compare this adoption preference to the existing and expected future performance of these suppliers.

POSSIBLE RESEARCH TOOLS AND METHODOLOGY

We suggest that the research tools for studying the adoption of new u-commerce technologies can base on the following:

1. A minimum of two sets of questionnaire-based surveys targeting at the current IT merchants (potential suppliers of u-devices) and currently active e-shoppers (potential u-shoppers) respectively, about the benefits brought along by adopting the new technologies of u-commerce, from the perspective of users.
2. Another set of questionnaire, coupled with follow-up interviews, can be sent to sample IT merchants, requesting them to disclose

the current performance of their companies, as well as the expected competitive advantages gained from the introduction of new technologies of u-commerce, from the perspective of suppliers.

MEASUREMENT OF DEPENDENT AND INDEPENDENT VARIABLES

We suggest taking the currently active e-shoppers and computer merchants, as proxies of potential u-shoppers and suppliers of u-devices respectively. A seven-point Likert type scale, described by "Strongly Agree" (= 5 or 7) and "Strongly disagree" (=1), will be used in measuring the various constructs.

First of all, researchers can collect data on whether potential u-shoppers and suppliers of u-devices will consider the adoption of new technologies based on a medium term view (3 to 5 years) and at the same time, they are asked to provide response from a long term view (more than 5 years). They are also requested to provide reasons why they adopt or do not adopt, in terms of timing, irrelevant opportunities, changing trends and applications.

Researchers can then collect data on the significance of the dimensions of u-commerce by asking potential u-shoppers, as well as potential suppliers of u-devices, to express their views on the relations between each of the dimensions of u-commerce (i.e. ubiquity, universality, upgrading, undertaking, usefulness, and uniformity, which are independent variables) and the adoption of each of the four identified new technologies for u-commerce (i.e. technologies related to new wireless, new voice recognition, new digital TV and new microprocessor, which are independent variables). Respondents are required to give their views on these variables, with reference both to medium term and long term.

Researchers can measure 6 U's for the six dimensions of u-commerce. First, ubiquity can be measured by the perception of the need of access to ubiquitous networks. Universality can be measured by the usability and perceived functions of the new u-devices. Ultra-yield can be measured by the perception of users regarding the extent that the new technologies can provide significant improvement. Ultimacy can be measured by the perception of users about the extent to which the current new technologies can be further upgraded. Usefulness can be measured by the effectiveness and efficiency of the applicability of u-commerce. Last but not least, uniformity can be measured by the extent of recognition by peer groups in adopting the new technologies of u-commerce (Watsons et al, 2002; Galanxhi-Janaqi and Nah, 2004; Bessen, 1999); Venkatesh and Davis, 2000).

Researchers can collect data of the perceived competitive advantages of u-commerce by the suppliers of u-devices (expressed in terms of four perceived constructs, namely, employee productivity and operating efficiency (A1), enhanced customer service (A2), personalization of services (A3) and supply chain connectivity (A4), which are independent variables), and relate each of them to the adoption of each of the four identified choice of new technologies for u-commerce (i.e. technologies related to new wireless (C1), new voice recognition and radio frequency (C2), new digital TV (C3) and new microprocessor (C4)). They can also collect information about the financial performance (P) (e.g. ROI) of these suppliers, and their perceived company growth in respect of both the medium and long term perspectives.

Researchers can measure some important control or moderating variables, such as price (E) (expressed in terms of a five or seven-point Likert scale from (5 or 7) very expensive to (1) not expensive), male and female potential u-shoppers and their education levels as well as occupations, nature of businesses of u-devices suppliers, and last but not least, social influence by peer groups (S) (to see the moderating effects as suggest by information cascades theory).

CONCLUSION AND CONTRIBUTION TO LITERATURE

We adopt an ambidextrous approach because on the demand side of u-commerce, we consider it is useful to explore how the perceived dimensions of u-commerce (i.e. ubiquity, universality, upgrading, undertaking, usefulness, and uniformity) by organizations and u-shoppers can affect their adoption of new technologies in relation to u-commerce (i.e. technologies related to new wireless, new voice recognition and radio frequency, new digital TV and new microprocessor). On the supply side, we plan to exploit the competitive advantages of the adoption of new technologies related to u-commerce can be enhanced with reference to of employee productivity and operating efficiency, enhanced customer service, personalization of services and supply chain connectivity.

We contribute to literature by identifying the relative importance of six dimensions of u-commerce, the six U's. We make use of the relative applicability of options model and TAM in the context of U-commerce and we develop relevant constructs for the development of our proposed model, based on these two models. We further contribute by relating the adoption of new technologies to the potential company performance of suppliers in u-commerce.

Our proposed conceptual framework represents a theory-driven examination of the organizational response to the adoption of new technologies. The powerful tool of u-commerce can allow for faster and easier response to market demand. A good example can be seen in the case of Johnson & Johnson. Since 2004, the banner ads for Johnson &Johnson's Tylenol headache reliever unfurl on e-brokers' web sites whenever the stock market falls by more than 100 points (Birkinshaw & Gibson, 2004).

We expect that our framework can provide important implications about the significance of new technologies, both from the perspectives of u-shoppers (buyer) and suppliers of u-devices (seller). We foresee that our model can contribute to literature by ascertaining the most significant variables, among all those key variables that we have identified based on our literature review, that can determine which and how new technologies are likely to be adopted in the next generation u-commerce.

ACKNOWLEDGMENT

This research was supported in part by The Hong Kong Polytechnic University under grant number A-PA6E.

REFERENCES

Bagozzi, R.P., Davis, F.D., & Warshaw, P.R. (1992). Development and test of a theory of technological learning and usage. *Human Relations, 45*(7), 660-686.

Bessen, J. (1999). *Real Options and the Adoption of New Technologies.* On-line working paper at http://www.researchoninnovation.org/online.htm#realopt

Bikhchandi, S., Hirschleifer, D., & Welch, I. (1992). A Theory of Fads, Fashion, Custom and Cultural Change as Informational Cascades. *Journal of Political Economy, 100*(5), 992-1026.

Birkinshaw, J., & Gibson, C. (2004). Building Ambidexterity into an Organization. *Sloan Management Review, 45*(4), 47–55.

Chari, V., & Hopenhayn, H. (1991). Vintage human capital, growth and the diffusion of new technology. *Journal of Political Economy, 99*(6),1142-1165.

Chircu, A., & Kauffman, R. (2000). Reintermediation Strategies in Business-to-Business Electronic Commerce. *International Journal of Electronic Commerce, 4*(4), 7-42.

Cowles, D.L., Kiecker, P., & Little, M.W. (2002). Using key informant insights as a foundation for e-retailing theory development. *Journal of Business Research, 55*, 629-636.

Dahlbom, B., & Ljungberg, F. (1998). Mobile Informatics. *Scandinavian Journal of Information Systems, 10*(1,2), 227-234.

Davis, F.D., Bagozzi, R.P., & Warshaw, P.R. (1989). User acceptance of computer technology: A comparison of two theoretical models. *Management Science, 35*, 982-1003.

Doraszelski, U. (2004). Innovations, improvements, and the optimal adoption of new technologies. *Journal of Economic Dynamics & Control, 28*, 146–1480.

Ellis-Chadwick, F., McHardy, P., & Wiesnhofer, H. (2000). Online Customer Relationships in the European Financial Services Sector: A Cross – Country Investigation. *Journal of Financial Services Marketing,* (June, 6/4), 333-345.

Frankel, M. (1955). Obsolescence and technological change in a maturing economy. *American Economic Review, 45*(3), 296-319.

Fram, E. (2002). E-Commerce Survivors: Finding Value amid Broken Dreams. *Business Horizons,* Jul. /Aug., (pp. 15-20).

Galanxhi-Janaqi, H., & Nah, F. (2004). U-Commerce: Emerging Trends and Research Issues. *Industrial Management and Data Systems, 104*(9), 744-755.

Gallaugher, J. (2002, July). E-Commerce and the Undulating Distribution Channel. *Communications of the ACM, 45*(7), 89-95.

Gort, M., & Klepper. S. (1982). Time paths in the diffusion of product innovations. *The Economic Journal, 92*(3), 630-653.

Jallat, F., & Capek, M. (2001 Mar/Apr.). Disintermediation in Question: New Economy, New

Networks, New Middleman, *Business Horizons*, (pp. 55-60).

Jovanovic, B., & Lach, S. (1989). Entry, exit and diffusion with learning by doing. *American Economic Review, 79*(4), 690-699.

Jovanovic, B., & MacDonald, G. (1994). Competitive Diffusion. *Journal of Political Economy, 102*(1), 24-52.

Junglas, I.A., & Watson, R.T. (2003). U-Commerce: A Conceptual Extension of E- and M-Commerce. *International Conference on Information Systems*, Dec 14-17th, Seattle, WA.

Kiang, M., & Chi, R. (2001). A Framework for Analyzing the Potential Benefits of Internet Marketing. *Journal of Electronic Commerce Research*, 4(2), 157-163.

Lyytinen, K., & Yoo, Y. (2002). The Next Wave of Nomadic Computing: A Research Agenda for Information Systems Research. *Information Systems Research*, 13(4), 377-388.

Lumpkin, G.T., & Dess, G.G. (1996). Clarifying the entrepreneurial orientation construct and linking it to performance. *Academy of Management Review, 21*(1), 135-172.

Miller, A.I. (2002). *Einstein, Picasso: Space, Time, and the Beauty That Causes Havoc*. New York, Basic Books.

O'Reilly, C.A. III., & Tushman, M.L. (2004, April). The ambidextrous organization. *Harvard Business Review*, (pp. 74-81).

Parente, S. 1994. Technology adoption, learning by doing and economic growth. *Journal of Economic Theory*, 63(2): 346-369.

Salter, W. 1969. *Productivity and Technical Change*, Cambridge: Cambridge University Press.

Sheasley, W.D., 2000, Taking an Options Approach to New Technology Development, *Research Technology Management*, 43 (6): 37-43(7)

Stevens, G.R. and McElhill, F. 2000, A qualitative study and model of the use of e-mail in organizations, *Electronic Networking Applications and Policy*, 10 (4): 271-283.

Struss, J., El-Ansary, A. and Frost, R. 2003, *E-Marketing*, 3rd edition, Prentice Hall, New Jersey.

Venkatesh, V., & Davis, F.D. (2000). A theoretical extension of the technology acceptance model: Four longitudinal field studies. *Management Science*, (46:2), 186-204.

Viswanathan, S. 2000. Competition across Channels: Do Electronic Markets Complement or Cannibalize Traditional Retailers? *Proceeding of International Conference on Information Systems*, 513-519.

Watson, R. T., Pitt, L. F., Berthon, P. and Zinkhan, G. M. 2002. U-Commerce: Extending the Universe of Marketing, *Journal of the Academy of Marketing Science*, 30(4): 329-343.

Zwass, V. 1996. Electronic Commerce: Structures and Issues, *International Journal of Electronic Commerce*, (1)1, 3-23.

KEY TERMS

Ubiquity: The possibility of allowing users to access networks from anywhere and at any time.

Ubiquitous Commerce (U-Commerce): Defined as the use of ubiquitous networks to support personalized and uninterrupted communications and transactions between a firm and its various stakeholders, including customers, to provide a level of value over and above other types of traditional commerce.

Ultimacy: The perception of users that the current new technology will be the ultimate one and it is unlikely that there will be significant subsequent improvement.

Ultra-Yield: Is about the degree to which a buyer believes that the new technology can provide significant improvement.

Uniformity: The degree to which a person can make the best use of the new technologies with appropriate recognition by his/her peer groups.

Uniqueness: Allows users to be uniquely identified, in terms of their identity and preferences.

Unison: Covers the idea of integrated data across multiple applications so that users have a consistent view on their information, irrespective of the devices to be used.

Universality: Means mobile devices are universally usable and multi-functional.

Usefulness: Related to the perceived value in the adoption of new technologies.

Chapter II
Service–Level Roaming:
A New Virtual Home Environment Concept

Giovanni Frattini
Atos Origin Italia S.p.A., Italy

Ivano De Furio
Atos Origin Italia S.p.A., Italy

Roberto Russo
Atos Origin Italia S.p.A., Italy

Luigi Romano
Atos Origin Italia S.p.A., Italy

Federico Ceccarini
Atos Origin Italia S.p.A., Italy

ABSTRACT

We will discuss on new methods and tools for building high personalized, virtual e-business services. A new service provisioning architecture based on web services has been conceived, taking into account issues related to end-user mobility. The following pages deal with a proposal for creating real localized, personalized virtual environments using web services and domain ontologies. In particular, to overcome interoperability issues that could arise from a lack of uniformity in service descriptions, we propose a way for controlling and enforcing annotation policies based on a service registration authority. It allows services to be advertised according to guidelines and domain rules. Furthermore, this solution enables enhanced service/component discovery and validation, helping software engineers to build services by composing building blocks and provision/deliver a set of personalized services.

STATE OF ART

The advent of wireless and mobile technology has created both new opportunities and new challenges for the business community. Our aim is to present a possible solution for enabling new mobile services inherently ubiquitous.

The penetration of mobile device in western countries is still increasing. The Italian case is really surprising: every single Italian has more than one mobile terminal. Thus, considering this large potential audience, and the increasing power of new generation terminals, a large space for innovation exists. The magnitude of the mobile penetration has the potential to create a substantial pressure on the current business models (not only on the e-commerce business models). It could generate a substantial change of the value propositions in many industries. Nevertheless, m-commerce has to face several limitations. Among the others: uniform standards, ease of operation, security of transactions, minimum screen size, display type and bandwidth, billing services, connectivity costs and, above all, the role that all the actors are currently playing in the value chain. A successful m-commerce provider must usability is a fundamental requirement for a successful m-business. Wireless users demand hyper-personalized information, not reduced versions of generic information. Therefore, new models for exploiting at the best the unique characteristics mobile terminals are more than necessary.

To summarize, m-commerce is not a new distribution tool, a mobile Internet or a substitute for personal computers. Rather, it is a new aspect of consumerism and a much more powerful way to speak with consumers. Unleashing the value of m-commerce requires understanding the role that mobility plays in people's lives. That calls for a radical shift in thinking (Nohria & Leestma, 2001).

M-commerce, as defined by Muller and Veerse (1999), stands for conducting commercial transactions via a "mobile" telecommunications network using a communication, information and payment (CIP) device such as a mobile phone or a palmtop unit. In a broader sense, m-commerce can be defined simply as exchanging products, ideas and services between mobile users and providers.

Let us consider the m-commerce from another perspective: the telecom operators point of view. Telecom operator are facing difficulties due to more and rapid change of the business scenarios. The revenues per minutes from voice traffic have steadily decreased in the last 10 years (see Figure 1). The so-called Value Added Service (VAS) revenues are following the reverse path: the growth ratio is almost 35% per year.

This is the main reason that drives telecommunications industries to invest in new value added services. Actually, Value Added Services revenues come mostly from content provisioning. Typical services are based on the download of contents like: logos, ring tones, games. The value chain for VAS is shown in Figure 2.

Mobile operators are in the middle of the value chain and control provisioning and billing processes. It means that, if goods vendors want to

Figure 1. Average revenue per user (ARPU) for voice are slowly decreasing while VAS are constantly increasing their importance (Italian case. ©2008-2009 Assinform. Used with permission)

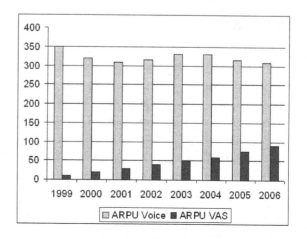

sell a product using the mobile network operator payment system, they are completely dependant on the operator. A telecommunication business model is mostly based on a operator-centric approach.

Legal barriers have strengthened the position of the mobile operators in the value chain limiting, as a consequence, the growth of the mobile service offering. Technology issues also have contributed to enforce a closed business model approach, despite the market demands for a more open and collaborative business approach.

In the latest years telecommunications monopolies have been abolished in Europe. Telecommunications operators are facing increasingly fierce competition with new operators. It has

become imperative for such companies to reinvent themselves and adopt the nimbleness that makes their new competitors so successful. Innovation requires embracing a new way of doing business (open garden), where spotting and cultivating new technologies is fundamental. This includes the systematic identification of new technologies and business models, detailed evaluation, aggressive prototyping, and, last but not least, implementation and operations.

For example, the next generation of services should take localization into account. In other words: services are increasingly based on *user position*. An efficient mobile-ticketing service, where a user can buy, for instance, bus tickets using its telecom account, should allow user mobility

Figure 2. Today's value chain. Operators are in full-control of the delivery process.

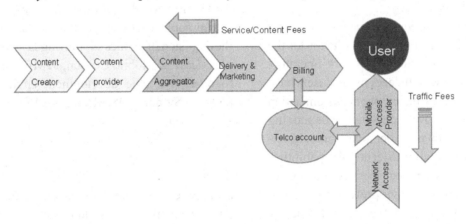

Figure 3. Today services are based on telecommunications accounts. Future services must be billed differently.

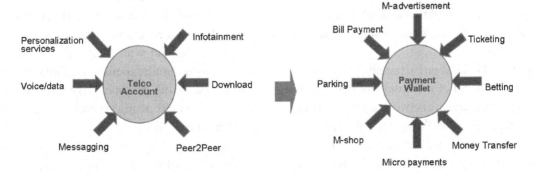

from both a geographical and a service provider point of view. Imagine users routinely traveling within his town by metro or bus and paying via mobile-ticketing service. When users move to another country, the same operator should offer the same service localized in the new town or should have a service roaming agreement with a local operator that allows users to access the service in the same way (interface and procedures) they are accustomed. Notice that in this case roaming is used in a wider sense: it is not referred just to the core services of the network operator, but it also covers service processes. Addressing the problem of roaming services to an higher level of abstraction is a first step turned towards opened business models. Furthermore, in almost all the European countries, telecommunications operators generally offer services that are strictly related to their core business, and services like mobile-ticketing are not widely deployed.

The tailoring of services to customers' preferences and profiles is a key success factor for the service offerings of mobile network operators and service providers. Indeed, mobile users have shown their interest in mobile phone customization by buying colored covers, personal logos and ring tones. The next step is the personalization of services: content adaptation to terminal capabilities, context and location based services and content filtering on the basis of user preferences.

This scenario leads us to the Virtual Home Environment (VHE) concept. Basically it means that telecommunications companies users can access services with the same personalized features and user interface customization in whatever network, whatever terminal (within the capabilities of the terminal and the network) and wherever the user may be located.

3GPP (3rd Generation Partnership Project) has defined the concept of a Virtual Home Environment. Its key features are network and protocol independence (achievable through standard abstract interfaces), terminal independence (via standard execution environments on terminal, Mobile Ex-

ecution Environment, MExE, specifications) and an abstract data structure for expressing customer personal profiles. It is not specified, however, how to roam high level applications, built on top of a virtualized network, from one geographical region to another. Neither it is specified how to extend the home environment to services based on collaborating partners that cannot export customers' personal data.

The VHE concept, thus, should be extended. Voice, SMS, etc. are services that are always independent on the serving network and position of the user. The same could apply to services like ticketing, m-shopping, etc, provided that a system for making them independent from the user position exists.

In order to address customer mobility, e-business (or better a m-business) solution should follow the terminal capabilities evolutions. Most of the commercial handsets on the market are able to run applications. It is especially relevant for the diffusion of phones supporting Java technologies, (Java 2 Mobile Edition, J2ME) compared to other available development environments (notably, Symbian OS, Microsoft Mobile Edition/CE, Linux).

It is possible to think about services based on a client acting as an agent for mediating among different devices with different communication capabilities (Moreno, Valls & Viejo 2003). User-friendlier application should take into account dynamics in content and services (e.g. the possibility to update service menus as well as accessing dynamic content), the interaction among mobile devices and smart cards and the possibility to interact with other networks. In other words, in a mobile service environment, devices should be able to interact with local networks as well as with usual (and expensive) cellular network connection, using protocols like ZigBee, IEEE 802.11x, Bluetooth, using, where possible, a single, uniform approach.

Actually, techniques that provide users with services and information that are adapted to individual needs (according to user specific preferences and interests) are still at a early stage.

Our experience suggests that web services are a good solution to support transparent service roaming (extending the concept of roaming that is traditionally referred to network services like pre-paid accounts, connectivity and voice services) and localized services. In general, methods and technologies for building a flexible service oriented delivery platform is a key challenge for software industry. Web services have a great potential as an enterprise application integration technology. They can be also used to streamline business-to-business processes that in turn could foster service provider coalition and could enable service-level roaming.

Problem Statement

Let us consider a mobile bus ticketing service. Generally this kind of service is localized: a local bus company operates in a specific geographical area. What happens when a mobile-ticketing service user leaves, for some reason, its "home" location and moves to another area? He would not be able to use the service. But, if we assume a business agreement among, for example, different public transport service providers ("roaming" agreement), it is possible to offer the same service independent of the customer position, provided that a platform for supporting cooperation among partners exists. Enabling flexible mobile business, in other words, means that service roaming, as known to every mobile user, must be enhanced in a wider sense, preserving customer preferences (user should feel at "home" using the services while roaming). The key idea is that services should have a "standard behaviour" while user is roaming from one provider to another. Just like the handset can automatically choose the best network based on signal power, an ad-hoc service environment should be automatically set up based on a user profile.

A key issue in service roaming is establishing the best service provider, within a set of providers, with a given customer profile (including user's location information).

Since the number of services and service providers increase, automated service discovery is a key feature for service provisioning. Service discovery should enable users to automatically discover and use services through their devices. Furthermore, a mechanism for advertising newly delivered services must be provided to Service Providers.

Semantic Web and Semantic Web technologies offer a new approach to managing information and processes, by means of semantic metadata, that can significantly improve service discovery.

Using Semantic Web technologies brings several benefits. Considering semantic reasoning capabilities, first of all, a reasoning system could extend an existing knowledge-base by making new inferences and could highlight semantic ambiguity in service description (allowing, in this way, a safer publishing method and an advanced and effective service discovery). Semantically defined services are more clearly defined, allowing a reasoning system to mitigate interoperability issues that can arise in a traditional, text-based service matchmaking system, due to ambiguous descriptions. Indeed, matchmaking approaches based on syntactic service description are not able to express the semantics of service functionality but just their signature. Several matchmaking approaches based on semantic descriptions have been proposed. Ontologies have been identified as a core technique for semantic aspects of these descriptions. Moreover if services are provided with metadata describing their function and context, then services can be automatically selected and invoked. Thus, such a semantic description is likely to become a key factor for large-scale SOA implementations.

In the second place, we can organise and find information based on meaning, not just text. Through semantics, systems could understand that different words are semantically equivalent. When searching for 'Garibaldi', for example, in a semantic search engine we may be provided with an equally valid document referring to 'Hero of the Two Worlds'. Conversely it can distinguish where the same word is used with different meanings. When searching for references to 'Garibaldi' in the context of Travel Ticketing, the system can disregard historical references to the Italian patriot and soldier of the Risorgimento and propose travel options referring to the Garibaldi Square railway station. When not much can be found on the subject of a search, the system can try instead to locate information on a semantically related subject.

Last but not least, personalized services matching user preferences with service descriptions can be delivered. Using semantic matchmaking a more efficient selection could remove from consideration services that do not fit the user profiles. Services could be delivered mediating among different devices, personalizing content delivery further, by prioritizing information to be displayed and delivering the one predicted to be most pertinent first.

To enable such a roaming mechanism, semantics is not the only ingredient. Even if services could be presented to the user using standard environments (WAP), the use of applications for presenting menus and contents in the most appropriate way should be taken into account. Such an approach ensures the highest service usability (service environment designed following usability methodologies) and avoids inappropriate network interactions (saving money that the user does not want to pay). Furthermore, as discussed above, services that are geographically localised must interact with the local environment in most of the business scenarios (e.g. for passing through an automatic barrier). These are requirements that must be taken into account for building effective mobile business services.

PROPOSED SOLUTION

As we mentioned before, the VAS market demands for new services and new business models that require new architectural and technological solutions for building highly personalized, mobile virtual service environments. Next generation services should implement business processes that tightly integrate actors in the value chain from a business point of view, while keeping them loosely coupled from a technological point of view. The proposed solution, based on SOA and Web Service technology (Booth et al. 2004), enhanced with semantic support (De Furio and Frattini 2006), best fits these needs.

Let us consider the possible roles that a telecommunications operator can play within a collaborative business model. The telecommunications operator could be the ideal actor for mediating among its subscribers and service providers. It is better able to control the heterogeneity of the terminals and customer preferences and, at the same time, it can act as a technology provider for a large variety of business actors, no matter the market segment they are working in.

According to Gisolfi (2001), a telecommunications operator can play different business roles in SOA:

- **Service requestor:** Also called consumer, the service requestor could be a company needing a specific service.
- **Service provider:** The entity that implements a service specification or description.
- **Registry:** A software entity that acts a service locator. It implements the discovery and order functions for the requestor for a specific service, and where new services are published and delivered.
- **Broker:** A special service that can pass service requests to other service providers. In service-oriented architectures, service description and metadata play a central role

Figure 4. Telecommunications operator like mediator

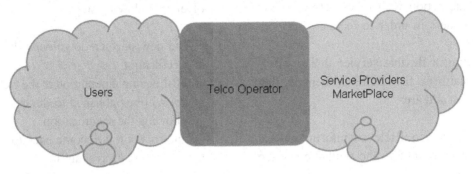

in maintaining a loose coupling between service requestors and service providers. The role of the broker extends the registry, as it offers additional metadata about the partners' services and, based on this metadata, the functionality for searching and classification of services. In addition, industry-specific taxonomy data helps the customers find service providers and enables service providers to describe service offerings precisely.

- **Aggregator/Gateway:** This extends the capabilities of the broker by the ability to describe actual policy, business processes and binding descriptions that form the standard way of operation on the marketplace, and which are fulfilled by service-providing partners. It would be the logical place to find standard Web Service interface definitions for common business processes in the industry. Marketplace customers then can use these as a reference to use the services.

In our solution, the telecommunications operator plays the role of a service broker, collecting requests coming from other business entities and providing services offered by its partners. More specifically, the broker interacts with the partners in order to offer composite services to the customers, and therefore can be seen as an intermediary providing service aggregation. It also offers context-support. Semantic technology

is fundamental as long as it provides methods and tools for representing information that can be used for effective service discovery and composition.

Acting as a mediator between service users and providers, the operator could offer a standardized way of interacting with the required services. In other words, the mediator should be able to hide the heterogeneity of interacting with different service providers, which makes service usage easier for the customers and, at the same time, offers flexibility in choosing the most suitable provider. Services from multiple parties can be compounded to form comprehensive service bundles.

A mobile telecommunications operator can personalise services considering the terminal features and the customer profiling. The role of the broker extends the registry, as it offers additional metadata about the partners' services and, based on this metadata, the functionality for searching and classification of services. In addition, industry-specific taxonomy data helps the customers find service providers and enables service providers to describe service offerings precisely.

Objectives

The proposed solution faces some critical issues such as: dealing with different devices and with different capabilities; delivery of dynamic contents and services to the telecom operator's customers (e.g. the possibility to update services menus as well as accessing dynamic contents), fulfil the interaction with other networks and service providers in order to realize a service-level VHE.

In building a flexible service delivery/provisioning platform, the additional benefits that semantics can add are:

- Better access to all relevant information and functionality, due to the semantic service registry.
- Better quality of business services, due to standardization in service descriptions and publishing.
- Semantic user profiles representing the current working context of the user which can be used to guide service searching, browsing, filtering and alerting.
- Faster response to market changes, due to component reuse.
- Savings in resources, time, and money, as processes will be modelled and run automatically, and centralized computer assisted management capabilities.

Until now, a fully semantic approach has been far from viable. However, it is possible to combine semantic technology with standard tools in order to exploit the additional features it offers.

Figure 5 represent a typical case in which a company B must set-up an agreement with other companies with a similar business, geographically bounded to specific regions, in order to achieve effective service roaming.

The fundamental processes that must be considered are:

- Agreement setup
- Service localization upon explicit customer update
- Run-time service discovery and presentation
- Run-time service delivery
- Billing the service

The agreement setup, in turn involves (or could involve) the following steps:

- The new partner downloads the technical specification
- Off-line implementation of the web services that will be published to the external world following the specification
- Once ready it will come back to the system and declare its availability
  - The system, according to the domain ontology, asks for additional information (e.g rating information, terminal class supported, multimedia formats supported, location area for the service, etc.).
  - Test the whether the web service enforces the interoperability rules (as described in the technical specification).
  - Insert the information into the metadata repository
  - Activate the partner

Figure 5. The service roaming scenario

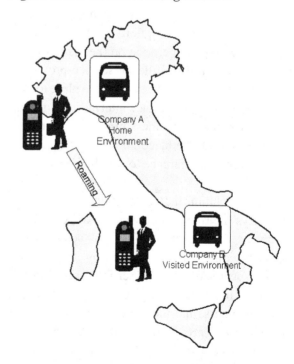

In other words a service provider must first register itself, declaring its availability to collaborate with the others according to collaboration rules, and during the provisioning phase insert all the additional information that the system requires. This additional information will be used during the run-time operations for service delivery.

Thus, our approach to semantics includes the introduction of a semantic-enabled validation layer to check the advertisement of new services and the extension of the standard discovery mechanisms exploiting the additional information that such a publishing environment allows. Furthermore, in order to make the knowledge manageable, we lay out some boundaries to ontology management, its evolution and target domain complexity. We assume that an enterprise, possibly the telecommunications operator, playing the role of broker in the value chain, defines its own business ontology model and that every partner of software services is required to adopt it. This constraint greatly simplifies the discovery and composition of services while reducing interoperability problems.

A thorough domain analysis is necessary in order to devise a suitable ontology model. Such a model encompasses the enterprise vocabulary, the main concepts, the service and operations taxonomy up to the level of detail for which properties, attributes and operational constraints about each service are defined.

A contract must be defined for each operation, specifying the operation and the messages it can exchange. Defining a contract for each available operation ensures interoperability between all instances of that operation category so that a service that satisfies the search criteria will also meet all interoperability requirements.

When a set of domain ontologies has been defined, Web services can be formally described by using common meanings from that pool. Services can then be published in registries according to interoperability constraints, thereby becoming available for process composition.

In order to do that, we use our front-end, the Service Registration Authority (SRA). It has to be used by both external service providers and internal publishers, indifferently.

The SRA allows them to advertise their services according to fixed guidelines and domain rules. The SRA also allows publishers to navigate the domain ontology and proposes service category slots available for publishing. By using the SRA, any publisher can download service/component technical specifications, implementation instructions, and all the required technical documents (e.g. WSDL template and required business data such as XML schemas). SRA also informs the publisher about the properties and attributes that can be or must be provided to correctly annotate the service/component. It also transparently generates the semantic annotation according to the domain ontologies and validates the service annotation highlighting both syntactic and semantic errors. Finally, the service description is published on a standard SOA registry, UDDI (2004) or ebXML (2005), and synchronized with the metadata store.

This kind of publishing of Web services delivers interoperable business services, which means that services will exhibit consistent accessibility to any composite business process that wishes to use it.

Thanks to SRA, the service providers are not forced to invest in tools or people reskilling for using semantic technologies. What they see and use are always well known web pages.

A telecommunications operator, working on a pool of loosely-coupled, homogenously and well annotated Web Services is able to aggregate services and switch among similar services according to end-user requests, avoiding any human intervention. This greatly simplifies the service delivery processes. Services participating in a composite process are now selected from common pools (service registries). Business processes are composed and executed at a higher semantic (abstract) level.

Once a common repository of semantics has been established, inclusive of user profiles, device profiles, etc., it will be possible to apply personalization to Service Discovery. This will allow optimization of the service itself, as only the relevant services will be presented to the user, according to his context and preferences.

General Description

The general architecture we adopted is shown in Figure 6. It is a general reference model widely adopted when analysing telecom oriented new generation service delivery platforms. The picture underlines how every software layer must be used by means of interfaces (Service Provider Interface).

The solution fits the needs of an effective partner management (service provider management layer) as well as the customer requests for the delivery of the services (service platform).

It is important to stress the role of the client side for implementing the concept of VHE for high-level services: the client must be able to act as an access point for the local service environment. This role can be enabled using the technology we have developed and concisely described below.

Thus, the client is a fundamental part of the VHE architecture we have implemented.

The Mobile Domain

We have designed and developed a solution for enabling inexpensive, customizable, usable and secure vertical services. Figure 7 shows the terminal domain subsystem.

As shown in the Figure 7, we have developed several software modules. We will not discuss them one by one, but we will show a few characteristics. In the m-commerce arena, where the bandwidth of mobile devices is low and large data transfers would not be possible, the discovery of new information and retrieval techniques that would filter through thousands of services or millions of pages to return only relevant information, is a key element.

We have focused our attention on these main directions:

1.   Simplify as much as possible the mark-up for service, trying to identify the minimal set of information needed for an optimal navigation.

Figure 6. Reference architecture

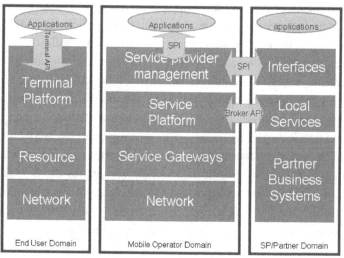

End User Domain	Mobile Operator Domain	SP/Partner Domain

2. Abstracting as much as possible application from the mark-up, to achieve an higher degree of flexibility.

3. Selecting the best rendering mechanism, to avoid as much as possible unwanted network accesses.

4. Maximum exploitation of the terminal short range communication capabilities, for both service access and service security.

5. Combining keyword queries with ontology, in order to achieve better and more effective query formation.

Terminal technologies are evolving continuously and more and more attention is dedicated to the definition of service environments designed by considering special usability issues. It is likely that in the near future technologies like J2ME (Java FX)1 and/or Mobile Ajax2 will aid in implementing new and more usable mobile applications. Furthermore, both mobile operators and terminal manufactures are working to new proximity protocols for interacting with local service point. These are facts that must be taken into account for building next generation services.

The Mobile Operator/Service Aggregator Domain

In Figure 8 gives a view of the main platform modules. Even though it could be interesting to discuss all the modules, we will concentrate our attention on Semantic Support Services, the ones for managing the service lifecycle, using semantic annotation.

The type of semantic information that would be useful in describing a Web Service encompasses the concepts defined by the Semantic Web community in OWL-S (Martin et al., 2004) and other efforts METEOR-S (Rajasekaran, Miller, Verma and Sheth 2004), WSMO (Roman, Keller and Lausen 2004). The idea is to extend service descriptions by adding context information, (i.e. what the service does, how it behaves, security policies, etc.). The potential benefits of Semantic Web Services (SWS) include better usability by means of a more expressive Web service description, and it is well-known how it enables the automated Web service discovery, execution, composition and interoperation.

Ontologies provide a large extent of flexibility and expressiveness, the ability to express semi-

Figure 7. Mobile domain modules and server side specific services

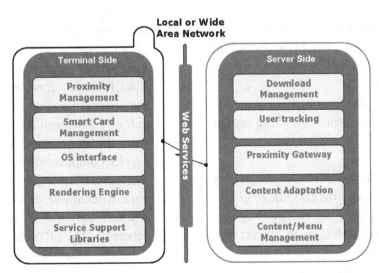

Figure 8. Architectural view of the service platform

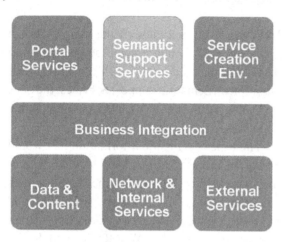

structured data, constraints, and support types and inheritance. The industry's Web service standards, however, provide better manageability, scalability, and modularization. We moved towards an evolutionary approach to Web Service architecture that combines the two worlds and their potential benefits. So we designed a delivery platform that tries to benefit from both technologies.

SEMANTIC SUPPORT SERVICES: DETAILS

This subsystem can be decomposed into several components. All these components have been designed for ensuring interoperability with existing solutions, enabling an efficient service creation mechanism.

Figure 9 depicts the layout of the semantic subsystem. The main components of the system are:

- The *Registry/Repository*: as our component repository we chose the ebXML Registry/ Repository. In fact, the ebXML registry provides a persistent layer for service description, supporting a wide variety of objects and metadata.

- The *Metadata Store subsystem* manages metadata expressed in XML format. Furthermore, this subsystem handles the domain ontology in OWL format and the service annotations extracted from the main repository (ebXML). Some reasoning is pre-computed for improving performances. For that we use Jena3 extensively. Jena is a Java framework for building Semantic Web applications developed at HP Bristol's laboratory.

- *Sync tools*: tools are provided to export part of the OWL domain conceptualization to ebXML taxonomies, ensuring compatibility with a standard ebXML service discovery. We have also developed tools for data synchronization between the metadata-store and the ebXML registry. These components have been developed for allowing external queries to a standard registry. This additional requirement was inspired from the need to be as standard as possible.

- *ESDL (Enhanced Service Discovery)*: this is our matchmaker agent. ESD-WS exposes interfaces for computing matching scores on a pre-agreed ontology using well-known rules. When requested, the ESD-WS will execute a service query on the metadata store applying query-specific reasoning.

- *ReAL (REgistry Abstraction Layer)*: this software layer allows, in perspective, the reuse of the overall architecture using a different registry (e.g. UDDI).

- *SRA (Service Registration Authority):* has been shortly described in the previous sections. In brief, it allows publishers to navigate the domain ontology and proposes service category slots available for publishing. By using the SRA, any publisher can download service/component technical specifications, instructions to implement it, and all the needed technical documents (e.g. WSDL template and required business data as XML schemas). The SRA also informs the publisher about the properties and attributes that

Figure 9. Semantic subsystem layout

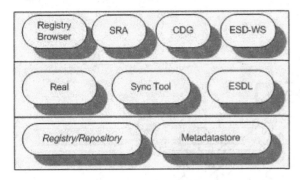

Figure 10. Component description generator GUI

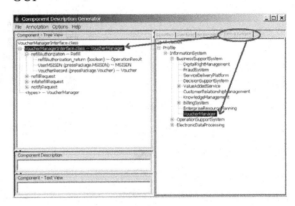

can be or must be provided to annotate the service/component correctly. It also transparently generates the semantic annotation according to the upper domain ontology and validates the service annotation highlighting both syntactic and semantic errors. Finally, the service description is published on an ebXML registry and synchronized with an external metadata store.

- *CDG (Component Description Generator):* The goal of the CDG is to create an application that assists the user in semantically annotating components already available in the customer organization like legacy components. CDG using a point-and-click interface (Fig 10) enables the user to semantically annotate pre-existing Web Services, but also other software components (Plain Old Java Objects (POJO), EJBs, etc.). The key feature of CDG is the ability to suggest which ontological class to use to annotate each element of the component description. The recommendations are based on a machine learning algorithm like in Heß, Johnston, and Kushmerick (2004).

This modular architecture is backward compatible with standard ebXML registries in order to ensure interoperability with existing solutions. A core component of the architecture is an authority whose role is to enforce the respect of

enterprise policies while publishing new services. Furthermore, it has been designed in such a way as to be able to deal not only with web services, but also with other software components (POJO, EJBs, etc.). This is one of the main reasons for selecting the ebXML registry, being the latter also a repository. We would like to be ready for publishing not only Web services but also annotated components. In other words, we would extend the concept of the semantic enabled registry to a central repository of "servicelet". We define a service let as everything that could be composed and reused for building a service. We believe that semantics could add a huge value in helping enterprises to build new services, reusing existing servicelets - borrowing the same approach used for Web Services. Anyway this chapter will not deal with this topic.

Considering that UDDI registries are available on the market with similar capabilities, we have given thought to an abstraction layer for achieving a "registry independence" and eventually plug a different registry whenever requested.

In short, we devised a set of software tools that allow the end user (software designer) to take advantage of the descriptive power of semantic languages and tools, while shielding, at least partially, their complexities.

Figure 11. A semantic SOA

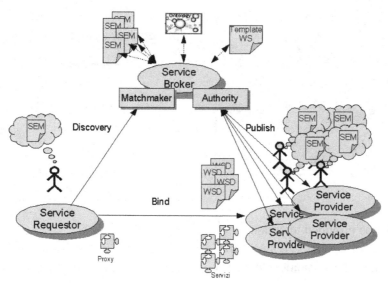

In the medium term we expect that similar approaches will foster service/component reuse. In fact associating services/ components with a significant knowledge body, expressed in standard languages, ensures that such services/components are completely documented and hence much easier to reuse.

The Service Registration Authority

Our research (De Furio and Frattini 2006) was hence focused on how to provide effective tools for annotating (adding semantically relevant information) software services and components while publishing them in the registry. The publishing service manages the domain ontology internally and, thus, it is able to annotate the service by adding semantic annotation.

To ensure interoperability among domains:

- The publisher must first contact an authority in order to obtain (download) the service specifications for any given service category.

- The publisher will have to create the service, conforming to the specifications obtained.

- Finally, the publisher will notify the authority about the availability of the new service.

It is worth noting that the authority will prevent publishing of services not included in the domain taxonomy. Every service to be published will therefore adhere to specific domain policies. Upon confirmation of the success of the publishing operation, the authority will automatically generate the OWL annotation for the service and transfer it to a suitable metadata repository, making the service available for semantic discovery.

The Matchmaker

An Enhanced Service Discovery Web Service (ESD-WS) exposes interfaces for computing matching scores on a pre-agreed ontology using domain rules. The ESD-WS is our matchmaker agent that can resolve service queries applying OWL reasoning with custom rules.

The ESD-WS implements a flexible service discovery algorithm that can be used:

- To resolve business workflow templates at run time, replacing service tasks depicted by criteria for service selection with service instances.

- To substitute a service instance at run time with an equivalent one.
- To compose service menus for terminals matching services with user profiles (preference-dependant), matching services with terminal characteristics (terminal dependant) and matching services with user context (context-aware).

On top of this platform we have built a system for m-ticketing, considering the possibility that a user could roam from a city to another, accessing seamlessly to the same service, providing just its position. The system enables two or more hypothetical transportation companies to establish a relationship that enables the service virtualization when the user is roaming. The system is able to identify the requested service using its semantic description and, if necessary, it infers the best service given both the customer and the service profile (matchmaking). The ticketing service itself is a Web Service that returns a ticket identifier and its representation as a bar code. When the user is at "home" the "local" ticketing service is invoked; when the user declares a new position the system updates its profile and, at run-time, discovers the external partner service trying to find the one that best matches the customer profile. Other QoS criteria, given the customer profile, could be applied for selecting the best service. It is important to notice that, even if we have implemented the system assuming a central brokering platform (a mobile telecommunications operator), every single local service provider could act as a broker for its roaming customers, keeping control of the customer profile and even of the customer billing.

The system covers all the relevant processes. For avoiding any lack of clarity, in the remainder of this section we describe the relevant phase for complete service provisioning.

Design-Time

The system relies upon a number of design-time activities that must be carried out in order for the system to work correctly at run-time. As depicted before, the actor playing the role of broker must set-up its SRA. As broker, he must define the ontology that will be partially shown as service taxonomy in the SRA (see Figure 12). Furthermore the company must define its specific policies and produce a template for providing its partners a technical specification for interacting with the partner at run-time. Furthermore, the partner downloads a specification of the specific message exchange pattern for correctly interacting with the other parties.

Considering the fact that only services respecting the domain policies are enabled to participate to business processes, a workflow designer needs to face just two problems: coding the criteria for service selection and invoking the service. Other problems vanish since structural and semantic differences between services are eliminated during the publishing phase.

Publishing-Time

We assume that a commercial relationship exists amongst parties. Once an agreement is signed among the parties, it is possible to set-up the collaboration infrastructure.

The partner connects to the SRA after having obtained the credentials for accessing the web site. A page presenting the service taxonomy of the services is presented.

When a new service provider (i.e. a new local transportation company) joins the business community, he uses the SRA to select the service category slots available for its business category. By using the SRA, the new partner can download service specifications, instructions to implement it, and all the needed technical documents.

The SRA also informs the publisher about the properties and attributes that can be or must be

Figure 12. SRA a) Technical specification download b) Aided service annotation

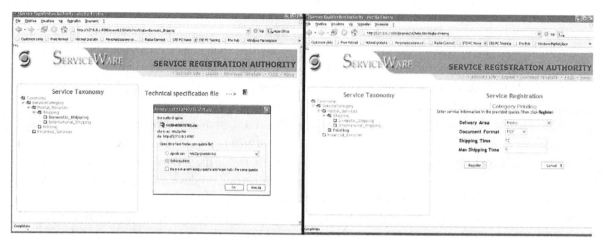

provided to annotate the service correctly and enable the run-time service provisioning.

The publisher will have to create the service, conforming to the specifications obtained, using standard tools to develop Web Services.

Finally the publisher has to notify the authority about the availability of the new service, completing the registration. The SRA then, transparently, generates the semantic annotation according to the upper domain ontology and validates the service annotation highlighting both syntactic and semantic errors. The service description is published on the registry and synchronized with the metadata store. The publishing workflow could also include the testing of the partner interface in order to avoid run-time fault. At this time, the service is discoverable and it can participate in the business.

The SRA facilitates the discovery of a Web Service that cannot only be based on its name or description; but also has to account for its operational metrics and its interfaces.

In fact the composition of e-workflows cannot be undertaken while ignoring the importance of operational metrics. Trading agreements between suppliers and customers modelled with e-workflow include the specification of QoS items such as products or services to be delivered,

deadlines, quality of products, and cost of service. The correct management of such specifications directly impacts both the success of organizations participating in e-commerce and the success and evolution of e-services itself.

Run-Time

A client on a mobile phone using Java technology (J2ME) is allowed to use Web Services for interacting over the Internet (via GPRS) and eventually store data locally, avoiding expensive accesses to the mobile network. In a typical scenario, the java client has been downloaded and installed on the customer mobile phone at the end of his/her service subscription procedure to the service and, thus, that the customer has a service geographical region and a "billing home". When the application on the mobile starts, the client downloads and presents a menu of the "home" services. The user can change the home using the application itself.

In the implemented scenario, having a dedicated client on his/her mobile the user can buy a "home" public transportation ticket. This is only an example of a possible service: the same approach could be easily applied in several different e-business scenarios. A normal ticket acquisition flow encompass: (1) the loading of the customer profile, (2) the calling of an authorization service according to the ticket price (billing), (3) the production of a ticket code, (4) the rendering of the code in a visual format (bi-dimensional bar code), (5) the accounting of the ticket on the home payment system.

To implement the service flow we have used our own orchestration engine. The orchestration engine is able to bind dynamically the components needed for completing the task. So we experienced dynamic selection of the most appropriate services among the available ones, and replacement of services by equivalent ones (i.e. in case of failure). The business designer composes a template workflow where just the selection criteria for the services are coded. At run time a workflow engine will discover services suitable for the assigned task. The construction of dynamic services is, thus, simplified due to the fact that equivalent services have the same interfaces. The registration procedures, mediated using the SRA are, thus, very effective for enabling such a degree of dynamicity.

After receiving an "update position" command, the system executes the following tasks: (1) loading the user profile, (2) acquire terminal position depending on the user selection (real GPS position, cell-ID or a string), (3) update the service menu on the mobile phone. Since the user profile contains also the current service localization (e.g. Milan-company A) every change must be tracked. When the user requests an update location, the system tries to solve the request by matching the user profile against the metadata store, trying to find the best service providers against the user preferences and position. If a service provider exists the system retrieves an appropriate service menu, downloads it on the customer device and updates the user service profile for taking into account the updates.

The flow for a ticket request, during a roaming, does not differ from the normal one except for the Web Services invocation that is transparent

for the user: the ticket code is produced remotely according to its internal rules and, finally, the accounting service is both local and remote (for reconciliation purposes). Thus, exploiting the metadata stored during the publishing phase, creating partnerships is very simple and has very small impacts on the business: the system does not have to adapt messages or calls to the partners since they have been forced to comply to the domain policies: as in the "home" flow, the system loads the user profile, evaluates the ticket cost and asks for authorization to the home payment system. Then, the system requests a valid ticket identifier to the remote partner, commits the payment transaction and notifies the partner for future reconciliation.

It is worth noting that the customer data, including sensible data, are always in the home environment: the agreement among the companies allows a transparent service roaming. In other words, the roaming mechanisms that every mobile user knows very well for telecommunications services, are reproduced for other kind of services. The key ingredients are: Web Services; ontologies for describing accurately the service, the user profile and the user context; and a platform for building an effective client environment, based on dynamically reconfigurable service menus.

OTHER SOLUTIONS

The growth of Web services and service oriented architecture (SOA) offers attractive basis for realizing dynamic architectures, which mirrors the dynamic and ever changing business environment. With the help of industry wide acceptance of standards like Business Process Execution Language for Web Services (BPEL4WS), Web Service Description Language (WSDL) and Simple Object Access Protocol (SOAP), Web Services offers the potential of low cost and immediate integration with other applications and partners.

Several commercial platforms are available for building Web Service enabled SOA, like IBM

WebSphere, webMethods Fabric, BEA WebLogic Enterprise Platform and others. All these products have in common that they do not facilitate semantic annotation of the published services. All these products are based on a pure syntactical approach. This implies that the corresponding Web service architectures built on Web Service SOA exhibit little flexibility and expressiveness and that restrict the usability of Web services mostly to human users rather than machine agents. However, SOAs will not scale without significant automation of service discovery, service adaptation, negotiation, service composition, service invocation, and service monitoring; and data and process mediation. For the latter one would need, e.g., Web service description languages that support semi-structured data, constraints, types and inheritance.

The Semantic Web is fundamental to enabling the services and applications outlined above by providing a universally accessible platform that allows data to be shared and processed by automated tools, and by providing the machine-understandable semantics of data and information that will enable automatic information processing and exchange. Experts have already developed a range of mark-up frameworks and languages, notably the revised Resource Description Framework (RDF) and the Ontology Web Language (OWL) which mark the emergence of the Semantic Web as a broad-based, commercial-grade platform. Combination and enhancement of Semantic Web and Web Service technologies is expected to produce a new technology infrastructure — Semantic Web Services.

Several research initiatives focused on mechanisms to applying semantics in annotation, quality of service, discovery, composition, execution with Web services like OWL-S (Martin et al., 2004), METEOR-S (Rajasekaran, Miller, Verma and Sheth 2004), WSMO (Roman, Keller and Lausen 2004), European Semantic Systems Initiative (ESSI 2007) , and OASIS Semantic Execution Environment (OASIS 2007). The idea is to extend service descriptions by adding context information (i.e. what the service does, how it behaves, security policies, etc.), that add semantics to service descriptions.

Some other effort has been spent by the international community to apply Semantic Web technology to Business architecture, for example in (Werthner, Hepp, Fensel and Dorn 2006), it is discussed a B2B architecture that uses intelligent mobile agents to provide automatic negotiation with less cost and time within open and heterogeneous environments like the Internet.

The mentioned research can be exploited to automate Web services-related tasks, like discovery, selection, composition, mediation, monitoring, and invocation, thus enabling seamless interoperation between them while keeping human intervention to a minimum. Nevertheless many major challenges still need to be addressed and solved in this field to allow a real-world implementations of SWS applications, so until now, a fully semantic approach has been far from being viable. Academic and research institutions worldwide are strongly supporting this effort but some other research work needs to be done before the Semantic Web Services vision can make a reality. However, it is possible to combine it with standard tools in order to exploit the additional features it offers.

We propose an open modular architecture that enables an efficient service creation mechanism, a publishing method for fully semantic annotated services, and enhanced service discovery using OWL reasoning. This modular architecture is backward compatible with standard ebXML registries in order to ensure interoperability with existing solutions. A core component of the architecture is an authority whose role is to enforce respect of enterprise policies while publishing new services. Furthermore, it has been designed in such a way as to be able to deal not only with web services but also with other software components (POJO, EJBs, etc.).

In short, we devised a set of software tools that allows the software designer to take advantage of the descriptive power of semantic languages and tools, while shielding, at least partially their complexities .

In the medium term we expect that similar approaches will foster services/components reuse. In fact associating services/ components with a significant knowledge body expressed in a standard language ensures that such services/ components are completely documented and hence much easier to reuse.

COST AND BENEFITS

As discussed in section 1, telecommunications operators are facing a strong competition due to new entrant. This simple fact implies that they need to reduce costs.

As stated in Duke and Richardson (2006) "The costs of integration, both within an organisation and with external trading partners, are a significant component of the IT budget. A Forrester survey (Koetzle, 2001) found that average spending on integration by the top 3500 global companies was $6.3 million and 31% was spent on integrating with external trading partners."

Service Oriented Architectures are particularly suitable for implementing VAS, since they reduce the integration costs for both internal and external systems. Especially for integrating external partners using web services, a big problem is to enforce integration rules. Integrating every single potential partner could imply changes to the security rules, business logic (especially when aggregating recursively services). Thus, in a market that is increasingly federated, due both to regulatory pressures and to companies' attempts to catch market opportunities with tailored, bundled services, a solution for controlling a possible integration complexity explosions is more than necessary. The solution we propose addresses this problem, considering the position of telecom-

munications operator in the value chain: they are always the first user point of contact and they can play a central role in building new Value Added Services. Furthermore, services like m-ticketing are built aggregating equivalent service providers. Ontology is the best way for describing service providers equivalence class, and, at the same time, for managing efficiently information that cannot be simply included in the service description language selected (generally WSDL).

As introduced above, most of IT decision makers are sceptics with respect a massive introduction of semantics in their software architectures. The solution we propose tries to overcome this problem. This solution, while using semantics for expressing additional knowledge on services, tries to shield both Telecom operators, playing the role of brokers/aggregators in the business ecosystem, and service providers, whose main objective is to exploit the best new marketing channels, from the need to invest in tools and training.

It is important to notice that the concepts like service level VHE are fundamental for implementing m-business services. The bus ticketing example is again very representative: a user does not need to use its mobile for buying a bus ticket, changing his habits from one day to another. A normal user is likely to use its mobile while travelling: this would really help him. Implementing such a mechanism, while theoretically possible using standard technologies, would create huge interoperability problems and introduce costs for aggregating/adapting potential partners to let them participate to the business. On the other hand, a service provider, such as a mass transportation company, whose core business is not IT intensive, does not want to invest in new software systems; what they want is something easy. Apart from the example of bus ticketing, this is true for many other business categories: m-shopping, event ticketing (cinema, theatre, etc.), m-advertising, m-couponing, amongst others. It is important to find a solution that makes it as easy as possible to participate and, at the same time to offer a service that is there when needed.

RISK ASSESSMENT

Semantics and all the related technologies are not well known in the IT environment. Most of the IT people day by day problems are related to the maintenance of their platforms and services. That is why introducing new technologies is always difficult. This is particularly true for semantics since it is perceived as still immature: few big players are now marketing semantic enabled products.

Nevertheless, the telecom market is asking for innovation. A simple internet like approach to mobility does not face the real problems related to user mobility. Our solution tries to face some of the relevant issues: usability, usefulness, simplicity, service benefit/cost ratio boosting. We are absolutely conscious that many factors could influence the market: political decision could enlarge the possibility to pay for goods and services using telecommunications accounts, terminal manufacturers could enable new proximity mechanisms enabling new business scenarios, new telecommunications operators could introduce new business models. A strategic analysis is difficult since most of the IT and Telecom market big players could influence the future and take advantage from their dominant position in the market. At the moment, real revenues are coming from traditional services: logo, ring-tone, games, etc. Since an investment for creating a network of service providers could be large and the estimation of the return of investment (ROI) not easy, most of the big players are delaying decisions. Furthermore the IT big players are concentrated in marketing service oriented solutions, keeping eventual more advanced solutions in their lab. In other words, at the moment, we suggest to keep moving very carefully. That is one of the reason for introducing semantic technologies gradually, masking it to operational people. In other words, considering the value that semantics could add, it is easier to introduce new solutions starting from real issues: governance, total cost of ownership reduction, new revenue streams. Hence, even if it is still felt as unsafe to apply semantic technologies in an open environment where domain knowledge is uncontrollable and ontology is not pre-defined and agreed upon, it is possible to focus on internal service life cycle, where even operational people could appreciate the benefit of an improved IT governance. Thus, the idea we have followed aims to exploit semantic annotation in a restricted domain in order to improve service oriented architectures as currently implemented using standard tools and products: from service creation and publishing, to service discovery mechanisms

We would like also to suggest to pay attention to scalability issues and, thus, to consider carefully what are the customer requisite. Some of the technologies we have used for implementing our trial system are not able to scale enough for serving a large number of concurrent users (e.g. Using Jena it is not possible to open more than a single connection while updating). Nevertheless, this is not the major problem: it is of fundamental importance to implement semantic enabled architectures reusing as much as possible products having strong market penetration in the telecommunications worlds (especially for what concern RDBMS). This will open new real marketing perspectives. It is possible to use alternatives solutions reusing software products usually well known by IT people (e.g. rule engines) without renouncing to an ontological representation of the domain.

FUTURE TRENDS

In the last few months new investment in the telecommunications market are coming from Mobile Virtual Network Operators. This is a relatively new phenomenon: they are well known all over the world. What is really new is that some of these new players are financial institutions (e.g.

Rabobank in Holland, Poste Italiane in Italy). It is likely that they will exploit their core business for enabling payments using mobile terminals. M-payment is not new and by itself is relatively interesting: what is really new is the fact that new services will be enabled by a single business actor. This could create the conditions for an explosion of the m-business market, considering that at least one of the barriers is falling. This would be the ideal condition for proposing a new, more flexible architecture for semantic enabled service provisioning like the one we dealt with in this chapter.

The need for new research is huge. Our research group will further proceed by extending the set of tools needed to support services/components along all their lifecycle. More specifically, we intend to develop visual tools for reusing components/ services using an intelligent service/component environment. This should improve the service creation phase allowing non technical people to create services reusing as much as possible the existing software component and services. The idea is to use the Service Registration Authority as a front-end for a configuration management system, enabling one to keep track not only of the software components/services but also of their meaning. This system should improve the service creation process and enable large companies to save large amounts of money.

Moreover, a more direct link to enterprise architecture methodologies and tools must be studied and developed. We believe that in the near future enterprise software architectural models will have to include domain ontologies. Thus tools for simplifying this prominent design task will become an absolute priority for the software research community.

It could be said that, from our point of view, the new frontier of the IT industry is strictly related to semantics. This is the main way to really introduce innovation and to justify future investment in this sector.

CONCLUSION

We have presented a solution for enabling a more effective service provisioning all along the service lifecycle. We started from considering the need to open the mobile operator business, trying to identify a solution for enabling a more flexible service publication mechanism and a more effective service discovery. Such a platform can be used for enabling a higher level of service personalisation, allowing service roaming among a coalition of business partners, reproducing the well-known concept of roaming at a higher abstraction level. The core subsystem of the overall infrastructure is the Service Registration Authority, a component based on a pre-engineered domain ontology, that plays the role of entry point for publishing new partner services. The idea underneath the SRA could be used for improving the service creation process, enabling the reuse of services and components for creating new value-added services.

The market is evolving rapidly and signs of a wide adoption of semantic enabled services architecture are more and more frequent. We have adopted an approach that mixes together semantic annotation along with traditional tools aiming to overcome some of the cultural barriers that could frighten conservative IT people.

REFERENCES

Booth D., Haas H., McCabe F., Newcomer E., Champion M., Ferris C., & Orchard D. (2004). *Web services architecture*. Retrieved February 2004, from http://www.w3.org/TR/ws-arch

De Furio, I., & Frattini, G. (2006). A semantic enabled service provisioning architecture. In *Proceedings of the 6th Business Agents and the Semantic Web (BASeWEB) Workshop*, Hakodate, Japan, May 2006.

Duke, A., & Richardson, M. (2006). A semantic service-oriented architecture for the telecommunications industry. In J. Davies, R. Studer, & P. Warren (Eds.), *Semantic Web technologies: Trends and research in ontology-based systems.* John Wiley & Sons.

EbXML. (2005). OASIS ebXML RegRep Standard. Available at http://docs.oasis-open.org/regrep/v3.0/regrep-3.0-os.zip

ESSI. (2007). The European semantic systems initiative site. Retrieved June 2007, from http://www.essi-cluster.org/

Gisolfi, D. (2001). *Web services architect, Part 2: Models for dynamic e-business.* Retrieved January 2007, from http://www-128.ibm.com/developerworks/webservices/library/ws-arc2.html

Heß, A., Johnston, E., & Kushmerick, N. (2004). ASSAM: A tool for semi-automatically annotating Semantic Web Services. In *Lecture Notes in Computer Science 3rd International Semantic Web Conference (ISWC 2004).* Springer-Verlag.

Koetzle, L. (2004). *IT spends follows organizational structure.* Retrieved from, http://www.forrester.com/

Martin, D., Burstein, M., Hobbs, J., Lassila, O., McDermott, D., McIlraith, S., et al. (2004). *OWL-S: Semantic markup for Web services, version 1.1.* Available at http://www.daml.org/services/owl-s/1.1/overview/

Moreno, A., Valls, A., & Viejo, A. (2003). *Using JADE-LEAP to implement agents in mobile devices.* Retrieved from http://jade.tilab.com/papers/EXP/02Moreno.pdf

OASIS. (2007). The OASIS semantic execution environment TC site. Retrieved June 2007, from http://www.oasis-open.org/committees/tc_home.php?wg_abbrev=semantic-ex

Rajasekaran, P., Miller, J., Verma, K., & Sheth, A. (2004). Enhancing web services description and discovery to facilitate composition. In *Proceedings of SWSWPC2004: International Workshop on Semantic Web Services and Web Process Composition.* Retrieved from, http://lsdis.cs.uga.edu/lib/download/swswpc04.pdf

Roman, D., Keller, U., & Lausen, H. (2004). *Web service modeling ontology - Standard (WSMO - Standard), version 0.2.* Available at http://www.wsmo.org/2004/d2/v1.0

UDDI Version 3.0.2. (2004). OASIS standard. Available at http://www.oasis-open.org/committees/uddi-spec/doc/tcspecs.htm#uddiv3.

Werthner, H., Hepp, M., Fensel, D., & Dorn, J. (2006). Semantically-enabled service-oriented architectures: A catalyst for smart business networks. In *Proceedings of the Smart Business Networks Initiative Discovery Session*, June 14-16, Rotterdam, The Netherlands

ADDITIONAL READING

Akkiraju, R., & Goodwin R. (2004). Semantic matching in UDDI, external matching in UDDI. In *Proceedings of IEEE International Conference on Web Services (ICWS)*, July 2004, San Diego, USA

Davies, J., Studer, R., & Warren, P. (2006). *Semantic Web technologies: Trends and research in ontology-based systems.* West Sussex: Wiley Publishing, John Wiley & Sons

Dogac, A., Laleci, G. B., Kabak, Y., & Cingil, I. (2002). Exploiting Web service semantics: Taxonomies vs. ontologies. *IEEE Data Engineering Bulletin, 25*(4).

Dogac, A., Kabak, Y., & Laleci, G. (2004). Enriching ebXML registries with OWL ontologies for efficient service discovery. In *Proceedings of RIDE'04*, Boston, March 2004.

Mahmoud, Q. (2005). *Service-oriented architecture (SOA) and Web services: The road to enterprise application integration (EAI).* Technical

Articles, Sun Development Network. Retrieved October 19, 2005, from http://java.sun.com/developer/technicalArticles/WebServices/soa/

Salam, A.F., & Stevens, J. R. (2006). *Semantic Web technologies and E-Business: Toward the integrated virtual organization and business process automation.* Hershey, PA: Idea Group Publishing.

Sivashanmugam, K., Verma, K., Sheth, A. P., & Miller, J. A. (2003). Adding semantics to Web services standards. In *Proceedings of The 2003 International Conference on Web Services (ICWS'03)* (pp. 395-401).

ENDNOTES

[1] See java.sun.com/javafx/

[2] AJAX (Asynchronous JavaScript and XML), or Ajax, is a web development technique used for creating interactive web applications. The intent is to make web pages feel more responsive by exchanging small amounts of data with the server behind the scenes so that the entire web page does not have to be reloaded each time the user requests a change. Some of the commercial mobile browser are able to support Ajax. The idea is to overcome some of the issues related to mobile application usability using the Ajax approach. One of the issues that Ajax solve is the latency of the over-the-air communication (12-15 sec for UMTS networks)

[3] See http://jena.sourceforge.net/

Chapter III
Planning for the Introduction of Mobile Applications to Support the Sales Force:
A Value–Based Approach

Chihab BenMoussa
Åbo Akademi University, Finland

ABSTRACT

Performance gains from SFA investments have often been obstructed by the sales force's unwillingness to accept and use available systems. Studies show that a strong reason for resistance by the sales force to the technology is the failure to convince salespeople of the advantages and benefits of the new technology. Consequently firms face the challenge of selecting SFA technologies that their sales force will perceive as valuable and accept to use to enhance its performance. This issue becomes more challenging when it comes to introducing emerging technologies such as mobile technologies, where there is a risk of falling into the trap of overestimating/underestimating their potential value. The present study proposes a value-based approach for planning the introduction of Mobile applications to support the sales force. The approach suggested provides guidelines on how to determine whether or not mobile technologies would add value to the sales force before those technologies actually get selected and implemented. Good planning of SFA investment would help firms avoid resistance of the sales force towards the implemented systems, rather than having to treat it at the post-implementation stage.

INTRODUCTION

Despite the impressive advances in hardware and software capabilities the troubling problem of underutilized systems continues. Low usage of installed systems has been identified as a major factor underlying the "productivity paradox" surrounding lacklustre returns from organizational investments in information technology. (Venkatesh and Davis, 2000, p 186).

The above problem is highly relevant to the sales force. In recent years the issue of motivating the sales force to adopt sales force automation (SFA) technology has come to the forefront in both practitioner publications and academic research.

SFA occurs when firms apply information and communication technologies to improve the effectiveness and efficiency of sales-related-activities, notably the sales force channel. SFA can be applied to support many sales force's tasks such as contact management, scheduling, targeting, forecasting, mapping out sales routes, prospecting, making sales presenting, reporting sales encounters, collaborating with colleagues, retrieving sales information, documenting buyers' objections and gathering important customer and competitor data that feed marketing decisions (Widmier, Jackson, & McCabe, 2002; Engle & Barnes, 2000). In 1996 SFA was a US$ 1.5 billion industry (Rivers & Dart, 1996) and the global market for SFA software was predicted to reach $4.5 billion by 2004 (Rangarajan et al.2005), and was predicted to grow significantly in the future. The cost per sales person for SFA is estimated to be US$5000 to US$15000 per year (Honeycutt et al.2005).

To date 55-80 per cent of SFA projects have been unsuccessful (Honeycutt, 2005; Rigby et al. 2002).According to a leading IT consulting agency, 60 per cent of sales personnel report not using available SFA technology (Dulaney, 1996). The main reason cited by sales representatives is that SFA did not help them in the most important aspects of their job: face-to-face customer meetings. As a result, given that firms invest between US$5000 and US$15,000 per salesperson in SFA projects, failure rates at even one half of this magnitude indicate that firms may not be recouping their technology investment (Honeycutt, 2005). Aside from the obvious negative effect on company profits such failure can also hinder sales force performance and potential customer satisfaction (Jones et al., 2002)

The Problem of Motivating the Sales Force to use the Company-Initiated SFA Systems

Firms planning the introduction of new SFA to support their sales force face the challenging problem of how to convince their salespeople about the usefulness of the new technology so that they adopt it and use it to enhance their performance.

Studies on SFA adoption have shown that perceived usefulness is the strongest factor that influences salespeople's adoption of new technology. For instance Schillewaert et al. (2005) studied 229 salespeople from different industries in order to investigate their adoption of information technology. The results of their studies indicate that usefulness is a fundamental driver of sales technology usage by the sales force and ease of use is a secondary driver. Similarly Avlonitis et al. (2005) found that salespersons are more likely not to adopt and use implemented information systems in day-to-day activities if they believe that such systems are not useful and/or are difficult to use. Jones et al. (2002) examined factors leading to SFA use. The results of their study show that usage of the technology may depend on its benefit as perceived by the individual salesperson. The authors also found that salespersons who demonstrate a low level of personal innovativeness may experience problems in adopting the technology. Likewise a study by Buehrer et al. (2005) investigated reasons why sales representatives use technology and barriers that may impede their successful adoption of SFA systems. Their findings indicated that sales representatives use technology because it is useful.

The Problem of Predicting the Value of an Emerging SFA Technology

Given the importance of perceived usefulness for SFA adoption, firms planning the introduction of new SFA face the challenging problem, "how to determine the potential value of a new SFA so that the sales force would perceive it as useful and accept to use it to enhance its performance?"

Indeed, a number of studies showed how SFA technologies have failed because of inappropriate planning of the SFA initiative. Poor planning has led a number of firms to investing in technologies that may not fit their sales force's work requirements. As a result, the sales force may not perceive the technology as useful for its work and thus regard it as an imposition from the management. Erffmeyer et al. (2005) investigated companies' expectations and outcomes from SFA investment in a study involving 43 companies. They found that a very limited number of firms participating in their study were able to offer details with regard to the goals of their sales force automation. For example, the majority of the respondents mentioned improving the sales force efficiency as a goal of SFA. However, when asked what specific areas that need improvement, a typical response was "our goal is to get as many things automated as possible". They also observed that in some cases planning efforts were made with little or no involvement of the sales force. Among their recommendation to managers is to set explicit goals for the SFA investment and make sure that they are accepted by both the sales force and the customers.

In another study Speier & Venkatesh (2002) conducted a longitudinal study on the sales force's adoption of SFA systems. Their study revealed that sales representatives reacted favourably to SFA immediately after release. However, negative perceptions of SFA emerged six months after implementation. The technology was widely rejected by the sales force. In addition, absenteeism and voluntary turnover had significantly increased. They also reported a significant decrease in perceptions of organisational commitment, job satisfaction, person-organisation fit, and person-job fit. The authors conclude that for a SFA project to succeed; sales representatives should be actively involved with management in understanding the degree to which SFA will augment their sales activities before purchase and implementation.

A noteworthy study by Gohmann et al. (2005) investigated the difference between the perceptions of SFA systems held by management and the sales force. Their findings revealed a discrepancy between the management and the sales force in terms of their perceptions of SFA. This led to the management having productivity expectations higher than what the sales force can achieve with the system. The authors conclude that when salespeople are excluded from the decision-making process they may view the adoption of SFA technology as an imposition at best or an odious addition to a job at worst. Thus the issue of determining the potential value of a new SFA prior to implementation is crucial not only to understanding why new SFA technology has been introduced, but also to influencing what the organization gets out of the SFA investment. As Preece (2003) observed, managers at the early stages of new technology adoption/introduction, have some degree of choice over the associated social, organizational, and technical aspects and issues. They have much wider "design space" than they do at later stages, when key decisions have already been taken.

The need of a good planning of SFA introduction becomes more important when it comes to an emerging technology whose potential value is merely hypothetical and the chances are high for management to fall into the overestimation/ underestimation trap with regard to assessing the potential value of the technology. Ingram et al. (2002) indeed made a point when they asserted that predicting the impact of specific technologies and productively applying new technologies within a sales organisation is a challenge that firms have to deal with in the new millennium.

The Case of Mobile Information and Communication Technologies (M-ICT)

The advent of mobile information and communication technologies (M-ICT) continues to trigger an ongoing debate in both the academic and the practitioner communities. For enthusiasts, the introduction of M-ICT into the workplace marks a new era that will revolutionise the way of working and collaborating. They believe in the ability of M-ICT to provide anytime, anywhere support to any task, and thus the mobile device could act as a small desktop computer that would allow users to run various applications with the same functionality.

Sceptic analysts show a concern about whether or not M-ICT can be introduced successfully into the workplace. That is whether firms will be able to develop and roll out mobile applications that employees would value and accept to use in order to increase their performance. Those analysts points to the potential constraints of M-ICT in terms of security, reliability, privacy protection and form factors, e.g., display, bandwidth, memory, length of battery. They believe that those constraints would prohibit M-ICT from delivering appropriate support to targeted users compared to its stationary counterpart.

Moderate analysts take a more realistic position. They believe that the hunt for mobile killer applications that would replace the stationary ICT support is a vain endeavour. Companies should rather work on understanding how M-ICT given its key features and limitations could create a value to the members of their workforce. Indeed a number of studies on the work force's adoption of M-ICT point to the need for a balanced view that would take into account both the key features of M-ICT and its limitations when it comes to distilling the value-adding mechanisms of such technologies. For instance Gebauer & Shaw (2004) investigated success factors and the impacts of a mobile electronic procurement system implemented at a Fortune 100 company. The results of their study indicate that several factors inhibited the usage of the mobile application, especially by the managers that operate in a mobile work setting. The inhibiting factors include screen and keyboard size of the mobile devices, set up and login procedures, as well as training and support.

The authors' conclusions, based on the lessons derived from the case study, are that users of mobile applications need simple yet functional solutions. They argued that mobile technologies can compliment existing applications by adding an ad hoc element for data-processing, information access, communication and notification (Gebauer & Shaw, 2004).

Likewise, Nielson (2001) argued that mobile technology support should be examined as one component among the "web-of-technologies" available to support the user's tasks and routines. Hence, she suggested that mobile devices need to fulfil at least one of the following demands in order to be successful: (i) expand existing services or systems by giving them mobility and making it possible to solve a set of specific tasks in a specific context; (ii) offer a solution to a well-defined, targeted task, i.e. provide here-and-now related information. Thus the key question for firms wishing to introduce M-ICT to support their sales force is "how M-ICT given its key features and limitations would create value to the sales force?"

All of these points to the need for a new approach, that could model how M-ICT given its key characteristics and constraints could provide a value adding support that the sales force will be willing to adopt and use to enhance its performance, in such a way to be understood by managers and developers.

BenMoussa (2008) formulated a Barrier-To-Support (BTS) Model of new ICT's value creation. It draws upon Fernand Braudel's (1979) work on the mechanisms through which new technologies could add value to potential users. BTS framework analytically characterises the four types of new ICT based on their potential value to prospective users: Freedom, opportunity, convenience and feature technologies. This chapter projects BenMoussa's (2008) general framework onto the specific question of: *"How can we determine whether or not M-ICT could be a freedom or opportunity ICT support for the sales force?"*

The aim of the chapter is therefore to suggest a value-based approach that would help managers determine prior to implementation whether or not M-ICT could provide a value adding support to the sales force. The suggested approach builds on BenMoussa's (2008) BTS framework and proposes a Barrier-Technology-Fit (BTF) that complements the BTS model. The two models are then merged and translated into methodological guidelines for helping mangers at the planning stage determine whether or not M-ICT could create value to their sales force.

The remainder of this chapter is organized as follows. In the next section we introduce BenMoussa's (2008) BTS framework. In section 3 we link BTS framework with the issue of motivating the sales force to adopt new SFA. Section 4 introduces BTF framework. Section 5 translated the two models into methodological guidelines on how to determine the value adding potential of M-ICT in providing useful support to the sales force.

HOW TO DETERMINE THE VALUE POTENTIAL OF NEW ICT SUPPORT?

The general framework suggested by BenMoussa (2008) characterises a barrier-based model of new ICT's value creation. It draws upon Fernand Braudel's work on the mechanisms through which new technologies could add value to potential users. Braudel is one of the most influential historians of the last century. Since his first publication in 1949, Braudel's subject of investigation has always been the forces that shape people's everyday life. He did that across a vast panorama of technologies, time, space and societies (Keen & Mackintosh 2001). Braudel's (1979) view of new technologies' value adding mechanisms is based on the concepts of barriers within the structure of everyday life and effectiveness of existing technologies in helping people deal with the barriers

they face. Braudel's idea is basically that a new technology could create value if people perceive it as expanding their limit of the possible within the structure of their everyday life. That is making it possible for people to achieve what was taught to be impossible. His view also outlines how the new technology could expand users' limit of the possible. Braudel (1979) argued that a new technology could expand people's limit of the possible by *breaking barriers* or *opening up new opportunities* within the structure of their everyday life. He showed that as long as the everyday life runs without problems, people will not have any economic motivation to induce a change; innovations are left unexploited. It is only when people face obstacles and barriers that they start looking for technological inventions that would support them in breaking those barriers as well as in opening up new opportunities.

Earlier attempts to characterize new technologies' value based on Braudel's work have been done by Keen & Mackintosh (2001). In their book, the Freedom Economy, they draw upon Braudel's first volume of his Civilisation and Capitalism: 15th-18th Century trilogy to define what they labelled the Braudel Rule. They specifically used Braudel's two concepts of "the structures of everyday life" and "the limit of the possible". They define the Braudel Rule as "changing the limit of the possible within the structures of everyday life". They then use this rule as a tool to analyse the value of a number of technologies for people, based on the extent to which those technologies can change the limit of the possible within the structures of individuals' everyday life, i.e. to provide people with new sources of freedom. Using the "Braudel rule" as a framework, Keen & Mackintosh (2001) classified technology impacts into Freedom, Convenience and Features. Freedoms are technologies that pass the Braudel Rule. They change the limit of the possible in the structures of everyday life. Conveniences and features, on the other hand, do not fit the Braudel Rule. They are neat ideas that are solutions to problems that no one may care about (Keen & Mackintosh, 2001).

BenMoussa's (2008) continues Keen & Mackintosh's (2001) work by translating the Braudel Rule into a framework characterising new ICT support's value potential. His framework that he labelled Barrier-to-Support (BTS) matrix for new ICT artefacts is based on Braudel's two conditions for a new technology to expand the limit of possible for end-users that we discussed earlier. Those conditions are (i) there should be barriers that hinder the structures of people's everyday life, and (ii) the available technologies have reached their "ceiling" in terms of helping them to deal with the barriers they face. Although used at their maximum capabilities, the existing technologies fail to provide the appropriate support to people in terms of dealing with the barriers that hamper their everyday life.

The resulting framework (cf. Figure 1) characterises the potential value of new ICT support by matching the frequency with which prospective users face certain barriers within the structures of their everyday life, and the effectiveness of the existing support available for dealing with the barriers. This resulted in four categories of new ICT value, *freedom, opportunity, convenience* and *feature*. Additionally the BTS framework described the potential reaction of end-users towards the new ICT support as *"help me"*, *"show me"*, *"don't disturb me"* and *"why not?"*. The following outlines those four analytical values of new ICT:

- **Freedom new ICT:** These create value by expanding the limit of the possible within users' structure of every day's life. This happens by freeing people from the barriers that people face frequently; and for which existing technologies fail to provide the required support (cf. lower- right quadrant in Figure 1).
- **Opportunity new ICT:** These compete with existing technologies in terms of helping people to deal with their everyday life barriers. Their success rests on their abili-

ties to provide new and innovative support that outperforms existing technologies and would thus justify their adoption (cf. upper-right quadrant in Figure 1).

- **Conveniences new ICT:** These are technologies that are merely a convenience to people. They offer support for barriers that individuals do not face frequently. Hence, a new technology would be "nice to have" rather than a "must have" technology (cf. lower- left quadrant in Figure 1).
- **Feature new ICT:** These provide some new functions that help people to deal with certain barriers that they face occasionally and for which the support of existing technologies is appropriate. For these barriers, the new technology may have a disturbing rather than a supportive effect on potential adopters, if they have to invest time in learning how to operate a new technology that would not provide them with sufficiently tangible values (c.f. upper-left quadrant in Figure 1).

IDENTIFYING THE POTENTIAL VALUE OF NEW SFA USING THE BTS FRAMEWORK

The BTS framework aims at finding the targeted needs where a new ICT support is required based on both prospective users' barriers that hamper their performance and the effectiveness of existing ICT support available to them. The purpose is to uncover the areas where a new ICT is needed and could provide a value adding support to users. The ultimate objective is to ensure that the new technological support offered to people makes sense to them, and that they find it useful to integrate into their every day life routines (BenMoussa, 2008). These can be useful within the context of introducing new SFA where perceived usefulness has been found as a dominant factor influencing sales force's adoption. In the following the four

Figure 1. The barrier-to-support framework (BenMoussa, 2008)

Frequency of the barrier to performance

types of new ICT support's value (cf. Figure 1) will be discussed within the context of introducing new SFA to support the sales force.

Freedom New SFA **(High Barrier Frequency; Low Effectiveness of Existing SFA Systems)**

This refers to situations where salespeople frequently face certain barriers despite the support of the existing arrays of technologies they have. For those barriers, the available technologies have reached the limits of the possible without helping the sales force remove the barriers. Hence, a new SFA is needed and its value-adding potential rests on its ability to free the sales force from the barriers that still hamper them in their everyday life routines.

Detecting those barriers would make it possible to build value-based ICT support on the premise of freeing the sales force from something negative,

i.e. providing salespeople with a useful ICT that has the potential to free them from the barriers that still hinder them within the structure of their everyday life. This is important within the context of a sales force's work where employee resistance has been identified by many researchers as a major risk associated with SFA implementation. According to Xu et al. (2002) in most companies, SFA efforts often never get off the ground because they encounter stiff resistance from users. Among the many reasons for resistance by the sales force to the technology is the failure to convince salespeople of the advantages and benefits of the new technology (Gilbert, 2004; Patton, 2001; Bush et al. 2005; Gohmann et al. 2005). Consequently, salespeople question the benefits of the SFA system. For example, according to Patton (2001), many SFA projects falter because the sales force needs to be sold on the idea. The nature of their job means that salespeople are autonomous decision-makers who are accustomed to assessing the features, advantages, and benefits of a new product or service. Therefore, they are more likely to be influenced by their own perceptions of the benefits of the technology than their peers, their superiors or their clients (Patton, 2001). Providing the sales force with new ICT support to free them from the barriers that hinder their every day life routines, would make it possible for management to show the sales force the benefits of the new ICT support. It would also enable the sales force's members to assess the potential usefulness of the new ICT support for freeing them from the barriers that hinder their sales job.

In terms of selecting a new SFA, the identification of the barriers requiring new ICT support would allow organisations to assess, before implementation, whether or not, a specific SFA given both its key characteristics and limitations could be an appropriate form of ICT support to help their sales force deal with those barriers. If the new SFA under study proved to meet the requirements of the barriers in terms of support, then its value would be clear and rests on meeting an unanswered need among the members of the sales force since it would provide them with freedom from the barriers that still impede their performance.

Opportunity New SFA (High Barrier Frequency; High Effectiveness of Existing SFA Systems)

In this situation, the sales force frequently faces certain barriers within the structures of their everyday life. However, the existing technology provides appropriate technology support. In this case the new SFA must offer superior capabilities (e.g. easier use, better performance, lower cost) that would entice the sales force to adopt it. In other words, the sales force should be "sold" on the opportunities offered by the new SAF compared with the existing one in order for them to consider a change.

Convenience New SFA (Low Barrier Frequency; Low Effectiveness of Existing SFA Systems)

In this situation salespeople occasionally faces certain barriers and the existing technologies do not provide them with appropriate support to deal with them. In this case the new technology would be merely a convenience for the sales force since it offers support for barriers that prospective users do not care a lot about. Thus, the new SFA would be a "nice to have" rather than a "must have" technology. Moreover, if this type of SFA is introduced it will be difficult for companies to demonstrate its usefulness the sales force's members, especially if it requires time and effort from them in order to master the new technology. According to Honeycutt et al. (2005), organisations must understand that time devoted to learning a new technology is a sacrifice that salespeople will undertake only if they understand how the technology will help them serve their customers and meet their sales goals.

Feature New SFA (Low Barrier Frequency; High Effectiveness of Existing SFA Systems)

This refers to the situation where people occasionally face certain barriers and the existing technologies provide an appropriate support to deal with them. In this case, the new technology would have merely a feature impact. It would add new features to technologies that support people appropriately in dealing with the barriers that they face occasionally. Moreover, the new technology may have a disturbing impact on people if they have to spend time learning how to operate it.

For the sales force, a main goal of SFA is to re-direct less productive time and effort toward the sales force's main priority: selling (Honeycutt et al.2005). However, if the new SFA proposes solutions to barriers that the sales force face only occasionally and existing ICT support is effective in helping them deal with those barriers, then it would be difficult to justify its usefulness. Moreover, providing those technologies to the sales force may be value-eroding if the sales force has to spend time learning how to operate the new SFA at the expense of selling.

To sum up, the barrier-to-support matrix (cf. Figure 1) does not aim to specify which new technology would create freedoms or provide superior technology support for the sales force. Rather, it enables a scan of the barriers sales people face in relation to the effectiveness of the technological support available to them to deal with those barriers. The goal is to sort out targets barriers where new technology support could provide a value-adding support to the sales force. The value would stem from freeing prospective users from target barriers, i.e. freedom new SFA, or offering them a better support compared to what is available to them, e.g. opportunity new SFA The ultimate objective is to ensure that the new technological support, e.g. freedom ICT, opportunity ICT offered to salespeople makes sense to them, and that they find it useful to integrate it into the structures of their everyday life.

HOW TO DETERMINE WHETHER OR NOT M-ICT IS SUITABLE TECHNOLOGY FOR DEALING WITH THE TARGET BARRIERS?

The purpose of this section is to introduce a model that builds on the output of the BTS framework. The model which is labelled the Barrier-Technology-Fit (BTF) would help determine whether or not M-ICT given its key characteristics and limitations could provide the sales force with appropriate support in terms of dealing with the barriers identified through the BTS matrix.

The BTF framework draws upon Goodhue & Thompson's (1995) general theory of task/technology fit, and Zigurs & Buckland's (1998)

specific theory of task/technology fit for group support systems. The model followed Goodhue & Thompson's (1995) recommendation that task/technology fit, when decomposed into its more detailed components, could be the basis for a strong diagnostic tool to evaluate whether information systems in a given organisation meet users' needs. In the proposed BTF framework, the focus is on the barriers that impede the sales force's efforts to carry out their everyday tasks.

Figure 2 depicts the BTF framework. The arrows indicate sequence in a process way. Starting at the top left of the figure, the BTF framework involves pre-defining a profile of ICT support for the target barriers. The next step in the model is to analyse the degree of fit between the constructed profile of the ICT support and both the key features and limitations of M-ICT. If the fit is achieved, then useful M-ICT solutions will be designed to support the sales force in dealing with the identified target-barriers; otherwise an alternative candidate for ICT support has to be considered. Moving clockwise in Fig.2, as the prospective adopters will perceive the M-ICT applications as useful in supporting them to deal with the target barriers; they will integrate their usage into the structure of their everyday life routines. This is intended to be consistent with the work of Davis et al. (1989), and Adams et al. (1989), who have used perceived usefulness to predict IS use. In the BTF framework, however, perceived usefulness is interpreted in a process way (an event that necessarily precedes the outcome) rather than in a variant way (variance in the independent variable is necessary and sufficient to cause variance in the dependent variables). Moving again clockwise, if prospective users perceive M-ICT solutions useful, then they will use it to deal with the target barriers that hinder their performance within the structure of their everyday life.

In the following we will discuss the constructs of the BTF framework described in Figure 2.

Figure 2. The barrier-technology fit framework (BTF)

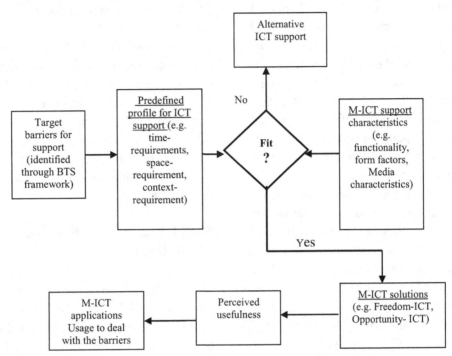

Target-Barriers

The target-barriers construct refers to the list of barriers detected as requiring new ICT support based on a scan through the BTS framework (cf. Figure 1). They refer to the barriers that the sales force faces frequently during the structure of their everyday life. However, the available ICT support reached the limit of the possible without providing the necessary support; new ICT support is therefore needed. Additionally, the target-barriers construct includes the barriers identified as frequently faced by the sales force and for which existing ICT provides appropriate support for the workers. For those barriers, the value of a new technology rests on its ability to propose new and innovative support compared to the existing one.

Predefined Profile for ICT Support to Deal with the Target-Barriers

This construct refers to building a predefined profile of the ICT support that can help the sales force deal with the target barriers identified through the BTS framework.

Depending on the nature of the identified barriers, the analysis might include such dimensions as time, space, and the context of the required ICT support. The *temporal* dimension concerns analysing the mobilisation urgency required for the support to create a value for the prospective users. As an example, these involve analysing the value of getting the support "Now" in order to establish the time relevance of the prospective ICT support (Keen & Mackintosh, 2001).

The *spatial* dimension refers to analysing the implications of the workers' spatial movement for the characteristics of the prospective ICT support. In the modern era, workers perform their work in different places including stationary work settings and mobile work settings. *A stationary work* setting means workers do their job mostly in a physical space that does not involve geographical movement locally or globally (Han, 2005). *Mobile work settings* involve different degrees of geographical movement, depending on the nature of the job. For example, Kristoffersen & Ljungberg (1998) propose a generic model of mobile IT use that aims at understanding mobile work and designing new mobile technologies to support it. By identifying what they call "typical instances" of a type of mobility, they created a classification with three distinct types of mobility: travelling, visiting and wandering. Travelling denotes the kind of mobility where you move from one place to another using a vehicle, like commuters. Visiting denotes the type of mobility where you spend some time at one physical location before going somewhere else, e.g. consultants. Wandering denotes local mobility within a smaller area such as a building with very little time spent in any one place e.g. the night watchman going on his round. Sarker & Wells (2003) pointed out that the modalities of users' mobility have implications in terms of the characteristics of the required mobile support. They suggested that the optimal size requirement of a device is lower when wandering compared to travelling or visiting. Similarly, larger network coverage is needed more when travelling than when visiting.

The *contextual* dimension refers to the characteristics of the use situation for ICT support, which may include cultural factors such as usage etiquette (e.g. you should not use the IT support during a face-to-face encounter with a customer) or power distance. Power distance refers to the symbolic meaning of what communication a medium carries depending on the nature of the relationship between individuals. For example, in countries with a high power-distance culture, such as Korea, text messaging to supervisors might be seen as a serious offence (Sarker & Wells, 2003). The contextual dimension may include distraction factors characterizing the use situation. Tarasewich (2003), for example, found that users operating in a mobile work setting tend to be distracted more often compared with those in a typical office environment. This is because in a mobile setting many activities compete for the attention of the mobile user. According to Tarasewich (2003) safety issues can also limit the attention that the user can give to the IT support (e.g. driving the car).

M-ICT Characteristics and Limitations

This involves analysing the key features and limitations of M-ICT in order to find out how well it fits the predefined multidimensional ICT profile constructed for the target barriers. The analysis might include such dimensions as functionality, form factors and media-richness.

The use of functionality as a dimension to characterise technology has been employed in applications of the task/technology fit theory. Zigurs & Buckland (1998) used the functional view of technology and defined group support systems technology as "the set of communication, structuring, and information processing tools that are designed to work together to support the accomplishment of group tasks". Goodhue & Thompson (1995) focused on functionality when they used information systems as a proxy for their technology construct.

Form factors may include the analysis of the M-ICT in terms of portability and interface characteristics.

Media-richness as developed by Daft & Lengel (1986) is a prescriptive model positing that achieving a match between information-processing requirements (e.g. uncertainty and equivocality reduction) and communication media (e.g. face-to-face interactions and writing memos) is essential for organisational effectiveness (Markus, 1994). According to the media-richness theory rich media, including the telephone and face-to-face meetings, are needed to process complex situations, such as setting organisational goals, strategies, communicating managerial intentions, and managing employee motivation. Media low in information richness, such as written information sources, technical manuals and mathematical formula were best to deal with simple topics, such as inventory control. The media-richness theory has been validated in a number of studies. For example, Lim & Benbasat (2000) use the media-richness theory as a framework for investigating whether or not a rich representation of information (multimedia) can better support the information-processing needs of decision-makers. The results of their studies indicated that task analysability influenced both the type of information representation that was most appropriate for equivocality reduction, and the usefulness of an information system. Specifically, they found that multimedia support them in coping with less analysable tasks.

Fit

The concept of fit has been widely used in a variety of models that deal with contingencies among variables (Zigurs & Buckland, 1998). Within the framework of strategy research, Venkatraman (1989) identified six perspectives of fit: fit as moderation, as mediation, as matching, as gestalts, as profile deviation and as covariance.

In GSS research, achieving a fit between a group's tasks and GSS technology was suggested as a principle for effective use of group support systems (Zigurs & Buckland, 1998). Dennis et al. (2001) performed a meta-analysis to summarise and synthesise the results of 15 years of research on GSS effectiveness. The results of their study indicate that when there is a fit between the GSS structures and the tasks, GSS had the greatest

impact on outcome effectiveness (decision quality and idea). They also found that the support the group receives had the highest impact on the process (time required and satisfaction).

Zigurs & Buckland (1998) applied the task/technology framework to examine GSS effectiveness. They considered the conceptualisation of fit as an adherence to an ideal profile to be the most appropriate for task/technology fit in a GSS context, compared with the other perspective of fit (fit as matching, moderation, gestalts and covariance). They argued that the perspective of fit as an ideal profile, allows for a holistic approach to examining complexity in an organisation (Zigurs & Buckland, 1998). Zigurs & Buckland's TTF theory in the context of group support systems was later tested by Zigurs, Buckland, Connolly and Wilson (1999) on a selected set of published GSS experiments. They found that GSS groups perform better than non-GSS groups when the GSS and the task fit. Their study also revealed that GSS either performs worse or the same as non-GSS groups, when there is a mismatch between the GSS and the task.

Dishaw & Strong (1999) used the task/technology fit framework to assess the fit between the characteristics of a maintenance task and a software maintenance tool. The fit was assessed by comparing the actual functionality of the maintenance tool with the anticipation of users regarding the functionality required to complete various tasks. The greater the number of anticipation functionalities available in an actual tool, the better the fit was determined.

The concept of fit can be employed as a degree of adherence to a predefined ideal profile. Therefore the analysis of the fit in the BTF framework involves the following three steps: (1) predefining a multidimensional profile of ICT support for the target barriers; (2) analysing the characteristics of M-ICT support, and (3) finding out how well the M-ICT fits the predefined multidimensional profile.

M-ICT Solutions

This refers to solutions enabled by the M-ICT that will help prospective users deal with the target barriers. If M-ICT proved to fit the predefined profile discussed in 4.2, those solutions could be *freedom M-ICT* solutions, designed to free the users from the barriers identified as frequently faced and for which the existing ICT fails to provide appropriate support. They could also be *opportunity M-ICT* developed to provide superior support to prospective users.

Perceived Usefulness

Davis (1989) defines perceived usefulness for a specific IT to be "the degree to which a person believes that using a particular system would enhance his or her job performance". In the BTF framework, perceived usefulness refers to *"the degree to which the sales person believes that using the new ICT support, e.g. M-ICT solutions will help him/her in dealing with the barriers and thus will enhance his or her job performance or his or her organizational performance.*

ICT Usage to Deal with the Barriers

ICT usage refers to the degree to which the users actually use the implemented ICT solutions, e.g. M-ICT solutions to deal with the target barriers they face within the structure of their everyday life.

METHODOLOGICAL GUIDELINES

In the following we will translate the BTS and the BTF frameworks (cf. Figure 1) into an approach that would make it possible for management to understand the potential value of M-ICT support before introducing it into the workplace (cf. Figure 3).

Step 1: Understand

The aim of this step is to understand the nature of the barriers to performance the sales force faces. In this first step, management should assign a team of both representatives of the sales force to work and information systems specialists on collecting data related to the barriers to work performance the sales force faces. The team could then use qualitative, e.g. shadowing of prospective users and /or quantitative methods, e.g. surveys to build the list of prospective users' barriers to performance. During this step the team should also investigate how effective the available ICT support, e.g. desktop-based application, laptop-based application, in helping prospective users in breaking the barriers identified. The output of this first step is (i) the ranking of the barriers based on how frequent the sales force are facing them, and (ii) the ranking of available existing ICT support based on how effective, from the perspective of end-users, the support is in terms of helping then in breaking the barriers.

Step 2: Identify Target Barriers

The identification of target barriers for new ICT support is the aim of the second phase. This can be done by scanning the barriers through the BTS matrix (cf. Figure 3).

Here the aim is to detect gaps where a new ICT support is needed, based on both salespeople barriers to performance and the effectiveness of existing ICT support available to them. The purpose is to sort out target barriers where a new ICT is needed and could provide a value adding support to users. A value-adding support means freeing the users from something negative. That is, providing users with a freedom ICT that has the potential to free them from the barriers that they the face frequently and for which the ICT support they have fail in supporting them effectively (cf. Freedom new ICT quadrant in Figure 1).

Figure 3. The BTS and BTF frameworks translated into an approach for analysing the potential value of M-ICT support

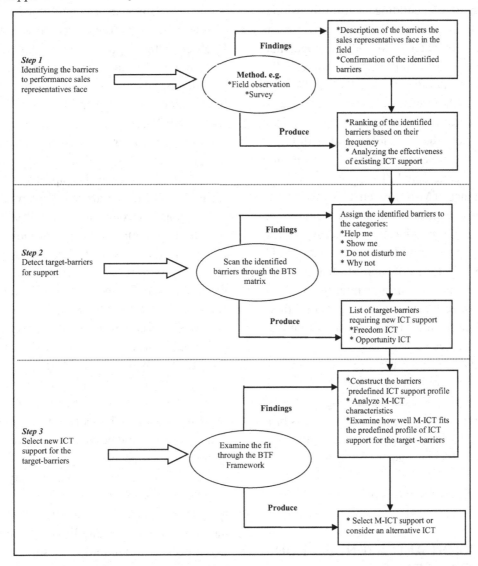

A value adding support would also rest on the expansion of possibilities that an ICT could give to prospective users in terms of support in order to deal with the barriers that they face frequently. However, the existing technology provides appropriate technology support (cf. Opportunity new ICT quadrant in Figure 1). In this case the new technology would be an opportunity ICT and must offer superior capabilities (e.g. easier use, better performance, lower cost) that would entice people to adopt it. In other words, people should be "sold" on the opportunities offered by the new technology compared with the existing one in order for them to consider a change.

Step 3: Analyze the Suitability of M-ICT in Helping the Sales Force Deal with Target Barriers

In the third phase the team should work on assessing whether or not M-ICT could be a "freedom" ICT or "opportunity" ICT in terms of helping the sales force deal with the target barriers. In the analysis the team could employ concept of fit. This will involve (i) building a multidimensional profile of ICT support for the target barriers; (ii) analysing the characteristics of M-ICT support and (iii) finding out how well the candidate ICT fits the predefined multidimensional profile. If M-ICT turns out to fit the requirements of predefined profile, then the team should design mobile solutions that would help the sales force deal with target barriers. Otherwise, step 3 should be repeated with another candidate ICT support.

For instance, if M-ICT given its key characteristics, e.g. timely information support, ubiquitous terminals, and limitations, e.g. usability issues, processing power proved to be a "freedom ICT" (cf. Figure 1) in terms of support, then its value would be clear and rests on meeting an unanswered need of prospective users since it provides them with freedom from the barriers that still impede their performance.

Similarly If M-ICT can serve as an "opportunity ICT", i.e. providing prospective users with better support than existing technologies; then its value potential would rest on expanding possibilities that the ICT support could give to potential users. Indeed, there would be no reason to provide the sales force with M-ICT unless doing so adds better possibilities in terms of support.

CONCLUSION AND AVENUES FOR FURTHER RESEARCH

Investments in SFA have often been fraught with pitfalls. Performance gains from SFA investment aimed at enhancing the sales force's performance have often been obstructed by the end users' unwillingness to accept and use available systems. In addition, even if firms can get the sales force to adopt the technology; there remains the problem of how much of this technology is actually used. For SFA systems to yield any benefits for the organization, sales people must accept and utilise

them. Given the alarming failure rate of SFA projects, managers need practical guidelines that would help them plan effectively the introduction of new technology to support their sales force. As Buehrer (2005) argued given the failure rate of SFA, the pressing question now seems to be "How we can prevent repetition of any firm's failures in information technology investment?" The present study contributes to filling this void by presenting and illustrating a value based approach for planning the introduction of M-ICT applications to support the sales force. The approach suggested starts by identifying targeted gaps where a new ICT support is needed, based on both sales force's barriers that hamper their performance and the effectiveness of existing ICT support available to them. The purpose is to sort out target barriers where a new ICT is needed and could provide a value adding support to end-users.

The identification of the barriers requiring new ICT would allow the management to determine proactively whether or not M-ICT could be an appropriate form of ICT to help their sales force deal with target-barriers. If M-ICT proved to fit the requirements of the barriers in terms of support, then its value would be clear and rests on meeting an unanswered need among the members of the sales, i.e. freedom M-ICT, opportunity M-ICT.

The approach suggested places the sales force at the centre of the analysis. It starts from the sales force's everyday life work barriers and works back to the technological support required to help them, while taking into consideration the effectiveness of existing technology support. As such, the approach achieves the balance between the work system and the information system that Alter (1999) has called for. Indeed Alter (1999) made a point when he builds the analogy between the work system and the information system that supports it as Siamese twins that are distinguishable but still so deeply connected that examining them separately is meaningless.

Finally, in line with the objective of the chapter, some methodological guidelines are described.

The author is currently working on some case studies where the approach is applied in order to test its operational aspect. The approach suggested will hopefully enable and stimulate other researchers to empirically investigate how to help mangers plan effectively before embarking into the cloudy waters of introducing new SFA technologies.

REFERENCES

Adams, D.A., Nelson, R.R., & Todd, P.A. (1992). Perceived usefulness, ease of use, and usage of information technology: a replication. *MIS Quarterly, 16*(2), 227-247.

Ahearne, M., Jelinek, R., & Rapp, A. (2005). Moving beyond the direct effect of SFA adoption on salesperson performance: Training and support as key moderating factors. *Journal of Personal Selling and Sales Management, 34*(4), 379-388.

Alter, S. (1999). The Siamese twin problem: a central issue ignored by dimensions of information system effectiveness. *Communications of AIS, 2*(20), 40-55.

Avlonitis, G., & Panagopoulos, N.G. (2005). Antecedents and consequences of CRM technology acceptance in the sales force. *Industrial Marketing Management, 34*(4), 355-368.

BenMoussa, C. (in press). A barrier-based model for justifying new ICT support: Focusing on mobile support. In *Proceedings of 7th International Conference on Mobile Business*. Barcelona, Spain. July 7-8, 2008.

Braudel, F. (1979). *Civilisation matérielle, économique et capitalisme XV-XVIII siécle-les structures du quotidian: le possible et l'impossible*. Librairie Géneral Francaise.

Buehrer, R. E., Senecal, S., Bolman E.P. (2005). Sales force technology usage—Reasons, barriers, and support: An exploratory investigation. *Industrial Marketing Management, 34*(4), 389-398.

Daft, R., & Lengel, R.H. (1986). Organizational information requirements, media richness and structural design. *Management Science, 32*(5), 554-571.

Davis, F.D. (1989). Perceived usefulness, perceived ease of use, and user acceptance of information technology. *MIS Quarterly, 13*(3), 319-340.

Dennis, A.R., Wixom, B.H., & Vandenberg, R.J. (2001). Understanding fit and appropriation effects in group support systems via meta-analysis. *MIS Quarterly, 25*(2), 167-193.

Dulaney, K. (1996, October). The automated sales force. *American Demographics*, 56-63.

Engel, R.L., & Barnes, M.L. (2000). Sales force automation usage, effectiveness and cost-benefit in Germany, England and United States. *Journal of Business and Industrial Marketing, 15*(4), 216-241.

Erffmeyer R.C., & Johnson, D.A. (2001). An exploratory study of sales forces automation practices: Expectations and realities. *Journal of Personal Selling and Sales Management, 21*(2), 167-175.

Gilbert. (2004, July). No strings attached. *Sales and Marketing Management*, 22-27.

Gebauer, J., & Shaw, M.J. (2004). Success factors and impacts of mobile business applications: Results from a mobile e-procurement study. *International Journal of Electronic Commerce, 8*(3), 19-41.

Gohmann S.F., Guan, J., Barker, R.M., & Faulds, D.J (2005a). Perceptions of sales force automation: Difference between sales force and management. *Industrial Marketing Management, 34*(4), 337-343.

Goodhue, D.L., & Thompson, R.L (1995). Task technology fit and individual performance. *MIS Quarterly, 19*(2), 213-236

Han, S. (2005, April). Understanding user adoption of mobile technology: focusing on physicians in Finland (Doctoral Dissertation). *TUCS Dissertations, 59.*

Honeycutt, E.D. (2005). Technology Improves sales Performance-doesn't it? *Industrial Marketing Management,34*(4), 301-304.

Ingram, T.N., LaForge, R.W., & Leigh, T.W. (2002). Selling in the new millennium: A joint agenda. *Industrial Marketing Management,31*(7), 559-567.

Jones, E., Sundaram, S., & Chin, W. (2002). Factors leading to sales force automation use: A longitudinal analysis. *Journal of Personal Selling and Sales Management, 22,* 145-156.

Keen, P., & Mackintosh, R. (2001). *The freedom economy: gaining the m-commerce edge in the era of the wireless Internet.* Berkeley, CA: Osborne/Mcgraw-Hill.

Kristoffersen, S., & Ljungberg, F. (1998). Representing modalities in mobile computing. In *Proceedings of Interactive applications of Mobile Computing.*

Lim, K.H., & Benbasat, I. (2000). The effects of multimedia on perceived equivocality and perceived usefulness of information systems. *MIS Quarterly, 24*(3), 449-471.

Nielsen C., & Sondergaard, A. (2000). Designing for mobility: an integrative approach supporting multiple technologies. In *Proceedings of Nordic CHI 2000.* Royal Institute of Technology, Stockholm, Sweden.

Patton, S. (2001). The truth about CRM. *CIO Magazine, 14,* 16-23.

Rangarajan, D., Jones, E., & Chin, W. (2005). Impact of sales force automation on technology-related stress, effort, and technology usage among salespeople. *Industrial Marketing Management, 34*(4), 345-354.

Robinson, L., Jr., Marshallb, G.W., Stamps, M.B. (2005). An empirical investigation of technology acceptance in a field sales force setting. *Industrial Marketing Management, 34*(4), 407-415

Rigby, D.K., Reichheld, F.F., & Schefter, P. (2002). Avoid the four perils of CRM. *Harvard Business Review, 80*(2), 101-108.

Rivers, L.M., & Dart, J. (1999). The acquisition and use of sales force automation by mid-sized manufacturers. *Journal of Personal Selling & Sales Management, 19*(2), 59-73.

Sarker, S., & Wells, J.D. (2003). Understanding mobile handheld device use and adoption. *Communications of the ACM, 46*(12), 35-40.

Schillewaert, N., Ahearnw, M., Frambach, R.T., & Moenaert, R.K. (2005). The adoption of information technology in the sales force. *Industrial Marketing Management, 34,* 323-336

Speier, C., & Venkatesh, V. (2002). The hidden Minefields in the adoption of sales force automation technologies. *Journal of Marketing, 66*(3), 98-111

Tarasewich, P. (2003). Designing mobile commerce applications. *Communications of the ACM, 46*(12), 57-60.

Venkatesh, V., Morris, M.G., & Davis, F.D. (2003). User acceptance of information technology: toward unified view. *MIS Quarterly, 27*(3), 425-478

Venkatesh, V., & Davis, F.D. (2000). A theoretical extension of the technology acceptance model: four longitudinal field studies. *Management Science, 46*(2), 186-204.

Venkatraman, N. (1989). The concept of fit in strategy research: Towards verbal and statistical correspondence. *Academy of Management Review, 14*(3), 423-444

Widmier, S. M., Jackson, D.W., & McCabe, D.B. (2002). Infusing technology into personal selling.

Journal of Personal Selling and Sales Management, 22(3), 189-198.

Xu, Y., Yen, D.C., Lin, B., & Chou, D.C. (2002). Adopting customer relationship management technology. *Industrial Management and Data Systems, 102*(8), 442-452.

Zigurs, I., & Buckland, B. K. (1995). A theory of task-technology fit and group support systems effectiveness. *MIS Quarterly, 22*(3), 313-334.

Zigurs, I., Buckland, B.K., Connoly, J.R., & Wilson, E.V. (1998). A test of task technology fit theory for group support systems. *The Database for Advances in Information Systems, 30*(3-4), 34-50.

KEY TERMS

Barriers to Performance: They refer to the difficulties and disturbances that hinder individuals from carrying their work-related tasks effectively and efficiently.

Barrier-Technology-Fit: It refers to the objective correspondence between the requirements of the barriers to performance in terms of a new ICT support, and the actual characteristics of a candidate ICT systems, designed to help individuals deal with the barriers to performance.

Braudel Rule: An approach for distilling the potential value-added of a new technology. Derived from the work of the economic historian Fernand Braudel, the Braudel Rule builds on the assumption that a new technology would be perceived as a value-adding technology, if it is designed and implemented in such a way that it will expand the limits of the possible within the structure of people's everyday life routines.

Convenience New ICT: This refers to technologies that are merely a convenience to people. They offer support for barriers that individuals do not face frequently. They are "nice to have" rather than "must have" technologies.

Feature New ICT: They provide some new functions that help people to deal with certain barriers that they face occasionally and for which the support of existing technologies is appropriate. For these barriers, the new technology may have a disturbing rather than a supportive effect on potential adopters, if they have to invest time in learning how to operate a new technology that would not provide them with sufficiently tangible values

Fit: Degree of adherence of an ICT solution to a predefined ideal ICT profile. Assessing the degree of fit as an adherence to a predefined profile would involve (1) predefining a multidimensional profile of ICT support for the target barriers; (2) analysing the characteristics of a candidate ICT support, e.g. M-ICT, and (3) finding out how well the candidate ICT fits the predefined multidimensional profile.

Freedom New ICT: A metaphor that attributes a new technology's value-adding effect to the technology's ability to free potential users from the barriers they face within the structure of their everyday's life routines; and where available technologies fail to provide the needed support in terms of removing those barriers.

Mobile Information and Communication Technologies (M-ICT): They refer to information and communication applications run over a wireless network using a mobile device and in a wireless environment. A mobile device is any lightweight device connected to the Internet or other networks through wireless networking using any standard wireless communication protocol. They may include such devices as PDAs, communicators or smart-phones.

Opportunity New ICT: A metaphor that attributes a new technology's value-adding effect to the technology's abilities to provide new and innovative support that outperforms existing technologies and would thus justify their adoption. Potential users should be persuaded as to the opportunities, e.g. cost, functionalities, usability offered by the new technology compared with the existing one in order for them to consider a change.

Sales Force Automation (SFA) Systems: Information and communication applications designed to support the sales force in carrying out sales-related tasks, including, contact management, scheduling, targeting, forecasting, mapping out sales routes, prospecting, making sales presenting, reporting sales encounters, collaborating with colleagues, retrieving sales information, documenting buyers' objections and gathering important customer and competitor data that feed marketing decisions.

Chapter IV
Virtual Economy and Consumer:
How do Consumers Perceive and use Virtual Currency in Web 2.0 Communities?

Dong Hee Shin
Towson University, USA & Sung Kyun Kwan University, South Korea

ABSTRACT

By expanding the technology acceptance model, this study analyzes the consumer purchasing behaviors with virtual currency in Web 2.0 drawing data from 311 users. This study focuses on which variables influence the intention to transact with virtual currency in Web 2.0. Individuals' responses to questions about attitude and intention to transact in Web 2.0 were collected and combined with various factors modified from the technology acceptance model. The results of the proposed model show that subjective norm is a key behavioral antecedent to use virtual currency. In the extended model, subjective norm's moderating effects on the relations among the variables are found significant. The new set of variables can be virtual environment-specific factors, playing as enhancing factors to attitudes and behavioral intention in Web 2.0 transactions. This study provides a more intensive view of Web 2.0 system users and is an important step towards a better understanding of the consumer behavior in Web 2.0.

INTRODUCTION

Web 2.0 encompasses a variety of different meanings that include an increased emphasis on user-generated content, data and content sharing, and collaborative effort, together with the use of various kinds of social software, new ways of interacting with Web-based applications, and the use of the Web as a platform for generating, re-purposing and consuming content (O'Reilly, 2006). One of the most recent examples is the virtual world Second Life. A downloadable software program enables its users (Residents) to interact with each other through motional Avatars, providing an advanced level of a social network service combined with general aspects of a metaverse. Residents can explore, meet other Residents, socialize, participate in individual and group activities, and create and trade items (virtual property) and services from one another. Second Life's population is drastically climbing. Currently there are about 7 million users, and forecasts project more than 25 million users by 2008 (Fetscherin & Lattemann, 2007). New business models in virtual worlds have been growing with the popularity of virtual currency. For example, the Second Life economy is growing so fast that the number of Second Life users making more than $5,000 (US) a month continues to grow (Reuters, 2007). Second Life processes over $400,000 worth of virtual currency transactions per day, supports more than 7,000 profitable businesses, and allows top entrepreneurs to earn more than $200,000 per year (Boyd & Moersfelder, 2007).

Residents can make objects and sell them for Linden Bucks (virtual currency in Second Life), which can then be redeemed for cyber-cars, clothes, and houses. Perhaps most important, the virtual currency can be converted into U.S. dollars. The growing popularity of virtual currency is a worldwide trend. The volume of virtual currency has reached several hundred million U.S. dollars a year in China. The so-called QQ coin has become so popular that the country's central bank is worried that it could affect the value of the real currency. In Japan, over 100,000 users are working as "gold farmers" —playing online role playing games and selling the virtual currency, items, and experience they generate for real world money. Many online game sites in Web 2.0 allow players to exchange virtual currency and items for real money.

This study explores the variables influencing the transaction behaviors with virtual currency in Web 2.0 through user survey research. An empirical assessment of the proposed research model in the Web 2.0 context was conducted for this study. It applies the modified technology acceptance model (TAM) approach incorporating trust, perceived risk, and subjective norm as enhancing constructs to predict users' motivations for economic activities (transactions, purchasing,

and spending using virtual currency) in Web 2.0. Focusing on why users decide and continue to purchase virtual items in Web 2.0, a research question seeks to answer what the motivations are to transact with virtual currency in Web 2.0. This research aims to provide a basic model that predicts consumers' acceptance of virtual currency by explaining their intentions when using Web 2.0 technologies for transactions. The main research issues are:

1. Predicting the drivers of consumer intentions to accept virtual currency and engage in the transaction behavior in Web 2.0.
2. Deciding whether and how to integrate TAM with the trust and risk literature to jointly predict consumer behavior in Web 2.0 space.

This study applies the structural equation modeling approach, supported by LISREL software, to assess the empirical strength of the relationships in the proposed model. The results of this study should be of interest to both academics and practitioners. From a theoretical perspective, while drawing upon the extended TAM, this study provides a model that identifies antecedents of consumer intention to purchase in the virtual market of Web 2.0. From a practical standpoint, the findings should guide managers in selecting more effective strategies to the virtual consumers in Web 2.0. Implications and directions for future studies are discussed.

LITERATURE REVIEW: DEFINITION AND CURRENT TRENDS OF WEB 2.0

Web 2.0 and Social Commerce

Web 2.0 describes a paradigm shift from the Web as a "passive information resource" to the Web as a "platform for the delivery of engaging services and experiences" (Kelly, 2006). The advent of the Web 2.0 paradigm has significant implications to the development of the electronic repertoire of contention. Within the Web 2.0 approach, the Web is seen as a platform for service delivery – a model that emphasizes user control, architectures of participation, and emergent behavior (O'Reilly, 2006). With an increase of re-mixable, collectible, hackable systems of loosely joined pieces, the Web has the potential to become an even more critical tool for social movements.

This potentiality will be enabled by the key concept of Web 2.0, that is, the notion of "social software" that facilitates the building and maintenance of virtual communities, self-expression, participation and dialogue (Wilson, 2006). This feature of social software opens a window of opportunity for Web 2.0 "social commerce." Web 2.0 as a social commerce means creating virtual places where people can collaborate, get advice from trusted peers, find goods and services and then purchase them with virtual currency. One example of social commerce in Web 2.0 is Trenonaut's blog, which provides rich tips, tricks, advice and news about products and services. Big sites like Amazon, Froogle, and Yahoo are developing virtual stores in Web 2.0, integrating the nature of social commerce into blogs. It is a trend that e-commerce sites partner with the major blogging platforms to make co-branded social commerce even easier.

Three companies lead virtual users in the high technology-based online world: Cyworld, Second Life, and There.

Virtual Currency in Web 2.0

Digital money, which includes cyber-money, game-money, and mileage points, is evolving into a real currency. Web technologies have brought down the walls between what is real and what is not, and now money used in online games, such as Lineage can easily be exchanged into real cash via virtual game item trading sites on the Web.

Dedicated gamers can even pay for bills or tickets with game-money. As it becomes more useful, the virtual currency is proliferating. Game item broker Itembay increased its total trade size from $45 million (US) in 2005 to 280 billion (US) in 2006, or six times more in two years. It is estimated that the total amount of cyber-money is about $1 billion (US) (Boyd & Moersfelder, 2007). Cyber money in Korea, such as Dotori of SK Communications, Daumcash and Byeol of Daum Communications, Naver Mileage and Eunhwa of NHN, is estimated to be worth about $200 billion (US) each.

There are unexpected side effects. Fraudulent activity through stolen IDs and hacking is increasing, and the possibility of money-laundering via virtual money has been pointed out. Moreover, even though digital money is partly replacing the functions of real money, nobody knows exactly how much of it there is. With the increasing vulnerability in Web 2.0, the roles of trust and perceived risk in virtual currency become critical in Web 2.0 transaction.

Cyworld

Cyworld is a Web community site operated by SK Communications in Korea. Literally translated, "Cyworld" can mean "cyber world," but cy also means relationship in Korean, so it also means "relationship world." The Cyworld Website had the highest ranking of all blog sites in 2006 Korea (Bourdeau & Kim, 2007). As of April 2005, the number of Cyworld users exceeded 13 million (Jung et al., 2007).

Cyworld provides mini-homepages for their users to post, update and maintain bulletin boards, diaries, photos, messages, and other information. Its distinctive characteristics are services such as a mini-room, buddy relationship services and other decorating functions. Users decorate their mini-homepages and mini-rooms with tens of thousands of digital items—homepage skins, background music, pixelated furniture, and virtual appliances. To buy these items, users must first exchange their real world currency with Cyworld money called "acorns." Cyworld generated $67 million in 2005 from those items. In 2007, Cyworld expects to contribute $140 million in sales, with acorns accounting for 70 percent, which means Korean consumers will shell out more than $100 million this year for Cyworld virtual inventory.

Second Life

Second Life is a three-dimensional virtual world where millions of dollars are spent. The number of businesses operating in this virtual world increases. Companies such as Reebok, American Apparel, Warner Music, Adidas, Toyota, Nissan, and IBM have also set up virtual stores in Second Life. The rationale behind these transitions ranges from attracting press coverage to brand engagement with potential clients. SL is a unique and cutting-edge business platform that facilitates virtual conferences, training, sales meetings, consumer research. The Second Life economy runs on Linden dollars, convertible to U.S. dollars (via the LindeX service), and has an annual GDP of 64 million USD. In November 2006, Linden Labs began releasing metrics on Linden dollar amounts on the Second Life Website. The Economist writes on "virtual economies" driven by Second Life and suggested the size of the total virtual economy market was $1bn USD in 2005, and would grow to over $7bn US Dollars by 2009 (The Economist, 2006).

There, Inc.

There, Inc. (http://www.there.com) is an entertainment and communications platform company that has created a new application for online interaction, which combines chat with the fun of online games. There leverages the popularity of two mass-market activities: online socializing, such as chat rooms and instant messaging, and online casual games, like cards, trivia and board games. The Web-based, 3D environment provides con-

sumers with greater online connections through a broader, more sophisticated range of competitive, social, and creative activities when compared with conventional chat rooms or online games.

There uses its own currency, called Therebucks. Users have 20,000T when signing up for a year, or 10,000T for the monthly plan. Additional Therebucks can be purchased with U.S. currency, at the rate of 1,787T per dollar. The average users spent $7 per month on "in-world" goods. Most items such as furniture are designed to be used within houses or zones, although some items such as vehicles and dogs are not due to their mobile nature. Monetary transactions in There's economy are done using Therebucks, virtual currency with real world value. Therebucks can be purchased directly from There, from other members, or from any of the third party online "banks" which usually offer competitive exchange rates. Members can also sell their Therebucks to banks in exchange for real world currency, usually USD.

USERS' BEHAVIOR TO VIRTUAL TRANSACTION IN WEB 2.0

TAM was inspired by the theory of reasoned action (TRA), which argued that both the attitude towards an action and subjective norm have an impact on behavioral intention, which in turn affects how people perform the action. TAM was an early attempt to apply psychological factors to information systems (IS) and computer adoption. It assumed that perceived usefulness and perceived ease of use were major influences of an individual's attitude towards using the technology and thus, ultimately, relating to actual use (Davis, 1989). As many researchers have proposed various extended TAM, there is a growing trend to approach TAM with various motivations.

Figure 1 presents the proposed model, referred to as the Web 2.0 transaction acceptance model. Following the application of modified TAM to a technology-driven environment, the classical

Figure 1. Proposed research model

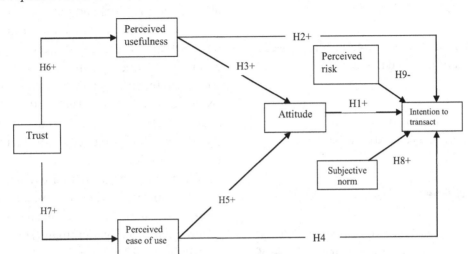

TAM variables (perceived usefulness and perceived ease of use) are posited as key drivers of virtual currency acceptance. In consideration of TRA, the proposed model integrates additional key drivers of Web 2.0 acceptance, such as trust, perceived risk, and subjective norm.

This model, based on TRA, is well suited to reflect the nature of Web 2.0 as it embodies the evolutionary progression of technology and usage dynamics toward a more fluid and agile "social" existence (O'Reilly, 2006). All the key drivers are defined and explained, and their relationship with transaction intentions and acceptance of Web 2.0 transaction is proposed. The practical utility of considering TAM stems from the fact that Web 2.0 is heavily technology-driven, as well as user-oriented. Web 2.0 is not so much about new Web technology as it is about the way that these technologies are being used to enhance human interaction and behavior (O'Reilly, 2006).

Trust and perceived risk are considered given the uncertainty of the Web 2.0 environment. Placing these variables under the nomological structure of TRA and precisely describing their interrelationships justifies the proposed integration of the hypothesized key Web 2.0 drivers into a coherent and parsimonious research model. Given the wide applicability of TAM in emerging technologies, it is expected that the general causalities found in TAM are also applicable to the Web 2.0 context. In particular, the relation between attitude and intention in a virtual community has been largely confirmed. Thus, it is hypothesized:

H1: Attitude toward Web 2.0 is positively related to the intention to use virtual currency.

Perceived Usefulness

In the present study, the definition of perceived usefulness starts with a classical definition of Davis (1989): the degree to which a person believes that using a particular system would enhance his or her job performance. Applying Lin's (2007) definition of perceived usefulness in virtual community, this study defines perceived usefulness in the context of virtual reality as user belief in their ability to obtain information and services, share their experiences with others, and enhance their performance in information exchange while using the virtual reality. In other words, this study follows the classical definition from Davis (1989) and also highlights the capability of being used advantageously.

H2: There is a positive relationship between perceived usefulness and intention to use virtual currency.

H3: There is a positive relationship between perceived usefulness and attitude towards virtual currency.

Perceived Ease of Use

TAM suggests that perceived ease of use has a direct effect on positive attitude. Perceived ease of use refers to the degree to which the prospective user expects the technology to be free of effort, and perceived usefulness refers to the prospective user's subjective probability that using the technology will increase his or her job performance (Davis, 1989). Empirical studies applying TAM have verified that perceived ease of use has significant effect on attitude and intention (Lin & Lu, 2000; Mathieson & Chin, 2001). In addition, the easier a technology is to interact with, the greater should be the user's sense of efficacy, and efficacy is thought to operate autonomously from instrumental determinants of behavior (Chung, 2005). Accordingly, it is hypothesized:

H4: There is a positive relationship between perceived ease of use and intention to purchase in Web 2.0.

H5: There is a positive relationship between perceived enjoyment and attitude towards transaction in Web 2.0.

Trust

Trust in IS research has been defined as a belief that Web vendors will perform some activities in accordance with consumers' confidence (Pavlou & Gefen, 2004). Because the online environment is impersonal, consumers often feel more uncertain about online vendors and the outcome of online transactions. Online vendors must therefore act purposefully to help consumers overcome uncertainty by building trust in vendors' Websites and in the Internet as a medium for transactions (Nijite & Parsa, 2005; Liu et al., 2005). McKnight et al. (2002) show that trust is the foundation of e-commerce and is the most important factor in the success of online vendors.

When it comes to virtual currency, trust is critical, especially when the transaction is not immediate, tangible, or when the money receiver cannot be physically identified (Hoffman et al., 1996). Pavlou (2003) shows a positive impact of trust on perceived usefulness and perceived ease of use also. The higher consumers trust in the Website, the less effort the consumer has to make to scrutinize the details of the site to asses the benevolence of the merchant. On a trusted site, because consumers assume the benevolence of the online merchant, the consumer will not waste time and cognitive effort to read the privacy policy, the term of use, and the conditions of sale, and thus will experience higher ease of use. The impact of trust on perceived usefulness is based on the credibility dimension of the trust. Consistent with the empirical evidence by Pavlou (2003), the following hypotheses are proposed:

H6: Trust in Web 2.0 is positively related to perceived usefulness.

H7: Trust in Web 2.0 is positively related to perceived ease of use.

Subjective Norm

Social norm is defined as the degree to which users perceive that others approve of their participating in the online community (Hsu & Lu, 2007). It is a similar concept with subjective norm, which involves referent identification and norm compliance (Hsu & Lu, 2004). Referent identification occurs when an individual adopts an opinion held by people who are important to that individual: friends, peer groups, coworkers, and schoolmates (Ahuja & Thatcher, 2005; Brown & Venkatesh, 2005). Norm compliance occurs when an individual performs some activities in accordance with the expectations of important others to strengthen relationships with them or to avoid their rejection and hostility (Shin, 2007).

Based on previous studies on subjective norm, the research model proposes a positive relationship between subjective norm and intention. This was confirmed by a theoretical model such as TRA, theory of planned behavior, and empirical studies (Lucas & Spitler, 2000; Venkatesh & Morris, 2000). Users may strongly want to use Avatar because they desire to gain acceptance from the external reference group and are already assimilated to the group norm. Accordingly, it is hypothesized:

H8: Subjective norm positively influences users' behavioral intentions to transact.

Perceived Risk

Consumers consciously and unconsciously perceive risk when evaluating products and services for purchase and/or adoption. IS adoption has been shown to create anxiety and discomfort for consumers and employees alike (Igbarria, 1993). The complexity of the human-computer interaction (HCI) also adds to implementation and adoption problems (Moore et al., 1991). Web 2.0-delivered virtual services add additional uncertainties and potential risks of the perceived unsecured transaction and delivery medium. These factors add great uncertainty to virtual services adoption for consumers.

Perceived risk enters the buying/adoption decision when circumstances of the decision create feelings of uncertainty, discomfort and/or anxiety conflict arouses in the consumer concern and psychological discomfort feelings of uncertainty,

pain due to anxiety and cognitive dissonance (Featherman & Fuller, 2003). When paying with virtual currency, people may feel insecure of the way the card will be used (Miyazaki & Fernandez, 2001). Likely, a psychological risk can also be observed. It is a feeling of unease or embarrassment during or after the transaction (Black et al., 2001). It can stem from the fear to be abused from the fear of abuse, or from a simple rejection of this payment mode which is incongruent with the consumer's way of being and behaving. The lack of physical contact and missing the human side of the purchase can also be major sources of perceived risk (Liebermann & Stashevsky, 2002). All these dimensions of perceived risk are all the more important in that users still do not have enough information about virtual currency in Web 2.0.

H9: Higher levels of perceived risk are associated with reduced purchasing intentions.

STUDY DESIGN

A Web-based survey was administered because a primary focus of this research is to understand the purchasing behavior regarding the use of Web 2.0-based service. The survey questionnaire was posted onto discussion forums of virtual reality/augmented reality/immersive reality and professional associations from March to June 2007, and all the members of each community were cordially invited to support this survey. A cover letter was attached to explain the purpose of this study and to ensure the confidentiality. By the time this survey was closed, 698 visitors browsed the survey, of which 312 completed and usable questionnaires were analyzed. Subjects were recruited from various Web 2.0 communities, such as Second Life, Cyworld, and There, Inc. Table 1 presents the sample demographics. For analysis of descriptive statistics, SPSS 10.0 was used. LISREL 8.72 was used for factor analysis reliability analysis, and the structural equation model (Joreskog & Sorbom, 1996).

Measurement Development

The variables in the model are well-established in IS and HCI literature. Prior to further study, the pilot test for measures was conducted. The wording of items was reviewed and modified based on the pilot test outcomes by professors in the quantitative research area. The participants indicated their agreement with a set of statements using a 7-point Likert-type scale (ranging from strongly disagree to strongly agree) drawn from previously validated instruments, as shown in the Appendix. The measures of behavioral intention to use and perceived usefulness were adapted from previous studies related to TAM model, mainly from the study of Davis (1989), which measured respondents' intentions to use virtual currency. Perceived usefulness was measured with six items from Davis (1989), measuring the extent to which a person believed that Web 2.0 was capable of being used advantageously and provided positive expected outcomes (alpha = .90). To address the elements of perceived ease of use, this study uses a four-item scale which was developed by Venkatesh (2000). Perceived risk and trust were measured with the items used by Pavlou (2003). Subjective norm was measured with the items of Song and Kim (2006). The final scales used in this study consisted of 20 items, four of which represented intention to use, three of which represented trust, two perceived risk, two subjective norms, three perceived ease of use, three perceived usefulness, and three attitudes.

Pretest

A pretest was undertaken to examine test-retest reliability and construct reliability before conducting fieldwork. Ninety undergraduate students majoring in Information Sciences and who have had Web 2.0 experiences (and other similar

Table 1. Characteristics of respondents (total=311)

Age	Number	Percentage (%)
Under 20	72	23.1
21-30	171	54.9
31-40	53	17.0
41-50	13	4.1
Over 51	2	0.6
Education		
High school or below	46	14.7
College	187	60.1
Graduate school or above	78	25.0
Gender		
Female	132	42.4
Male	179	57.5
User Experience		
1-3 months	27	8.6
3-6 months	36	11.5
6 months -1 years	49	15.7
1-2 years	130	41.8
2-3 years	40	12.8
More than 3 years	29	9.3
Web 2.0 Communities		
Second Life	127	40.8
Cyworld	110	35.3
There, Inc.	49	15.7
Other Web 2.0 sites	25	8.0

virtual services) participated in the pretest with a two-week interval. Cronbach's alpha test was employed to identify poor item-to-total correlation measure items. After eliminating the measure items that failed in either test, retest or alpha test, the remaining measure items were measured with Cronbach's alpha, which ranges between 0.84 and 0.91, suggesting acceptable construct reliability. These pretests are useful in the early stages of empirical analysis, where theoretical models do not exist and the basic purpose is exploration.

Data Analysis

Measurement Instrument

The reliability and validity of the measurement instrument was evaluated with LISREL 8.72, using reliability and convergent validity criteria. Reliability of the survey instrument was established by calculating Cronbach's alpha to measure internal consistency. As shown in Table 3, all values were above the recommended level of 0.7. The convergent and discriminant validity of the model were examined using the procedure suggested by Fornell and Larcker (1981). A confirmatory factor analysis (CFA) was conducted to test the convergent validity of each construct. This analysis showed that most items had factor loadings higher than 0.7, which were considered to be very significant by Fornell and Larcker (1981). Each item loaded significantly (p<0.01 in all cases) on its underlying construct. Therefore, all constructs in the model had adequate reliability and convergent validity.

To examine discriminant validity, this study compared the shared variance between constructs with the average variance extracted of the individual constructs. This analysis shows that the shared variance between constructs were lower than the average variance extracted of the individual constructs, confirming discriminant validity (Table 2). In summary, the measurement model demonstrated adequate reliability, convergent validity, and discriminant validity.

Structural Model

The test of the structural model was performed using the LISREL procedure. As this study collected a relatively large sample, LISREL is more capable of constructing structural relations than Partial Least Squares or other SEM techniques. Since the sample data set in this study was assumed to be normally distributed, LISREL provided a good estimation technique for this study. In particular, as this study aims to build new theory and attempts to validate it, LISREL is useful because it is designed to evaluate the fit between a theoretical model and observed data.

To assess how well the model represented the data, five goodness of fit indices were evaluated: the X^2 test statistic, the goodness-of-fit index (GFI), the normed fit index (NFI), Root mean square error of approximation (RMSEA), and the

Table 2. Discriminant validity

Construct	1	2	3	4	5	6	7
Perceived usefulness	0.71						
Perceived ease of use	0.25	0.19					
Perceived risk	0.33	0.23	0.57				
Subjective norm	0.16	0.24	0.45	0.71			
Trust	0.05	0.14	0.14	0.29	0.59		
Intention	0.34	0.15	0.10	0.29	0.28	0.62	
Attitude	0.42	0.16	0.18	0.14	0.24	0.34	0.61

Notes: Diagonals represent the average variance extracted. Other entries represent the shared variance

comparative fit index (CFI). Table 5 shows that the research model provides a very good fit to the data. Although the NFI value was a little lower than the commonly accepted value of above 0.90, researchers have recommended CFI as a better fit index than NFI. The CFI value for the structural model was clearly above the cutoff value of 0.90. Therefore, it is concluded that goodness of fit indices exceeded the recommended levels, suggesting that the research model provided a good fit to the data. Internal consistency for the three scales was also strong, evidenced by a coefficient alpha of 0.94 for the scale indicating the perceived enjoyment, 0.89 for the perceived usefulness, 0.89 for the perceived quality, and 0.84 for the perceived availability. Given a satisfactory measurement model fit, the path coefficients of the structural model were assessed.

RESULTS

Structural Paths and Hypotheses Tests

To test the structural relationships, the hypothesized causal paths were estimated and eight hypotheses were supported. The results are reported in Table 4. The overall fit of the model is acceptable because the goodness-of-fix statistics (CFI = 0.912, GFI =0.876, AGFI = 0.89, and RMSEA = 0.071) are satisfactory, with the X^2/df ratio close to 2.0. The results generally support the proposed model, confirming the classical roles of perceived usefulness and perceived ease of use in TAM. All but one of the paths in the model appear to be statistically significant. The importance of perceived ease of use is weakened

Table 3. Reliability checks for constructs

Construct	Initial items	Final items	Variable	M (SD)	Measurement error	Composite factor reliability	Cronbach's Alpha	AVE
Perceived usefulness	5	3	PU1 PU2 PU3	4.871 (1.263)	0.22 0.21 0.17	0.8982	0.8883	0.75
Perceived ease of use	3	3	PoEU1 PoEU2 PoEU3	5.906 (1.353)	0.23 0.31 0.24	0.8821	0.8962	0.69
Perceived risk	3	2	PR1 PR2	4.231 (1.321)	0.12 0.18	0.8933	0.8478	0.73
Subjective norm	3	3	SN1 SN2 SN3	6.613 (1.532)	0.59 0.38 0.23	0.9011	0.8510	0.77
Trust	4	3	T1 T2 T3	6.319 (1.684)	0.08 0.29 0.18	0.8781	0.9100	0.72
Intention	3	3	I1 I2 I3	5.993 (2.113)	0.86 0.32 0.28	0.8101	0.8876	0.70
Attitude	4	3	A1 A2 A3	5.892 (1.391)	0.19 0.29 0.27	0.8927	0.8671	0.79

in this study probably because users experience less difficulty using Web 2.0 services. Users consider the ease of use to be less important in the adoption decision. Further, the results highlight the important roles of subjective norm and perceived risk in determining the users' attitudes and intentions to purchase in Web 2.0. Perceived usefulness posited a significant direct effect on attitude (beta=0.31, t=6.717), and a significant effect on intention (beta=0.29, t=2.021), supporting H2 and H3. Likewise, perceived ease of use had a substantially moderate effect on attitude (beta=0.20, t=2.459) and a marginally significant effect on intention (beta=0.17, t=2.001), supporting H4 and H5. Supporting H6 and H7, trust had a significant effect on perceived usefulness and

perceived ease of use (beta=0.28, t=2.113 and beta=0.59, t=1.923 respectively). Subjective norm shows the greatest impact. The results support the influence of subjective norm on intention (b=0.52, p < 0.001), supporting H8. There is no significant support for H9: perceived risk on intention (b = -0.19, p < 0.001).

An Extended Research Model

It can be inferred that there are unexpected moderate relationships between perceived risk and subjective norm and between trust and subjective norm. Perceived risk is found to have negative relationship with intention to transact. However, as in previous studies, the significant levels and

Table 4. Fit indices for the measurement model and structural model

Fit statistics	Measurement Model	Structural Model	Recommended value
Normed Chi-Square	1.15	1.77	<5 (Bagozzi & Yi, 1988)
p-value	0.000	0.000	< 0.05 (Bentler, 1990)
AGFI	0.88	0.80	> 0.8 (Etezadi-Amoli et al, 1996)
RMSEA	0.031	0.076	> 0.06 (Joreskog & Sorbom, 1996)
CFI	0.93	0.93	> 0.90 (Brown & Cudeck, 1993)
NFI	0.91	0.89	> 0.90 (Bentler, 1990)
Incremental fit index	0.95	0.94	> 0.90 (Bentler, 1990)

Table 5. Summary of hypothesis tests

Hypothesis	Path coefficient	t-value	Support
H1: Attitude →Intention	0.39**	5.120	Yes
H2: PU → Intention	0.29*	2.021	Yes
H3: PU → Attitude	0.31**	6.717	Yes
H4: PEoU →Intention	0.17	2.001	Yes
H5: PEoU→ Attitude	0.20*	2.459	Yes
H6: TR → PU	0.28*	2.113	Yes
H7: TR → PEoU	0.39**	1.923	Yes
H8: SN → Intention	0.52**	3.981	Yes
H9: PR → Intention	-0.19	4.231	No

*p<.05; ** p<.001*

Figure 2. Result of the research model

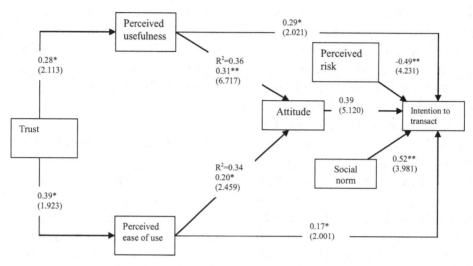

Figure 3. Estimation of extended research model

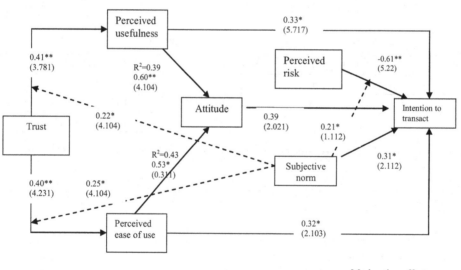

$* p<0.10; ** p<0.05.$

------→ : Moderating effects

the magnitude of the influences of perceived risk are small. Given the minimal contribution of perceived risk to the explanation of behavioral intention, what should be considered is its moderating effect with subjective norm. The same effect can be inferred between subjective norm and trust.

It may be said that the effect of perceived risk to behavior intention and the level of trust are influenced by word-of-mouth from users' peers or other members in a Web 2.0 community to use Avatar. Users tend to voluntarily spread word of their experiences to peers who may be assured by their online peers about the possible risk in transaction in Web 2.0. Accordingly, this study extends the proposed research model to include the interaction effect (1) between subjective norm and perceived risk, and (2) between subjective norm and trust. In the extended model, the moderating effects of subjective norm are shown in Figure 3.

The fit indices of the extended research model are reported in Table 6. All indices are well above or below the cut-off points. Interestingly, these results are similar to those of Song and Kim (2006) who identify additional links in their extended model. In the present study, it is also found that the extended model has the same major links as identified by the proposed research model. The normed chi-square for the extended model was 1.96. AGFI, CFI, and IFI indices were 0.93, 0.94, and 0.96, respectively. NFI and NNFI were 0.89 and 0.94 with RMSEA at 0.031. These results suggest that the measurement model adequately fits the data. The notable aspect in the extended model may be that the significance of subjective norm on intention to use is greatly increased. It appears that the impact of perceived risk on intention to transact is moderated through subjective norm. This finding is nicely congruent with the significance of the moderating role of subjective norm on trust. It appears that the impacts of trust on perceived usefulness/ease of use are enhanced through subjective norm, which jointly influence attitude. This finding can help explain the mixed results regarding the influence of subjective norm on attitude and behavioral intention in HCI research. The results indicate that Web 2.0 users do care what experts' and other buyers' opinions when they have a perceived risk in buying and spending in Web 2.0. In summary, when the user behavior is more social or networked than purely individual, the effect of subjective norm may clearly be shown. Not only does subjective norm affects the intention directly, but it also moderates the influences of trust on perceived usefulness and ease of use. In addition, under the presence of tendency to subjective norm, the influence of perceived risk on behavioral intention becomes weaker.

Table 6. Fit indices for the extended model

Fit statistics	Structural model
Normed Chi-Square	1.96
p-value	0.000
AGFI	0.93
RMSEA	0.031
CFI	0.94
NFI	0.89
Incremental fit index	0.96

DISCUSSION

The goal of the present study was to empirically extend TAM that can explain the development of individuals' behavioral intentions to buy and spend in Web 2.0. For this goal, new constructs modified from TAM were employed, and the results offer help in understanding the users' attitude and intention of Web.2.0 in a new field of Web paradigm and in understanding the implications for development of effective virtual applications. The results of the measure and structural model test lend support for the proposed research model as well as the extended model. Overall, the results show that the models demonstrate good predictive power and explain behavioral intentions of Web 2.0.

Among the constructs, the users' subjective norm shows a much stronger impact on intention than previous studies (Hsu & Lu, 2007; Venkatesh & Morris, 2000). This suggests that Web 2.0 users are more influenced by their peers in their decisions to purchase than Web1.0 users are. Users enjoy having subjective norm, and it increases the intention to use. Users are more reliant on subjective norm in the process of transaction in Web 2.0. From the high level of effect on the intention, it can be inferred that the variable of subjective norm plays a role in moderating effects to perceived risks as well as a direct reinforcement to intention. From the extended model, it is notable to see the significant role of subjective norm in purchasing decisions. With the wide diffusion of social networking channels, information communicated through Web 2.0 becomes an additional trigger to induce spending and buying. Many people make buying decisions based on more specific and detailed information available via Web 2.0. Web 2.0 provides forum spaces where consumers can obtain word-of-mouth information and product reviews provided by other consumers. Within the Web 2.0 environment, subjective norm can be seen as reinforcement that user intention is strengthened, directed, and moderated. Perceptual relationships of subjective norm have been included as integral aspects of the user behavior in a virtual environment, and innate or latent influences need to be further investigated.

Inconsistent with the broader research on perceived risk, it is shown that a negative effect of perceived risk on purchasing intention is not significant. This result may be interpreted that as consumers become more Web 2.0-oriented (i.e., gain more experience with purchasing using virtual currency), their concerns are more about the usefulness of purchasing than the risks. Their perception of usefulness becomes stronger than their perception of risk in parallel with their trust. An additional analysis supports this inference that the difference between perceived usefulness and perceived risk is positively correlated with consumers' degree of trust ($r = .243$, $p < .00$). It was found that the user's trust, as an external antecedent, contributes to the ease of use and usefulness of his or her experience. Furthermore, while it was not examined whether trust in Web 2.0 has a direct effect on intention but is based on the significant result and the moderating effect of subjective norm, it can be reasonably argued that trust does have an indirect effect through attitude toward using virtual currency.

The findings support previous research on trust as users reported that being confident was important and stressed the value of being able to explore new things in Web 2.0. It can be inferred that enhanced feelings of trust will result in im-

proved perception of usefulness and enjoyment. Recent findings in the intrinsic motivation and trust research indicate that ease of use and trust play important roles in determining a person's behavioral intention and actual behavior (Wu & Liu, 2007; Pavlou, 2003). These studies, however, did not address the relation between the intrinsic motivation and trust, or the possible underlying effects of subjective norm on other motivational variables. Identifying the gap in these studies, the current research finds that subjective norm has significant effects on both perceived usefulness and perceived ease of use, a central dimension of extrinsic and intrinsic motivations. This finding can be a theoretical improvement for TAM. As an antecedent variable, the role of trust is of importance because one of the limitations of TAM is that it does not help understand and explain acceptance in ways that guide development beyond suggesting that system characteristics impact enjoyment and usefulness perceptions. Therefore, as Venkatesh and Davis (2000) argue, in order to be able to explain user acceptance and use, it is essential to understand the antecedents of the key TAM.

IMPLICATIONS FOR THEORY AND PRACTICE

The results highlight several implications for TAM researchers as well as Web 2.0 service providers. The empirical findings demonstrate that employing trust and subjective norm would be a worthwhile extension of TAM as both were found to be influential in predicting the attitude and behavioral intention to use Web 2.0 currency. A primary contribution of this study is that it highlights the roles of trust and subjective norm in a new context of Web 2.0. Prior research in e-commerce in Web1.0 examined the impact of trust and subjective norm on shopping intentions, assuming that trust in online retailer Websites and subjective norm of shopping would have an effect on intention to purchase online (i.e., Thatcher & George, 2004). The present study indicates that trust and subjective norm also exert important influences in users' intentions to buy and spend with virtual currency in Web 2.0. According to the research related to TRA, behavioral beliefs could be viewed as an underlying individual's attitude and ultimately determine behavioral intentions via attitude (Ajzen, 1991). Thus, this study contributes additionally to the literature on TRA and TAM by confirming that trust, as one of those salient behavioral beliefs (Pavlou, 2003), can influence behavioral intention indirectly through attitude.

Related to this implication, an interesting contribution of this empirical study is the directionality of the relationship between trust and perceived risk. As Pavlou (2003) argues, trust and risk are interrelated constructs, and, thus, many studies have somewhat over-researched the causal relationship of the two. Other than the causal relationship, however, it seems that the relationship is not quite apparent in virtual context. Given the unique nature of Web-intermediaries in Web 2.0, the relation of trust and risk should be considered along with the mechanism of how trust and risk are related with other variables. The research suggests that subjective norm play intermediary roles in establishing positive attitude by affecting the relation of trust and perceived usefulness and ease of use. Subjective norm also plays intermediary roles in facilitating transaction by affecting the path of perceived risk to intention. Drawing upon the empirical findings for trust and risk, it may be inferred that trust also acts indirectly on intention to transact through the mediating effect of perceived risk, on which it has a direct effect. However, future studies should further investigate the complex interrelationship among trust, perceived risk, and subjective norm to clarify the intricate relations.

Overall, findings from the study suggest the modified TAM to be an appropriate model to explain users' behaviors of participating in the Web 2.0 community. The model provides a conceptual depiction of what motivates people to participate in Web 2.0 with reasonably strong empirical support. In terms of theory advancement, this study sheds light on developing a new theory by grounding new variables in a well-established TAM and applies it in a new context of virtual reality. The buying and spending in Web 2.0 is considerably different from other technological environments in terms of capability, experience, and behavior. In Web 2.0, users can be buyers, sellers, producers, consumers, and mediators in the dynamic supply-chain of Web 2.0 by constantly adding values to content and services. It is important to note this new context and Web 2.0-specific factors accordingly. The results in this study ensure a consistent model of the drivers of Web 2.0 and stable theory development for the emerging phenomenon. Hence, the model makes an important contribution to the emerging literature on immersive and augmented environments. Given the dearth of research on Web 2.0, this study contributes to the literature by modeling the behavioral processes that lead to intention to use.

Practical implications for industry can be drawn. Industry implications have to do with strategies and new business models pursued by virtual business. From the finding that trust impacts behavioral intention indirectly through attitude, vendors should establish user trust in Web 2.0 transactions by ensuring that their services perform in accordance with users' expectations that virtual currency in their services is reliable, accurate and changeable to real currency, and that promises and commitments are kept. In addition, as this study shows that users in Web 2.0 who are engaging social interactions in Web 2.0 have significantly lower perceived risk than other online communities, vendors may facilitate users' communications among Web 2.0 communities by providing a forum for customers to interact and share information, which eventually will lead to lower perceived risk. In the social commerce enabled and facilitated by Web 2.0, communities are comprised of socially involved individuals who share values or feel involved with a line of services. The shared trust among users clearly has the potential to be a powerful means of communication and persuasion in Avatar-enriched computer-mediated communication, and Web 2.0 in particular.

In conclusion, considering the ever-changing nature of Web 2.0 environment, this study offers help in understanding the user behaviors of virtual currency in this dynamic technology environment and in understanding the implications for development of effective business models. As users accept Web 2.0 as a new way and channel to commerce, communicate, collaborate, and cooperate and firms provide enabling platform capabilities to users, virtual worlds via Web 2.0 might become next generation platform for Internet users. However, in order to become popular, virtual currency and Web 2.0 have several challenges to overcome, and user acceptance is probably the most important one. The challenges include to better understand individual perceptions concerning the level of trust and the influence of subjective norm in transaction and in behavioral intentions. From this aspect, this study suggests that the findings provide a good basis for industry developing a service evaluation framework to determine the adoption potential of new mobile services. A modified TAM framework can be a good tool to understand market potential through an analysis of users' demands and prototyping market profiles.

LIMITATIONS AND FUTURE STUDIES

The results of this study should be interpreted and accepted with caution for several reasons. First, this study bears weaknesses of reflecting only limited aspects of user experiences in Web 2.0. As Web 2.0 is still in the early stages of evolving, this research is exploratory and it excluded individual differences as factors in virtual reality acceptance (e.g., demographics, user experience, personal innovativeness, etc.). Although this study did not consider demographics for parsimony, it may be essential to include individual variables given a significant increase variance of usage in many studies. A closer investigation of individual differences and their direct and indirect effects on Web 2.0 usage offers rich opportunities for future research. Second, the other difficulty is the limitation on generalization. Since intrinsic motivation, perceived synchronicity, and self-efficacy are additional antecedents of attitude, it is impossible to generalize the findings to other virtual reality contexts. Finally, this study collected data from various Web 2.0 communities and thus user experiences in different Web 2.0 communities cannot be treated equally as was the case in this study.

In all, this study took a first step at exploring user experience on virtual currency and found a number of metrics to be reliable and nomologically valid. Despite several limitations, an important contribution of this study is the exploring and testing of metrics for user behavior in Web 2.0 transactions. In addition to the fact that all the scales used in the study showed high reliability, those of trust, subjective norm, and perceived risk also demonstrated high nomological validity. Therefore, future research can use these metrics with some assurance. Testing them against other important factors not included in this study will advance our understanding of new user behavior in the virtual commerce in new virtual environments.

REFERENCES

Ahuja, M.K., & Thatcher, J. (2005). Moving beyond intentions and toward the theory of trying: effects of work environment and gender on post-adoption information technology use. *MIS Quarterly, 29*(3), 427-459.

Ajzen, I., & Fishbein, M. (1980). *Understanding attitudes and predicting social behavior.* Englewood Cliffs, NJ: Prentice-Hall.

Ajzen, I. (1991). The theory of planned behavior. *Organizational Behavior and Human Decision Processes, 50*(2), 179-211.

Bagozzi, R. P., & Yi, Y. (1988). On the evaluation of structural equation models. *Journal of the Academy of Marketing Science, 16*(1), 74-94.

Bentler, P.M. (1990). Comparative fit indexes in structural models. *Psychological Bulletin, 107* (2), 238-46.

Black, N.J., Lockett, A., Winklhofer, H., & Ennew, C. (2001). The adoption of Internet financial services: a qualitative study. *International Journal of Retail & Distribution Management, 29* (8/9), 390-398.

Brown, S.A. & Venkatesh, V. (2005). Model of adoption of technology in households: a baseline model test and extension incorporating household life cycle. *MIS Quarterly, 29*(3), 399-426.

Brown, M., & Cudeck, R. (1993). Alternative ways of assessing model fit. In K.A. Bollen and J.S. Long (Eds.), *Testing structural equation models* (pp. 136-162). Newbury Park, CA: Sage.

Bourdeau de Fontenay, A., & Kim, D. (2007). Interview with President and CEO of SK Communications. *Communications & Strategies, 65,* 1st quarter, 119-124.

Boyd, G., & Moersfelder, M. (2007). Global business in the metaverse: money laundering and securities fraud. The SciTech Lawyer, 3(3), Winter.

Chung, D. (2005). Something for nothing: Understanding purchasing behaviors in social virtual environments. *CyberPsychology & Behavior, 8*(6), 538 -554.

Davis, F. (1989). Perceived usefulness, perceived ease of use, and user acceptance of information technology. *MIS Quarterly, 13*(3), 319-340.

The Economist (2006). Living a second life: Virtual economy. *The Economist,* 28 April, 2006.

Etezadi-Amoli J, & Farhoomand AF. (1996). A structural model of end user computing satisfaction and user performance. *Information and Management, 30,* 65-73.

Featherman, M., & Fuller, M. (2003). Applying TAM to E-services adoption: The moderating role of perceived risk. In *Proceedings of the 36th Hawaii International Conference on System Sciences (HICSS'03),* 191.

Fetscherin, M., & Lattemann, C. (2007). *User acceptance of virtual worlds: an explorative study about second life.* June 2007. Report prepared by SL Research Team.

Fornell, C., & Larcker, D.F. (1981). Evaluating structural equation models with unobservable and measurement error. *Journal of Marketing Research, 18,* 39-50.

Hoffman, D.L., & Novak, T.P. (1996). Marketing in hypermedia computer-mediated environments. *Journal of Marketing, 60*(3), 50-117.

Hsu, C., & Lu, H. (2007). Consumer behavior in online game communities: A motivational factor perspective. *Computers in Human Behavior 23,* 1642-1659.

Hsu, C.L., & Lu, H.P. (2004). Why do people play on-line games? An extended tam with social influences and flow experience. *Information & Management, 41*(7), 853-868.

Igbarria, M. (1993). User acceptance of microcomputer technology: An empirical test. *Omega, 21*(1), 73-91.

Joreskog, K. G., & Sorbom, D. (1996). *LISREL 8: Users reference guide.* Chicago: Scientific Software International.

Jung, T., Youn, H., & McClung, S. (2007). Motivations and self-presentation strategies on Korean-based Cyworld weblog format personal homepages. *Cyberpsychology & Behavior, 10*(1), 24-31.

Kelly, K. (2006). We are the Web 2.0. *Wired.* August, 2006.

Liebermann, Y., Stashevsky, S. (2002). Perceived risks as barriers to Internet and e-commerce usage. *Qualitative Market Research, 5*(4), 291-300.

Lin, H. (2007). The role of online and offline features in sustaining virtual communities. *Internet Research, 17*(2), 119-138.

Lin, H. & Lu, I. (2000). Toward an understanding of the behavioral intention to use a Web site. *International Journal of Information Management, 20,* 197-208.

Liu, C., Marchewka, J., Lu, J., Yu, C. (2005). Beyond concern: a privacy-trust-behavioral intention model of electronic commerce. *Information & Management, 41*(2), 289-304.

Lucas, H. C., & Spitler, V. K. (2000). Implementation in a world of workstations and networks. *Information and Management, 38*(2), 119-128

Mathieson, K. & Chin, W.C. (2001). Extending the technology acceptance model: the influence of perceived user resources. *The Data Base for Advances in Information Systems, 32*(3), 86-113.

Miyazaki, A.D., & Fernandez, A. (2001). Consumer perceptions of privacy and security risks for online shopping. *The Journal of Consumer Affairs, 35*(1), 27-44.

McKnight, D.H., Choudhury, V., & Kacma, C. (2002). Developing and validating trust measures for e-commerce: An integrative typology. *Information Systems Research, 13*(3), 334-359.

Moore, G. C., & Benbasat, I. (1991). Development of an instrument to measure the perceptions of adopting an information technology innovation. *Information Systems Research 2*(3), 192-222.

O'Reilly, T. (2006). *What is Web 2.0: Design patterns and business models for the next generation of software.* O'Reilly Website, 30th September 2005. O'Reilly Media Inc. Available online at: http://www.oreillynet.com/pub/a/oreilly/tim/news/2005/09/30/what-is-Web-20.html [Accessed Jan. 17, 07].

Pavlou, P.A. (2003). Consumer acceptance of electronic commerce: integrating trust and risk with the technology acceptance model. *International Journal of Electronic Commerce, 7*(3), 69-103.

Pavlou, P.A. & Gefen, D. (2004). Building effective online marketplaces with institution-based trust. *Information Systems Research, 15*(1), 37-59.

Reuters, A. (2007). Hi-end Second Life profit growth stalls. Feb 8, 2007. *Second Life news center.* http://secondlife.reuters.com/stories/2007/02/08/hi-end-second-life-profit-growth-stalls

Shin, D. (2007). User acceptance of mobile Internet: Implication for convergence technologies. *Interacting with Computers, 19*(4), 45-59.

Song, J., & Kim, Y. (2006). Social influence process in the acceptance of a virtual community. *Information System Frontier, 8,* 241-252.

Thatcher, J., & George, J. (2004). Commitment, trust, and social involvement: An exploratory study of antecedents to Web shopper loyalty. *Journal of Organizational Computing and Electronic Commerce, 14*(4), 243-268.

Venkatesh, V., & Morris, M.G. (2000). Why don't men ever stop to ask for directions? Gender, social influence, and their role in technology acceptance and usage behavior. *MIS Quarterly, 24*(1), 115-139.

Venkatesh, V. (2000). Determinants of perceived ease of use: integrating control, intrinsic motivation, and emotion into the technology acceptance model. *Information Systems Research, 11*(4), 342-366.

Venkatesh, V., & Davis, F.D. (2000). A theoretical extension of the technology acceptance model: Four longitudinal field studies. *Management Science, 46*, 186-204.

Wilson, J. (2006). 3G to Web 2.0? Can mobile telephony become an architecture of participation? *Convergence, 12*(2), 229-242.

Wu, J. & Liu, D. (2007). The effects of trust and enjoyment on intention to play online games. *Journal of Electronic Commerce Research, 8*(2), 128-140.

APPENDIX

Constructs	Measure items	Source
Perceived usefulness	• PU1: I think that virtual currency is very useful to my life in general. • PU2: I think that virtual currency is helpful to improve my performance in Web 2.0. • PU3: I think that virtual currency is helpful to enhance effectiveness of my life in Web 2.0.	Davis (1989); Moon and Kim (2001)
Perceived ease of use	• PEoU1: I find service clear and understandable. • PEoU2: I find service doesn't require a lot of mental effort. • PEoU3: I find service easy to use.	Venkatesh (2000)
Subjective norm	• SN1: Experts whose comments I rely on for the use of Avatar in the virtual community have provided supporting evidence for use. • SN2: My friends whose opinions I think important for the use of Avatar in this community have provided supporting evidence for use	Song and Kim (2006)
Perceived risk	• PR1: As I consider to purchase a product through Web 2.0 marketplace, I become concerned about whether sellers: will commit fraud and will swindle • PR2: offer products that will not perform as expected	Pavlou (2003)
Trust	• TR1: This Web retailer is trustworthy. • TR2: This Web retailer is one that keeps promises and commitments. • TR3: I trust this Web retailer because they keep my best interests in mind.	Pavlou (2003)
Attitude	• I would have positive feelings towards buying a product from this site • The thought of buying a product from this Website is appealing to me • It would be a good idea to buy a product from this Website	Heijden (2004)
Intention to use	• I intend to transact with virtual currency in the future. • I intend to use virtual currency as much as possible. • I recommend others to use virtual currency in Web 2.0. • I intend to continue using virtual currency in the future.	Davis (1989)

Chapter V
U–Commerce in the Financial Marketspace

Alexander Y. Yap
Elon University, USA

ABSTRACT

The mission of this chapter is to investigate (1) how u-commerce is made available by online brokerage agents and the different interfaces they provide via mobile phone transactions, computer transactions, and/or land-line telephone transactions (either thru broker assisted transactions or interactive voice-response phone systems), (2) how the anytime anywhere demand and supply of financial knowledge and availability or non-availability of ubiquitous trading tools and systems affect the behavior of traders and investors in the financial market, and (3) to what extent ubiquity of information and systems tools are regulated in relation to stock trading, stock manipulation, and global volatility of financial markets.

BACKGROUND OF U-COMMERCE IN FINANCIAL MARKETS

One of the most natural applications for U-Commerce is enabling anytime anywhere transactions, communications, and dissemination of knowledge in electronic financial markets. U-Commerce is a critical and necessary business platform in the arena of financial markets, because financial markets cross international and time-critical boundaries. Global financial markets can affect each other in merely a matter of seconds and minutes. Any volatile movements in the Dow (USA), FTSE (UK), Nikkei (Japan), NASDAQ (USA), Hang Seng (Hongkong), Dax (Germany), and Shanghai (China) stock indices can almost have an instantaneous effects on the global prices of stocks, options, futures, bonds and other financial instruments. Traders, investors, fund managers, and hedge funds need to react to these price movements anytime anywhere or they could lose a substantial amount of money in a few seconds or minutes. The volume of stocks, options, futures, forex, metals and commodities traded run in the trillions of dollars worldwide everyday, and ubiquity of information systems is a critical requirement in this area.

The use of Blackberries, Palm Pilots, and mobile phones with good LCD screens in trading stocks has become more prevalent in today's trading environment. The need for instant information anytime anywhere is becoming common. However, one may also question the problems or issues related to ubiquity. Is it really necessary to be trading stocks while you are driving, or on vacation, or when you are not in your office? To what extend can users benefit from ubiquity? What are the effects of ubiquitous computing on the trading behaviors of traders and investors?

RESEARCH APPROACH

The movement of stock prices and options in financial markets are fickle and many traders and investors often need to act quickly when buying and selling stocks, options, and other financial securities. To evaluate applications for u-commerce, three online brokerage systems that have u-commerce interfaces for computers, mobile devices, and land-line phone transactions will be evaluated in this chapter. The researcher has two solid years of experience in the usage of ubiquitous trading systems for Scottrade, Ameritrade, and Interactive Brokers and has qualitative data to illustrate how their ubiquitous trading systems platforms are operationalized. Trading stocks at home, on the road, or even in remote areas are possible due to these u-commerce systems. Each broker has unique solutions and innovations for u-commerce that will be discussed and compared in this chapter.

In addition, the research will also investigate the regulatory issues in financial markets and how u-commerce is affected by these issues. Global financial markets are brutal and billions of dollars can be wiped out in a few seconds due to the combination of program trading and ubiq-

uitous trading capabilities of different systems. Regulatory bodies, such as the US Securities and Exchange Commission (SEC), have tried to regulate financial markets from becoming too volatile or from being too prone to manipulative trading practices. For this research, information on regulatory issues will be obtained from the SEC and linked to issues of u-commerce.

A CONCEPTUAL TREATISE OF U-COMMERCE IN THE FINANCIAL MARKET

For u-commerce to help facilitate the financial marketspace, there are two important components for ubiquitous electronic trading to take place – (1) *demand and supply of financial knowledge* – the demand for instantaneous knowledge or information is critical because knowledge/information appears to be limited most of the time, and (2) *the information systems tools and the appropriate user-interface* - for ubiquitous electronic transactions to happen in the financial marketspace, users demand the proper type of information systems tools and user-interfaces for them to safely execute transactions anytime anywhere. There is a need to look at whether or not the systems capabilities and tools are adequate for the users' needs or not.

Without up-to-date or real-time knowledge of what is happening in the financial marketspace, it is difficult for traders and investors to make informed decisions and act on any ubiquitous financial transactions. And this is where the gap in the demand and supply of knowledge can hamper ubiquitous decision-making. Traders and investors need to make buy/sell decisions anytime anywhere and most of the time they do this with incomplete knowledge or information of the market situation. However, most traders and investors would prefer to get the most accurate picture of the market space before making any decision and transaction ubiquitously. Based on unfounded fear, some traders and investors sell their favorite stocks when prices are plunging fast, only to buy it back later at a higher price when the market stabilizes.

Research questions:

1. Is u-commerce beneficial or detrimental to traders or investors when there is a huge gap in the supply and demand of financial market knowledge/information to make informed instantaneous decisions for ubiquitous buy or sell transactions?

2. Is there a danger of "over-trading" with ubiquitous trading systems in financial markets?

3. To what extent is u-commerce regulated in the financial marketspace? Or should it be regulated at all?

4. How should users plan the use of ubiquitous systems in financial markets, knowing that in exchange for ubiquity, some interfaces are incomplete? The use of interactive voice-response systems over land-line phones has a very different interface compared to using a trading systems installed on a computer.

5. What are the improvements needed for u-commerce to be more effective in the financial marketspace?

Figure 1. Wireless/mobile interface for Ameritrade

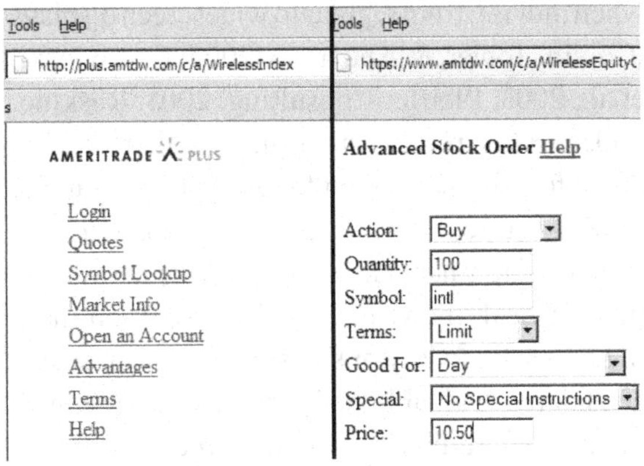

The demand for financial knowledge/information anytime anywhere is very high, but the supply has always been short of the demands. Often, investors and traders just do not have any clue why the prices of stocks are going down or going up. They search for knowledge/information on stock ratings, reports, and rational explanations but sometimes there are none, and they are just left to speculation on several possible variables affecting the financial marketspace.

In Figure 1, the mobile/wireless interface for Ameritrade shows a 'bare bone' or scaled-down interface that allows traders to get stock quotes and also trade stocks. It allows traders and investors to trade anytime anywhere as long as there is a cellphone signal.

Whether knowledge is publicly available or not, it is highly possible that the supply of knowledge/information can also be constricted by the interface provided by the information delivery platforms in the u-commerce space. If a trader compares the interface of Ameritrade that is available for use on a desktop or laptop computer (Figure 2) vis-à-vis the mobile/wireless interface available on the phone, a trader will immediately notice that full desktop/laptop interface version allows users to do research on different markets, stocks, options, bonds, and mutual funds. It also allows the trader to use different real-time trading platforms that have streaming data that changes by the second.

Clearly, this shows that the delivery of information and knowledge is not the same across different interfaces for u-commerce. There are advantages and limitations of different information delivery mechanisms in the u-commerce platform in financial markets and the balance is a trade-off between the richness of information vs. the ubiquity of trade executions.

The question therefore is when should a trader use the mobile interface (Figure 1) as oppose to the full interface (Figure 2)? Let us look at a situation where a trader's stock price sudden starts falling by $1.00 as the trader access the

Figure 2. Research and trading tools in the full interface

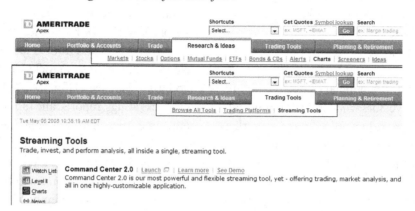

stock quote on his/her cellphone. The trader has limited access to news about his/her stock. The trader may see a few lines of news saying that the stocks' profits have declined by a $0.50 cents per share this quarter. Will it be wise for the trader to use the cellphone interface to sell and unload his/her stock or not? Some traders might just hit the sell button and unload their stocks. However, some traders will wait to see if there is additional news about stock. Maybe the reason why there was a profit decline was that the company heavily invested in some assets during the last financial quarter. However, this particular information is not available on the mobile phone. This information needs to be downloaded from the Securities and Exchange Commission (SEC) regulatory filings showing detailed financial reports about the company. In such case, it is possible that the stock market over-reacted to one piece of news, not knowing that there are mitigating circumstances that could actually be beneficial to the company in the future as they acquired assets that could dramatically improve future profits. Take for example the breaking news that Bear Stearns was about to go bankrupt and that they were bought out by Lehman Brothers for $2/share. Many shareholders sold their stocks immediately in a panic, but it turns out that Bear Stearns prices went back up to $11. In such case, having access to a ubiquitous system, combined with 'limited

knowledge and panic selling', would result in a big loss for investors and traders.

In Table 1, the different features of financial systems interfaces are described to provide u-commerce capabilities that allow financial trading anytime anywhere. Different devices or channels are needed to enable true ubiquitous trading capabilities.

Desktops and laptops have full complete interfaces for trading tools, streaming news, and charts. The main advantage of desktops is that traders can opt for having a dual-monitor display and have a more information and financial knowledge accessible at a given point in time. Dual displays allow one monitor to be used as a trading platform and the other monitor to view real-time charts and breaking news in the stock market.

Previous research have shown that office tasks routinely show productivity gains of 10%-25% when moving from regular to widescreen displays (Colvin, Tobler, & Anderson, 2004; Czerwinski, et al., 2003; Pfeiffer Consulting, 2005; Raskino, 2005). This poses an argument that scaling down to a smaller screen for ubiquitous financial trading purposes means giving up some access to real time financial information and valuable time-critical knowledge used for decision making on where to buy or sell stocks. Screen size is considered 'valuable real estate' when it comes to financial trading, so U-commerce in the finan-

Table 1. Comparing different trading interfaces for ubiquitous trading

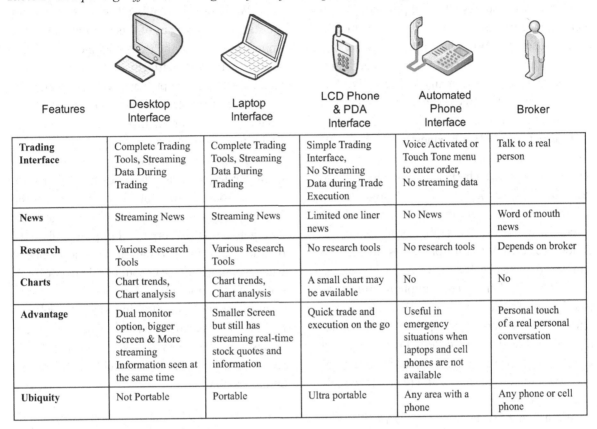

Features	Desktop Interface	Laptop Interface	LCD Phone & PDA Interface	Automated Phone Interface	Broker
Trading Interface	Complete Trading Tools, Streaming Data During Trading	Complete Trading Tools, Streaming Data During Trading	Simple Trading Interface, No Streaming Data during Trade Execution	Voice Activated or Touch Tone menu to enter order, No streaming data	Talk to a real person
News	Streaming News	Streaming News	Limited one liner news	No News	Word of mouth news
Research	Various Research Tools	Various Research Tools	No research tools	No research tools	Depends on broker
Charts	Chart trends, Chart analysis	Chart trends, Chart analysis	A small chart may be available	No	No
Advantage	Dual monitor option, bigger Screen & More streaming Information seen at the same time	Smaller Screen but still has streaming real-time stock quotes and information	Quick trade and execution on the go	Useful in emergency situations when laptops and cell phones are not available	Personal touch of a real personal conversation
Ubiquity	Not Portable	Portable	Ultra portable	Any area with a phone	Any phone or cell phone

Figure 3. Advantage of dual monitor desktops in financial trading

cial marketspace need to consider what is being given up when using smaller devices. Later, we will analyze what group of traders or investors general benefit or not benefit from this, and what they are giving up for ubiquity.

Laptops basically have the same functionality as desktops but with a smaller screen area to monitor stock prices, charts, and news. However, laptops are more mobile as it can easily be carried for traveling. Being able to bring a laptop to Wi-

Fi-enabled hotspot area such as Starbuck's coffee shops and trade stocks while sipping coffee is a convenience that is becoming a norm. Some car dealers also offer Wi-Fi hotspots that customers can use when are having their car serviced for oil change or repairs. And many airports, like Las Vegas airport, offer free hotspots for travelers to get online and access information on the Web.

Internet-enabled Cellphones and PDA phones are becoming standard issue for those buying new phones today. The PDA phones have complete QWERT keyboards that are able to access different financial trading websites. Since LCD screens used for PDAs and phones are small, the different electronic trading platforms have a more simplified interface for PDAs and Cellphones. Interactive Broker's PDA/Cellphone interface (see Figure 4) allow traders to (1) trade stocks, options, futures and futures options, (2) see quote, (3) review the status of orders, (4) modify and cancel orders, (5) monitor account information, (6) view execution reports, and (7) review one's financial portfolio.

What is not available in the PDA/Cellphone interface at the time of this writing is real-time streaming stock quotes, real time news, intra-day chart of how stock prices are performing. Displaying real-time information requires a fast Internet

connection and wireless data feeds are commonly slow. Widespread broadband wireless networks are still in the offing as of this writing and it may improve the use of the PDA/Cellphone interface as serious trading platforms in the future. In the later part of this chapter, we will try to analyze what type of traders will be disadvantaged and what type of traders will benefit from this type of trading channel and interface.

Some brokers offer a backup automated telephone systems in case it is not possible to use their web-base trading platform. This is not the best way to trade stocks at all and is only good for emergencies. However, it still improves ubiquity by allowing traders to call and use a payphone whenever necessary. Discount brokers like Scottrade and full-time brokers like Fidelity offers their clients the privilege of talking to a real broker (a real person) to provide advice or handle certain trades. They have geographic offices that station real brokers to talk to local clients. This also enhances ubiquity.

U-COMMERCE AND DIFFERENT USER NEEDS

There are different types of traders or investors in the stock market (Yap and Synn, 2008). Different financial brokerage services and trading interfaces respond to the needs of different types of traders or investors. The following are different groups of traders/investors:

Figure 4. Using a PDA phone to access stock information from Interactive Broker

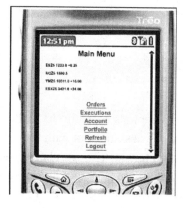

1. **Long-term investors:** These are investors who "buy and hold" and keep their stock portfolio for months or years. These investors believe that over a few years, the market will go up, and they assume that their investment returns will outperform inflation rates and the bank's savings rate.

2. **Swing traders:** These are traders who do not keep stocks for more than a week. They take advantage of the upswing and downswing

of stock prices over the course of a few days. They look for patterns in stock price movements and time its rhythm. Some swing traders may observe that stocks can go up in two days and go down in three days and then up again in two or three days. And they take advantage of the small price swings.

3. **Pattern day traders:** These are traders who buy and sell stocks during the same day. If day traders follow their own rule, they would have to sell stocks at the end of each market's closing. These traders believe that the following day is a different scenario and that would be dealing with a different market behavior. After all, one day the bulls of the market can triumph and the next day the bears can overpower the bulls of the market.

4. **Micro-day traders:** There is a growing number of traders who only look at intra-day stock price charts. They buy and sell stocks in a smaller time window. This means that their buy and sell trading activities are done within seconds or minutes. They are not concerned about the health of the company of which stocks they buy into. Their objective is to take advantage of small fluctuations in the market and make a small spread with these fluctuations. Most of these traders have a larger capital to play because their spreads are small. So, even if they only make five cents a share, if they bought and sold 100,000 shares, that still translates to $5,000 of profit in a few seconds of trading.

5. **Penny stock and small cap traders:** There are traders who trade only micro-caps or small caps stocks. Micro-cap stocks are often referred to as penny stocks because they can be traded for less than a dollar. Small caps stocks are also cheap and usually below $5. Most of these stocks trade as a pink slip stock (PK) or as an over-the-counter (OTC) stock. Various online trading systems handle these stocks differently from stocks traded with

NASDAQ or NYSE. Traders who deal with these stocks have a unique need that not all systems can address.

6. **Large cap and middle cap traders:** There are a group of traders who believe that they should only buy stocks above $10 or $20. They believe that micro-cap and small cap stocks are cheap for a reason; they are risky and trading for what they are worth.

7. **Institutional traders:** Large institutions that invest their capital in stocks have different needs. Some traders provide certain features to address unique needs of larger institutional traders.

This research maps the experience collected from using different trading systems to the different trading behavior of various traders and investors (see Table 2).

For long-term investors to have access to a Cellphone or PDA so they can trade is not really beneficial. The objective of long-term investors is to buy and hold for a long time. Having access to a Cellphone or PDA can cause investors to panic sell. During the research period, having the ability to access stock prices over a Cellphone or PDA and see that the price of your stock has just plummeted, it can be very tempting to punch a few buttons on your Cellphone and sell your stocks. Long-term investment should never be about haphazard buying and selling of stocks, so doing it on a PDA and Cellphone while travelling runs counter to this type of investing strategy. Long term investors do not buy or sell on a whim.

Swing trading is holding a stock position for a few days or a week. This type of trading is normally based on technical up and down price movements and not based on the intrinsic price value of the stock. Swing traders monitor the moving price averages and trends in price fluctuations. So the frame of mind of traders executing this type of strategy is their preparedness for quick buying and selling of stocks. This type of investing strategy takes good advantage of hav-

Table 2. Fit of u-commerce interface for different investors

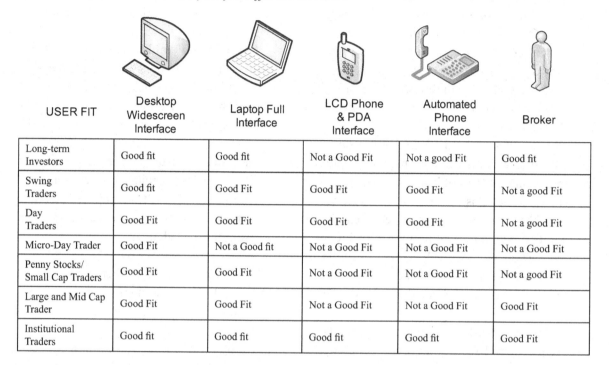

USER FIT	Desktop Widescreen Interface	Laptop Full Interface	LCD Phone & PDA Interface	Automated Phone Interface	Broker
Long-term Investors	Good fit	Good fit	Not a Good Fit	Not a good Fit	Good fit
Swing Traders	Good fit	Good Fit	Good Fit	Good Fit	Not a good Fit
Day Traders	Good Fit	Good Fit	Good Fit	Good Fit	Not a good Fit
Micro-Day Trader	Good Fit	Not a Good fit	Not a Good Fit	Not a Good Fit	Not a Good Fit
Penny Stocks/ Small Cap Traders	Good Fit	Good Fit	Not a Good Fit	Not a Good Fit	Not a good Fit
Large and Mid Cap Trader	Good Fit	Good Fit	Not a Good Fit	Not a Good Fit	Good Fit
Institutional Traders	Good fit	Good fit	Good fit	Good fit	Good Fit

ing ubiquitous trading capabilities. U-commerce provides traders the ability to quickly buy and sell stocks. The only communication channel that does not fit well with this strategy is talking to a real broker. Brokers normally do not advice quick buying and selling.

Day trading is also another strategy that takes advantage of u-commerce's transaction ubiquity. Day trading is the strategy of buying and selling stocks on the very same day. Whether day traders gain or loss, they have to dispose of their stock position before the end of the day. So day traders really need to strategize which stocks are opening at very undervalued prices and will gain some upward price momentum sometime during mid-day or early afternoon. Day traders usually buy early when there is good news about the stock and they see it as news that will substantially add intrinsic value to the stock prices. Since most traders will not be on their computer screen monitoring the stock prices all day, it is good to have a Cellphone or

PDA in hand to quickly dispose of the stocks. The mentalities of these traders are very different from long-term 'buy and hold' investors. These traders will not risk having a stock position overnight. They always look forward to closing their portfolio at the end of the day and holding to 100% cash. These traders have a certain timeframe limit and they will execute their trades anytime anywhere before the end of the trading day.

Micro-day traders is the buying and selling of stocks within a few seconds or within a minute. The ideal trading system for this type of strategy needs to have multiple monitors, because traders are watching different and separate electronic markets simultaneously looking for small gaps in the price of stock being bought and stocks being sold. Trade execution thru a Cellphone or a PDA will be too slow to take advantage of the split second trading window. And it is almost impossible to monitor different electronic markets in a small LCD screen.

Figure 5. Unique interface needs for micro-day trader (arbitrage trader)

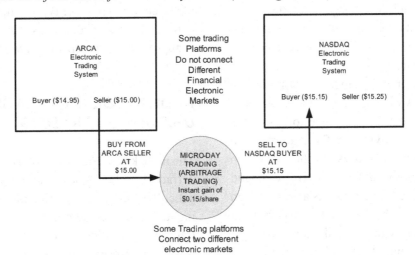

For example, a trader could be monitoring the NASDAQ trading system where the price of stock XYZ has a buyer for $15.15 and a seller for $15.25. And that same trader may also be monitoring the ARCA trading system where there is a buyer at $14.95 and a seller at $15.00 (see Figure 5 for this illustration).

The trader may notice that there is a seller at $15.00 in ARCA and there is a Buyer for $15.15 in NASDAQ. The trader can immediately buy the $15.00 stock in ARCA and sell it immediately to the Buyer at $15.15 in NASAQ. What is happening here is that the buyer who intends to buy the stock at $15.15 in NASDAQ does not have access to the ARCA system. And the seller at $15.00 in ARCA does not see the buyer of $15.15 at NASDAQ. Some trading systems do not automatically connect some electronic markets together, while other trading platforms do.

The micro-day trader in our example is able to see and monitor two electronic markets (NASDAQ and ARCA) on a big dual screen monitor and sees the small price discrepancies between the bid/ask price in one market and the bid/ask price in another market. Once the micro-day trader sees this price discrepancy, they immediately make a split-second buy and sell transaction in

two different electronic markets. If they bought and sold 10,000 shares within 60 seconds with a profit of $0.15/share, that's an instant total profit of $1,500.00. In finance terms, this is also called 'arbitrage trading'. There are traders that specialize in monitoring multiple market price inefficiencies so they can profit from these small price gaps.

Based on Figure 5, smaller screen or screen-less communication device cannot satisfy micro-day traders or arbitrage traders. So ubiquitous anytime anywhere trading does not fit the needs of this trader group.

Penny stock buyers are traders/investors who buy very cheap stocks. These are stocks below $1.00. Small-cap stocks are also cheap, mostly below $3.00 or $5.00. Most penny and small cap investors also prefer to hold on to their stocks for a long time hoping it will reach $20-$30 in a few years. So these traders may not really require ubiquitous trading capabilities. Penny stocks or small-caps are very risky stocks and very volatile. Even if a trader buys a penny stock at $0.30/share, it can still drop to $0.05/share. It is very common to see Penny stocks to go from $0.15/share to $0.75/share and then drop back to $0.30/share. So, if we combine a very volatile stock group and an investor group that wants to buy and keep that stock for a longer period of time, then there is a lot of temptation for panic selling. Having access to a PDA or Cellphone can be very tempting for panic selling.

Large cap and mid-cap stock investors are also the type of users who would not act on a whim. Most large cap and mid-cap investors look for stocks that give out dividends. For example, if an investor buys Coca-cola, an established blue-chip stock, that investor would be expecting dividend earnings. So these types of stocks are not traded frequently due to the fact that investors treat them like as assets with yearly dividend earnings. So the need for ubiquitous trading is not highly demanded.

Institutional investors are a different breed as they have billions of dollars in their coffer. Normally, institution investors are represented by mutual fund managers, hedge fund managers, and managers that can invest their money in bonds, US treasuries, and foreign exchange. These managers are extremely knowledgeable individuals who are responsible for multi-million dollar portfolios which they monitor around the clock. These managers are paid well, but they are known to trade at 3:00 a.m. or 1:00 a.m. in the

morning in global markets across the other side of the continent. These type of individuals need to have a PDA device, because ubiquitous trading is appropriate for their line of work.

KNOWLEDGE, REGULATIONS, AND UBIQUITOUS TRADING

The more knowledge and experience an investor or trader has about stocks, options, futures and the general economy means that the danger of trading anytime anywhere is less risky. Ubiquitous trading capabilities can be very risky if a trader is not well informed. It is safe to say that the benefits of ubiquitous trading are proportional to the knowledge and experience of a trader.

The ability to trade stocks anytime anywhere can be compared to the analogy of carrying a loaded gun. It is a very powerful tool that can make or break a financial portfolio. A huge sum of money could be gained or lost through a PDA or cellphone trade. A person in a wrong frame of mind, possibly trigger happy or have itchy trigger fingers, should not be carrying a loaded gun. In the same analogy, if a trader does not have the 'right frame of mind', that trader should not engage in

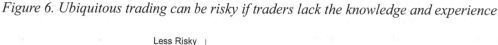

Figure 6. Ubiquitous trading can be risky if traders lack the knowledge and experience

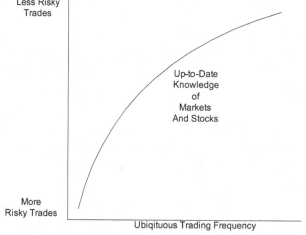

sudden ubiquitous trading activities via a PDA or cellphone if those actions are triggered by fear, panic, excitement, anger or other emotions. The feeling of being overwhelmed by sudden market movements can cause traders to immediately buy or sell stocks and later feel remorseful about such action. Base on the hands-on research for this paper, these emotions are very real among traders.

In addition, having ubiquitous access to trading tools creates the temptation of "over-trading". The better a trader's access is to the electronic markets, the higher the temptation is to buy and sell. Overtrading is a common mistake that most traders fall into. The term "overtrading" was originally a devious and manipulative ploy by many stock brokers to make more commissions. By formal definition, overtrading is the "excessive buying and selling of stocks by a broker on an investor's behalf in order to increase the commission the broker collects" (Investopedia.com, 2008). Overtrading drains investors and traders of commission fees, because each trade activity incurs trading fees and fattens the earnings of online brokers. So when online brokers provide ubiquitous trading capabilities, online brokers are subconsciously encouraging traders and investors to overtrade by giving them the ability to trade anytime anywhere, knowing that inexperience traders will normally panic in a volatile market.

The question is—how experienced and knowledgeable should a trader be before he or she should have the powerful ability to trade ubiquitously? At the very least, traders/investors should have a good knowledge and the mind-set to deal with a very volatile market. They should have thoroughly researched the stocks and other financial securities they hold. They should have a game plan on how to trade. Traders with a good plan need to have a target buy and sell price at a given period of time and that they should have the strict discipline of staying with their trading plan. The less knowledge an investor or trader have, the more they should be cautious in using

ubiquitous trading capabilities in an uncertain and volatile market. Emotions and rash decisions rule the majority of the market and ubiquitous trading capabilities can magnify "regretful and erroneous split-second trade decisions".

To lessen the element of risk, a trader should have access to up-to-date financial knowledge and information about the company being traded before a final decision to buy and sell is made. Stocks could go up or down for no sound logical reason at all. In many situations, the culprits are big hedge funds that are either distributing (selling) or accumulating (buying) stocks. Knowledge on how institutional traders affect the stock market is a very important factor that all experience traders/investors monitors. Hedge funds, many of whom are big institutional investors, are known to manipulate the market. In fact, to many traders, institutional investors are 'the market'.

In the late 1990s, former Prime Minister of Malaysia Mohammed Mahatir accused billionaire-investor George Soros of suddenly taking out billions of dollars from the Asian financial market and causing the financial crisis in Asia. However, hedge fund trading is very illusive and deceptive that it is difficult to actually find proof to what extent they control the market, because hedge funds do not report all their trading activities and therefore these activities may not be public information. Brown, Goetzmann and Park (2000) could not find conclusive evidence that George Soros did indeed caused the Asian market debacle. Fox (2008) argued that "there are problems with the data on hedge funds' currency exposures used by Brown, Park, and Goetzmann. Because hedge funds released no data on their holdings, the three researchers had to estimate exposures to the ringgit [*Malaysian currency*] and other currencies by correlating the hedge funds' returns with exchange rate changes". Brown, Park, and Goetzmann acknowledge that these calculations may misrepresent the funds' true exposures. And that is why the U.S. Securities and Exchange Commission (SEC), as of this writing, is still lobbying the US Congress to have Hedge funds report all their trading activities. Since individual investors and traders are always up against the big players that have deceptive and stealth trading activities, individual traders/investors are more susceptible to fall into the manipulative strategies of these "big sharks" who out to "devour the small fishes".

When stocks fall hard even without any tangible news, it could be a 'head fake' played by hedge funds that are forcing stock prices to artificially go down. Sometimes hedge funds can artificially lower a stock price so they can buy cheap before any anticipated good news comes. Or they could play it the other way around, where Hedge funds may pump up the stock prices they are already holding and then sell massive amounts of stocks when good news is out. There is a common trader motto that says "Buy on the rumor, Sell on the news". Head fakes are games that billion-dollar hedge funds can play against small investors who only have $5,000 or $30,000 in their portfolio. These small investors are normally at a disadvantage when trading against the big players. Their only means of surviving is if they do not panic trade.

If we then go back to the research question of whether U-commerce should be regulated in the financial marketspace, the discussion above provide some answers to this question. It is almost impossible to regulate u-commerce in the financial market space unless governments intervene and set certain limiting parameters for online trading. The US Congress has reaffirmed time and again that Hedge fund trading will remain unregulated (SEC, 2008). Below is a statement from SEC showing how the SEC wants to regulate hedge funds but is opposed by the US Congress:

The private adviser exemption was not intended to exempt advisers [hedge funds] to wealthy or sophisticated clients. It appears to reflect Congress' view that there is no federal interest in regulating advisers that have only a small number of clients and whose activities are unlikely to affect national

securities markets. Today, however, a growing number of investment advisers take advantage of the private adviser exemption to operate large investment advisory firms without being registered with the Commission. Instead of managing client money directly, these advisers pool client assets by creating limited partnerships, business trusts or corporations in which clients invest. In 1985, we adopted a rule that permitted advisers to count each partnership, trust or corporation as a single client, which today permits advisers to avoid registration even though they manage large amounts of client assets and, indirectly, have a large number of clients.

Financial markets, by their nature, needs to remain relatively free from government intervention. However, large investors can play manipulative games that can be termed as 'unfair trading' practices for small investors. This analogy is similar to the case of David versus Goliath. Investors with hundreds of millions or billions of dollars can always manipulate market prices to a certain extent, because they can create a huge artificial demand or supply of stocks and thereby affect prices temporarily. So a balance needs to be in check somewhere.

The SEC has already taken action in regulating day trading activities in 2001 when the Dot.com bubble collapsed and many traders and investors lost billions of dollars. Currently, only traders with $25,000 or more are able to day trade. So we could say that ubiquitous day trading also has its limits. If a trader does not have $25,000, then ubiquitous trading is limited to three consecutive trades within five trading days. Cadway (2001) summarize these new rulings:

As some of you might be aware, the NASD has come out with some new margin rules for day-trading accounts effective September 28th, 2001. Among these rules is the requirement for all pattern daytrading accounts to have a minimum equity of $25,000. Currently, all accounts are classified *as investment accounts until a pattern daytrading account status is triggered.*

A "pattern daytrading account" is classified as an account that has four or more daytrades in a consecutive five day period. A daytrade is a buy and sell of the same security in the same trading day. There is no limit on other types of trades. For example, you could buy 10 stocks today and sell those 10 stocks tomorrow. Because you held them overnight they are not considered daytrades. Once an account is determined to be a pattern daytrading account, it will forever be classified as that and will have specific guidelines it must follow.

Investment accounts that do 4 or more daytrades in a 5 day period will be considered pattern daytrading accounts and will be required to bring the account up to $25,000 in equity. Those accounts will have three days to do this. If the account has not been brought up to the minimum equity of $25,000 after three days, the account will be considered frozen and limited to liquidating transactions only.

Regulations like this protect inexperience traders who have little capital from overtrading via u-commerce. So any type of trading regulation can restrict how u-commerce is conducted in the financial marketspace. SEC will continue to look at different issues that need to be regulated if it creates too much volatility in the market. The reason why daytrading was regulated by SEC was that it was creating a lot of volatility in the financial markets. Teenagers, college students, and nine-to-five workers were using their lunch money to bet on stocks and they overtraded in the late 1990s. Imagine if they now had the capability to daytrade with cellphones, PDAs, and laptops in Wi-Fi hotspots, then the global financial e-markets will be extremely volatile as it becomes a huge virtual gambling casino for just about everyone on this planet with an online trading account and ubiquitous trading access anytime anywhere.

Good knowledge and information about stocks and the market in general is not always available. And to some extent, having access to a broadband network on a nicely setup desktop allows a trader to have better access to financial knowledge due to the screen size available as oppose to a small screen PDA that is only able to access one-liner news or no news at all. Let us remember that websites made for wireless handheld devices do not contain the same information as websites made for viewing in a large desktop screen. Websites accessible through PDA or mobile phones have only a very limited amount of information and news. Base on the possible trade off between having knowledge and mobile trading capabilities, we can also say that devices that provide better knowledge representations (bigger screen, streaming news, research-friendly interface) may be less risky trading channels for ubiquitous trading.

Figure 7 illustrates the possible trade off between having a big screen and a small screen assuming that the effectiveness of real-time information and multiple knowledge sources depends on the screen size and the presence or absence of a screen. The use of interactive voice-response or touch-tone land-line phone systems has a very different interface, because it is a trading system without any interactive screen interface. As such, it can be one of the riskiest systems to use, because one assumes that the user has no access to a computer and real-time news at the time a trade is executed. At best, one can assume that users using a touch-tone or voice-response phone system could be seeing financial news from a television and suddenly decides to sell or buy stocks using a land-line phone.

Mobile screen devices can also incur more risky trades than bigger screens devices, because news, financial information and research capabilities are limited with mobile websites. The less risky types of devices for financial trading are still devices that offer full screen and access to all types of research knowledge and real time financial news. As long as a trader understand the tradeoff

Figure 7. Knowledge interface vs. risk

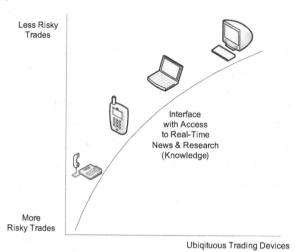

between the lack of information and knowledge in using some devices at the time they execute a trade, then ubiquitous trading would have serve its purpose for that particular user.

Traders need to assess what kind of financial knowledge they need and demand compared to what is supplied by their brokers and other research sites on the Internet. The higher the gap between the information demanded by the trader and the information supplied by their broker or the Internet, the more risky it is to trade (see Figure 8). Traders who feel that they did not have enough knowledge, research or information on the stocks they purchased or sold will psychologically have more reason to feel jittery about sudden price movements and will therefore have more tendencies to panic trade. And having access to ubiquitous trading facilities will further aggravate an already nervous trader that did not have enough background research on a stock. In such case, panic trading can easily occur given ubiquitous trading capabilities.

Traders who feel that the supply of knowledge adequately meets their demand for knowledge would normally feel confident that they made the right decision to purchase or sell the stock at a particular price, and therefore they would have

less chances of panic trading. In this scenario, u-commerce is just another tool for executing a rational trading strategy anytime anywhere, and not a tool that negatively encourages panic buying or selling. If traders are always demanding real-time news, information, and research knowledge, small screen mobile devices may fall short of providing such demand for knowledge. Knowledge and research about financial markets and stocks is what gives traders and investors the confidence to plan when to buy and when to sell financial securities.

SUMMARY ANALYSIS AND CONCLUSION

To answer the first research question, the research analysis is that traders and investors that have not done enough research or acquired enough information on the stocks they buy or sell should be discouraged from having ubiquitous trading capabilities. A large gap in the supply and demand of financial knowledge could cause investors/traders to easily doubt or have second thoughts about their buying/selling decisions. And giving them ubiquitous access to dump or acquire

Figure 8. Lack of knowledge is risky with ubiquitous trading capabilities

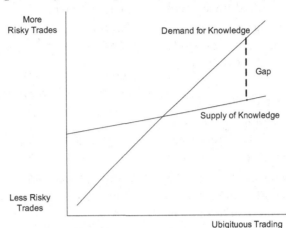

shares while traveling on the road may not be a good decision.

The second research question regarding overtrading tends to be a true temptation for having ubiquitous trading access. Based on the emotional trading experience from this research, nervous and amateur traders tend to buy and sell more often when the market is volatile. Giving traders access to trading facilities anytime anywhere will only bolster the itch to sell when the market is taking a dive and buy when the market looks like it is going up. However, day traders and swing traders that trade frequently have a trading strategy that is prone to overtrading. Since overtrading is common in their trading strategies, the bottom line shows that it is better for these types of traders to have ubiquitous trading access. Daytrading and swing trading is not for everyone. To win using these types of trading strategies require a tremendous amount of knowledge, research, and experience.

When we looked at the research question of how u-commerce in the financial marketspace is regulated, our research experience shows that it is only regulated to the extent that governments regulate the financial markets. The US SEC has attempted to regulate day trading and hedge fund manipulative trading activities. They have

succeeded in regulating day trading activities, so that limits certain daytrading habits in the u-commerce space. That should limit amateur traders from gambling their 'lunch money' on the stock market using their cellphones or PDAs. SEC has not been successful in regulating hedge fund activities, so hedge funds will continue to create heavy volatility in global markets. Market volatility and having access to ubiquitous trading means that there are more chances for hedge funds to scare and intimidate the small traders to dump their stocks or manipulate them to buy overpriced stocks. The temptation to buy and sell in a volatile market is very real and strong. In this manner, ubiquitous trading extends the reach of market manipulators to scare or entice traders and investors to sell or buy stocks respectively. Again, traders that have access to ubiquitous trading should base their trading strategy on good knowledge and research rather than emotions that can overwhelm them.

Users planning on using different devices for ubiquitous trading should understand what limited information, research, and trading capabilities they get from the different interfaces being used. Experience traders know that the information and knowledge they get from mobile phones and PDAs are limited, and automated response land-line phone systems should only be used for emergencies. Lastly, traders should understand that real-time broadband trading speeds are not currently available in PDAs and cellphones. Trade executions can be delayed without high-speed Internet connection.

In summary, for u-commerce to be an effective and positive trading platform for traders/investors, traders and investors need to have a good amount of knowledge, information, and experience in the stock market and also a good trading strategy. Without a good trading strategy, ubiquitous trading in the financial marketspace is very risky. Lastly, traders and investors need to be aware of the interface limitations of different devices that enables anytime anywhere trading. Not all interfaces can provide complete trading and research information and that can put some traders/investors at a disadvantage. Ubiquitous trading is a convenient and powerful tool for trading, but it is not appropriate for all types of users.

REFERENCES

Brown, S.J., Goetzmann, W.N., & Park, J.M. (2000). Hedge funds and the Asian currency crisis. *Journal of Portfolio Management, 26*(4), 95-101.

Cadway, R. P. (2001). *New daytrading rules.* Retrieved from, http://www.princetondaytrading.com/newsletter-princeton/NL-9-31-2001.html

Colvin, J., Tobler, N., & Anderson, J. A. (2004). Productivity and multi-screen displays. *Rocky Mountain Comm. Review 2*(1), 31-53.

Czerwinski, M., Smith, G., Regan, T., Meyers, B., Robertson, G., & Starkweather, G. (2003). Toward characterizing the productivity benefits of very large displays. In *Proceedings of INTERACT 2003* (pp. 9-16). IOS Press.

Fox, J. (2008). Retrieved from, http://www.nber.org/digest/oct98/w6427.html

Galanxhi-Janaqi, H., & Nah, F. (2004). U-Commerce: Emerging trends and research issues. *Industrial Management and Data Systems, 104*(9), 744-755.

Junglas, I. A. (2003). *U-Commerce: An experimental investigation of ubiquity and uniqueness.* Doctoral Dissertation, University of Georgia.

Junglas, I. A., & Watson, R.T. (2003, Dec. 14-17). *U-Commerce: A conceptual extension of e- and m-commerce.* Paper presented at International Conference on Information Systems, Seattle, WA.

Lyytinen, K., & Y. Yoo (2002). The next wave of nomadic computing: A research agenda for information systems research. *Information Systems Research, 13*(4), 377-388.

Pfeiffer Consulting (2005). *The 30-inch Apple Cinema HD Display. Productivity Benchmark.* Retrieved from, http://www.pfeifferreport.com/Cin_Disp30_Bench_Rep.pdf

Raskino, M. (2005, April 1). *Bigger and better display will boost productivity at last.* (Report G00126172). Gartner Research.

Robertson, G., Czerwinski, M., Baudisch, P., Meters, B., Robbins, D., Smith, G., & Tan, D. (2005). The large-display user experience. *IEEE Computer Graphics and Applications: A Special issue on Large Displays, 25*(4), 44-51.

Roussos, George (2006). *Ubiquitous and pervasive commerce: New frontiers for electronic business.* London: Springer.

Watson, R.T. (2000). U-Commerce: The ultimate. *Ubiquity: An ACM Magazine.* Retrieved from, http://www.acm.org/ubiquity/views/r_watson_1.html

Weiser, M. (1991). The computer for the 21st century. *Scientific American.*

Yap, A., & Synn, W. (2008). Evolution of online financial trading systems: E-service innovations in the brokerage sector. In A. Scupola (Ed.), *Cases on Managing E-services*. Hershey, PA: IGI Global.

Web Sites

http://biz.yahoo.com/rb/080508/cablevision_wireless.html (Website accessed in 2008)

http://www.interactivebrokers.com (Website accessed in 2008)

http://www.investopedia.com/terms/o/overtrading.asp (Website accessed in 2008)

http://www.scottrade.com (Website accessed in 2008)

http://www.sec.gov/rules/final/ia-2333.htm (Website accessed in 2008)

http://www.tdameritrade.com (Website accessed in 2008)

KEY TERMS

Day Trading: The act of buying and selling stocks on the same day. Ubiquitous trading capabilities often attract these types of users, because they only have a small time window to make profits.

Electronic Financial Markets: Global financial markets are now linked by several information systems network that automate and facilitate the trading of stocks, futures and options worldwide.

Online Discount Brokers: These are stock brokers that have created online systems for trading stocks and options with a low transaction cost. The cost is normally less than $10 per trade.

Overtrading: Ubiquitous trading capabilities can result in the excessive buying and selling of stocks that may not have been necessary. The temptation to buy and sell stocks when a trader is in a emotional state is greater when one has access to ubiquitous trading systems, and this tends to result in overtrading.

Ubiquitous Trading: The capability to trade (buy and sell) stocks anywhere anytime. Stock brokers have developed several trading interfaces for their clients that allow them to trade using different devices.

Ubiquitous Trading Interfaces: There are different devices and software interfaces for the ubiquitous trading of stocks and options. This could range from a dual-monitor screen to a handheld device to a standard phone.

U-Commerce: The ability to make commercial transactions anytime anywhere. This is viewed as an evolution of e-commerce as this concept provides more hardware and software accessibility for users to make online transactions anytime anywhere. Ubiquitous trading systems that are able to fulfill online transactions fall under the u-commerce framework.

Chapter VI
Context Related Software Under Ubiquitous Computing

N. Raghavendra Rao

SSN School of Management & Computer Applications, India

ABSTRACT

The advancements in information and communication technology (ICT) have resulted in the new concepts being developed in this discipline. Ubiquitous and pervasive computing are among the number of other concepts provided by the ICT. Especially these concepts are providing scope for radical changes in business processes of organizations. It would become a necessity for integrating business with these concepts to face the new realities in business process in organizations. This chapter describes the historical background of commerce in electronic environment, the concepts related to context computing, ubiquitous computing and pervasive computing, and Grid computing. Further it explains the recent trends and also talks about the three business models with these concepts incorporated in three different contexts.

INTRODUCTION

Information technology has advanced by delivering exponential increase in computing power. Telecommunication technology has like wise advanced communicating capabilities. Convergence of these two technologies has become possible due to rapid advancements made in the respective technology. This convergence has been termed as information and communication technologies (ICT) as a new discipline. ICT is the major

stimulus for facilitating business organizations to adapt themselves to the changes in business environment. Mobile computing is one of the concepts in ICT discipline has helped globalization to become successful. Mobile computing which is used in different contexts with different names. Asoke L Talvkder and Roopa R Yavangal (2005) list the different names related to mobile computing. They are 1- Anywhere Anytime Computing 2-Virtual home environment 3-Normadic computing 4-Pervasive computing 5-Ubiquitous computing 6-Global service portability and 7-Wearable computers. While talking about wearable computers Paul Luckowiz, Andreams Timm-Giel, Michael Lawo and Otthein Herzoz (2007) state that in wearable computers are often cited as an enabling technology for out-of office application. The concepts of ubiquitous computing and pervasive computing are providing the scope for innovations and radical changes in applications related to business and home environments. The dictionary meaning of the words "Ubiquitous" and "Pervasive" convey the similar meaning. The word ubiquitous is referred as "Found Everywhere". The word "Pervasive" is referred as "Spread Throughout". Ubiquitous computing blends computing devices with environmental objects. It means integration of computing devices into practically all objects in our everyday environment. Ubiquitous computing is based on pervasive computing which has computing activities. It will be interesting to note the complex concepts of ubiquitous and pervasive computing have hidden behind a friendly user interface. These concepts would facilitate creation of new applications and services for the benefit of individuals and business in the ensuing paragraphs.

COMMERCE IN ELECTRONIC ENVIRONMENT

Convergence of money, commerce, computing and networks has laid the foundation for electronic commerce. Effraim Turban Jay E. Arunson and Ting pang Liang (2006) narrate the various applications related to e-commerce. Many large organizations used to make use of the application electronic fund transfer (EFT) for electronic fund fund transfer. Another application electronic data interchange (EDI) has been used for direct exchange of documents from one business computer systems to another. Communications through internet and introduction of the web sites during nineties have led the applications related to

electronic commerce to make rapid progress. The year 2000 has witnessed many dotcom companies going out of business. As a consequence to this electronic commerce was affected. Due to globalization policy followed by many countries across the globe the applications related to electronic commerce have started gaining momentum from 2003. Now many organizations irrespective of the size of their organizations have been making use of electronic commerce applications. In the present business scenario, it may be noted that e commerce business models are being developed for various segments of business and industries. These models can be classified under three purposes such as organization purpose, people oriented and society purposes.. The advancement in mobile communications have made mobile commerce (m- commerce) popular. m-commerce can be considered as one or more features in e commerce. Mobile commerce is the successor of today's PC based e-commerce. Two more concepts are emerging under electronic environment. They are space commerce and ubiquitous commerce (u-commerce). Commercial satellite systems are made use of developing system models in multiple domains such as health, education and business. Ubiquitous commerce focuses in the development of location based application software.

CONTEXT COMPUTING

Generally business models developed under information systems follow two methods. They are "Push" and "Pull" methods. When information is thrust on end users it is considered as "Push Method". The classic examples for this method are advertisements (print and electronic media), telemarketing and information through email and snail mail. End users when they browse websites and go through hard copies for specific information, it is termed as "Pull Method". It has been the practice among end users to understand the information provided under the above methods and relate it to the particular context. This means end users are proactive to context computing. Now attempts are being made to make the information systems proactive to the context. Now the trend is developing context aware applications. The word "context" has its origin in the Latin verb "Contexere". It means to weave together. This meaning has more reference in context computing. The main feature of context computing is the ability to sense and process information as per the requirements of end users. It relates to a particular context relevant to end users. There are many definitions in respect of "Context Computing". They fall under two categories such as "Enumeration Based" and "Role Based". The former category talks about context in terms of its various categorization. The second category is very specific in terms of its role in context aware computing.

It would be apt to note the definition of context under "Enumeration – Based" in terms of various categories by Chen and Kotz's (2000). They have refined Schlitz's definition of context. They have classified context under five categories. (1) Computing context consists of network connectivity, communication band width and local resources. (2) User context considers user profile, location and people in the vicinity of the user. (3) Physical context includes lighting and noise levels, traffic conditions and temperature. (4) Temporal context talks about time of day, week, month and season of the year. (5) Context history is the recording of computing, user and physical context across the time span. Further they define context under "Role Based" as the set of environmental status and settings that either determines an application behavior or in which an application event occurs and is interesting to the user. It can be inferred from the above definitions that context aware computing applications are developed to respond to changes in the environment in an intelligent way for the benefit of end users. Ubiquitous and pervasive computing concepts support in developing context aware computing applications. Context aware is also referred as Local aware by some authors. It

would be apt to recall the observation of Denise Anthony and David Kotz and Tristan Henderson (2007) on location aware technology. They state that local aware technologies such as sensor networks enable everyday devices to become increasingly and often invisibly interconnected with one another and with the internet.

UBIQUITOUS AND PERVASIVE COMPUTING

It is interesting to note the research work related to context-aware computing started in 1990's. The credit goes to Xerox Parc Laboratory and Olivetti Research Ltd (now part of AT & T Laboratories Cambridge) for initiating the research on context–aware computing. Under the vision of ubiquitous computing, mid 1990's ubiquitous computing has also been known as pervasive computing. Rajkamal (2007) clearly explains that ubiquitous computing refers to the blending of computing devices with environmental objects. It is a term that describes integration of computers into practically all objects in everyday environment endowing them with computing abilities. Ubiquitous computing is based on pervasive computing "(p-26). Further he says: pervasive computing is a trend towards increasingly ubiquitous computing and it entails computing by devices connected to the environment by a convergence of advanced electronic and wireless technologies and the internet. Pervasive computing devices are not PCs. These are handheld, very tiny, or even invisible devices which are either mobile or embedded in almost any type of object." (p-27).

"Environment: in ubiquitous computing is reference to location, surrounding devices, computing systems and network." The role of pervasive computing is to make devices adaptable to "Environment". It would be apt to recall the observation of Marckweiser (1991) who stated that in accordance to Moore's law , future computing environments would consist of very cheap (disposable) interconnected specialized computers all around us , some embedded in our surroundings and others worn by us . Moore's law has given the name "Future computing" for ubiquitous and pervasive computing. It can be inferred that ubiquitous computing and pervasive computing are inter dependent.

The aim of ubiquitous computing is to design computing infrastructures to integrate them seamlessly with the environment. It has the ability to sense and process context for making a system proactive and self tunable. Further it supports mobility of computing devices. Pervasive computing expects information and communication technology to be an integral part of "Environment" in ubiquitous computing. The demand for ubiquitous personal communication is making new networking techniques to support end users who move in multi complex buildings, cities and countries.

UBIQUITOUS COMPUTING AND GRID COMPUTING

There is a common feature in ubiquitous and grid computing. The function of the both computing is to provide information services regardless of place. The other important characteristic is to support computing capabilities and database wherever situated globally. They link systems and resources together. It is complementary to each other.

Devices

Information and communication technology is the driving force for the production of new generation devices working on wireless technology. These devices have been providing workable solutions in virtual environment scenario. While talking on mobile and wireless devices Jochen Schiller (2004) rightly states: Even though many mobile and wireless devices are available, there will be

many more in the future. There is no precise classification of such devices by size, shape, weight or computing power. Currently mobile devices range in sensors, embedded controllers, pagers, mobile phones, personal digital assistant, packet computer and notebook/laptop (pp 7-8). All these devices become more useful when they support personal and business applications. Bruno Giussani (2001) classifies these devices into four categories. They are (1) Dedicated devices – designed for a particular functionality; (2) Integrated devices – integration of functions of different devices;. (3) Modular devices – bringing devices into one shell; and (4) Federated devices – connecting different parts of devices.

There are other segments such as embedded systems, consumer electronics and hand – held devices which are expected to grow and support pervasive computing devices. Embedded systems are not visible to end users; they are embedded in products and appliances. Consumer electronics have pervasive computing elements in digital cameras, video recorders, electronic books and MP3 players / recorders with wireless modems, and direct internet access. Hand-held devices are mobile phones, pagers, PDA's and mobile PC's. These systems are enablers in ubiquitous computing.

The pervasive computing market is a typical innovation market. Markets are emerging with products specially developed with the elements of pervasive computing. They are already pervasive devices available in the market. Need of the hour is to identify the devices and use them efficiently for personal and business applications. While explaining on device technology Jochen Burkhardt, Dr Hurst Henn, Stefan Hepper, Klaus Rintdorff and Thomas Schack (2005): there is a limit to the size of mobile devices that is imposed by the need to input and output data. The size of the input and output components, such as the keyboard and the Liquid Crystal Display (LCD), influences the total size of a mobile device. While both are integrated into the same package, we cannot expect them to become any smaller than mobile phones of today. Once separated, the advances in integration will deliver even smaller device. The display may be worn like a wristwatch or a head-mounted display. In the future, alternatives to the keyboard as the main input technology will appear. The devices might not even be visible any more because they will be integrated into the fabric of our clothes or hidden in glasses, pens or jewellery (p.57).

Present Scenario

In recent times handset makers have been queuing up to launch devices which have unique features. The most valued current paradigm however is the ability of business application system developers to make use of these devices in ubiquitous computing environment. Some of these devices with their unique features are developed for particular applications. Jankrikke (2005) rightly observes that potential for possible applications is limited only by the imagination. Some of the devices recently introduced in the market are described below with their special features:

- **GPRS enabled mobile hand set:** This hand set supports GPRS. It will be helpful for sales persons who work in the location where they are not familiar with. It has one more feature, when they key in data on their mobiles it is immediately converted into graphical format and sent to the head office. It can update in the company's ERP or SCM system.
- **Electronic bracelets:** This is an electronic ankle-tracer bracelets system. It has global positioning system embedded in the device. It will be helpful for people who go for trekking.
- **Mobile handsets supporting retail management:** There are mobile handsets supporting Retail Purchase activity. The feature in retail purchase activity takes care of purchase and payment for items purchased.

A SMS is sent to the mobile user at the point of purchase, once the user responds with a confirmatory SMS and user's authorization code then the transaction in completed. This service essentially enables high security cashless transactions while still hiding the user's debit or credit card details from the retailer. It requires that users should link their mobile phones to their bank account or credit card account. This link facilitates mobile users to use SMS or a simple application to enter a security code and authoring transaction.

- **Mobile handsets supporting academic activity:** This device provides a platform for teachers to send parents SMS updates of their child's academic performance, homework and attendance. Further it helps to inform parents about PTA meetings and holidays at school.
- **Mobile multimedia:** Mobile multimedia device provides access to rich world of entertainment and information. It also facilitates creation and sharing of the content through this device. It has a feature of video recording.
- **Home theatre watch:** Home theatre watch is designed to provide the experience of watching a film sitting in a chair at home, waiting at the doctor's clinic or traveling in a train. It has functionality of a watch also.
- **Voice enabled mobile phones:** This device has a feature to announce the caller's identity and also reads out SMS. This is designed for visually impaired, senior citizens, illiterate and people who are not comfortable using cell phones. It supports many different languages at global level. It will also be useful for executives who are very busy with their work.
- **E-book reader:** E-book reader is a portable reader system. It is expected to supplement conventional books. Users can carry a collection of books around. It has high resolution

electronic paper display which provides a comfortable reading experience. Users can connect e-book store for downloading the required material for reading.

- **Camera Sunglasses:** This is a digital camera embedded in the frame. It can snap pictures.
- **Electronic Shelf Labeling:** This system transmits from a retailer's product price file to wireless electronic shelf labels that are located o products shelf. Retailers can select among different display sizes as well as choose labels that can be mounted on peg hooks, existing store fixture, refrigerator units and freezers.

Device Management

The need for device management is obvious in ubiquitous computing environment. Heterogeneous devices, applications and users need to be administrated. The core functionality of pervasive device is to platform a task with high speed. Memory management has to address spaces for each application and type of device. It has to support different kind of user interfaces. The main requirement of device management is to take care of operating system structure, memory protection, operating system size, security and multitasking.

Emerging Trends

It will be interesting to note the usage of ubiquitous computing concept has started in some parts of the globe. The following examples indicated the trends in this direction.

Hong Kong

Jenani Gopalakrishnan Vikraman (2007) inputs from Chiaki Ishikawa describes that T-Engine / kernel based ubiquitous communicator terminals are used by the visitors to the veno Zoo in Tokyo, Japan for guidance in the Zoo for information about the animals.

India

Vandana Sharma (2007) says to improve the service to their customers, Menu Taxis-Mumbai a service provider has fitted with GPS based tracking device in their cars. It helps them to identify the taxis closest to a customer pick up point.

Japan

Matsushita Electric Industry Co Ltd is planning to launch two HDD car navigation system models in Japan in the month of June 2008. These will be fitted in cars. These will allow drivers to remotely operate lighting and air conditioners at home, monitor conditions at home via images captured with a network camera and record TV programmes by controlling a Panasonic DVD recorder from the car.

USA

A GPS unit fitted inside the cabin of a farmer's tractor in Tallulah, Illinois USA. GPS technology at the farm helps to keep costs by making it possible to spray less fertilizer and fewer herbicides a benefit in these times of rising costs of fuel ,seed, fertilizers and just about everything else it takes to grow crops.

South Korea

South Korea justice ministry is planning to make use of electronic bracelets from October 2008 to track down the wearer via global positioning system. The government has decided to make repeat sex offenders wear the devices.

BUSINESS MODELS

The following three business models related to travel sector, trading sector and home environment are explained in ubiquitous computing environment.

Case Illustrations for Travel Sector

Travel World Services (TWS) the travel agency business over two decades. They have been providing services for vacation packages and making airline, hotel and rental car reservation. Their innovative ideas in providing services to their customer helped them to become a leader in travel services. They always make use of the advancements in information and communication technology in their business. This is one more reason to be a leader in their business. They provide services also through websites to their customers. Some of their customers have been availing themselves of their services over a decade. They are considered as "Privileged Customers" by them. They want to extend personalized travel service to the privileged customers under the ubiquitous computing environment. They have identified two types of customers (1) Who do trekking during their vacation and (2) who hire cars going around the places. Three types of devices have been identified for the above type of customers. Bracelet is embedded with global positioning system. Sunglass is embedded with a digital camera. Handheld terminal is to be used

for the process of returning rental cars. Figure 1 – privileged customer model gives an overview of ubiquitous computing environment.

Ubiquitous computing is aimed at designing computing infrastructure integrating with the environment through devices. In this case illustration computing infrastructure is referred as the infrastructure at the office of Travel world services. The environment means (1) Travel plan booking, (2) Trekking, and (3) Rental car. The devices are mobile phone, bracelet with GPS and rental car recording device for usage.

Travel Plan Booking

Privileged customers will browse at their convenience through the mobile phone the various travel options, once it is decided by them. They can book on line with their Preferences. Their preferences can be either with Bracelet with GPS or Rental car recording device.

Bracelet with GPS

This device will help them to guide in the route for their trekking. In case any guidance is needed,

Figure 1. Privileged customer model

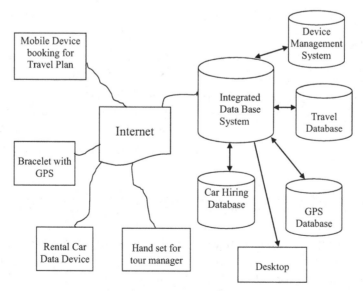

the office at TWS can be contacted. This type of device will be useful for people even if they are not familiar with the area of places visited by them.

Rental Car Recording Device

The starting mileage and ending mileage of the car used by the customer can be obtained by a person standing near the car. The customer need not spend more time at Rental car office. The Rental car office will transfer the data to the database at TWS office.

Ubiquitous Computing at TWS

The computing infrastructure at TWS office and the devices used by their customers and devices used by car rental office are integrated by TWS under ubiquitous computing environment.

Case Illustration for Trading Sector

ROA Mart is the largest marketer and distributer of consumer durables, consumer goods, spare parts for automobiles, drugs and electronic devices. They have a head office in Madras and 20 outlets across India. They have been in the business over three decades. Their relationship with the vendors and customers has been excellent. They have been procuring the products for their mart direct from the source. The sources of procurement are from Farmers, Pharmaceutical companies, manufacters, consumer durable manufacturers, electronic devices and automobile spare parts. The outlet for their requirements is their retail outlets. Further they are also authorized distributors for the products procured by them. They have tie up with some selected transporters for transporting their products to their retail outlets and authorized distributors. They have integrated information system for all their business activities. Their sophistication information system has helped them to take timely business decision and to provide user friendly service to

their customers. Their policy is to make use of the advancements in information and communication technology in their business. The integration of the above business activities at RoaMart are shown in the Figure 2, ubiquitous trading model. Further it gives an idea of integrating the devices for business activities.

Warehouse

Warehouse consists of packages that are ready for dispatch, pasted with a slip containing certain characters. It is not easily decoded by human beings. A device that can read these characters is known as MICR (Magnetic Ink Character Recognition). OCR (Optical Character Recognition) is another device which is also used for this purpose. This device helps to transmit the data to ubiquitous trading model. This facilitates the process of documentation for the packages to be dispatched.

Retail Outlet

Electronic shelf labeling system transmits information from a retailer's product price to wireless electronic shelf labels that are located on a products shelf. Retailers can select among different display sizes as well as choose among labels that can be mounted on peg hooks and store fixtures.

Distributor

Electronic devices are invading the market with the new features almost daily. Information pertaining to special features in the electronic devices after market release can be sent to specific prospective customers to their devices.

Wholesale Grocer

At the time of placing orders with the farmers for their products, the actual product can be viewed on a handheld device with multimedia feature.

Figure 2. Ubiquitous trading model

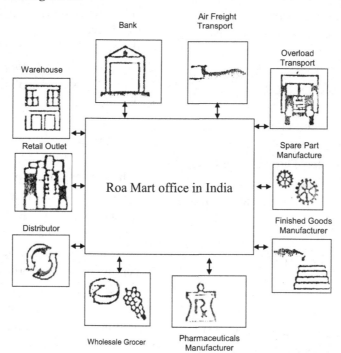

Pharmaceutical Manufacturer

They can be provided with an access to the database at ROA Mart for the movement of their products and can know the stock position. Accordingly despatches can be organized by pharmaceutical manufacturers to ROA Mart.

Consumer Durables

The packages of consumer durables occupy more space. Exact availability of space can be seen through a device with a multimedia feature. Executives at the head office can view the space available at warehouse and place orders accordingly with the manufacturers of consumer durables.

Spare Part Manufacturers

ROA Mart is an authorized agent for specific automobile parts from the renowned automobile

spare part manufacturers. The understanding of RoaMart with automobile spare part manufacturers is to obtain the drawing from their customers and sent to them. Specifications of the parts to be manufactured are designed by using CAD software by ROA Mart. The design generated by CAD software is sent to the manufacturer.

Transporters

The movement of trucks carrying their products from ROA Mart to their outlets and their customers can be monitored through GPRS system installed in the trucks.

Air Freight Transport

The movement of packages booked through aircraft can be traced in the websites provided by the respective airfreight carriers.

Banks

All the banking transactions can be carried out through e-banking system by ROA Mart.

Grid Computing in Ubiquitous Trading

Coordination of various resources such as computing power, data, hardware, devices, software, applications and networking services are needed for ubiquitous trading model. This coordination facilitates (1) application partitioning; (2) ascertaining and scheduling tasks; (3) data communication distributing the data where and when it is required; and (4) providing and distributing application codes to specific system devices. Grid computing supports the above requirements. Johy Joseph and Craig Fellenstein (2004) rightly state: one of the most valuable aspects of Grid computing systems are that they attract the business they

are intended to address (pp 12-13). Figure 3, Grid computing in ubiquitous trading model, gives an overview of the features explained above are taken care.

Case Illustration for Home Environment

Senior citizens who stay alone in their houses need various types of information for their day to day activities. They need to necessarily know about the climate conditions. Their decision to go out of their houses depends on the information pertaining to climate conditions. One should have patience to browse the web sites providing the above information. To make their life easy, devices can be provided at convenient places in their houses that draw their attention to plan their activities for that day. Climate digital display device can be installed in a living room to display

Figure 3. Grid computing in ubiquitous trading model

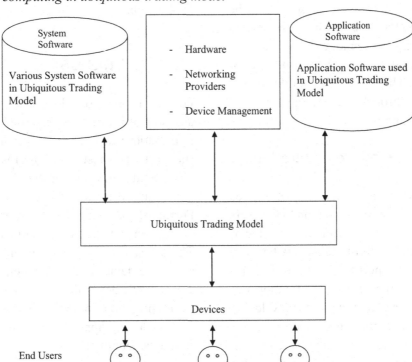

Table 1. Requirements in the business models

Name of the Application	Database	Devices at their Respective Offices	Pervasive Devices	Environment
Travel Sector	Existing Database at their office	Desktop terminals at their office	-Sunglass with digital camera -Bracelets with GPS -Handheld terminals	-Office -Customers place of convenience -Places visited by customers during vacation
Trading Sector	Existing Database	Desktop terminals at their office	-Scanner -Mobile device with Multimedia feature -GPR Systems in Mobile devices -Hand Held devices with internet facility	-Office -Vendor Place of Business -customers place of retails outlets -Roads
Home Environment	Websites	-	Devices with special features for Climate Conditions	-Residential house -Objects in the houses

that day's likely temperature. A link needs to be established to climate digital display device to a website providing the information relating to the place where the senior citizens are living. Another digital display system has to mounted on wardrobes. This device would suggest the types of clothes to be chosen for the type of climate on that day. One more digital system is to be installed at umbrella and coat stand. The display on the system draws the senior citizens' attention whether it is required to carry an umbrella or raincoat or both. The above types of information can be provided through climate digital system by using web semantic concepts.

Summary of the above Illustrations

The above three business models give an idea in identifying the context in relation to the users benefit. The critical part in ubiquitous computing environment is establishing the link between the environment and pervasive devices. It is also interesting to note the existing information systems and websites are made use of for developing business models with the concepts in ubiquitous computing environment and pervasive devices. It is interesting to note that the existing information

systems and websites are made use of developing business models with the concepts in ubiquitous computing. The other important aspect is to identify the pervasive devices as per the requirements of specific applications. Table 1, requirements in the business models explain the various elements in ubiquitous computing for development of an application.

FUTURE TRENDS

Potentially everyone has access to enormous amounts of information now days. Much of the information available is however meaningless to a specific user at most of the time. Instead of relating the context to information, the choice of information required to the context is very important. Further display of information on very specific devices in the user's environment is required. There has been a strong trend in introducing pervasive devices in the market. These devices are going to determine the scope of ubiquitous computing environment. There is a good scope for developing application in this environment for the benefit of end users.

CONCLUSION

Macro level design of business models in ubiquitous computing environment is explained. Providing the specific information required by the end users at a place convenient to them is a very important aspect to be remembered by the developers of applications. Developers need to identify the pervasive devices that would be useful in ubiquitous computing environment. Even they can envisage the type of devices required. They may even suggest to Research and Development agencies. Ubiquitous computing is no longer confined to academic and research communities. It can create an efficient framework to leverage in business environment. Technology does not drive change. It enables change.

REFERENCES

Adelstein, F., Gupta, S.K.S., Richard III, G.G., & Schwiebert, L. (2005). *Context-aware computing, fundamentals of mobile and Pervasive Computing* (pp. 91-92). New Delhi: Tata McGraw-Hill Publishing Company.

Anthony, D., Kotz, D., & Henderson, T. (2007). Privacy in location –Aware computing environments. *IEEE- Pervasive Computing Mobile and Ubiquitous Systems, 6*(4), 64.

Burkhardt, J. Henn, H., Hepper, S., Klaus Computing, & Schack, T. (2005). *Device technology, pervasive computing* (pp. 57). New Delhi: Pearson Education

Cheng.G , & Kotz, D. (2000). *A survey of context aware computing research* (TR 2000-381). Hanover, NH: Dartmouth Computer Science Technical Report.

Giussani, B. (2001) .*The intimate utility, roam making sense of the wireless Internet* (pp.12-24). London: Random House Business Books.

Joseph, J., & Fellenstein, C. (2004). *Introduction to grid computing* (pp. 12-13). New Delhi: Pearson Education.

Krikke, J. (2005). T-engine: Japan's ubiquitous computing architecture is ready for prime time. *IEEE Pervasive Computing* .

Lukowicz, P., Timm-Giel, A., Lawo, M., & Herzog, O. (2007). Wearable computing. *IEEE-Pervasive Computing Mobile and Ubiquitous Systems, 6*(4).

Rajkamal (2007). *Mobile communications, mobile computing* (pp. 26-27). New Delhi: Oxford University Press.

Schiller, J. (2004). *Telecommunication systems, mobile communications* (pp. 7-8). New Delhi: Pearson Education

Sharma, V. (2007, December). Case study – Meru Taxis driven by technology. *Information Technology,* 54-55.

Talukder, A.K. & Yavagal, R.R. (2005). *Introduction, mobile computing* (pp. 7-8). New Delhi: Tata McGraw Hill.

Turban, E., Aaronson, J., & Liang, T.P. (2006). *Electronic commerce, decision support systems and intelligent systems* (pp. 744-745). New Delhi: Prentice Hall of India Pvt Ltd.

Vikram, J.G. with Ishikawa, C. (2007). *The T-Engine tomorrow happening today* (pp. 75-76). New Delhi. Information Technology.

Weiser, M. (1991). The computer for the 21st century. *Scientific American, 265*(3), 94-104.

KEY TERMS

Enterprise Resource Planning (ERP): This is an application software that integrates several data sources and processes in an organisation.

General Packet Radio Service (GPRS): It is a packet oriented mobile data service available to users of global system for mobile communications.

Global Positioning System (GPS): It has a combination of text, graphics, icons and symbols on maps.

Grid Computing: This involves the actual networking services and connections of a potentially unlimited number of ubiquitous computing devices within a "GRD".

Nomadic Computing: The computing environment moves along with the mobile user.

Personal Digital Assistant (PDA): It is a handheld computer device and also known as palmtop.

Supply Chain Management (SCM): It is a process of planning, implementing and controlling the operations from supplier, to manufacturer and to customers.

Web Semantic: This is the extension of the World Wide Web. This helps data to be shared and reused across applications.

Chapter VII
Developing a Software Agent for Establishing a Convenient Customer–Driven Group–Buying Mechanism

Toly Chen
Feng Chia University, Taiwan

Yi-Chi Wang
Feng Chia University, Taiwan

Horng-Ren Tsai
Lingtung University, Taiwan

Yu-Cheng Lin
Overseas Chinese Institute of Technology, Taiwan

ABSTRACT

Group-buying (or volume discount) is a promising field in electronic commerce for applying software agent technologies. In a traditional group-buying mechanism, either a customer or the supplier calls up a sufficient number of buyers for a target item, and then coordinates the actions of all participants during the whole process. Most participants involved in a group-buying project are passive. Studies in this field were therefore focused on developing an effective mechanism so as to enhance the utility of every participant in a fair way. However, the utility of a customer can only be maximized if the customer can buy the item he/she personally needs at a possibly lowest price, not just an item recommended by another customer or the supplier that he/she is supposed to like. In other words, it would be more flexible if every customer can initiate a group-buying project of his/her own for the item he/she personally needs in a convenient way. As a result, there will be multiple group-buying projects for multiple target items at the same time. To this end, a software agent is developed in this study to make every customer easily reach the web page he/she browses for a target item for group-buying. The data of the item will be automatically extracted and uploaded onto a website which then informs every registered user of the group-buying project of this item. Requests for the same item will be combined, and there are always multiple target items on the website for group-buying at the same time. As a result, cross group-buying becomes possible. An experimental system is constructed in this study to demonstrate the applicability of the software agent. Its advantages and/or disadvantages are also discussed.

INTRODUCTION

The characteristics of e-commerce are different with various trading objects or applications. E-commerce can be classified into business-to-business (B2B), business-to-consumer (B2C), business-to-business-to-customer (B2B2C), consumer-to-consumer (C2C), peer-to-peer (P2P), mobile commerce, intra-organizational, business-to-employee (B2E), collaborative commerce, non-profit-making, digital learning, exchange-to-exchange (E2E), and e-government categories. According to Zwass's opinions (Zwass, 2003), e-commerce comprises five respects including commerce, collaboration, communication, connection, and computation. These respects can be exploited to find innovational opportunities to organize and address marketplaces, to offer innovative products, to collaborate with business partners, to transform business processes, and to organize the delivery of information-system services. If the five innovational opportunities are mapped to these categories, then a matrix showing the innovational opportunities in these e-commerce categories can be constructed as shown in Table 1. This study is focused on group-buying (or volume discount, aggregate sell/buy, buyer coalition, etc.), which belongs to both "organize and address marketplaces" and C2B EC. The concept of group-buying is that buyers can advantageously negotiate with sellers and purchase items at volume-discount prices by forming a coalition (Yamamoto & Sycara, 2001). Group-buying is also considered as a special type of reverse auction. For group-buying, an electronic market place usually a server computer) is a more convenient place than a traditional market, because it is very difficult to find a certain group of people with the same demand latter (Yuan & Lin, 2004).

In a traditional group-buying mechanism, either a buyer/customer or the seller/supplier calls up a sufficient number of buyers for a target item, and then coordinates the activities of all participants during the whole process. Most participants involved in a group-buying project are passive. Studies in this field were focused on developing an effective mechanism so as to enhance the utility

Table 1. Innovative opportunities in e-commerce categories

	B2B	B2C	C2C	C2B	Others
Organize and address marketplaces				█	
Offer innovative products					
Collaborate with business partners					
Transform business processes					
Organize the delivery of information-system services					

of every participant in a fair way. However, the utility of a customer can only be maximized when the customer can buy the item he/she personally needs at a possibly lowest price, not just an item recommended by the other customers or the supplier that he/she likes. According to Yamamoto & Sycara (2001), existing group buying schemes do not provide buyers any means to declare and match their preferences. In other words, it would be more flexible if every customer can initiate a group-buying project of his/her own for the item he/she personally needs in a convenient way. That will create a lot of group-buying projects at the same time for the buyers to choose from. To this end, an efficient group-buying mechanism needs to be established.

Group-buying is a promising field in agent technology applications in electronic commerce. However, owing to the computational complexity, it is difficult to deal with thousands of buyer agents which could join in practice. The objectives of a group-buying project usually include increasing each buyer's utility, allowing more buyers to obtain the items, a fair division of the surplus among buyers, etc. Tsvetovat et al. (2000) and Rha & Widdows (2002) showed that both buyers and sellers could both benefit from the group-buying project. Yamamoto & Sycara (2001) proposed the GroupBuy auction mechanism in which a buyer can post many items if he/she intends to buy any one of these items. Namely, the GroupBuy auction mechanism allows a buyer to announce his/her own group-buying projects which relationship is the OR operator. However, the GroupBuy auction mechanism is not convenient to the buyers because they have to collect the data of the items they need and then upload onto the group-buying website manually, which is not only laborious and might also infringe upon the property rights of the data sources.

To overcome these difficulties, a software agent is developed in this study. There are two types of agents in an electronic market place, seller agents and buyer agents. While a seller agent tries to sell

goods at a higher price, a buyer agent tries to buy goods at a lower price. The software agent developed in this study belongs to the buyer agents. With the software agent, every customer can easily turn an item on the web page he/she browses into a target item for group-buying. Some web page mining algorithms are proposed for this purpose. The data of the item will be automatically extracted and uploaded onto a website which then informs every registered user about the group-buying project of this item. Requests for the same item will be combined, and there are always multiple target items on the website for group-buying at the same time. As a result, cross group-buying becomes possible. An experimental system is constructed in this study to demonstrate the applicability of the software agent. Its advantages and/or disadvantages are also discussed.

The remaining of this paper is organized as follows. The next section reviews some existing group-buying mechanisms. In the third section, some web page mining algorithms are proposed for extracting the information of every item from a web page, so as to facilitate the initiation of a new group-buying project for any one of these items. The operation procedure of the new group-buying mechanism is then detailed in the fourth section. To evaluate the effectiveness of the proposed methodology, an experimental system is constructed in the fifth section, and a series of experiments have also been carried out. Finally, the concluding remarks and some directions for future research are given in the last section.

LITERATURE REVIEW

Group-buying is a volume-discount mechanism that aggregates customer demands to lower the unit price (Anand & Aron, 2003). The more the number of aggregated buyers is, the higher the bargaining power of these buyers becomes (Yuan & Lin, 2004). Group-buying is based on two basic principles:

1. The unit cost of marketing to many customers is usually lower than that to a single customer, and therefore the company becomes more willing to sell at a lower price.
2. To the customers, the willing to buy an item increases as the unit price of the item decreases.

The past studies in this field were devoted to three different categories:

1. **Demand aggregation:** With the popularity of Internet, the geographical boundaries of international trade have being eliminated. That facilitates the aggregation of demands for the same item even from distant regions. For example, Yuan & Lin (2003) and Li et al. (2004) both proposed new group-buying mechanisms to facilitate the gathering of sellers and buyers.
2. **Bargaining:** Though bargaining leads to save money for the buyers, it might take a lot of efforts and much time. The costs accumulated during the bargaining process are called the bargaining cost and have to be considered in evaluating the effectiveness of the group-buying mechanism (Zwick et al., 2000). Anand & Aron (2003) investigated the performance of a monopolistic group-buying website under a dynamic pricing mechanism and compared the results with that under a fixed pricing mechanism.
3. **Volume discounting:** In the electronic market, a seller agent can sell multiple items. Each item has a price table, a deadline, and

the number of the item in stock (Ito et al., 2002). A price table represents the discount rates for various numbers of buyers (see Table 2).

There are various ways to measure the utility of each participant in a group-buying project. If there is only one item for sell, then the utility of a buyer is usually inversely proportional to the deal price, while the utility of a seller goes high with the increase in the deal price:

$$U_b(X) = N(X) / P(X)$$
$$U_s(X) = N(X) \cdot P(X)$$

where X is an item; U_b and U_s indicate the buyer utility and the seller utility, respectively; $N(X)$ is the acquired quantity; $P(X)$ is the deal price of X, and has to be smaller than the price desired by the buyer, i.e. the reservation price. The difference is called the surplus that has to be aggregated and then distributed among the participating buyers. Other formulae for them include:

$$U_b(X) = N(X) \cdot (P_b(X) - P(X))$$
$$U_s(X) = N(X) \cdot (P(X) - P_s(X))$$

where $P_b(X)$ and $P_s(X)$ denote the prices desired by the buyer and the seller, respectively. In the multiple-item case, Ito et al. (2002) mentioned that the utility of an item to the buyer might depend on those of the other items. There exists complementarity between items X and Y if:

$$U_b(X, Y) > U_b(X) + U_b(Y)$$

It is also not uncommon that a buyer desires an item less if he/she has already bought another one. We say that there exists substitutability between the two items:

$$U_b(X, Y) < U_b(X) + U_b(Y)$$

In the group-buying mechanism proposed by Ito et al. (2002), exchanging items among sell

Table 2. A price table

The number of items sold	Unit price
1~5	10,000
6~10	9,500
11~20	9,000
20~	8,600

agents was allowed. In this way, the quantity for sale can be further increased and the final deal price might be very low, which is beneficial to the success of the group-buying project. The same concept was also adopted by Tsai & Chen (2008). In their study, an online collaborative stock control and selling mechanism (OCSSM) among seller agents was constructed. In OCSSM, the stock levels of an item owned by multiple seller agents are monitored, virtually aggregated, and shared among these seller agents. According to their experimental results, the OCSSM mechanism improved the efficiency of selling items for the participating sellers by shortening the average time to stock depletion up to 14%. Yuan & Lin (2004) proposed the credit based group negotiation approach. The negotiation credit is a pre-specified number of negotiation times within which the negotiation must be finished. In their study, buyers and sellers can bargain with different strategies. With the negotiation credit, deals could be closed more efficiently but still achieved good payoffs. Yuan & Lin also mentioned the three difficulties with group-buying as neither communication nor negotiation really happens between the seller and the buyers, and thus the deal price might still be far beyond the buyers' expectation.

Buyers may pay different prices for the identical item, and therefore a stable manner is needed for measuring the division of the surplus. Here the stability means that the outcome is immune to the deviations by individual participants. The core of the game theory can be applied to assess the stability of surplus division (Yamamoto & Sycara, 2001).

The computation becomes very complicated if many buyers are involved. For this reason, some studies (e.g. Shehory & Kraus, 1996) restricted the size of the buyer coalition.

Mobshop.com utilizes two demand coordination engines, Collective Buying Service and PowerBuy, to group buyers with the same demands for price bidding. Software agent technology is applied in many studies in this field. However,

it will be very money and time consuming for the agents to reach the final decisions without restraining the process of negotiation (Yuan & Lin, 2004).

METHODOLOGY

The GroupBuy auction mechanism allows a buyer to list several items from which he/she could choose from. Such a concept is called cross group-buying (see Figure 1). The items are usually substitutes for each other, and buyers have to collect the data of the items by themselves. In the proposed methodology, the data of an item will be automatically extracted from the web page it is contained in and uploaded onto a website which then informs every registered user about the group-buying project of this item. Requests for the same item will be combined, and there are always multiple target items on the website for group-buying at the same time. As a result, cross group-buying becomes more flexible and automatic.

The first algorithm for mining the related information of every item from a web page is the distance-based approach described as follows:

1. Search for every picture embedded in the web page, and record the hyper reference of the picture.

Figure 1. The concept of cross group-buying

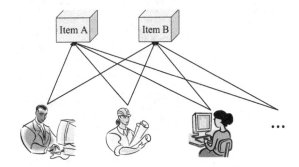

2. Record the position of each picture in the web page.

3. Determine whether the picture is related to an item or just for decoration according to its size, file name, position, etc. Reserve only non-decorative pictures.

4. Search for every text embedded in the web page.

5. Record the position of each text in the web page.

6. For each picture, calculate the absolute distance between the picture and each text as: Absolute distance $(p_i, t_j) = |P(p_i) - P(t_j)|$, where p_i and t_j indicate the i-th picture and the j-th text, respectively. $P(x)$ is the position of x.

7. A text is related with the picture if the absolute distance is less than a threshold, ε. Take Buy.yahoo.com.tw as an example. The web pages of ten items were randomly chosen. The absolute distance needed for each item to include all necessary description was obtained. The results were summarized in Figure 2. In this case, ε can be set to be 11.

The second algorithm is the hierarchical-relationship approach described as follows:

1. Search for every text, picture, or table part (including body, row, column, and grid) embedded in the web page.

Figure 2. Determining the value of ε

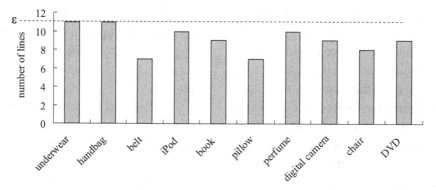

Figure 3. The hierarchical relationship web page mining algorithm

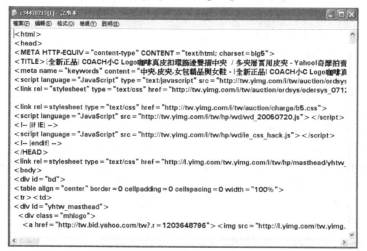

2. Number each of them with the following rules (see Figure 3):

   a. If it is a text or picture outside all tables, number it with positive integer numbers (1, 2, 3, etc.).

   b. If it is a table body (with html code <table ...>), number it also with positive integer numbers.

   c. If it is a table row (with html code <tr ...>), number it as *body number.row number*, where row number is also a positive integer number.

   d. If it is a table gird (with html code <td ...>), number it as *body number.row number.grid number*, where grid number is also a positive integer number.

   e. If it is a text or picture inside a table, number it as *body number.row number. grid number.text or picture number*, where text or picture number is also a positive integer number.

3. For each picture, find out the related texts with the following rules:

   a. A text is strongly related with the picture if they have the same grid numbers.

   b. A text is moderately related with the picture if they have the same row numbers but different grid numbers.

   c. A text is weakly related with the picture if they have the same table numbers but different row and grid numbers.

   d. A text and the picture might be unrelated if they do not have the same table numbers.

The third algorithm is the keyword-based approach described as follows:

1. Search for every picture embedded in the web page.

2. Number these pictures with positive integer numbers.

3. Search for every text embedded in the web page.

4. Number these texts with positive integer numbers.

5. Find out the keywords in every text.

6. If some successive texts have the same keywords, then they belong to the same text group.

7. Assign text groups to pictures in ascending order.

EXPERIMENT

There have been a lot of e-commerce sites for group-buying (e.g. Volumebuy.com, MobShop (i.e. Accompany.com), Mercata.com, etc.). However, the ways of operation on these websites are different. For example, MobShop clearly shows the initial price of an item, the discount for a certain number of buyers, and the accumulated number of buyers till now, while Mercata.com does not show how many buyers have been gathered until the end of the group-buying project. As a result, the buyers are not able to know the current price based on which the decision of joining or not can be made. The roles of buyers on these two websites are passive. Conversely, another group-buying website BazaarE allows every user to join or organize a shopping group that is composed of many users interested in the same item. There are also group-buying websites for B2B purposes spread around the world, such as C-Tribe, OnlineChoice, and DemandLine in US, LetsBuyIt and CoShopper in Europe, StockBuzz in Thailand, Chennai Online in Indian, Coshopper in Japan, CitiMart in Taiwan, etc. However, owing to the intensive competition in this industry, many of the aforementioned group-buying websites have ceased their operations in this field or even have been closed. Nowadays most group-buying services are offered online by shopping websites as one of many purchasing ways. In addition, a bulletin board system (BBS) becomes a new platform for conducting group-buying projects in which the role of the moderator is eliminated and one of the buyers in a group-buying project is responsible for initiating and administrating the project. The role of buyers becomes active. However, it is still a laborious task.

To evaluate the effectiveness of the proposed methodology, an experimental system with the following environment has been constructed:

1. **Platform:** Microsoft Windows XP and Internet Information Service (IIS) server installed on a PC.
2. **Architecture:** Three-layer (communication layer, application layer, and database layer) client-server architecture.
3. **Programming language:** The application layer is composed of several active server pages (ASP) coded using Visual Basic Script.
4. **Database management system:** Microsoft Access 2003.

The architecture of the convenient group-buying system is illustrated with its data flow diagram (DFD) in Figure 4. The system adopts the client-server architecture. On the client side,

a windows interface is provided for every buyer to browse the web page that contains items that the buyer is interested in, and therefore the necessity for these buyers to gather at the same place is relaxed, which is especially meaningful for items with global demand. The data of such items will be automatically extracted with the two aforementioned algorithms and uploaded onto the system server which then informs the other buyers about the group-buying projects of these items. The windows interface is developed using VB.NET and can be operated in the same way as the common browsers (see Figure 5). Its operation procedure is detailed in Figure 6. Conversely, on the server side (see Figure 7), the convenient group-buying system has the following components:

1. **The reception part of the web page miner,** which receives the information of items for group-buying from the client side, and then stores the received data into the system database.
2. **The item identifier:** Requests for the same item have to be combined, and therefore the item identifier will screen every incoming

Figure 4. The DFD of the convenient group-buying system

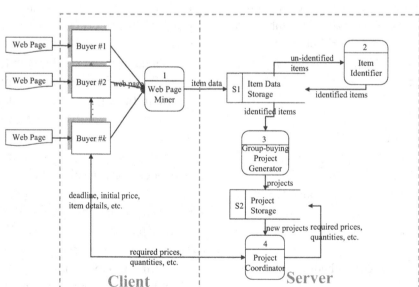

data and match them with those that have been stored in the system database to find out whether they indicate the same item or not. It is very common that the same popular item appear on different web pages spread on the Internet.

3. **Group-buying project generator:** After identifying new items for group-buying, the group-buying project generator generates a corresponding group-buying project for each of them including the originator, the project title, targeted item, possible deadline, possible quantity, price table, etc.

4. **Project coordination module:** After a group-buying project is launched, the project coordination model informs every registered user about the group-buying project, receives feedbacks from the users, and reports the status of the project to every user that might be interested in.

The DFD illustrates the operations of these components and the data flows among these components. These operations are also numbered according to their sequence. Most existing group-buying mechanisms also have their own websites.

Figure 5. The user interface on the client side

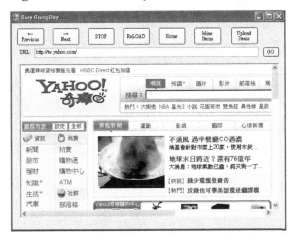

According to Yamamoto & Sycara (2001), there are three goals for evaluating the effectiveness of a group-buying mechanism:

1. Increasing the number of buyers that can purchase items, which can be measured in this study with the percentage of aggregated buyers over the required buyers = min (the number of aggregated buyers / the number of required buyers, 1) * 100%.

2. Increasing the total utility and each buyer's utility, which can be measured with the difference between the reservation price and the deal price in this study.

3. Dividing the total surplus among buyers in a fair and stable way.

To evaluate the advantages and/or disadvantages of the proposed methodology and to make

Figure 6. The procedure of web page mining

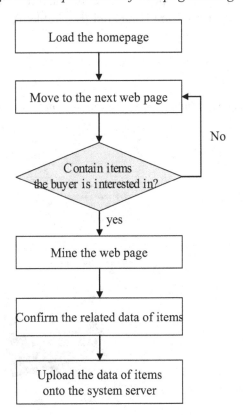

Figure 7. The server side of the convenient group-buying system

comparison with some existing group-buying mechanisms – GotoGroupBuy.com (Figure 8), PureNook.com, LetsGoShopping.com.tw, all of them were at first evaluated in several qualitative respects. The results are summarized in Table 3. Then the three performance measures of these mechanisms were compared (see Table 4). According to experimental results:

1. The convenient group-buying system automatically informs every registered user about the appearance of a group-buying project, and therefore is more likely to aggregate a sufficient number of buyers for the group-buying project. The percentage of aggregated required buyers with the proposed group-buying mechanism was then the highest one among the three compared mechanisms.
2. The easiness of gathering a lot of buyers lowers the unit price further possible, which is beneficial to elevate the buyers' utility.
3. All of the three group-buying mechanisms distribute the total surplus among the participating buyers in a fair way.

CONCLUSION

The existing group-buying mechanisms are not convenient to the buyers because they have to collect the data of the items they need and then upload onto the group-buying website manually. The operation of the mechnisms is not only labo-

Figure 8. Compared group-buying mechanism – GotoGroupBuying.com

rious and might also infringe upon the property rights of the data sources. To solve these problems, a software agent belonging to the buyer agents is developed in this study. With the proposed software agent, every customer can easily turn an item on the web page he/she browses into a target item for group-buying. The data of the item will be automatically extracted with some web page mining algorithms and then uploaded onto a website which then informs every registered user about the group-buying project of this item. Requests for the same item will be combined, and there are always multiple target items on the website for group-buying at the same time. As a result, cross group-buying becomes feasible.

To demonstrate the effectiveness of the proposed methodology and to make comparison with some existing group-buying mechanisms, an experimental system is constructed in this study. According to the experimental results:

1. The new group-buying mechanism indeed increased the number of buyers that can purchase items.
2. The total utility and each buyer's utility measured with the difference between the reservation price and the deal price were also improved with the new group-buying mechanism.

Table 3. Comparison among various group-buying mechanisms

	GotoGroupBuy.com	PureNook.com	LetsGoShopping.com.tw	The proposed mechanism
Originator	Buyer	Seller	Seller	Buyer
Show price table	Yes	Yes	No	Yes
Deadline	Yes	Yes	Yes	Yes
Countdown	Yes	No	No	Yes
Show number of buyers	Yes	No	Yes	Yes
Show retail price (& discount)	Yes	Yes	Yes	Yes
Show item details	Yes	Yes	Yes	Yes
Automatic item details uploading	No	No	No	Yes
Automatic cross group-buying	No	No	No	Yes

Table 4. The three performance measures of various group-buying mechanisms

	% of required buyers aggregated	Average saving percentage	Surplus division
GotoGroupBuy.com	0%	14%	Fair
LetsGoShopping.com.tw	98%	27%	Fair
The proposed methodology	100%	37%	Fair

More sophisticated group-buying mechanisms can be developed in future studies. For example, a peer-to-peer (P2P) architecture can be adopted so that every participant does not need to access a central server. All he/she needs is to put the favorite items into a pre-determined directory that will be virtually aggregated to respond to the same requests. On the other hand, the new mechanism has to be applied to group-buy more items to further evaluate its effectiveness.

REFERENCES

Anand, K. S., & Aron, R. (2003). Group-buying on the Web: a comparison of price-discovery mechanisms. *Management Science, 49*(11), 1546-1562.

Ito, T., Ochi, H., & Shintani, T. (2002). A group buy protocol based on coalition formation for agent-mediated e-commerce. *International Journal of Computer & Information Science, 3*(1).

Li, C., Chawla, S., Rajan, U., & Sycara, K. P. (2004). Mechanism design for coalition formation and cost sharing in group-buying markets. *Electronic Commerce Research and Applications, 3*(4), 341-354.

Rha, J-Y, & Widdows, R. (2002) The Internet and the consumer: countervailing power revisited. *Prometheus, 20*(2), 107-118.

Shehory, O., & Kraus, S. (1996) Formation of overlapping coalitions for precedence-ordered task-execution among autonomous agents. In *Proceedings of the 2nd International Conference on Multiagent Systems*.

Tsai, H.-R., & Chen, T. (2008). Online collaborative stock control and selling among e-retailers. *Lecture Notes in Computer Science, 4947*, 613-620.

Tsvetovat, M., Sycara, K., Chen, Y., & Ying, J. (2000). Customer coalitions in the electronic marketplace. In *Proceedings of the 3rd Workshop on Agent Mediated Electronic Commerce*.

Yamamoto, J., & Sycara, K. (2001). A stable and efficient buyer coalition formation scheme for e-marketplaces. In *Proceedings of International Conference on Autonomous Agents*, Canada.

Yuan, S.-T., & Lin, Y.-H. (2004). Credit based group negotiation for aggregate sell/buy in e-markets. *Electronic Commerce Research and Applications, 3*, 74-94.

Zwass, V. (2003). Electronic commerce and organizational innovation: aspects and opportunities. *International Journal of Electronic Commerce, 7*(3), 7-37.

Zwick, R., Weg, E., & Rapoport, A. (2000) Invariance failure under subgame perfectness in sequential bargaining. *Journal of Economic Psychology, 21*(5), 517-544.

Chapter VIII
How Research can Help to Create Commercially Successful Ubiquitous Services

Teea Palo
University of Oulu, Finland

Kaisa Koskela
University of Oulu, Finland

Timo Koivumäki
VTT Technical Research Centre of Finland, Finland

Jaana Tähtinen
University of Oulu, Finland

ABSTRACT

Ubiquitous computing will change the way people live with technology. At the same time it will also affect the way people access and use services. It is obvious that these new ubiquitous services have a lot of business potential. However, before this potential can be fully exploited, we need to understand the crucial factors behind creating commercially successful ubiquitous services. To do so, research is needed in three important areas. Firstly, we need to understand the basic nature of ubiquitous services, i.e., their unique characteristics. Secondly, we need to know the needs of the customers in order to create value to them so that they will accept and use ubiquitous services. This can be done by involving users into the innovation process of ubiquitous services. And thirdly, we need to understand the value creating networks developing and commercializing the ubiquitous services as well as to find an appropriate business model for describing them. Value creation is impossible without a successful network business model which is yet to be found. Thus, the aim of this chapter is to describe, examine and give proposals for further research in these three important research fields which can be seen as the prerequisites for developing commercially successful ubiquitous services.

INTRODUCTION

The era of ubiquitous computing does not only change the way how people access and use information. It will also have a profound effect on the way people access and use services. The emerging technologies connected with ubiquitous computing will change the relationship between a business and its customers in terms of three important areas. The technology will offer new ways for achieving awareness; new channels for accessibility; and thirdly, new techniques for responding to customers. This will enable the birth of new kind of services that only make sense when being embedded in the surrounding environment. (Fano & Gershman, 2002.) The successful commercialization of these services is in the key focus of this chapter.

In order to create commercially successful ubiquitous services one must first understand the nature of ubiquitous services and the challenges and opportunities that the new ubiquitous computing technology brings along. This chapter will try to identify the important characteristics of ubiquitous services, which separate them from ordinary service. However, understanding only the nature of ubiquitous services is not enough to make them commercially successful, that is why in this chapter we also want to stress the importance of customer needs, user innovation, value creating networks and the concept of network business model in the creation of ubiquitous services.

Understanding consumers' needs is one essential part in creating commercially successful ubiquitous services. However, in the case of novel products or services characterized by rapid change, as ubiquitous services, typical market research analysis is not very reliable and companies might be having trouble in identifying correctly the future needs of users (von Hippel, 1989). Therefore, to create successful ubiquitous services a new approach of "user driven innovation" is needed to the usually quite technology driven innovation and development of ubiquitous services. The

study of user driven innovation regards users as a resource in the innovation process (Holmquist, 2004). In other words, "users are not considered as a reference group that sets the specifications of a system, but as a source of inspiration that can foster innovation in its own right" (Holmquist, 2004, pp. 1091). In this chapter, we propose involving users, especially those identified as lead users, into the company's innovation and development process, as a solution to overcome the problem of identifying users' needs correctly. This way the needs of the users are the basis of the innovation and design process of a new service from the beginning of its creation.

According to Henkel and von Hippel (2005) most of the users' innovation activity is concentrated among the "lead users" in a user population. Because of the unique characteristics of lead users, they are not as constrained with the present as are the ordinary users, who are unlikely to generate new product and service ideas. Instead, they experience needs that are not general in the market for months or years and for that reason can serve as needs/forecasting laboratory for the companies as well as resources in the innovation process. (von Hippel, 1986; von Hippel, 1989.) Thus, within the research of user driven innovation the focus of this chapter is especially on the theory of lead users. The concept of lead user will be brought to the new context of ubiquitous technology and a theoretical framework building of lead user characteristics in the context of ubiquitous services will be started. Also further research issues will be discussed especially in the fields of lead user identification and lead user integration.

Another key issue in creating commercially successful ubiquitous services is to examine the value creating networks and the way lead users can be integrated into them. The development of new ubiquitous services is changing the business environment in many ways: new possibilities for generating revenues occur and new kinds of benefits appear. But perhaps one of the biggest changes brought by the development of these new kinds of services concerns the way value is created. The development of new ubiquitous services requires companies to cooperate and develop competencies in networks. Individual companies cannot internally master all the relevant value activities, nor is it even economically desirable to try to do so (see e.g. Möller, Rajala & Svahn, 2005). In addition to the different business actors involved in the network, customers are also a crucial part of the value creation process. Thus value creation in these new ubiquitous services is impossible without a business network that creates value together successfully to all parties of the network.

Furthermore the aim is to examine the concept of network business model. The inherent value of new technology remains latent unless it is commercialized in some way, and a successful business model connects technical potential with the realization of economic value (Chesbrough & Rosenbloom, 2002). Analyzing and identifying business models in this context is important as practitioners are still trying to figure out what are the appropriate business models which can provide value as a new ubiquitous business or as converged with traditional businesses (Lee & Lee, 2005). But it is not only the business models of single companies that are changing in this new ubiquitous service environment but the whole network business models that are evolving. Therefore instead of focusing on the business models of single companies, a network view on the concept introduced by Komulainen, Mainela, Sinisalo, Tähtinen and Ulkuniemi (2006) is needed. It is important to model the whole network developing and commercializing the ubiquitous services in order to analyse the actors and their roles as well as the value activities among them.

Both value creating networks and their business models are crucial elements in developing commercially successful ubiquitous services. By examining the previous literature concerning these issues, this chapter aims to address important and challenging issues for further research in this field.

VISION OF UBIQUITOUS WORLD

The vision of ubiquitous world was first introduced by Mark Weiser already in the early 1990's. In his article, "The computer of the 21st century" (1991), Weiser describes how computing technology will eventually disappear into our everyday life and become invisible to its user the same way as the "literacy technology", writing, has done.

In the following we will present the main element of the ubiquitous world; the ubiquitous computing as well as the ubiquitous services and ubiquitous commerce emerging from it. Based on the unique characteristics of these phenomena some key areas in business and marketing are recognized in the end of the discussion which are affected by the ubiquitous world.

The New Computing Paradigm: Ubiquitous Computing

According to Fano and Gershman (2002) ubiquitous computing will change the way we live with technology. With ubiquitous computing, using information technology will progressively feel more like using everyday objects such as pencils or hinges, than using personal computers (Fano & Gershman, 2002). However, in order to realize these visions, there are several goals to address, such as understanding the everyday practices of people, augmenting the world through the provisioning of heterogeneous devices and finally orchestrating the networked devices in order to provide for a holistic user experience (Abowd, Mynatt & Rodden, 2002).

Because ubiquitous reality resides in our real surrounding environment, the human world, it should not be confused with virtual reality, which attempts to create a world inside the computer. Thus when the purpose of virtual reality is to simulate the world in the point where the outside world and its inhabitants cease to exist, ubiquitous reality instead aims at enhancing the already existing one and poses no barriers to personal interactions. If anything the transparent connections offered by ubiquitous vision might bring people closer together. (Weiser, 1991.)

According to Weiser (1991) ubiquitous computing, like personal computing, will not produce anything fundamentally new. However, it will have a huge impact on our world and transform the things that are apparently possible by making everything faster and easier to do, with less strain and mental gymnastics. Thus also the concept of a product and a service will change, when it is made ubiquitous.

According to Lyytinen and Yoo (2002) "in its ultimate form, ubiquitous computing means any computing devices, while moving with us, can build incrementally dynamic models of its various environments and configure its services accordingly". In other words, ubiquitous computing will integrate the advantages of mobile computing and pervasive computing. Though these two terms might seem interchangeable, they employ different ideas of organizing and managing computing services. While mobile computing aims at enhancing the capability to physically move computing services with us, pervasive computing refers to the ability of an embedded computing service to obtain information from its surrounding environment and use it accordingly. (Lyytinen & Yoo, 2002.)

As well as advantages these concepts also pose great challenges. The biggest limitation of mobile computing is the fact that the model of computing does not considerably change while on move and so cannot obtain information about the context and adjust it. On the other hand, in the case of pervasive computing the main challenge is the limited scope and great effort to teach a computer to understand its environment, thus making the pervasive services highly localized. Thus for ubiquitous computing to reach its ultimate form, it also has to tackle the integrated limitations of mobile and pervasive computing. (Lyytinen & Yoo, 2002.)

In addition to the ubiquitous availability of computing infrastructure there can also be seen new paradigms of interaction enabled by the constant access to information and computational capabilities. For the past decade there can be recognized three main interaction themes around ubiquitous computing research: natural interfaces, context-aware applications and automated capture and access. Natural interfaces facilitate a richer variety of communication capabilities between humans and computation. Context-aware applications adapt behavior according to the physical and computational environment. Ubicomp applications aim to automate the capture and access of life experiences. In addition to these themes, a fourth paradigm of interaction is suggested to be everyday computing where the relationship between humans and computers changes into continuous interaction. (Abowd & Mynatt, 2000.)

However, despite of the great vision, in recent years there has been more and more critique towards the field of ubiquitous computing research, as there have been little or no progress at all in realizing all these visions made by earlier research. Research in the field of ubiquitous computing has failed to produce visible results as well as the ubicomp research community has failed to create its own theoretical framework (see e.g. Sharp & Rehman, 2005; Bell & Dourish, 2007). Thus, there is still a rich and exciting opportunity for future research in the field of ubiquitous computing as it is currently in an early stage of development. Jeon, Leem, Kim & Shin (2007) see that the emergence of ubiquitous computing provides many exciting opportunities for future research although previous research has mainly focused on just technologies which are required in establishing the ubiquitous computing environment.

Ubiquitous Services and their Unique Characteristics

As said earlier, shift to the ubiquitous computing paradigm will enable the birth of new kinds of services. These services will have unique characteristics when compared to ordinary services. Because of these characteristics, also the way people use and access services as well as the relationship between a business and its customers will change. (Fano & Gershman, 2002.) A lot of research is needed in these new research fields of ubiquitous service characteristics, user situations and company-customer relationship. In this chapter we try to bring these issues into the spot light, give future research recommendations and start the theoretical framework building.

Because it is impossible to determine the most appropriate service in some situation without understanding services, it is vital to first answer to the question: what are ubiquitous services? (Yamazaki, 2004). Only after this we will be able to succeed in creating successful ubiquitous services that the consumers will use. According to Fano and Gershman (1992) ubiquitous computing will cause a fundamental change to our definition of a service. It will change what constitutes a service, how it is perceived and the value it provides the customer.

Because, ubiquitous services are enabled by ubiquitous computing, they will also integrate the opportunities and challenges of mobile and pervasive technology. Hence, as ubiquitous computing, also ubiquitous services are able to move with us and at the same time reach us from places and situations where the ordinary services cannot get. This, of course, widens the marketplace and offers all kinds of new opportunities as well as challenges for service providers.

Because of the pervasive computing characteristics, ubiquitous services are embedded into our surrounding environment. Hence, another key characteristic of ubiquitous services is that they are triggered based on physical conditions, thus they know the real world status and users' situations (Yamazaki, 2004). By using sensor and local resources, ubiquitous service providers can become more aware of their customers' needs and be more responsive (Fano & Gershman,

2002). For this reason, ubiquitous services have the ability to be unexpected to the user, because they are triggered by a system and not by the user's intention (Yamazaki, 2004). Because of the above characteristics of ubiquitous services, they should be intelligent enough to understand the real world. This phenomenon is sometimes called context-awareness.

Context-awareness is generally regarded as an enabling technology for ubiquitous computing systems. Although the term "context" is sometimes equated with "location", especially in the scope of mobile applications, it has also several other meanings. Schilit et al. (1994) decomposed context into three categories: computing context, user context, and physical context. Later, Dey and Abowld (2000) provided very general and widely referenced definition for context: "Context is any information that can be used to characterize the situation of an entity. An entity is a person, place, or object that is considered relevant to the interaction between a user and an application, including the user and applications themselves." Further, Dey & Abowld (2000) state that "a system is context-aware if it uses context to provide relevant information and/or services to the user, where relevancy depends on the user's task." A lot of research is still needed in this area and also in the area of sensing the real world, which is the prerequisite for understanding it.

In their ultimate form ubiquitous services are also invisible through natural interfaces. This means that the physical interaction between humans and service computation will be more like the way humans interact with the physical world, for example with speech and gestures, and less like the current desktop/keyboard/mouse/display paradigm (Abowd & Mynatt, 2000).

It is clear that when services become ubiquitous they enable businesses to redefine the key aspects of their customer relationships and offer a lot of new opportunities and ways to make money. However, these new capabilities also present new competitive challenges for businesses. (Fano &

Gershman, 2002.) The questions arising from the new opportunities and challenges of ubiquitous services are discussed more profoundly in the next part of the chapter dealing with ubiquitous commerce.

Next Big Step: U-Commerce

As ubiquitous computing changes the way people access and use services, it causes new classes of services embedded in the environment leading us to a world of ubiquitous commerce (Fano & Gershman, 2002). Watson, Pitt, Berthon and Zinkhan (2002) see that ubiquitous commerce, u-commerce, is the next big step in digitization as e-commerce and m-commerce are just way stations on the path. U-commerce can be defined as "the use of ubiquitous networks to support personalized and uninterrupted communications and transactions between a firm and its various stakeholders to provide a level of value over, above, and beyond traditional commerce". All in all, u-commerce can be seen as a new paradigm extending the internet era by providing ubiquity, universality, uniqueness and unison (Galanxhi-Janaqi & Fui-Hoon Nah, 2004).

U-commerce has broad implications as it will transform the business and marketing landscape in many ways. U-commerce will affect the customers and the firms as well as the products and services. It will change our view of business by transforming the interaction with customers in time and space. The connectivity created by ubiquitous networks affects the communication between an organisation and stakeholders changing it from simple and unidirectional model to a complex multi-directional one. Furthermore, the role of information will become the core of marketing and the nature of competition will change as the technology may enable new entrants to the marketplace. U-commerce can also have an effect on the structure of the firms and especially on the marketing functions. (Watson et al., 2002.)

All in all, u-commerce has implications to the nature of communication, competition, structure, marketing and the business model itself. It will also encourage innovation which is seen to be key to success in u-commerce. U-commerce will provide improved operating efficiency, enhanced customer services, increased services personalization, continuous supply chain connectivity and continuous interactivity. (Galanxhi-Janaqi & Fui-Hoon Nah, 2004.)

However, as u-commerce provides many opportunities it may also be a threat to some industries (Watson et al., 2002). U-commerce applications may face many challenges and raise new questions (Galanxhi-Janaqi & Fui-Hoon Nah, 2004). The new capabilities provided by ubiquitous computing present competitive challenges concerning how to extend services to every location, how to sense customer needs, how to use all the available resources at each location and how to be selective and precise in customer interaction without violating customer privacy. These challenges will define the competitive landscape of u-commerce and still need answering. (Fano & Gershman, 2002.)

However knowing the characteristics of ubiquitous services and the impacts of ubiquitous technology as well as u-commerce is not enough. To really succeed in creating successful ubiquitous services, we need to understand the human beings using them (Yamazaki, 2004) as well as the nature value creating networks responsible for their creation.

USER DRIVEN INNOVATION AND LEAD USERS IN THE CONTEXT OF UBIQUITOUS SERVICES

One of the many reasons, why we have failed in the mission to make ubiquitous computing an integral part of our lives, is the fact that the ubiquitous products and services developed and designed have been too technology driven. In other words the needs of the end users, the consumers, have been ignored and forgotten. This has happen even though Weiser (1991, pp. 66) himself argued that the ultimate goal of ubiquitous computing, the disappearance of technology, is not really a matter of the technology itself but of human psychology, because "whenever people learn something sufficiently well, they cease to be aware of it".

However, in order that a person will take the time and effort to learn to use for example a complicated, new device or service, he or she needs to benefit for it a great deal and the customer perceived value of these new ubiquitous products and services is many times invisible for the ordinary consumers, assuming that it even exist. This fact is justified in Åkesson and Ihlström-Eriksson (2007) that shows that in order to accelerate the adoption rate of mobile services, marketing communication of the content and the value of these services is very important as opposed to communicating only of the technological innovation. However, to succeed in creating value creating ubiquitous products and services to the consumers, one needs to understand their needs. Thus, it is needless to say that a new approach is required in order to be able to make the dream of ubiquitous world a reality. One possible and potential solution is to concentrate on user driven design and user innovation, especially in the form of integrating consumers in the innovation and development process of ubiquitous products and services. In the study of user driven innovation users are not considered just as a reference group, but as a source of inspiration that can foster innovation in its own right. (Holmquist, 2004.)

As stated earlier understanding consumers' needs is essential in the development of commercially successful products and services. However, in the case of novel products or product categories characterized by rapid change, as ubiquitous computing, typical market research analysis is not very reliable and companies might be having trouble in identifying correctly these future user needs. (von Hippel, 1989.) The same anal-

ogy can be applied to ubiquitous services. This is due to a fact that ordinary user's insights into new product or service needs and solutions are constrained with their own experience. In other words, ordinary users are unlikely to generate novel product ideas that conflict with the familiar. (von Hippel, 1986; von Hippel, 1989.) Lead users however have experiences of needs that are not general in the market for months or years, and thus are not constrained so much with the present. This is why they are very useful in the innovation or development process and can serve as needs/forecasting laboratory for the companies as well as for the researchers. (von Hippel, 1989.)

Even though the high value of using lead user data in the new product development process has been empirically shown in the previous research (see e.g. Lilien, Morrison, Searls, Sonnack & von Hippel, 2002), the lead user identification is still quite difficult and more research needs to be done in order to shed light in the specific characteristics of lead users. Furthermore, this time the research focus is on service development instead of product development as has usually been the case in lead user research.

Identification of Lead Users

According to Henkel and von Hippel (2005) and Morrison, Roberts and von Hippel (2000) most of the innovation activity of users is concentrated among the "lead users" in a user population. Lead users can be organizations as well as individual users. In this chapter the focus is more on consumers i.e. the individual lead users, because the consumer side has received far less attention in the study of lead users so far.

Originally the concept of lead user was proposed for new product development in the industries that deal with high technology and are subject to rapid change (von Hippel, 1986). Thus this theory is optimal to be applied also in the novel field of ubiquitous computing. Additional value can be provided by examining the role of lead users also in the new service development (NSD) in this given field, instead of the new product development (NPD).

According to Morrison et al. (2004) the lead user research emerged from research into sources of innovation. First, it was found that users rather than manufactures where the initial developers of ideas that would later become commercially significant (Morrison et al. 2004). Later, it was discovered that innovations made by users tended to concentrate among those users who experienced need for that given innovation earlier than others in the target market i.e. to the lead users (von Hippel, 1986; Morrison et al., 2004). Hence, the success of the lead user method lies in the ability to identify the right users as the sources of innovation (Intrachooto, 2004). However, one of the major challenges of applying the lead user method in practice is the reliable and efficient identification of lead users (Lilien et al., 2002, Lüthje & Herstatt, 2004, Olson & Bakke, 2001). Most severe this problem seems to be in the consumer goods fields where the user populations are very large. The lead user research so far has generated only limited advice to overcome this problem. Basically the only two known characteristics are the definitional characteristics of lead users that are being ahead of a trend and expecting high benefits from innovating. (Schreier & Prügl, 2006.) In this study a few other possible lead user characteristics are presented. However, future research still needs to address this gap of knowledge in order to facilitate the identification of lead users among from the more ordinary users.

Lead User Characteristics

In order to succeed in lead user identification, one must first know how lead users differ from the rest of the user population or in other words, what are the special characteristics of lead users? According to von Hippel (1986) there are two main characteristics of a lead user. Firstly, lead users are ahead of an important trend and face

needs before the others. Secondly, they benefit significantly when obtaining a solution to these needs and consequently are more likely to innovate. To prevent misunderstanding, it should be stressed that conceptually these two components of lead user definition are independent. They stem from different literatures and thus serve different functions in the lead user theory. (Franke, von Hippel & Schreier, 2006.) The two features and their measures are examined more profoundly in the following.

The first of the two main characteristics and identification criteria of lead users is fact that they face new needs substantially earlier than the bulk of the market (von Hippel, 1986). In other words lead users are being in advance of the market with respect to some important dimension that is changing over time. Thus to be able to identify lead users this underlying trend has to be specified in the case of each different context. (von Hippel, 1989.)

The second main characteristic of lead users is that they benefit significantly from obtaining a solution to their needs. The greater the expected benefit is for the users, the greater his or hers effort is to obtain a solution (von Hippel, 1986). Therefore, this characteristic also serves as indicator of innovation likelihood (Franke et al., 2006). In other words lead users are found to innovate i.e. develop new products more likely than non-lead users (Urban & von Hippel, 1988). Here it should be noted that the term "innovate" has different meanings for example in the R&D and diffusion/adoption literatures. In R&D the term can be applied to individuals as well as in organizations and it means "to develop a new product or service". However, in the diffusion/adoption literature an "innovator" refers to an individual who is one of the very first to adopt a new product or service. Thus the term relates more to the timing of the adoption of a new product or service. (Morrison et al., 2004.) In the case of lead users, this term is used to refer for the development of a new product or service. However, also the early adoption behavior is very common for individuals identified as lead users.

According to Urban and von Hippel (1988) three types of proxy measures are useful when measuring the potential user benefit from solving a need. These are user's tendency toward product development or product modification, user dissatisfaction with existing product and the speed of adoption of innovations.

In addition to these two main characteristic identified by von Hippel (1986), Schreier and Prügl (2006) found in their study that consumer's leading edge status depends also variables which can be categorized as field-related as well as field-independent variables. The identified field-related variables are consumer's basis of knowledge and use experience gained in the underlying field. The relevant field-independent variables were individual's innovativeness and "locus of control" i.e. the tendency to believe that outcomes depend primarily on person's own actions.

Other possible lead user characteristics might include either innate innovativeness, use innovativeness or domain-specific innovativeness of a person or all of these types of innovativeness. Also demographic and psychographic characteristics, such as age, education, opinion leadership and greater social participation, might be helpful when identifying lead user among a user group. However, a lot of further research and empirical validation is needed before lead users can be easily and positively identified in the context of ubiquitous services.

Integrating Lead Users into the Innovation Process

Integration of external innovation ideas, such as lead user input, into company's R&D and innovation processes is a challenging task which has puzzled companies ever since the introduction of open innovation paradigm. There are some success stories, such as Lego, that can serve as benchmark cases for other innovative companies.

Unfortunately, the formula to success is not as straightforward as mimicking the innovation processes of these companies. The innovation processes vary significantly based on the company, the market environment it operates in, the product/service offered by the company, its customer profile, etc.

Integration of lead user into the innovation process of a firm has been studied in the past for some extent (see e.g. Urban & von Hippel, 1988). However, there is still a need for both empirical theoretical research to assist companies in selecting and tailoring the most appropriate management strategy for open lead user driven innovations depending on their context. We envision an approach by which each organization can define or select a suitable strategy, considering parameters such as type of innovation, partnership models, product complexity, available expertise and degree of maturity. There is also need for theoretically sound, empirically grounded knowledge to assist companies to better manage the execution of its innovation projects in a swiftly changing development environment, monitoring and updating the status and progress of the projects and obtaining the necessary and sufficient knowledge to enable quick response and innovation evaluation and decision making concerning the projects' performance and business goals.

VALUE CREATION IN UBIQUITOUS SERVICES

As stated earlier, because of the unique characteristics of ubiquitous services, the business environment will be changed in many ways. The development of new ubiquitous services requires companies to cooperate and develop competencies in networks as individual companies cannot internally master all the relevant value activities, nor is it even economically desirable to try to do so (see e.g. Möller et al., 2005). Thus value creation in these new ubiquitous services can be seen as a more dynamic and interactive process involving a network of individual companies. In addition to these business actors, customers and especially lead users are also a crucial part of these networks as it is increasingly important to involve them in the innovation and value creation of the services. Therefore, a crucial aspect in creating commercially successful ubiquitous services concerns business networks including the different business actors and customers involved in the development and commercialization of these services. Research is needed in this field especially to find out how value is created in networks and how customers identified as lead users can be integrated into the value creation process.

However, the inherent value of new technology remains latent unless it is commercialized in some way, and a successful business model connects technical potential with the realization of economic value (Chesbrough & Rosenbloom, 2002). Therefore it is also important to analyze and identify the new business models in this context and thus describe the value creation process of the network. Therefore it is not only the business models of single companies that are changing in this new ubiquitous service environment but the whole network business models that are evolving. It is important to describe the whole network developing and commercializing the ubiquitous services in order to analyse the value creation process of the network. Although there has been a lot of research concerning business models especially in the fields of m- and e-business, further research is still needed in the field of network business models as the concept is viewed from the network viewpoint and is therefore a rather new field of interest. Furthermore, the business models around ubiquitous services are strongly shaped by the unique characteristics of the services and therefore it is important to yet study what kind of network business models are appropriate in this new business environment.

Both these elements of value creating networks and their business models are crucial elements in developing commercially successful ubiquitous services. By examining the previous literature concerning these interrelated fields, important and challenging issues for further research can be made and some theoretical insights discovered. Furthermore, the ways, in which customers identified as lead users can be integrated into the networks, are another important issue in the creation of commercially successful ubiquitous services and are still an unexplored area of interest.

Value Creating Networks: Value Co-Creation with Customers

Value is an economic concept making people engage in business relationships (Shin & Lee, 2005). Theoretically viewed value can be seen as the trade-off between benefits and sacrifices relative to competition (Walter, Ritter & Gemünden, 2001). In practice, value can be viewed in different forms. Allee (2000) for example identifies three currencies of value, which are the firm's offering in the form of products or services, knowledge and intangibles. Furthermore, ubiquitous services can offer also other unique values for customers (Shin & Lee, 2005). Fano and Gershman (2002) for example talk about improved awareness, accessibility and responsiveness. Watson et al. (2002) introduce the concepts of ubiquity, universality, uniqueness and unison. Other special characteristics of ubiquitous services, such as context-awareness, mobility and embeddedness can also be seen as unique values for customer. Thus ubiquitous services can offer new dimensions of value to the customer. However, this value cannot be created solely by one single company, but there are various business actors involved in the process of creating value to the customer as well as to all the business actors involved.

Therefore it is understandable that the focus of value creation has moved from beyond individual firms to value creating networks formed by the key firms in the value chain (Kothandaraman & Wilson, 2001). As the traditional value chain thinking has been gradually replaced by the new enterprise model of the value network, a major challenge today is to reconfigure business from value chain organisation to value network structure (Allee, 2000). Technical innovations turn value creation more interactive and less linear and this value co-production among two or more actors forces organisations to rethink their structures and managerial arrangements (Ramirez, 1999). Hence, value for the customer is more often created through value networks which are formed in order to generate economic value in dynamic engagements among all business stakeholders of a firm (Shin & Lee, 2005).

According to the traditional value chain concept, value creation can be seen as sequential and value is considered as added. In industrial value creation customers were considered to destroy the value that producers had created. Therefore customers and the producers were separated from each other. An alternative view on value creation implies that value creation is synchronic and interactive, not linear and transitive. Instead of destroying value, customers create it. Furthermore, value is not added but it is mutually created and re-created among different actors with different values. (Ramirez, 1999.) This is seen to be the case in developing ubiquitous services. The customers identified as lead users, are an integral part of the innovation process of the services and therefore they are also essentially involved in the value creation with the other business actors in the network in the innovation stage of creating commercially successful ubiquitous services.

Prahalad and Ramaswamy (2004a) see that the co-creation of unique value with customers is the answer to the challenges faced by management as the leaders need a new frame of reference for value creation. Value co-creation with the customer begins by recognising that the role of the customer is becoming more connected, informed and active. This means that companies can no longer act autonomously but customers influence in every part of the business. They want to interact

with firms and the use of interaction is a basis for value co-creation. Customers are engaged in defining and creating value. This co-creation experience of the customer is the very basis of value. Management needs to attend to the quality of co-creation experiences, not just the quality of the products and processes. The roles of the company and the customer converge toward a unique value co-creation experience. (Prahalad & Ramaswamy, 2004a.) Because of ubiquitous computing the customers are able to be more connected, get easier and broader access to information and this way also be more active. Ubiquitous computing can also have many other unique effects on the role of the customer and especially on the interaction between the organisation and the customer, which needs further examination.

However, this kind of changing nature of the consumer-company interaction as the locus of value co-creation is redefining the concept of value and the process of value creation. The building blocks of interaction between the firm and the consumers are dialog, access, transparency and risk-benefits. Through dialog the consumer and the firm become equal and joint problem solvers. This however is impossible without access and transparency of information to both parties. Due to ubiquitous connectivity it is possible for a consumer to get as much information as needed. On the basis of these three building blocks, dialog, access and transparency, the consumer can make a clear assessment of the risk-benefits of a certain action or a decision. This personalized value co-creation experience is seen as a source of unique value, but it is separated from the concept of customers as innovators. As long as the process is firm centric and product centred, it is at best a variant of the current dominant logic. (Prahalad & Ramaswamy, 2004b.)

However, we see that value co-creation with customers especially in this specific environment can involve customers identified as lead users as part of the innovation process of the services. This way value is being created at the innovation and development stage of the services and the customers are an integral part of the value creating networks. Value creation is not firm-centric if the customer is tightly involved in the network developing and commercializing the services. It can be seen to be network-centric as all the actors in the network are part of the value creation process. Furthermore, ubiquitous services could not exist without active participation of customers and moreover, the consumption of these kinds of services involves several users at the same time.

In addition to just examining the interaction between the company and the consumer, there are also other parties involved in the process of value creation from the services. Companies can no longer just examine one major competitor, but they need to examine the whole network related to that competitor. Competition is argued to be shifting from the firm level to the network level with value creating networks. Satisfying customer needs is no longer enough but firms need to create better or superior value compared to their competitors. Core capabilities, which are rare within most firms, are crucial in delivering superior value. Therefore there is a need for de-integrating operations and building strong relationships. Forming a network of firms in order to assembly the competencies needed to build a market offering that delivers high value to the customer is a major strategic issue to the firm. Therefore it can be argued that firms are moving into an environment in which they are not competing against each other but where networks of firms are competing against each other. Superior customer value, core capabilities and relationships are considered to be the building blocks of value creating networks. (Kothandaraman & Wilson, 2001.)

Matthyssens, Vandenbempt and Berghman (2006) also recognise that building new marketing competencies requires cooperation among a network of actors. They identify the construct of value innovation as a specific strategy to create

superior customer value which involves a redefinition of the industry or business where the roles of different companies and relationships among firms are redesigned. Successful value innovation should be embedded in the company's network relationships as it involves the cooperation and commitment of external parties too. Therefore the authors propose that value innovators and their network partners must cooperate in order to build jointly new marketing competencies and synergistic relations to exploit the new value concepts.

It is important to combine the two aspects of value co-creation introduced here: the co-creation of unique value with customers and value creating networks composed of different business actors. Integrating customers and especially customers identified as lead users into the value creating networks is a crucial task in creating commercially successful ubiquitous services. Research is needed in this field to find out how this can be done and what are the building blocks of this integration. The building blocks of customer-company interaction have been identified as dialog, access, transparency and risk-benefits (Prahalad & Ramaswamy, 2004b). Value-creating networks are seen to consist of three main building blocks: relationships, superior customer value and core capabilities (Kothandaraman & Wilson, 2001). However, in order to integrate customers into the value-creating networks, these building blocks need to be integrated or new kinds of elements developed.

Network Business Models

The concept of business model is concerned about how technological innovations can be commercialized by firms. As business around ubiquitous services is still rather unexplored and shaped by the technological innovations, analysing the business models in this field is important. Furthermore, as the development and commercialization of ubiquitous services is done in value-creating networks, it is important describe the whole networks and their value creating activities and exchanges among the actors of the network. Therefore the concept of business model needs to be explored from the viewpoint of network theory. Network business models are seen as useful in describing the networks.

There are various definitions of the concept of business model including different components, flows and relations. Often a business model can be seen as a mode for generating revenues (Komulainen et al., 2006). Afuah and Tucci (2001) define business model as an organisation's core logic for creating value representing the system of components, linkages, and associated dynamics to produce value. Timmers (1998) defines business model in three interrelated parts: as (1) an architecture for product, service and information flows including the various business actors and their roles, (2) a description of the potential benefits for business actors and (3) a description of the sources of revenues. Weill & Vitale (2001) also describe business model as the roles and relations among the firm's customers, allies and suppliers identifying the major flows of product, information and money and the major benefits for the actors. Furthermore, a business model can be seen as an important locus of innovation and a crucial source of value creation for the firm and its suppliers, partners and customers (Amit & Zott, 2001). Hedman and Kalling (2003) propose a generic business model that includes different components which are (1) customers, (2) competitors, (3) offering, (4) activities and organisation, (5) resources, (6) supply of factor and production inputs and (7) a longitudinal process component which can be referred as scope of management. Most of all the concept of business model can be seen to represent the logic for value creation including all the above mentioned components, flows, relations and linkages. And especially in this specific context of new ubiquitous services the

main idea behind the concept is the value creation logic of this new technology, in other words how value can be created from the technology.

However, the concept of business model is generally examined from the viewpoint of single companies and therefore there is not much literature concerning network business models. The concept is still a new field of interest. The network viewpoint on business models draws on network theory. Opposite to the viewpoint of Amit and Zott (2001) who see that each business model is centred on a particular actor, network business model is not limited to one core actor but explore the concept from network perspective (Komulainen et al., 2006). According to Komulainen et al. (2006) there are three core elements of a network business model; the product/service, the business actors and their roles and value-creating exchanges among the actors. In this field, the product or service component of network business model is seen to represent the technology, ubiquitous computing and the unique characteristics of ubiquitous services. The business actors and their roles implies to the actors involved in the development and commercialization of the services. In addition to the various business actors, customers and especially lead users are a crucial part of the network in the innovation process of the services. Value-creating exchanges among the actors of the network can include different kinds of economic and non-economic flows that create value, e.g. money, product or service, information and other resource flows.

These three core elements of a network business model are a good starting point for identifying and analysing network business models in the specific field of ubiquitous services. In order to create commercially successful ubiquitous services, further research is needed in the fields of developing the concept of network business model further and identifying possible and appropriate network business models around ubiquitous services.

CONCLUSION

This chapter has introduced three main research fields, which are important prerequisites for creating commercially successful ubiquitous services. All these fields are interrelated and need to be taken into account in order to develop and commercialize new ubiquitous services. First of all, understanding the basic nature of ubiquitous services is important in both the innovation of the services and the value creation. Secondly, the needs of the consumers must be known in order to create value to them. For this reason including lead users in the innovation of the services becomes essential. However, the development and commercialization of ubiquitous services is impossible without a business network which creates value to the members of the network including the customers and especially the lead users. Thus, thirdly value co-creation with customers in the networks is important in order to innovate and develop commercially successful ubiquitous services. This chapter has connected these three elements; unique characteristics of ubiquitous services, lead users and value creating networks, to develop ground for further research in the field of creating commercially successful ubiquitous services.

There are many special characteristics of ubiquitous services that differentiate them from more traditional technology-intensive services. These characteristics offer new possibilities but also pose many challenges to the development and commercialization of ubiquitous services. This birth of new kinds of services embedded in the environment leads us to a world of u-commerce (Fano & Gershman, 2002) which transforms the business environment in various ways. The perception of services changes along with the consumption of them. Interaction and communication between the companies and its customers and other stakeholders are transforming into more complex and dynamic forms. Competition becomes tenser as there are new entrants and net-

works of companies involved in the business. The usage and access to information is easier because of ubiquitous networks. Ubiquitous services and u-commerce provide new values for customers and value creation is changing into more complex and interactive. Especially the innovation of the services can provide a special source for value creation. All in all the whole business models are changing around u-commerce.

Special attention need to be also given to the innovation of ubiquitous services. The traditional technology driven innovation and design will not produce commercially successful ubiquitous services for consumer markets. Instead, service producers should concentrate in understanding consumer needs and developing new services based on these needs. A good way to do this is to identify lead user from the user population and then integrate them into the innovation and development process of the firm.

Value co-creation with customers an important prerequisite for commercial success of ubiquitous services. This chapter focused especially on the customers identified as lead users who are involved in the innovation of the services and this way also a crucial part of the value creating networks. In addition to the customers there are also many business actors involved in the development and commercialization of the services. The business actors and the customers form value creating networks which need to be examined further in the future. The concept of network business model is seen as useful in describing and understanding of the networks and how value is created in them. Therefore, research is needed in this field to examine the value creating networks and network business models.

We have now identified the crucial areas for further research which are important prerequisites for creating commercially successful ubiquitous services. By conducting research in these three main areas of interest, many crucial questions can be answered and this way the development and commercialization of ubiquitous services can be advanced. Identifying lead user characteristics and ways to integrate them into the innovation process as well as into the value creating networks would enable the successful co-creation of value for the customer and the business actors in the network. Furthermore, identifying and analyzing network business models would help to understand these value creating networks and the process of value co-creation.

ACKNOWLEDGMENT

This study is part of UbiLife research project funded by the Technology Agency of Finland, TEKES.

REFERENCES

Abowd, G. D., & Mynatt, E. D. (2000). Charting past, present and future research in ubiquitous computing. *ACM Transactions on Computer-Human Interaction, 7*(1), 29-58.

Abowd, G. D., Mynatt, E. D., & Rodden, T. (2002). The human experience – reaching for Weiser's vivion. *Pervasive Computing,* January-March, 48-57.

Afuah, A., & Tucci, C. (2001). *Internet business models and strategies.* New York: McGraw-Hill Companies, Inc.

Åkesson, M. & Ihlström-Eriksson, C. (2007). The vision of ubiquitous media services: how close are we? In M.J. Smith & G. Salvendy (Eds.) *Human Interfaces, Part II, HCII 2007.* Heidelberg: Springer-Verlag Berlin. (LNCS 4558 pp. 222-232).

Allee, V. (2000). Reconfigurating the value network. *Journal of Business Strategy, 21*(4).

Amit, R., & Zott, C. (2001). Value creation in e-business. *Strategic Management Journal, 22,* 493-520.

Bell, G., & Dourish, P. (2007). Yesterday's tomorrows: notes on ubiquitous computing's dominant vision. *Personal and Ubiquitous Computing, 11(*2), 133-143.

Chesbrough, H., & Rosenbloom R. (2002). The role of the business model in capturing value from innovation: Evidence from Xerox Corporation's technology spin-off companies. *Industrial and Corporate Change, 11*(3), 529-555.

Dey, A., & Abowld, G. (2000). *Towards a better understanding of context and context-awareness.* Paper presented at the CHI 2000 Workshop on the What, Who, Where, When, Why and How of Context-Awareness.

Fano, A., & Gershman, A. (2002). The future of business services in the age of ubiquitous computing. *Communications of the ACM, 45*(12), 83-87.

Franke, N., von Hippel, E., & Schreier, M. (2006). Finding commercially attractive user innovations: A test of lead-user theory. *Journal of Product Innovation Management, 23*(4), 301-315.

Galanxhi-Janaqi, H. & Fui-Hoon Nah, F. (2004). U-commerce: emerging trends and research issues. *Industrial Management & Data Systems, 104*(9), 744-755.

Hedman, J., & Kalling, T. (2003). The business model concept: theoretical underpinnings and empirical illustrations. *European Journal of Information Systems, 12,* 49-59.

Henkel, J. & von Hippel, E. (2005). Welfare implications of user innovation. *Journal of Technology Transfer, 30*(1/2), 73-87.

Holmquist, L. E. (2004). User-driven innovation in the future applications lab. In *Proceedings of the International Conference for Human-Computer Interaction (CHI2004)* (pp. 1091-1092). Vienna, Austria.

Intrachooto, S. (2004). Lead users concept in building design: its applicability to member selection in technologically innovative projects. *The TQM Magazine, 16*(5), 359-368.

Jeon, N., Leem, C., Kim, M., & Shin, H. (2007). A taxonomy of ubiquitous computing applications. *Wireless Personal Communications, 43*(4), 1229-1239.

Komulainen, H., Mainela, T., Sinisalo, J., Tähtinen J., & Ulkuniemi P. (2006). Business model scenarios in mobile advertising. *International Journal of Internet Marketing and Advertising, 3*(3), 254-270.

Kothandaraman, P., & Wilson, D. T. (2001). The future of competition: Value-creating networks. *Industrial Marketing Management, 30*, 379-389.

Lee, J., & Lee, S. (2005). Developing business models in ubiquitous era: exploring contradictions in demand and supply perspectives. In *Computational science and its applications – ICCSA 2005*. Heidelberg: Springer Berlin. (LNCS 3483 pp. 96-102).

Lilien, G. L., Morrison, P. D., Searls, K., Sonnack, M., & von Hippel, E. (2002). Performance assessment of the lead user idea-generation process for the new product development. *Management Science, 48*(8), 1042-1059.

Lüthje, C., & Herstatt, C. (2004). The lead user method: an outline of empirical findings and issues for future research. *R&D Management, 34*(5), 553-658.

Lyytinen, K. & Yoo, Y. (2002). Issues and challenges in ubiquitous computing. *Communications of the ACM, 45*(12), 62-65.

Matthyssens, P., Vandenbempt, K., & Berghman, L. (2006). Value innovation in business markets: breaking the industry recipe. *Industrial Marketing Management, 35*, 751-761.

Morrison, P. D., Roberts, J. H. & von Hippel, E. (2000). Determinants of user innovation and innovation sharing in a local market. *Management Science, 46*(12), 1513-1527.

Morrison, P. H, Roberts, J. H., & Midgley, D. F. (2004). The nature of lead users and measurement of leading edge status. *Research Policy, 33*(2), 351-362.

Möller, K., Rajala, A., & Svahn, S. (2005). Strategic business nets – their type and management. *Journal of Business Research, 58*, 1274-1284.

Olson, E. L. & Bakke, G. (2001) Implementing the lead user method in a high technology firm: A longitudinal study of intentions versus actions. *Journal of Product Innovation Management, 18*(6), 388-395.

Prahalad, C. K. & Ramaswamy, V. (2004a). Co-creating unique value with customers. *Strategy & Leadership, 32*(3), 4-9.

Prahalad, C. K., & Ramaswamy, V. (2004b). Co-creation experiences: the next practice in value creation. *Journal of Interactive Marketing, 18*(3), 5-14.

Ramírez, R. (1999). Value co-production: Intellectual origins and implications for practice and research. *Strategic Management Journal, 20*, 49-65.

Schreier, M. & Prügl, R. (2006). *Extending lead user theory: antecedents and consequences of consumers' lead userness*. Working paper. Vienna University of Economics and Business Administration.

Schilit, B., Adams, N., & Want, R. (1994). *Context-aware computing applications*. Paper presented at Workshop on Mobile Computing Systems and Applications, Santa Cruz, CA, U.S.

Sharp, R., & Rehman, K. (2005). The 2005 UbiApp Workshop: What makes good application-led research? *Pervasive Computing, 4*(3), 79-82.

Shin, B., & Lee, H.G. (2005). Ubiquitous computing-driven business models: A case of SK Telecom's financial services. *Electronic Markets, 15*(1), 4-12.

Timmers, P. (1998). Business models for electronic markets. *Electronic Markets, 8*(2), 3-8.

Urban, G.L. & von Hippel, E. (1988). Lead user analyses for the development of new industrial products. *Management Science, 34*(5), 569-582.

von Hippel, E. (1986). Lead users: a source of novel product concepts. *Management Science, 32*(7), 691-705.

von Hippel, E. (1989). New product ideas from 'lead users'. *Research Technology Management, 32*(3), 24-27.

Walter, A., Ritter, T., & Gemünden, H.G. (2001). Value creation in buyer-seller relationships: Theoretical considerations and empirical results from a supplier's perspective. *Industrial Marketing Management, 30*, 365-377.

Watson, R., Pitt, L., Berthon, P., & Zinkhan, G. (2002). U-Commerce: expanding the universe of marketing. *Academy of Marketing Science, 30*(4), 333-347.

Weill, P. & Vitale, M. (2001). *Place to space: migrating to e-business models*. Boston: Harvard Business School Press.

Weiser, M. (1991). The computer for the 21st century. *Scientific American, 265*(3), 66-75.

Yamazaki, K. (2004). Research directions of ubiquitous services. In *Proceedings of the 2004 International Symposium on Applications and the Internet (SAINT'04)*.

KEY TERMS

Lead User: According to von Hippel (1986) there are two definitional characteristics of a lead user. Firstly, lead users are ahead of an important trend and face needs before the others. Secondly, they benefit significantly when obtaining a solution to these needs and consequently are more likely to innovate.

Network Business Model: The concept of business model is perceived from a network perspective as the development and commercialization of ubiquitous services is done in value-creating networks. According to Komulainen et al. (2006) there are three core elements of a network business model; the product/service, the business actors and their roles, and value-creating exchanges among the actors.

Ubiquitous Commerce: Ubiquitous commerce or u-commerce can be defined as "the use of ubiquitous networks to support personalized and uninterrupted communications and transactions between a firm and its various stakeholders to provide a level of value over, above, and beyond traditional commerce" (Galanxhi-Janaqi & Fui-Hoon Nah, 2004).

Ubiquitous Services: In ubiquitous services the opportunities and challenges of mobile and pervasive technology are integrated. Hence, they are mobile, embedded in the surrounding environments as well as context-aware. In their ultimate form ubiquitous services can be also invisible through natural interfaces.

User Driven Innovation: User driven innovation refers to a situation, where the innovation is developed by users (either end users or organizations) rather than manufacturers.

Value Co-Creation: This chapter takes an alternative view on value creation which suggests that customers are involved in value creation and thus co-create value in an interaction with the companies. Furthermore, this value co-creation in the specific environment of ubiquitous services can involve lead users as part of the innovation process of services taking place in value creating networks.

Value Creating Network: Value creating networks are composed of different business actors involved in the process of value creation.

According to Kothandaraman & Wilson (2001) the building blocks of value creating networks are relationships, superior customer value and core capabilities.

Chapter IX
Framework for Proximity Aware Mobile Services

Jon T.S. Quah
Nanyang Technological University, Singapore

V. Jain
Nanyang Technological University, Singapore

ABSTRACT

This chapter discusses a service oriented framework to realize proximity aware services for mobile devices. It describes the architecture at both client and server ends. Using the proposed framework we develop a prototype to realize a real world application. The chapter ends with a discussion on the framework and possible future enhancements.[1]

INTRODUCTION

In recent years, demand for value added services has shown tremendous growth. Yet another trend which is on an upswing is of mobile phones being perceived as means of reaching almost anyone, anytime, anywhere. These ubiquitous devices have proliferated beyond the confines of just means to exchange conversation. These are the devices which unite the communication space and mobility. Services coupled with context aware handset could make quite a convenient combination. Users want to be able to do more with fewer hassles and

definitely without carrying dedicated device for each task. Apart from being a convergence device, mobile handsets are something that all of us carry at all times. They are perfect candidates to tap into information on the go. Context has various interpretations. Proximity is one of the contexts which can be used to trigger exchange of data/ services. Although we focus on mobile handsets, there are plenty of other devices which may not be as capable but nevertheless can be instrumental in variety of other ways. Mobile handset is typically at the service consumer's end and a more capable device acts a service provider. We do not necessarily lack the technology to provide this capability but what we do lack at the moment are collaborative technologies, standardized application development framework, wide array of sensor technologies to name a few. Over the past decade, researchers have put forth various proposals to tackle some of these hindering factors. This chapter reports one such attempt, i.e. by emphasizing on the service-oriented perspective of delivering context aware information.

Proximity-aware services are applications that are capable of delivering certain information whenever we are in the vicinity of a service provider. It is different from the notion of Location Based Services (LBS) in that it does not necessarily cater to absolute GPS like positioning but instead relies on relative positioning with respect to the other services in the present vicinity. Global Positioning System (GPS), Triangulation techniques can provide positioning accuracy of within 10 feet. This kind of accuracy would be useful if we were to be in a remote location and needed to convey our co-ordinates to someone. But, coming to think of our day-to-day routine, we live in the concrete jungle and we have plenty of other mobile devices that come in close proximity to each other. Here, we would be interested in what is present in our immediate vicinity and how we can interact with it. This kind of interaction can be related to Ad-Hoc networking where devices form a community on the fly. To this concept, if we were to add multiple sensors and context-aware information exchange we have proximity-aware services.

By targeting at services present in a small area, we bring down the equipment setup costs. The simplest of the services should be such that it can be setup by just about anyone with limited resources and tight budget. This is another design goal which is considered in our framework. Services can be built and offered to the consumers at a much faster rate by the localized service providers than say, a telecommunication operator setting up the service and offering it to its subscribers. Since, the risks are much lower and the service can be modified to cater to variety of consumers.

LITERATURE REVIEW

Most notable works on this topic have been from Dey et al(2000), Abowd G.D et al(1997) and Schilit et al(1994). Active Badges (Want, Hopper et al. 1992) is perhaps the first implemention of context aware application. This was an infrared transmitter that transmitted a unique identity code. As users moved throughout their building, a database was being dynamically updated with information about each user's current location, the nearest phone extension, and the likelihood of finding someone at that location (based on age of the available data). Servers are designed to poll the Active Badge sensor network distributed throughout the building and to maintain current location information. Applications that use these servers simply poll the servers for the context information that they collect. This was an application specific implementation and offered little scope for applying the same design for some other application.

Another specific application is the Cyberguide (Long et al., 1996) that served as an intelligent tour guide. Visitors were given handheld computing devices. The device displayed a map of the laboratory, highlighting interesting sites to visit and making available more information on those sites. As a visitor moved throughout the laboratory, the display re-centered itself on the new location and provided information on the current site. The Cyberguide system suffered from the use of a hardwired infrared positioning system, where remote controls were hung from the ceiling, each with a different button taped down to provide a unique infrared signature. This tight coupling of the application and the location information made it difficult to make changes to the application.

Moving to frameworks, Dey et al.(1998) implemented CyberDesk, a component based framework that allows flexibility in terms of new applications that can be integrated into the framework. As pointed out by the authors themselves, this framework lacks seamless application integration, limited variety of contexts handled and interface that may not be available/applicable for every purpose. In his doctoral thesis, Dey (2000) proposes an architecture consisting of context widgets and interpreters. Context widgets collect information from its environment using sensors. Widgets provide the much needed abstraction between the application and the underlying hardware layer. The information extracted out of the widgets is raw and it is processed to provide rich and higher level of information. Apart from these two, there are the aggregators that collate various contexts and provide this to applications. The system treats the services and entities that consume the services alike. The actual framework description is quite elaborate. However, creating distributed and collaborating services has been left out of scope since it is regarded by the author as something more to the perspective of service providers, even though including this perspective can help identify many more real life applications which are both viable and easy to develop.

Some of the issues associated with defining a framework for context aware applications are:

- Frameworks invariably become specific to certain genre of applications or too general requiring lot of customization to suit a new application.
- Application development is not straight forward.
- Focusing on client side specific frameworks rather than overall architecture.

In light of these shortcomings, we attempt to propose a new framework emphasizing the service oriented perspective. Base on this philosophy, we also try to add features that will make way for seamless integration of applications and are capable of being developed easily.

SYSTEM ARCHITECTURE

We focus on using proximity as the context to provide/access services. Proximity is a relative term and it makes sense as well given the fact that, both service provider and the client device could be mobile. It is different from location based services (LBS) since LBS would usually mean absolute physical location whereas, when we refer to proximity, we are referring to the possibility of a service provider in the vicinity. We can divide the tasks into 4 broad categories:

1. **Device/Service discovery:** To initiate any kind of data transfer, we need to ascertain other devices in the vicinity with which we can start 'conversing'. This is termed as Device and Service discovery since; these two processes could be separate tasks in their own right.

2. **Connection setup:** The Devices which are retrieved after the Device/Service discovery may optionally be presented to the user to determine user preference. Connection setup is purely dependent on the underlying sensor technology used. The concept of connection will differ from one device to another in terms of the interface presented by the sensor itself.

3. **Data exchange:** Once the connection is established, next step would be to initiate the data exchange. Data exchange would typically include exchanging device identity, credentials, information each of them seek etc. Two things we need to note here:
   o Mobile devices may have limited message processing capabilities.
   o Interoperability is an issue and concern.

4. **Processing and rendering:** The data received at the device end may be for one of the several applications running in parallel. We would need to separate them and direct them towards respective applications. We

may have to further process the information to make them 'presentable'. This refers to displaying on perhaps some kind of graphical user interface (GUI). It is optional since we are trying to address all mobile devices and some of them may not have the conventional user interface.

The framework is based on the service oriented architecture (SOA). We continue elaborating the architectures at both Client and Server ends and also try to fit these building blocks into them.

The client part of the framework is lightweight compared to the server counterpart to allow a wider variety of devices to contribute and interact with the system. 'Intelligence' has been placed more in the server than the client. However, applications can be developed such that client can also make 'smart' decisions. Till now we have discussed server as an independent entity; however, it can network and collaborate with other services in turn and act as an interface to those servers for the clients. This allows us to extend the reach of a service provider through suitable channels. Hence, one server can essentially host several services at one place for user convenience.

Client Architecture

The Client devices are typically less capable, low power, memory constrained entities which interact with a server counter-part to 'consume' services offered by the server. 'Dumb' as they might look, they have an important role to play in facilitating relevant information to the user by means of deriving contexts and invoking suitable services. The overall client framework is illustrated in Figure 1.

The main components of the client side are:

- User interface (UI)
- Applications
- Data exchange/parser
- Device/service discovery

These components will be elaborated in the following sections.

User Interface

This is the component with which the user interacts with the system. It's generally an input/output interface which allows manipulation of the system. These interfaces could be Graphical, Limited text interface or custom built devices. The main objectives of this component are:

- **Render:** The information parsed and sent up from the application needs to be presented to the user. The means of conveying the information to the user may differ from one device to another but, the common part is recognizing the way information needs to be presented.
- **Relay user input:** The input provided by the user needs to be accepted and relayed to the application. Based on the user interaction certain actions are triggered. These actions shape the behavior of the application.

Figure 1. Client architecture. © 2008 Jon T.S. Quah. Used with permission.

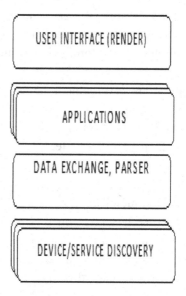

The component can be illustrated by Figure 2.

Applications

This component controls the actions of all other components within the system. The main objectives of this component are:

- **Stateless operation:** The client devices are highly susceptible to frequent breaks in connection to the server counterparts owing to the medium of communication in general. The applications need to be designed in such a way that their operations are stateless, i.e. independent of any previous message exchanges.
- **Small footprint:** The memory starved client devices require the individual applications that it hosts to be of smaller footprint and less processing intensive. This could mean writing very simple and efficient programs which are capable of receiving instructions/information from the server to be relayed to the user. Not only the installation but runtime footprint should be within the limit.
- **Variety of output modes:** Owing to the varying capabilities of the user interfaces that may be available for the application to interact with, the design of the application should be such that it remains more or

less detached from the vagaries of the user interface components.
- **Derive contexts:** The application should be able to derive the context it is currently in by interacting with the other components.

Organization of this component is depicted in Figure 3.

Data Exchange/Parser

This is the component which fetches and writes data from/to the underlying layers. It also picks out application specific data and performs any necessary message transformations. The main objectives of this component are:

- **Data exchange interface:** It should provide an easy to use interface to the above lying applications such that connections to/from external entities can be established. The application may optionally specify what type of a sensor it needs to initiate a data exchange.
- **Handle encoding/decoding:** The data exchanged would generally be encoded in an appropriate format which would need transformation/translation. Apart from encoding/

Figure 3. Client application organization. © 2008 Jon T.S. Quah. Used with permission.

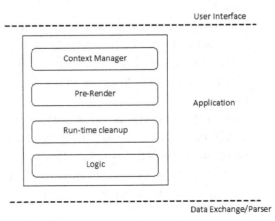

Figure 2. Organization of user interface component. © 2008 Jon T.S. Quah. Used with permission.

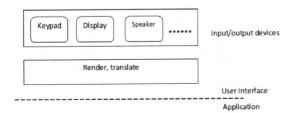

decoding, this component can also handle encryption/decryption and compression/decompression related activities.

- **Correlating function:** For data to be routed to-fro from the application to the underlying connection agent, we need a correlator that can keep track of the open connections and minimal state information regarding them.

Device/Service Discovery

This component is the closest layer to the underlying hardware. There are a variety of sensors that a client device may be built with, which this component is responsible for handling. The main objectives of this component are:

- **Hardware abstraction:** Being the closest layer to the hardware, this layer should provide an abstraction to the upper layer in terms of simplified view of the underlying hardware.
- **Proactive service searching:** It might be intuitive to have the client report available services in the proximity proactively. This dynamic discovery is necessary in deriving hidden contexts.
- **Power control:** Client devices are power starved and the device discovery/connection is a power intensive operation. We need to strike a balance between these two using power controls.
- **Security:** Security is a concern whenever we expose our device to external entities. These threats could be to compromise the client device into performing in ways it is not expected to.
- **Handling connections:** This component would interface with the sensor to communicate in a way that is sensor dependent. This would be the most hardware dependent operation that this component performs.

This component can be illustrated by Figure 4.

Server Architecture

Server devices are relatively more capable than their client counterparts. These are the entities that endow most of the 'intelligence' to the entire system. A full fledged server setup would include interaction with several other service providers. This would also allow propagating 'intelligence' to other service providers. However, a standalone server can also have a meaningful purpose. The four major components of the server architecture are:

- Application
- Proxy
- Data store
- Other services

There is no user interface (UI) depicted explicitly since typically a server would perform its operations repeatedly with little or no user intervention. UI however, would be useful in configuring the operation parameters of the server. The server architecture can be illustrated by Figure 5.

Figure 4. Organization of discovery component © 2008 Jon T.S. Quah. Used with permission.

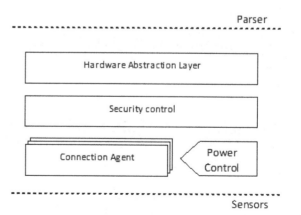

Application

This is the highest abstraction layer where the applications are developed and hosted. The main objectives of this component are:

- **Interface with the external components:** These external entities provide abstractions to essential functionality such as device discovery, low level interaction, accessing data store, other similar service providers etc.
- **Decide the core logic:** The core functionality or rather the 'brain' of the server resides in the application. Factors crucial for the application would be performance, scalability, simplistic user interaction, interoperability, cost etc. All these are achieved by the way the application is designed and configured.
- **Data transformation:** The data received from external components needs to be processed and relevant information extracted out of it. Information extracted could be input to some other functionalities or directed to a user interface.
- **Technology independent:** Although the external components assist with necessary abstractions, the application can still be written in a way that it is tied strongly to

the underlying implementation. This tight coupling would leave the application inflexible and unusable in another environment.

Proxy

This is the layer closest to the sensors which we treat as the lowest accessible hardware within the scope of this framework. The main objectives of this component are:

- **Provide an abstraction layer:** The underlying sensors can come from different vendors and building a common set of applications over them is not possible without using an abstraction layer. A part of this component would then be hardware dependent and together with other entities within the component provide a unified interface for the layers above to exchange data with little or no change.
- **Manage connections:** The applications above would interact with the external entities through possibly different sensor technologies. These sensors would have different connection semantics and hence we need an adaptation layer to handle connections.
- **Power management:** Mobile devices are power constrained devices; although the server may have no such constraints, it should take care of not burdening the client into expending unnecessary power.
- **Buffering and flow control:** It is possible that the server/client side overwhelm each other once in a while due to excessive data rates. There should be a known strategy of how it is being handled.

The overall component structure is illustrated in Figure 6.

Figure 5. Server architecture. © 2008 Jon T.S. Quah. Used with permission.

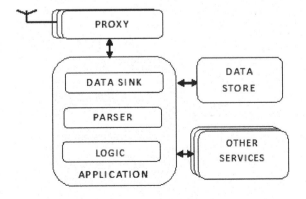

Data Store

This component is responsible for storing data in a manner that facilitates quick access by the applications. Usually a relational database management system (RDBMS) can accomplish this task in a manner that is easy to setup and very fast. Some of the desirable features of a data store are:

- Allow concurrent access to the data
- Efficient utilization of space to store user data
- Access control and security
- Fast and standardized access to data
- Data stored should be in a portable form
- Reasonable cost

Other Services

These are the other services that are accessible to the current server. They could be just for remote method invocation or hosting an entire application as a third-party service provider. This is a way of extending the service beyond the confines of a single server.

PROTOTYPE

Applying the concept of proximity aware smart applications, we took up a real world example for the purpose of prototyping. The Application is that of a Smart Shopping Assistant. User can invoke this application to jot down shopping lists as and when desired on their mobile handsets. When the user enters a shopping mall, the application detects a suitable service that it starts interacting with on its own; passing the users shopping list to the server. The server at its end analyzes the list and matches the entries with its own. All possible stores offering the items mentioned in the users list are identified and user is prompted for an option to sort the result based on factors such as: Lowest offered price, shortest billing delay, closest stores for pickup etc. Depending on users choice, corresponding result is prepared and passed over for the handset to display. Further, the shops suggested to the user are informed of the users requirements through its internal interface to the stores service agent. When the user approaches one of the suggested stores, the store's server recognizes the user and prompts a welcome message followed by information regarding where each of the listed items can be

Figure 6. Organization of proxy components. © 2008 Jon T.S. Quah. Used with permission.

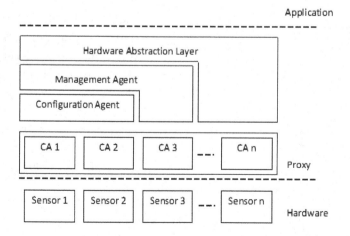

found within the store. User can make use of the information provided and check out the items of interest and on the way out request for a product catalogue. The server pushes an application that seamlessly integrates on the handset that offers several other services related to the store as well. This application also serves as an identifier for a returning customer.

The partial prototyping has been done using the Java Wireless Toolkit ver. 2.2 provided by Sun Microsystems. Prototype was developed with Bluetooth radio as communication medium. The toolkit provides full fledged simulator to test Bluetooth applications. For the purpose of prototyping, we developed 3 Java MIDlet applications; two of which are servers and another MIDlet for client application. This prototype demonstrates the use of web services perspective and the use of parser to render the user interface based on the data exchanged. However, real world applications would have more capable services instead of the MIDlets used here. Conceptually, there need not be any limit on the number of services looked up. Database limitations are not really a hindrance here; however, the client's user interface may be the point of concern. In our prototypes, we have limited the number of services that can be looked up to 7. This is due to the limitation of the Bluetooth piconet in the current setup. The data transfer speeds between the client and server have not been tested purely due to the fact that we are running these experiments on a simulator. The software simulation is no equivalent to the actual Bluetooth hardware which is affected by several factors such as obstacles, distance, mobility etc. Both the server applications have been developed as separate MIDlets and hence, we intend to use a more suitable toolkit to demonstrate the usage of collaborating services.

RESULTS

The MIDlets for the server(s) and client are run on the simulator. The server console in our prototype

allows for activating/de-activating the services offered by the server. This is depicted by Figure 7. Only the services activated on the server end are visible to the client application. On the client side, we have two basic operations that can be performed, i.e. 'Look for Services' and 'Note Shopping Items'. As the name suggests, the former option allows us to look for suitable services in the vicinity whereas the latter option allows us to feed new shopping items into the client application. This interface is depicted in Figure 8.

Figure 9 depicts screenshot of the client device discovering multiple services and allowing the user to choose from amongst them. Figure 10 illustrates the client device interacting with the shopping complex's main server. Figure 11 shows the screenshot on the client device where the application has retrieved the list of items noted down by the user and a subset of them can be selected to be sent over to the server. Also seen is the sort option which the server supports. Figure

Figure 7. Server console. © 2008 Jon T.S. Quah. Used with permission.

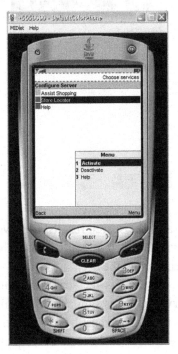

Figure 8. Client console

*Figure 9. Client device discovering services. ©
2008 Jon T.S. Quah. Used with permission.*

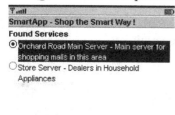

*Figure 10. Client device interacting with main
server. © 2008 Jon T.S. Quah. Used with permission.*

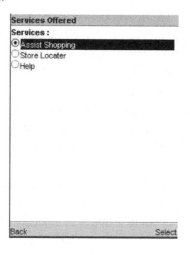

*Figure 11. Retrieving list of shopping items. ©
2008 Jon T.S. Quah. Used with permission.*

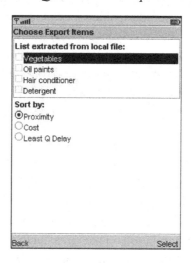

12 illustrates the search results sent over to the
client device by Main server based on the search
criteria chosen by the user.

Figure 13 depicts the server console of the
Store Server which is similar to the Main server
console with the difference being services offered.
Figure 14 illustrates the store server discovered
when the user is in the service providers proximity. Figure 15 shows the information relayed
by the Main server to the Store server regarding
the user's preferences. Figure 16 shows the Store
server assisting the user with directions within
the store to locate the items on the shopping list.
Figure 17 illustrates another sample service that
is related to only the store server and offered only
due to the proximity of the user to the service
provider.

Figure 12. Search results returned by the main server. © 2008 Jon T.S. Quah. Used with permission.

Figure 13. Screenshot of store servers console. © 2008 Jon T.S.Quah. Used with permission.

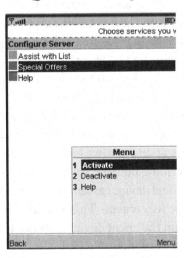

Figure 14. Client device discovering store server. © 2008 Jon T.S.Quah. Used with permission.

Figure 15. Services offered by the store server. © 2008 Jon T.S.Quah. Used with permission.

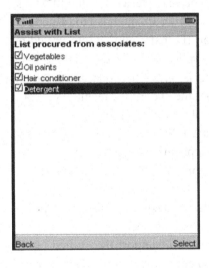

DISCUSSION

We introduced the proximity aware services with a real world shopping cart example. Although the prototype is yet to make complete use of the framework that has been suggested, we intend to dig deeper into understanding the intricacies of the proxy (link between the client and the actual service). XML also plays an important role into

making this communication platform independent; kXML libraries were used for the prototype. The task of designing a proxy agent boils down to developing a device driver for all available means of communication. Also, an abstraction layer that manages these connections in a scalable manner needs to be formulated. We have stressed on two-way communication; however, there could be cases where a passive service agent makes

Figure 16. Store server displaying relayed information. © 2008 Jon T.S. Quah. Used with permission.

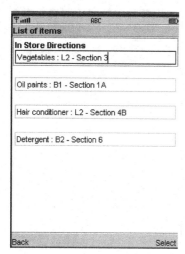

Figure 17. Store server assisting the user. © 2008 Jon T.S. Quah. Used with permission.

sense. For instance, a mesh of RFID tags laid in a locality which are intended to respond back with location ID that could be interpreted by an on-board application. These need to be investigated. Security is yet another concern and the framework assumes the underlying technologies take up this responsibility. The prototype has been developed as Java MIDlets which executes the services and client applications in a 'sandbox'.

In summary, the future works are:

- **Proxy design:** Designing a proxy can be a challenge because the underlying sensor may not support the unified interface that other proxy may provide. This might defeat the purpose of common interface across all proxies. On the other hand, the underlying sensor may be having extra capabilities that the usual interface may not be able to harness.

- **Support for devices with limited resources:** Our aim has been to include diverse devices to contribute to deriving contexts and also to offer/consume services. Moving away from mobile handsets, we would have

issues like severe memory crisis, limited processing, lack of OS like abstraction layer etc. Such devices may not be in a position to support a framework such as the one we suggested. In such a situation, we may have to tweak for lighter framework.

- **Device capability based adaptive services:** Although we have mentioned about server application logic, we have not ventured into describing how the server should ascertain the client device capability and based on that adapt its content. This would allow us to exploit the client devices' ability to convey the information.

- **scalable services:** The proxy design has another responsibility – support more and more users. Sensors might have their own limitations in supporting multiple clients at the same time. Effective utilization means keeping the service alive for a reasonable user load.

- **Agent based local execution:** Another emerging technique of mobile communication is to have dynamic objects which encapsulate data and functionality, carry its state from one mobile device to another, execute, collect data and relay information back to the user. This is another direction the framework could be researched upon.

CONCLUSION

We have described a conceptual framework for building proximity based services as well as an architecture that depends on continuous to-fro message exchanges; this approach might suit many scenarios; however, we would like to carry this work forward to designing the system that exchanges objects and execute locally. This can allow greater flexibility for the service provider to develop UI, reduce traffic exchanged, and increase capacity at the service provider's proxy end. Jini was one such technology we evaluated for implementation, however, it suffers from much needed support on J2ME and operate over contemporary communication mediums like Bluetooth. Moreover, such freely moving objects can transform into powerful mobile agents.

In summary, the chapter has described an end-to-end system architecture as well as the mapping of the components identified in the framework with real-world technologies and application designs. Finally, the chapter also suggest a programming model to assist application developers.

REFERENCES

Abowd, G.D. et al (1997). Cyberguide: A mobile context-aware tour guide. *ACCM Wireless Networks, 3,* 421-433.

Abowd, G.D., & Salber, D. (1998). *The design and use of a generic context server* (Technical Report GIT-GVU-98-32). Georgia Institute of Technology.

Bordini, R.H., & Hübner, J.F. (2007). *Jason Project Homepage.* Retrieved from http://jason. sourceforge.net/

Bovey, J.D., Chen, X. & Brown, P.J. (1997, October). Context-aware applications: From the laboratory to the marketplace. *IEEE Personal Communications.*

Cougaar Project (2007). *Cougaar: Cognitive Agent Architecture.* Retrieved from http://cougaar.org/

Dey, A.K. (2000). *Providing architectural support for building context-aware applications.* Doctoral Thesis, College of Computing, Georgia Institute of Technology.

Dey, A.K. (2001). Understanding and using context. *Personal and Ubiquitous Computing Journal, 5*(1), 4-7.

Dey, A.K., Abowd, G.D., & Salber, D. (1999). The context toolkit: Aiding the development of context-enabled applications. In *Proceedings of CHI'99* (pp.434-441).

Duri, S. et al (2001). An approach to providing a seamless end user experience for location-aware applications. In *Proceedings of the 1st International Workshop on Mobile Commerce* (pp. 20-25).

Hitachi Group. (2007). *Autonomous Mobility Support Project, Ubiquitous Location Information System Prototype Demonstration.* Retrieved from http://www.film.hitachi.jp/en/movie/movie562.html

IBM Research Labs. (2007). *Aglets.* Retrieved from http://www.trl.ibm.com/aglets

Jini Implementation Community (2007). *Apache River Project.* Retrieved from http://incubator. apache.org/river/

Kolari, J. et al (2004, June). The Kontti Project—Context-aware services for mobile users. *VTT Publications,* 539, 167-170.

Perttunen, M., & Riekki, J. (2005). *Introducing context-aware features into everyday mobile applications.* LoCA 2005. (LNCS 3479 pp. 316-327)

Schmidt, A., & Laerhoven, K.V. (2001, August). How to build smart appliances? *IEEE Personal Communications*, 66-71.

Shilit, B.N. (1995). *A context-aware system architecture for mobile distributed computing.* Ph.D. thesis, Dept of Computer Science, Columbia University.

Shilit, B.N., Adams, N., & Roywant (1994). Context-aware computing applications. In *Proceedings of the Workshop on Mobile Computing Systems and Applications*. IEEE.

Sun Microsystems. (2007). *Jini™ Technology Surrogate Home.* Retrieved from https://surrogate.dev.java.net/

Telecom Italia Labs (TiLab) (2007). *Jade: Java Agent Development Framework.* Retrieved from http://jade.tilab.com/

Want, R., Hopper, A., Falcao, V., & Gibbons, J. (1992, January). The active badge location system. *ACM Transactions on Information Systems,* 10, 91-102.

Zhang, D.Q., Pung, H.K., & Gu, T. (2005). A service-oriented middleware for building context-aware services. *Journal of Network and Computer Applications, 28*(1), 1-18.

ENDNOTE

[1] This research work is supported by the Singapore National Research Foundation Interactive Digital Media R&D Program, under research grant NRF2007IDM-IDM002-080.

Chapter X
A Study of the Relationship between PEOU and PU in Technology Acceptance in E-Learning

Vincent Cho
Hong Kong Polytechnic University, Hong Kong

Humphry Hung
Hong Kong Polytechnic University, Hong Kong

ABSTRACT

In models to study technology acceptance, the empirically validated path from perceived ease of use (PEOU) to perceived usefulness (PU) is usually rationalized by the argument that the less effort it is required to use a technology, the more useful the technology is. This argument is rather generic to fully account for the relationship between PEOU and PU. In this study we examine the effects of the common antecedents of PEOU and PU on their relationship. We first extensively reviewed the literature to identify the common antecedents of PEOU and PU. We then conducted a survey of users' acceptance of some common e-learning forums such as ICQ, WebCT, and MSN. Based on variance analysis we found that user-interface design (UID) explains 43% of the relationship between PEOU and PU, and that learners consider UID very important in deciding whether to accept an e-learning forum for their learning and communication. This chapter contributes to research by identifying the factors that account for the relationship between PEOU and PU, and provides e-learning developers with managerial insights on how to leverage UID for business success.

INTRODUCTION

In technology acceptance studies, there is a theoretical linkage between perceived ease of use (PEOU) and perceived usefulness (PU). It is usually argued that the ease of use of a system (i.e., a technology) will induce people to use the system more easily, and hence will make the system more useful (Davis, 1989; Szajna, 1996; Thong et al. 2002; Venkatesh and Davis, 2000). Davis et al. (1989) performed a study on a word processing program - WriteOne, and found that PEOU affects PU directly based on a regression analysis with a standardized coefficient of 0.23** and a R^2 of 0.05. They argued that PEOU is a direct determinant of PU, since all others being equal, the less effort it is required to use a system, the more useful the system is. However, this argument is too generic to fully account for the mechanism behind the relationship. There is evidence in other studies that the impact of PEOU on PU may vary and depend on the technology under study. Based on their proposed extended technology acceptance model (TAM2), Venkatesh and Davis (2000) found that the impact of PEOU on PU varies slightly among different systems after users have extensive experience in using them, namely 0.28** for a scheduling system, 0.34** for a Windows-based financial system, 0.35** for a Windows-based customer account management system, and 0.35** for a stock management system. Thong et al. (2002) found that the impact of PEOU on PU is 0.41** for a digital library system.

This chapter attempts to explain the theoretical linkage between PEOU and PU by making use of the construct user-interface design (UID), a common antecedent of both PU and PEOU. A good interface design will definitely make a system easier for users to use (Liang, 1987; Hay et al. 2004; Chimera and Shneiderman, 1993; Lederer et al. 2000; Thong et al. 2002); moreover, it will also make better navigation of different system functions (Davis et al. 1989; Parikh and Verma, 2002). In this regard, UID is an antecedent of

both PU and PEOU and is expected to explain the significant effect of PEOU on PU.

The objectives of this study are twofold: (i) to study the theoretical link between PEOU and PU in technology acceptance, and (ii) to study the influence of UID on the relationship between PEOU and PU. Using two theoretical models, namely (i) the original TAM, and (ii) a TAM-based model augmented with UID as an antecedent of both PU and PEOU, we investigate the role of UID in technology acceptance, through which we attempt to account for the theoretical linkage between PEOU on PU.

This chapter is organized as follows. We first re-formulate the technology acceptance model (TAM) by incorporating UID as an antecedent of both PEOU and PU. We discuss the methodology in the second section. We present the research findings and discussions of the role of UID in TAM in the third section. In the final section we conclude the study and suggest directions for future research.

THEORETICAL FRAMEWORK

Most past studies on technology acceptance were based on TAM, and substantial theoretical and empirical supports have accumulated in favour of TAM (Davis, 1989; Davis et al. 1989). The two fundamental constructs in TAM are PEOU and PU. PEOU deals with how easy it is to learn and use a system (Davis, 1989), while PU focuses on whether the user believes that the system would enhance his/her performance (Davis, 1989). First, people tend to use or not to use a system or a technology based on the extent they believe it will help them perform their job better. Second, even if potential users believe that a given system is useful, they may, at the same time, feel that the system is too hard to use and that the performance benefits of usage are outweighed by the effort of learning and using the system. All else being equal, the easier it is to interact with a system, the less effort is needed to operate it, and so one can allocate more effort to other activities, contributing to overall job performance (Davis, 1989). This provides the theoretical link between PEOU and PU. However, this argument is too generic to fully account for the PEOU-PU relationship. We attempt to identify the mechanism that links PEOU to PU via examining a common antecedent of PEOU and PU, i.e., UID.

The antecedents of PU and PEOU discussed in past technology acceptance studies can be grouped into three categories, namely system characteristics, environmental factors, and individual characteristics (Abdul-Gader and Kozar, 1995; Cho, 2006) (Table 1). System features, such as user-interface design, output quality, functionality, and accessibility, all fall under the system characteristics dimension (Davis et al. 1989). Environmental characteristics include system support, user training, management support, social presence, and subjective norms (Roger, 1995; Zmud, 1983). Computer experience and computer self-efficacy are grouped into individual characteristics (Agarwal and Prasad, 1998). It can

be seen that many antecedents examined in past technology acceptance studies mainly focus either on PU or PEOU. For example, functionality, output quality, subjective norm, and social presence have effects only on PU (Benbasat and Dexter, 1986; Davis et al. 1989; Davis et al. 1992; Venkatesh and Davis, 2000). Trialability, relevance, system support, and computer self-efficacy only influence PEOU (Chin and Gopal, 1995; Gefen and Straub, 2000; Davis, 1989; Venkatesh and Davis, 2000). However, these antecedents cannot explain the relationship between PEOU and PU because they have no impact on both of them.

In order to explain the relationship between PEOU and PU, a common antecedent should be investigated. In the literature, it appears that not many antecedents of this kind have been mentioned. User interface design, navigation, and accessibility are the few examples that affect both PU and PEOU (Benbasat et al. 1986; Davis, 1989; Thong et al. 2002; Davis et al. 1992; Kraemer et al. 1993; Karahanna and Straub, 1999; Venkatesh and Davis, 2000). Besides, there are some arguments that individual characteristics,

Table 1. Antecedents of PU and PEOU

Antecedent	Studies	PEOU	PU
System feature that affects PU only			
Functionality	Benbasat and Dexter (1986)		√
	Davis, Bagozzi and Warshaw (1989)		√
Output quality	Davis et al. (1992)		√
	Venkatesh and Davis (2000)		√
Result demonstrability	Venkatesh and Davis (2000)		√
System feature that affects PEOU only			
Trialability	Chin and Gopal (1995)	√	
Relevance (system fit to task)	Chin and Gopal (1995)	√	
	Keil, Berenek and Konsynsik (1995)	√	
	Gefen and Straub (2000)	√	
System feature that affects both PEOU and PU			
User Interface Design	Benbasat, Dexter, and Todd (1986)	√	
	Davis (1989)	√	√
	Thong Hong and Tam (2002)	√	

continued on the following page

Table 1. continued

Navigation	Davis, Bagozzi and Warshaw (1992)		√
	Thong Hong and Tam (2002)	√	
Accessibility	Kraemer et al. (1993)		√
	Karahanna and Straub (1999)		√
	Thong Hong and Tam (2002)	√	√
System quality/reliability	Igbaria et al. (1995)	√	√
	Gallivan (2001)		√
Type of IT/IS	Venkatesh and Davis(2000)	√	√
	Gefen and Straub (2000)	√	
Environmental feature that affects PU only			
Subjective norms	Karahanna and Straub (1999)		√
	Venkatesh and Davis (2000)		√
Social presence	Karahanna and Straub (1999)		√
Environmental features that affects PEOU only			
System support		√	
Environmental features that affects both PEOU and PU			
User training	Igbaria et al (1995, 1997)	√	√
External support	Igbaria et al (1995, 1997)	√	√
Management support	Igbaria et al (1995, 1997)	√	√
Individual feature that affects PEOU only			
Computer self efficacy	Davis (1989)	√	
	Venkatesh and Davis (1996)	√	
Individual feature that affects both PEOU and PU			
Gender	Venkatesh and Morris (2000)	√	√
	Morris, Venkatesh and Ackerman (2005)	√	√
Age	Morris and Venkatesh (2000)	√	√
Computer experience	Venkatesh and Davis (1996)	√	
	Adam, Nelson and Todd (1992)	√	√
	Jackson et al. (1997)		√

such as age, gender, and experience, would influence both PU and PEOU. Taylor and Todd (1995) stated that computer experience moderates the links between PU and PEOU towards behavior intention. In other studies, Adam et al. (1992) identified that computer experience has an influence on both PU and PEOU. PEOU will be more concrete once a user has hands-on experience of a system (Venkatesh and Davis, 2000). Morris and Venkatesh (2000) found that young workers pay more attention to the usefulness of a system, while old workers focus on the ease of use of the system for their acceptance of the system. Venkatesh and Morris (2000) argued that gender does moderate the link between PU and PEOU towards behavior intention of accepting a system. Nevertheless, we will ignore these individual characteristics in this study because we focus on studying the influence of PEOU on PU among different systems. Thus the system characteristic user-interface design is the most relevant. On the other hand, system quality (Igbaria et al. 1995; Gallivan, 2001) and type of IT (Venkatesh and Davis, 2000; Gefen and Straub, 2000) are too general to explain the relationship of PEOU and PU, and thus are excluded from our study.

The following expounds on the importance of UID on technology acceptance and its influence on PU and PEOU. Many technological innovations rely upon UID to elevate their technical complexity to a usable product. For example, the control and interface of a car, such as its steering wheel, is the most important input interface, while the large wind screen is the most effective output interface for a driver to control the car. Such user-interfaces directly affect the adoption of motor vehicle as a transportation tool. In terms of computer user-interface, it is broadly defined as the interface for users to work with a system, including documentation, training, and human support (Madsen, 2004). In particular, Peuple and Scane (2003) defined computer user interface as the point of contact that enables interaction between a human being and a system. In a review of the behavioural issues on computer systems, researchers (Lederer et al. 2000; Miller and King, 2003; Parikh and Verma, 2002) identified interface design as a major component that affects the human-computer interaction, which in turn affects the adoption of technology. Many user-interface features, such as menus, icons, and touch screens, are specifically intended to enhance usefulness, and ease of use of different functions in a system (Benbasat et al. 1986). For example, the Windows operating system is an interface that makes personal computers so popular. Bar code readers are a very effective input interface for inventory control systems and the point of sales systems (POS); without this interface, it is reasonable to expect that the level of acceptance of such ubiquitous systems will be substantially lower. As a medium between a system and users, the interface serves as the platform for user actions. Given the same content, the way the

information is presented on the user interface can greatly influence users' information search strategies (Thong et al. 2002), as well as their performance in using the system, which in turn will affect the successful acceptance of the new technology.

We speculate that innovative UID will push technology acceptance to new heights, primarily via its powerful influence on PEOU and PU. Technology alone may not win user acceptance. As a medium between the system and the users, the interface serves as the platform for user actions. A well-designed interface can help users to use the system more easily by reducing the effort to identify a particular object on the screen, or providing smooth navigation among screens. This supports the view that UID affects both PEOU and PU. The importance of good user-interface can be the difference between product acceptance and rejection in the marketplace. If end-users feel that an otherwise excellent product is not easy, or too cumbersome, to learn and use, then the product is likely to fail. Good user-interface can make a product easy to understand and use, and enhance user performance in using the product, which should result in greater user acceptance.

UID and PU

Many system features of user interface such as menus, icons, mice, and touch screens are specifically intended to enhance usability (Davis et al. 1989; Parikh and Verma, 2002). A good menu design with easy control toolbars and icons will make the functions of a system displayed in a handy manner; this will enhance the perceived usefulness of the system. Moreover, particular interfaces will make the system more useful. For instance, the bar code reader will make a POS more useful in terms of handling of transactions. In contrast, people may perceive POS less useful if they use keyboards for the input. In this way, we argue that UID will have an impact on PU and propose the following hypothesis:

H1: UID is a significant antecedent of PU.

UID and PEOU

A good interfaced system must be easy to use (Liang, 1987). Screen design, part of a user-interface design, has a strong impact on PEOU. For instance, poorly depicted buttons and icons can create confusion and misunderstanding. In contrast, a well-organized and carefully designed screen can help users to scan the screen and identify relevant information more easily (Hay et al. 2004). Moreover, the mouse interface reduces the task of controlling a system to a mere number of clicks. Certainly, a simple and flexible user interface will reduce the effort of using a system, i.e., it will be easier to use the system. Therefore, UID will have a positive effect on PEOU of a system, which has been empirically supported by Chimera and Shneiderman (1993), Lederer et al. (2000), and Thong et al. (2002). We therefore come up with the following hypothesis:

H2: UID is a significant antecedent of PEOU.

PU and PEOU

It has been reported in the literature that the ease of use of a system will induce people to use the system more easily and hence will make the system more useful (Davis, 1989; Szajna, 1996; Thong et al. 2002; Venkatesh and Davis, 2000). We echo the above argument by introducing an explanatory variable to the phenomenon, namely UID. A friendly user-interface design enables a user to command a system in an easy way and to understand the functions within the system in a better manner. That is, UID caters for the usefulness and ease of use of the system. Thus, we expect a high degree of overlapping between the common variances of UID and PEOU, and of UID and PU. These variances can help to partially explain the common variance of PEOU and PU.

This speculation naturally leads to the following hypothesis:

H3: The significant link between PEOU and PU is partially due to UID, and the variances of PEOU and PU can be partially explained by the variance of PEOU and UID and by the variance of PU and UID.

Other Hypotheses of TAM

The behavioural intention to use (BITU) a system is a measure of the likelihood a person will employ the system (Ajzen and Fishbein, 1980). Actually both PU and PEOU are found to be significant determinants of BITU. However, the relative strengths of their explanatory power are different. PU is a much stronger predictor of BITU with a magnitude of 0.52, as compared to 0.32 of PEOU (Thong et al. 2002). All in all, the easier it is for a user to interact with a system, the more likely he or she will intend to use it. And the more useful a system is, the more likely a user has the intention to use the system. As a result, the following hypotheses based on TAM are proposed:

H4: PEOU has a positive effect on BITU.
H5: PU has a positive effect on BITU.

E-LEARNING TOOL FOR EMPIRICAL INVESTIGATION

E-learning has received considerable attention from practitioners and information systems researchers (Ong and Lai, 2004; Im and Lee, 2004; Chiu et al, 2004; Selim, 2003; Piccoli et al. 2001). E-learning is defined as instructional content or learning experiences delivered by electronic technologies, including the Internet, intranet, and extranets (Ong and Lai, 2004). Forman et al. (2002) stated that e-learning is a new wave strategy, which complements comfortably with other strategies developed for the twenty-first century. In the US, it is projected that the annual growth rate in e-learning will increase from 31% in 1998 to 90% in 2007 (Edelson, 2001). According to IDC (2005), a North America-based research organization, spending on e-learning worldwide in 2001 was around US$5.2 billion. IDC predicted that the e-learning market will grow to some US$3.7 billion by 2006,. In other words, e-learning will become increasingly important in coming years, and is worthy of close scrutiny and detailed analysis. In this study we investigate e-learners' intention to use interactive discussion forums in the context of e-learning. This refers to discussion among friends or classmates on a particular topic, and is related to learning among learners through some e-learning communication tools such as ICQ, WebCT, or MSN.

DATA COLLECTION

We designed a questionnaire to collect data for this study. In order to ensure the questionnaire is valid and reliable, we conducted a focus group meeting in March 2005, where the group comprised end users (students), educators, system developers, and experts in the field of IT and behavioural science. Participants were invited to discuss open-ended questions related to e-learning features, the e-learning environment, as well as the antecedents that would affect e-learning acceptance. The meeting lasted for about two hours and the opinions of the participants were recorded and used to develop the research instrument. With the focus group's input and based on an extensive review of the literature on antecedences of technology acceptance, a questionnaire was constructed to investigate the antecedents of e-learning acceptance. The preliminary version of the questionnaire was then reviewed by five experts in the field of IT and behavioural science to assess its logical consistencies, ease of understanding, sequence of items, and task relevance. A number of suggestions were made

concerning the wording of several items and the overall structure of the questionnaire, like adding some headings for each construct, and these suggestions were incorporated into the revised instrument. A pilot study was then conducted in May 2005 by randomly selecting 100 higher education students in Hong Kong in order to gain additional feedback and to test the initial validity of the questionnaire. Factor analysis and reliability analysis were conducted after the pilot study. Some items were rephrased so as to remove ambiguity and some items like "the e-learning tool enables me to control my learning progress" and "I could always access the e-learning tool without any problems" were deleted.

A large-scale survey was launched in August 2005, whereby the questionnaires were randomly distributed in common rooms, libraries and canteens by hand to students of seven higher education institutions in Hong Kong, namely the Chinese University of Hong Kong, the City University of Hong Kong, Hong Kong Baptist University, Hong Kong Institute of Education, Hong Kong University of Science and Technology, Lingnan University, and the University of Hong Kong, at different time slots. The Open University of Hong Kong, which expect students using WebCT compulsorily, was excluded as our scope is to study e-learning tool adoption in a voluntarily basis. Given that some postgraduate students would only go to their institutions at night time, we invited them to fill in the questionnaires on the spot. Nevertheless, some respondents left the questionnaires blank. In order to gather more returns and to show our sincerity in conducting the survey, a donation of one Hong Kong dollar was made to a charity organization for every completed survey. We also explained to the respondents the purpose of the survey and motivated them to reply personally. The confidentiality of the results was stressed. To minimize data entry errors, all the collected data were checked for consistency. As a result, 370 valid questionnaires were collected to study the intention of students to use an e-learning discussion forum for their learning, and all duplicate responses and those responses that had too many missing values were removed.

The questionnaire consists of 17 items to assess four constructs, namely UID, PEOU, PU and BITU, of the proposed model. UID, consisting of five items, is measured using mainly the scale adapted from Wang (2003). The items used to construct PU and PEOU, each having four items, are based on the scale from Davis (1989) with appropriate modifications for e-learning adoption. Intention to use, consisting of four items, is measured by using the scale developed by Ajzen and Fishbein (1980). All the constructs

are measured on a five-point Likert scale ranging from (1) "strongly disagree" to (5) "strongly agree. Some demographic data, e.g., age, gender, level of education, etc., are collected at the end of the questionnaire.

FINDINGS AND DISCUSSIONS

Reliability and Validity

A factor analysis was carried out on all 17 items, i.e., five for UID, four for PU, four for PEOU, and four for BITU (Table 2). The factor analysis

Table 2. Descriptive statistics and reliability

Variables	Mean*	Std. Dev.	Cronbach's alpha
User-interface Design	**3.55**	**0.58**	**0.845**
Layout is user-friendly (UID1)	3.63	0.73	
Instruction is clear (UID2)	3.50	0.78	
E-learning tool is easy to follow (UID3)	3.60	0.74	
Layout is in good structure(UID4)	3.44	0.76	
Design is satisfactory(UID5)	3.58	0.67	
Perceived Usefulness	**3.44**	**0.62**	**0.872**
Enabled me to accomplish tasks more quickly (PU1)	3.42	0.72	
Improved the quality of my tasks(PU2)	3.38	0.76	
Enhanced the effectiveness of my tasks(PU3)	3.43	0.75	
E-learning tool is useful to me(PU4)	3.55	0.71	
Perceived Ease of Use	**3.54**	**0.64**	**0.854**
Use of the e-learning tool is simple (PEOU1)	3.60	0.76	
I have no trouble in using the e-learning tool (PEOU2)	3.48	0.83	
Provides information that is easy to comprehend (PEOU3)	3.48	0.76	
The e-learning tool is easy to use (PEOU4)	3.60	0.69	
Behavioural Intention to Use	**3.50**	**0.66**	**0.849**
I will use the e-learning tool in the future (BI1)	3.62	0.78	
I intend to use the e-learning tool more in the chosen subject (BI2).	3.50	0.81	
I intend to use the e-learning tool more in other subjects (BI3)	3.42	0.77	
I intend to increase my use of the e-learning tool(BI4)	3.44	0.80	

* 1- strongly disagree and 5 – strongly agree

is used to reduce the number of items in each construct while maintaining its reliability and discriminant validity. Factors are extracted using the principal component method and a varimax rotation. Variables are eliminated if they are not factorially pure.

Reliability refers to the extent to which a construct is free from errors and yields consistent results. Cronbach's alpha is used to measure the internal consistency of the multi-item scales used in this study. As the Cronbach's alpha values of all of the factors were over 0.7, it can be claimed that all of the variables are reliable. Moreover, as all of the measures of the constructs were used in previous studies and the questionnaire was screened by experts in IT and behavioural science before being adopted for conducting the survey, the content validity of the construct can be deemed to be acceptable.

The average variance extracted (AVE) of a construct measures the average variance shared between a construct and its underlying measures (Table 3). The AVE of a construct is calculated as the sum of its items' loadings squared, divided by the number of items in the construct. For example, the AVE of UID is $(0.69^2 + 0.77^2 + 0.77^2 + 0.71^2 + 0.81^2)/5 = 0.564$. In order for a construct to be reliable, its AVE should be higher than 50%.

The correlation matrix for the data set is shown in Table 4. All correlations were greater than 0.3 and significant at the 0.01 level. Moreover, the correlations between the measures of potentially overlapping constructs can also be examined. If the items comprising a construct do not overlap much with the other constructs, i.e., the average variance explained (AVE) of a construct is larger than the construct's squared intercorrelations with other constructs, then discriminant validity is established. From Table 3, the diagonal elements, which show the square roots of the AVE of the constructs, are all higher than the correlations between target constructs without exception,

Table 3. Factor analysis

	User Interface Design	Perceived Usefulness	Perceived Ease of Use	Behavioral intention to use
UID1	0.694			
UID2	0.768			
UID3	0.767			
UID4	0.711			
UID5	0.816			
PU1		0.750		
PU2		0.757		
PU3		0.807		
PU4		0.799		
PEOU1			0.801	
PEOU2			0.820	
PEOU3			0.686	
PEOU4			0.785	
BI1				0.703
BI2				0.636
BI3				0.686
BI4				0.836

Table 4. Correlation matrix

		1	2	3	4
1	UID	**0.751**			
2	Useful	0.310**	**0.780**		
3	Ease	0.500**	0.449**	**0.777**	
4	Intention	0.402**	0.645**	0.438**	**0.721**

**correlation is significant at the 0.01 level.*

Note: Diagonal elements (bold) are the square roots of the average variance extracted (AVE) between the constructs and their measures. Off-diagonal elements are correlations between constructs. For discriminant validity, diagonal elements should be larger than off-diagonal elements in the same row and column.

Table 5. Hierarchical regression results

Dependent variables	Independent variables	Coefficient (p-value)	Adjusted R^2
PEOU	UID	.55 (.000)	.248
PU	UID	.33 (.000)	.094
	PEOU	.44 (.000)	.199
	PEOU UID	.38 (.000) .12 (.033)	.207
BITU	PU PEOU	.59 (.000) .19 (.000)	.441

thus discriminant validity of all the constructs is established.

Regression Analysis

The results of regression analyses are presented in Table 5. Hypotheses H1, H2, H4, and H5 are evidently supported. UID has a significant impact on both PU and PEOU, which in turn have an impact on BITU. From the explained variance, which is the adjusted R^2, UID plays a more important role in explaining PEOU ($R^2 = 0.248$) than PU ($R^2 = 0.094$). Comparing the impacts of PU and PEOU on BITU, PU with ($\beta = 0.59$) is more important to predict BITU than PEOU ($\beta = 0.19$). This agrees with past technology acceptance studies by Davis (1989) and others. Moreover, PU is also dependent on UID and PEOU. For H3, we need to analyze the explained variances among the regressions on PEOU and PU. According to Hair et al. (1998), the Venn diagram (Figure 1) shows the relationship between the explained variances. The explained variance between PU and UID is represented by the overlapping area between PU and UID and is equal to $x + y$, where y is the common variance among PU, PEOU and UID. Similarly, $z + y$ is the explained variance between PEOU and UID, and $w + y$ is the explained variance between PU and PEOU. Moreover, the explained variance of PU in terms of PEOU and UID is equal to $x + y + z$. From Table 4, we have the following equations:

$$x + y = 0.094 \qquad (1)$$
$$z + y = 0.248 \qquad (2)$$
$$w + y = 0.199 \qquad (3)$$
$$x + y + z = 0.207 \qquad (4)$$

Solving the simultaneous equations 1-4, we obtain $x = 0.008$, $y = 0.086$, $z = 0.162$, and $w = 0.113$. The ratio $y/(y + w) = 0.43$ highlights the role

Figure 2. TAM model augmented with UID

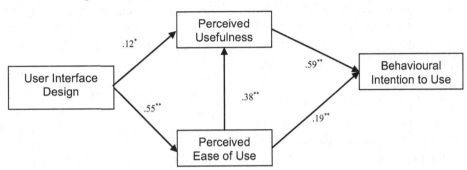

* stands for p < 0.05, ** stands for p < 0.01

Figure 1. The Venn diagram of the three constructs: UID, PEOU, and PU

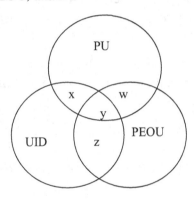

of UID in the relationship between PEOU and PU. This implies that UID plays an important role in the relationship between PU and PEOU; it explains 43% of the strength of the relationship.

Moreover, w = 0.113 > 0 indicates that UID cannot totally explain the relationship between PU and PEOU. As reflected in the regression of PEOU and UID on PU, with the addition of the variable UID, PEOU is still a significant factor affecting PU. In other words, if w = 0 or close to 0, we expect PEOU to be insignificant with the presence of UID in the same regression. Also w > 0 implies that there may be another common antecedent of PU and PEOU or PEOU intrinsically has an impact on PU. In this regard, we conclude that H3 is also valid. Nevertheless, we have only investigated the effect of one common

antecedent, i.e., UID, on PEOU and PU. The effect of other common antecedents such as navigation and accessibility may also play an important role in explaining the relationship between PEOU and PU.

Concerning students' intention to use an e-learning forum, we identify that UID does play an important role. It has a direct impact on PEOU, and has both a direct and an indirect impact on PU. In the path analysis with the model of Figure 2, its impact on PU is 0.55*0.38 + 0.12 = 0.329. Hence, the impact of UID on BITU is 0.329*0.59 + 0.55*0.19 = 0.30. Therefore, it is necessary to strengthen user-interface design in order to entice more students to use an e-learning forum for their learning and communication.

CONCLUSION

It has been argued in past studies on technology acceptance that the relationship between PEOU and PU is due to the fact that, all other factors being equal, the less effort it is required to use a system will induce more usefulness of the system,. Our study found that there are additional reasons to account for the relationship between PEOU and PU due to the effects from a common antecedent of PEOU and PU. In fact, our findings show that UID can explain 43% of the relationship between PEOU and PU in the context of students' intention to use an e-learning forum. Besides there are other antecedents, such as navigation and accessibility, that are common to PEOU and PU, which would further explain the relationship between PEOU and PU. Future studies should consider these additional antecedents.

This study highlights the importance of UID to students' intention to use an e-learning forum and it is urged that more focus should be placed on UID in order to encourage students to use an e-learning forum for their learning and communication. Nevertheless, e-learning is going to be a more important component in our learning systems, especially with the advance of the Internet technologies.

ACKNOWLEDGMENT

This research was supported in part by The Hong Kong Polytechnic University under grant number U040.

REFERENCES

Abdul-Gader, A.H., & Kozar, K.A. (1995). The impact of computer alienation on information technology investment decisions: an exploratory cross-national analysis. *MIS Quarterly, 19*(4), 535-559.

Adam, D.A., Nelson, R.R., & Todd, P.A. (1992). Perceived usefulness, ease of use, and usage of information technology, a replication. *MIS Quarterly, 16*, 227-250.

Agarwal, R., & Prasad, J. (1998). A conceptual and operational definition of personal innovativeness in the domain of information technology. *Information Systems Research, 9*(2), 204-215.

Ajzen, I., & Fishbein, M. (1980). *Understanding attitudes and predicting social behaviour*. NJ: Prentice-Hall.

Benbasat, I., & Dexter, A.S. (1986). An investigation of the effectiveness of color and graphical presentation under varying time constraints, *MIS Quarterly, 10*(1), 59-84.

Benbasat, I. Dexter, A.S. & Todd, P. (1986). The influence of color and graphical information presentation in a managerial decision simulation. *Human-Computer Interaction, 2*(1), 65-92.

Chan, Y., & Lou, H. 2002. Distance learning technology adoption: a motivation perspective. *The Journal of Computer Information Systems, 42*(2), 38-43.

Chimera, R, & Shneiderman, B. (1993). *Sparks on innovation in human computer interaction*. NJ: Ablex.

Chin, W., & Gopal, A. (1995). Adoption intention in GSS: relative importance of beliefs. *Data Base, 26*(2), 42- 63.

Chiu, C.M., Hsu, M.H., Sun, S.Y., Lin, T.C., & Sun, P.C. (2004). Usability, quality, value and e-learning continuance decisions. *Computers and Education*.

Cho, V. (2006). A study of the roles of trusts and risks in information-oriented online legal services using an integrated model. *Information & Management, 43*, 502-520.

Davis, F.D. (1989). Perceived usefulness, perceived ease of use, and user acceptance of information technology. *MIS Quarterly*, September, *13*(3), 319-340.

Davis, F.D., Bagozzi, R.P., & Warshaw, P.R. (1989). User acceptance of computer technology: A comparison of two theoretical models. *Management Science, 35*, 982-1002.

Davis, F.D., Bagozzi, R.P., &. Warshaw, P.R. (1992). Extrinsic and intrinsic motivation to use computers in the workplace. *Journal of Applied Social Psychology, 22*, 1111-1132.

Edelson, P.J. (2001). *E-learning in the USA: The Storm after the storm*. Paper presented at the Annual Conference of the University Association for Continuing Education, Glasgow, Scotland April 9-11.

Forman, D., Nyatanga, L., & Rich, T. (2002). E-learning and educational diversity. *Nurse Education Today, 22*, 76-82.

Gallivan, M.J. (2001). Organizational adoption and assimilation of complex technological innovations: Development and application of a new framework. *Database for Advances in Information Systems, 32*(3), 51-86.

Gefen, D., & Straub, D.W. (2000). The relative importance of perceived ease of use in IS adoption: a study of e-commerce adoption. *Journal of the Association of Information Systems, 1*(8), 1-28.

Hair, J.F., Anderson, R.E., Tatham, R.L., & Black W.C. (1998). *Multivariate data analysis*. NJ: Prentice Hall.

Hay, A. Hodgkinson, M., Peltier, J.W., & Drago, W.A. (2004). Interaction and virtual learning, *Strategic Change, 13*(4), 193-204.

Igbaria, M., Guimaraes, T., & Davis, G.B. (1995). Testing the determinants of microcomputer usage via a structural equation model. *Journal of Management Information Systems, 11*, 87- 114.

Igbaria, M., Zinatelli, N., Cragg, P., & Cavaye, A. (1997). Personal computing acceptance factors in small firms: a structural equation model. *MIS Quarterly, 21*(3), 279-305.

Im, Y., & Lee, O. (2004). Pedagogical implications of online discussion for preservice teacher training. *Journal of Research on Technology in Education, 36*(2), 155-170.

Jackson, C.M., Chow, S., & Leitch, R.A. (1997). Toward an understanding of the behavioural intentions to use an information system, *Decision Science, 28*, 357-389.

Karahanna, E., & Straub, D.W. (1999). The Psychological origins of perceived usefulness and ease-of-use. *Information & Management, 35*, 237-250.

Keil, M., Beranek, P.M., & Konsynski, B.R. (1995). Usefulness and ease of use: field study evidence regarding task considerations. *Decision Support Systems, 13*(1), 75-91.

Kraemer, K.L., Danziger, J.N., Dunkle, D.E., & King, J.L. (1993). The usefulness of computer-based information to public managers. *MIS Quarterly, 17*, 129-148.

Lederer, A.L., Maupin, D.J., Sena, M.P., & Zhuang, Y. (2000). The Technology Acceptance Model and the World Wide Web. *Decision Support Systems, 29*, 269-282.

Le Peuple, J., & Scane, R. (2003). *User interface design*. United Kingdom: Crucial.

Liang, T.P. (1987). User interface design for decision support systems: A self-adaptive approach. *Information & Management, 12*, 181-193.

Madsen, S.R. (2004). Academic service learning in human resource management education. *Journal of Education for Business*, 328-332.

Miller, T.W., & King, F.B. (2003). Distance education: pedagogy and best practices in the new millennium. *International Journal of Leadership in Education, 6*(3), 283-297.

Morris, M.G., & Venkatesh, V. (2000). Age differences in technology adoption decisions: implications for a changing work force. *Personnel Psychology, 53*(2), 375-403.

Morris, M.G., Venkatesh, V., & Ackerman, P.L. (2005). Gender and age differences in employee decision about new technology: An extension to the theory of planned behavior. *IEEE Transactions on Engineering Management, 52*(1), 69-84.

Ong, C.S., & Lai, J.Y. (2004). Gender differences in perceptions and relationships among dominants of e-learning acceptance, *Computers in Human Behavior.*

Parikh, M. & Verma, S. (2002). Utilizing internet technologies to support learning: an empirical analysis. *International Journal of Information Management, 22,* 27-46.

Piccoli, G., Ahmad, R., & Ives, B. (2001). Web-based virtual learning environments: a research framework and a preliminary assessment of effectiveness in basic IT skills training. *MIS Quarterly, 25*(4), 401-426.

Rogers, E. (1995). *Diffusion of innovation (4th ed.).* New York: The Free Press.

Selim, H.M. (2003). An empirical investigation of student acceptance of course websites. *Computer and Education, 40,* 343-360.

Szajna, B. (1996). Empirical evaluation of the revised technology acceptance model. *Management Science, 42*(1), 85-92.

Taylor S., & Todd, P. (1995). Understanding information technology usage: a test of competing models. *Information Systems Research, 6*(2), 144-176.

Thong, J.Y.L., Hong, W., & Tam, K.Y. (2002). Understanding user acceptance of digital libraries: what are the roles of interface characteristics, organizational context, and individual differences? *International Journal of Human-Computer Studies, 57,* 215-242.

Venkatesh, V., & Davis, F.D. (2000). A theoretical extension of the technology acceptance model: four longitudinal field studies. *Management Science, 46,* 186-204.

Venkatesh, V., & Davis, F.D. (1996). A model of the antecedents of perceived ease of use: development and test. *Decision Sciences, 27*(3), 451-481.

Venkatesh, V., & Morris, M.G. (2000). Why don't men ever stop to ask directions? Gender, social influence, and their role in technology acceptance and usage behavior. *MIS Quarterly, 24,* 115-139.

Wang, Y.S. (2003). Assessment of learner satisfaction with asynchronous electronic learning systems. *Information & Management, 41,* 75-86.

Zmud, R. (1983). The effectiveness of external information channels in facilitating innovation within software development groups. *MIS Quarterly, 7*(2), 43-58.

KEY TERMS

Environmental Characteristics: Environmental characteristics of a computer system include system support, user training, management support, social presence, and subjective norms

Perceived Ease of Use (PEOU): PEOU of a system (i.e., a technology) is the incentive that induces people to use the system more easily, and hence will make the system more useful.

Perceived Usefulness (PU): PU is the perception of users in utilizing a system or technology regarding the extent such a system or technology will achieve the stated objectives.

Technology Acceptance Model (TAM): TAM is an information systems theory that models how users come to accept and use a technology

User-Interface Design (UID): UID is the design of computer or reelated telecommunication technologies with a focus on the user's experience and interaction.

APPENDIX A

QUESTIONNAIRE ON LEARNERS' ADOPTION OF E-LEARNING TOOLS OR FACILITIES

This survey is to identify the characteristics of learners who are more likely to adopt e-learning and the factors behind e-learning adoption. To show our courtesy in conducting this survey, a donation of **$1** would be made to **HK World Vision (世界宣明會)** for you with every survey collected for this use. (As for your note and reference, a copy of the donation receipt would be available in the survey website http://158.132.84.133/ after research completes.) For any enquiry, please feel free to contact **Dr. Vincent Cho, Department of Management and Marketing, The Hong Kong Polytechnic University** by email (msvcho@inet.polyu.edu.hk) or phone 27666339. Respondents should apply e-learning tool for academic purposes.

Part I (E-learning Tool)

Please indicate the extent to which you agree/disagree with the following statements by choosing the appropriate boxes. The ratings are numbered from 1 to 5: 1 stands for strongly disagree; 2 stands for disagree; 3 stands for neutral; 4 stands for agree; 5 stands for strongly agree.

1. General E-Learning Situations

	Strongly Disagree	Disagree	Neutral	Agree	Strongly Agree	N/A
I am familiar with the e-learning system.	1	2	3	4	5	N/A
How frequently do you use e-learning tools?	Never	Several times a year	Several times a month	Several times a week	Several times a day	N/A

2. What is your *most familiar* e-learning tool?

Communications with the Instructor through Electronic Means	Interactive Discussion Forum among Learners	Self-paced Learning Tools
• e.g. An *online video presentation* from **an instructor**, elaboration through whiteboard or **email communications with instructor** on a particular topic. • It is related to the learning through *the communications with an instructor* through some e-learning tools.	• e.g. Discussion among friends and classmates on a particular topic. • It is related to *the learning among learners* through some e-learning communication tools.	• e.g. *Online quiz, or computer/online self-paced learning package.* • It is related to the learning *from a package through some e-learning resources, **but it is not related to purely download of materials**.*

*****Please answer the following questions according to your chosen e-Learning tool*****

Part II (Subject Details)

1a. What is **the subject area** of the most encountered e-learning tool as **chosen above**?

Subjects

IT		Language		Medicine		Business		Arts	
Social Science		Engineering		Art & Design		Science		Others	

1b. What is the **chosen subject level** of the most encountered e-learning tool?

Postgraduate		Undergraduate		Higher Diploma		Higher Certificate		Diploma		Certificate	

2. Subject Level

	Strongly Disagree	Disagree	Neutral	Agree	Strongly Agree	N/A
I often use the chosen e-learning tool to learn the basic terminology of a subject.	1	2	3	4	5	N/A
I often use the chosen e-learning tool to understand basic knowledge of a subject.	1	2	3	4	5	N/A
I often use the chosen e-learning tool to solve high level problems.	1	2	3	4	5	N/A
The chosen e-learning tool can inspire my creative thinking of the subject.	1	2	3	4	5	N/A
The chosen e-learning tool can inspire my critical thinking of the subject.	1	2	3	4	5	N/A

3. What is your learning mode in **the subject above**?

I study the chosen subject with face-to-face learning approach.	Never 1	2	3	4	Often 5
I study the chosen subject with e-learning approach.	Never 1	2	3	4	Often 5
I study the subject with mixed face-to-face and e-learning approach.	Never 1	2	3	4	Often 5

Part III (Learning Aspects)

1. General Learning Approach (Related to **your chosen learning tool/subject**)

	Strongly Disagree	Disagree	Neutral	Agree	Strongly Agree	N/A
You are actively in doing projects.	1	2	3	4	5	N/A
You do lots of thinking during the learning process.	1	2	3	4	5	N/A
You learn independently.	1	2	3	4	5	N/A
You are actively involved in creating your own ideas.	1	2	3	4	5	N/A

2. General Learning Characteristics (Related to **your chosen learning tool/subject**)

	Strongly Disagree	Disagree	Neutral	Agree	Strongly Agree	N/A
You have interests in your studies.	1	2	3	4	5	N/A
You have identified personal learning goals.	1	2	3	4	5	N/A
You have incentive to solve almost every problem.	1	2	3	4	5	N/A
You use time wisely in your studies.	1	2	3	4	5	N/A
You are able to find patterns and take effective notes to organize materials.	1	2	3	4	5	N/A

3. How can you describe your learning styles? (Related to **your chosen learning tool/subject**)

I understand something better when I	Think it through				Try it out
	1	2	3	4	5
In a study group working on difficult materials, I am more likely to	Sit back and listen			Jump in and contribute ideas	
	1	2	3	4	5
The idea of doing homework in groups, with one grade for the entire group,	Is not reasonable to me			Is reasonable to me	
	1	2	3	4	5
I prefer to study	Alone			In a study group	
	1	2	3	4	5
I would rather first	Think about how I'm going to do it			Try things out	
	1	2	3	4	5

4. Learning Performance (Related to **your chosen learning tool/subject**)

	Strongly Disagree	Disagree	Neutral	Agree	Strongly Agree	N/A
I am strong in **understanding new concepts**.	1	2	3	4	5	N/A
I am strong in **generalizing concepts into ideas**.	1	2	3	4	5	N/A
I am strong in **creating new ideas**.	1	2	3	4	5	N/A
I am strong in **presenting** my own ideas.	1	2	3	4	5	N/A

Part IV (Antecedents)

Functionality

	Strongly Disagree	Disagree	Neutral	Agree	Strongly Agree	N/A
The chosen e-learning tool responds fast enough.	1	2	3	4	5	N/A
The chosen e-learning tool provides sufficient features that I need.	1	2	3	4	5	N/A
The chosen e-learning tool enables me to learn the content that I need.	1	2	3	4	5	N/A
As a whole, the chosen e-learning tool enables me to achieve my learning goal effectively.	1	2	3	4	5	N/A

User Interface Design

	Strongly Disagree	Disagree	Neutral	Agree	Strongly Agree	N/A
The layout of the chosen e-learning tool is user-friendly.	1	2	3	4	5	N/A
The instruction provided by the chosen e-learning tool is clear.	1	2	3	4	5	N/A
The chosen e-learning tool is easy to follow.	1	2	3	4	5	N/A
The layout of the chosen e-learning tool is in good structure.	1	2	3	4	5	N/A
Overall user interface design of the chosen e-learning tool is satisfactory.	1	2	3	4	5	N/A

System Support

	Strongly Disagree	Disagree	Neutral	Agree	Strongly Agree	N/A
The service quality of the chosen e-learning tool is good.	1	2	3	4	5	N/A
The chosen e-learning tool provides **personalized** support (e.g. there are some options which enable you to specify your preference).	1	2	3	4	5	N/A
Overall system support is satisfactory.	1	2	3	4	5	N/A

Information Obtained

	Strongly Disagree	Disagree	Neutral	Agree	Strongly Agree	N/A
The chosen e-learning tool provides **sufficient** information for my study.	1	2	3	4	5	N/A
The chosen e-learning tool provides **accurate** information for my study.	1	2	3	4	5	N/A
The chosen e-learning tool provides **up-to-date** information for my study.	1	2	3	4	5	N/A
The chosen e-learning tool provides **useful** information for my study.	1	2	3	4	5	N/A
The information provided by the chosen e-learning tool is **easy to understand**.	1	2	3	4	5	N/A
The chosen e-learning tool provides **relevant** information for my study.	1	2	3	4	5	N/A
Overall information provided by the chosen e-learning tool is satisfactory.	1	2	3	4	5	N/A

Experiences

	Strongly Disagree	Disagree	Neutral	Agree	Strongly Agree	N/A
I am familiar with the use the chosen e-learning tool.	1	2	3	4	5	N/A
I have favorable experience in using the chosen e-learning tool.	1	2	3	4	5	N/A
I have favorable experience in using computer systems.	1	2	3	4	5	N/A
I am familiar with the use of Internet.	1	2	3	4	5	N/A
How frequently do you use computer systems?	Never	Several times a year	Several times a month	Several times a week	Several times a day	N/A

Perceived Usefulness

	Strongly Disagree	Disagree	Neutral	Agree	Strongly Agree	N/A
Use of the chosen e-learning tool enabled me to accomplish tasks more quickly.	1	2	3	4	5	N/A
Use of the chosen e-learning tool improved the quality of my tasks.	1	2	3	4	5	N/A
Use of the chosen e-learning tool enhanced the effectiveness of my tasks.	1	2	3	4	5	N/A
As a whole, the chosen e-learning tool is useful to me.	1	2	3	4	5	N/A

Perceived Ease of Use

	Strongly Disagree	Disagree	Neutral	Agree	Strongly Agree	N/A
Use of the chosen e-learning tool is simple.	1	2	3	4	5	N/A
I have no trouble in using the chosen e-learning tool to perform task that I needed.	1	2	3	4	5	N/A
The chosen e-learning tool provides information that is easy to comprehend.	1	2	3	4	5	N/A
As a whole, the chosen e-learning tool is easy to use.	1	2	3	4	5	N/A

Compatibility of Values and Beliefs

	Strongly Disagree	Disagree	Neutral	Agree	Strongly Agree	N/A
The chosen e-learning tool fits my learning style.	1	2	3	4	5	N/A
The chosen e-learning tool fits my practices in learning.	1	2	3	4	5	N/A
Studying with the chosen e-learning tool is as effective as the traditional face-to-face learning.	1	2	3	4	5	N/A
The chosen e-learning tool is add value to the traditional face-to-face learning.	1	2	3	4	5	N/A

Social Factor

	Strongly Disagree	Disagree	Neutral	Agree	Strongly Agree	N/A
My instructors think that I should use the chosen e-learning tool in learning.	1	2	3	4	5	N/A
My classmates think that I should use the chosen e-learning tool in learning.	1	2	3	4	5	N/A
My friends think that I should use the chosen e-learning tool in learning.	1	2	3	4	5	N/A
As a whole, the use of the chosen e-learning tool is a trend which I will follow.	1	2	3	4	5	N/A

Playfulness

	Strongly Disagree	Disagree	Neutral	Agree	Strongly Agree	N/A
I have fun in using the chosen e-learning tool.	1	2	3	4	5	N/A
Use of the chosen e-learning tool is pleasant.	1	2	3	4	5	N/A
Use of the chosen e-learning tool is interesting.	1	2	3	4	5	N/A
As a whole, I enjoy studying with the chosen e-learning tool.	1	2	3	4	5	N/A

Attitudes

	Strongly Disagree	Disagree	Neutral	Agree	Strongly Agree	N/A
It's a good idea to use the chosen e-learning tool.	1	2	3	4	5	N/A
Use of the chosen e-learning tool is convenient.	1	2	3	4	5	N/A
Use of the chosen e-learning tool can save time.	1	2	3	4	5	N/A
In general, use of the chosen e-learning tool is effective.	1	2	3	4	5	N/A

Behavioral Intention to Use

	Strongly Disagree	Disagree	Neutral	Agree	Strongly Agree	N/A
I will use the chosen e-learning tool in the future.	1	2	3	4	5	N/A
I intend to use the chosen e-learning tool more in the chosen subject.	1	2	3	4	5	N/A
I intend to use the chosen e-learning tool more in other subjects.	1	2	3	4	5	N/A
I intend to **increase my use** of the chosen e-learning tool in the future.	1	2	3	4	5	N/A
I intend to increase my use of the two other e-learning tools in the future.	1	2	3	4	5	N/A

Usage

	Strongly Disagree	Disagree	Neutral	Agree	Strongly Agree	N/A
I use the chosen e-learning tool whenever possible to study.	1	2	3	4	5	N/A
I use the chosen e-learning tool regularly in study.	1	2	3	4	5	N/A
I use the chosen e-learning tool frequently in study.	1	2	3	4	5	N/A
In general, I use the chosen e-learning tool in every aspect of my study.	1	2	3	4	5	N/A

Satisfaction

	Strongly Disagree	Disagree	Neutral	Agree	Strongly Agree	N/A
Using the chosen e-learning tool would give me a better opportunity to explore on the subject.	1	2	3	4	5	N/A
Using the chosen e-learning tool would give me a sense of self-control on my learning pace.	1	2	3	4	5	N/A
My decision to use the chosen e-learning tool was a wise one.	1	2	3	4	5	N/A
In general, using the chosen e-learning tool would give me a sense of satisfaction.	1	2	3	4	5	N/A

Performance Outcome

	Strongly Disagree	Disagree	Neutral	Agree	Strongly Agree	N/A
The chosen e-learning tool improves my grade on the subject.	1	2	3	4	5	N/A
The chosen e-learning tool enhances my understanding on the subject.	1	2	3	4	5	N/A
The chosen e-learning tool improves the competence of my studies.	1	2	3	4	5	N/A
Use of the chosen e-learning tool improved my overall learning performance.	1	2	3	4	5	N/A

Part V (Further Opinions)

1. What are the advantages and disadvantages of the chosen e-learning tool for your study?

Advantages: _____

Disadvantages: _____

2. Select TWO most important factors in each part (Part A & Part B) which encourage the adoption of e-learning.

Part A

Functionality	
User Interface Design	
System Support	
Information Obtained	
Experience	

Part B

Perceived Usefulness	
Perceived Ease of Use	
Compatibility	
Social Factor	
Playfulness	

Part VI (Demographic)

1. Age

18-25	
6-30	
31-36	
37-40	
41 or above	

2. Sex

Male	
Female	

3. Level of education

	Major
Post-graduate	
Undergraduate	
Secondary school	
Primary school	

4. Occupation

Student		Executive	
Professional		White-collar	
Teacher		Technician	
Self-employed		Others	

- End of questionnaire -

Chapter XI
Data Quality on the Internet

Vincent Cho
Hong Kong Polytechnic University, Hong Kong

ABSTRACT

This chapter will review the studies on the data quality on the Internet and will propose some suggestions to improve existing Internet resources. The layout of this chapter is as follows. First, the definitions of data quality will be visited. Next, the author would like to review the reasons of poor data quality. Framework and assessment based on the past literature will be reviewed and finally some recommendations are highlighted.

INTRODUCTION

Quality data on the Internet is getting more important as it is key resource for planning, producing, and communicating in the new millennium. However, the Internet data is never perfect. It is noisy, containing a lot of missing values, outdated, non-validated and heterogeneous. As such, the quality of Internet resources varies from one to another (Hawkins, 1999; Pack, 1999). With

the use of the Internet increasing dramatically, poor-quality data can be processed and distributed faster than ever and wider than ever. The impacts of using poor quality data on the Internet range from customer dissatisfaction, reduced revenue, weakening competitiveness or even to the termination of business operation (Huang et al. 1999; Redman 1996; Strong et al., 1997; Fuld 1998; Klein 2001; Teo and Choo 2001). Thus, the assessment and monitoring of data quality on the

Internet is emergingly essential. This would help an individual or organization to utilize high quality Internet resources for the decision making. This chapter will review the studies on the data quality on the Internet and will propose some suggestions to improve existing Internet resources.

The layout of this chapter is as follows. First, the definitions of data quality will be visited. Next, we would like to review the reasons of poor data quality. Framework and assessment based on the past literature will be reviewed and finally some recommendations are highlighted.

DEFINITIONS

The notion of data quality has been widely investigated in the literature. It is often defined as "fitness for use", i.e., the ability of a data collection to meet user requirements for his/her decision making on certain tasks. Both theoretical and experimental results indicate that data quality is a multi-dimensional concept (Ballou, 1998; Redman, 1996; Wang and Strong, 1996; Wand and Wang, 1996). Zmud (1978) empirically derived the data quality using factor analysis to examine the dimensionality of the construct of information. Four dimensions were derived: quality of information, relevancy of information, quality of format, and quality of meaning. Theoretically, Wand and Wang (1996) identified four dimensions of intrinsic data quality: completeness, lack of ambiguity, meaningfulness, and correctness. These dimensions are said to be applicable across different applications applied to different tasks. Hub et al. (1990) and Fox et al. (1994) identified four dimensions of data quality: accuracy, completeness, consistency, and currency.

In an early discussion of the quality of information systems, Davis and Olson (1985) identified three aspects of quality that refer to characteristics of data: accuracy, precision, and completeness. Lee et al. (2002) and Strong et al. (1997) grouped the information quality from an

information system into four categories, intrinsic information quality, contextual information quality, representational information quality, and accessibility information quality. Intrinsic information quality implies that information has quality in its own right. Contextual information quality highlights the requirement that information quality must be considered within the context of the task at hand; it must be relevant, timely, complete, and appropriate in terms of amount, so as to add value. Representational and accessibility information quality emphasize the importance of computer systems that store and provide access to information; that is, the system must present information in such a way that it is interpretable, easy to understand, easy to manipulate, and is represented concisely and consistently; also, the system must be accessible but secure.

Kim et al., (2005) defined data quality on the Internet using the concept of usability which data has to be quality in content (i.e. accuracy, relevance, completeness), presentable (interface structural quality, information packaging, and information accessibility), and time-concern (history maintenance quality, information delivery quality, and information currency).

In sum, quality data has been described as consisting of several attributes, including accuracy, accessibility, completeness, consistency, currency, and timeliness (Ballou, 1998; Redman, 1996; Wang and Strong, 1996; Wand and Wang, 1996; Fox et al., 1999; Lemire, 1995; Little and Misra, 1994). Accuracy is the measure of the closeness of the data to the actual event. Accessibility refers to the ability to obtain the necessary data. Completeness is the measure of whether the data contains all the relevant facts. Consistency addresses whether one set of data conflicts with a second related set of data. Currency refers to whether the data is up-to-date, and timeliness addresses the issue of how quickly the data can be obtained.

WHY POOR DATA QUALITY?

Klein (2002) stated that unlike professional journals and commercial publishers, who employ a system of editorial review and external referees to ensure the quality of information distributed, information can be spread over the Internet by anyone without regard to accuracy, validity, or bias. From time to time, the Internet data are contradicting each other. It is because of different data production workflows, different value representations, systematic errors which are introduced during data collection or analysis. and noise which may be introduced by chance while collecting, manipulating or analyzing data (Muller et al., 2004). Solomon (2005) also elaborated that data usually are copied or duplicated to allow for easier access due to a physical limitation. This replicated data will further enhance the chance of inconsistence among Internet data. Furthermore, Teo and Choo (2001) argued that the data quality of the Internet depends on the information and characteristics of the underlying system which provides the data.

FRAMEWORK FOR ASSESSMENT

In order to evaluate the data quality on the Internet, Janicke (1996) addressed three questions on resource selection and information evaluation: Is the resource or information likely to be found on the Internet? Where is the resource or information located on the Internet? Is the resource or information that exists accurate and reliable?

Hawkins (1999) discussed fourteen criteria that are included to evaluate the data quality on the Internet. The criteria include (1) currency/updating, (2) purpose/author/bias, (3) author/source, (4) scope, (5) accuracy/relevance, (6) design/format, (7) authority, (8) uniqueness/stability, (9) structure/indexing, (10) review/ratings, (11) writing quality, (12) data quality, (13) selection criteria, and (14) links to/from other sources. On the other hand, Alexander and Tate (1999) suggested five criteria for evaluating Internet-based information: authority, accuracy, currency, objectivity, and coverage.

In order to support effective data mining from distributed information sources, Wuthrich, Cho, Zhang and Pun (2000) developed a reliable and effective metrics to evaluate the data quality on the Internet. Based on the metrics, high quality information sources are selected to conduct data mining.

Wang et al, (1995) suggested attaching a label to every attribute value specifying the time when the value was recorded and a source from which it was obtained. Thus, the users can judge about the creditability of the data. As such, this technique addressed the timeliness and accuracy aspect of the data. Nevertheless, it seems that tagging all these data into the database would impose too much demand on data storage. The feasibility of applying this technique would be questionable.

DATA QUALITY ON THE INTERNET

Underlying the management of data, there are typically complex process and workflows. It is ideal to study data quality aspects for the entire data management process (Gertz et al., 2004). That is, one should focus on three components: (1) data producers (entities that generate data), 2) data custodians (entities that provide and manage resources for processing and storing data). (3) data consumers. For example, a major US Bank that administered the questionnaire found custodians (mostly MIS professionals) view their data as highly timely, but consumers disagree; and data consumers view data as difficult to manipulate for their business purposes, but custodians disagree (Pipino et al., 2002; Huang et al., 1999). A follow-up investigation into the root causes of differing assessments provided valuable insight on areas needing improvement.

However, past studies (Cappiello et al., 2004, Rieh and Belkin, 1998; Klein, 2002) are mainly focused on the degree to which data satisfy users'(consumers') needs. Rieh and Belkin (1998) found that the data on the Internet are perceived as less authoritative and credible than information generated from information systems. Klein (2002) compared user perceptions of the quality of information retrieved from Internet and traditional text sources (i.e. books, journals, magazines and newspapers). In this study, traditional text sources were rated as more accurate and objective than Internet sources. Users also found the reputation of traditional text sources to be better than that of Internet sources and the formatting of traditional text sources to be more consistent than that of Internet sources. In contrast, Internet sources were rated higher in terms of their timeliness and amount of available data.

RECOMMENDATIONS FOR ENHANCEMENT

In practice, from the assessment of the data quality on the Internet, we would identify some causes which would be further investigated for the improvement of the data quality. Winkler (2004) suggested controls on the input data using the business rules and data cleaning for finding duplicates before putting information on the Internet. Strong et al. (1995) and Shankaranarayan et al. (2003) presented a framework for managing data quality in such environments using the information product approach. Nowadays, the information products are likely to be posted on the Internet. This model explicitly represents the manufacture of an information product, quality dimensions and methods to compute data quality of the product at any stage in the manufacture, and a set of capabilities to comprehensively manage data quality and implement total data quality management. Manufacturing an information product is akin to manufacturing a physical product. Raw materials,

storage, assembly, processing, inspection, rework and packaging (formatting) are all applicable. Typical information products such as management reports, invoices, etc. are "standard products" and hence can be "assembled" in a production line. Also proven methods for TQM such as quality at source and continuous improvement that have been successfully applied in manufacturing can be adapted for total data quality management. Along with this approach, Pierce (2004) presented a control matrix which is adapted from the IS audit and control literature for use in analyzing the data quality to be posted on the Internet.

CONCLUSION

During the past decade, we have witnessed an explosion in the amount of information available through the Internet. This chapter reviews on the past studies on data quality on the Internet and summaries the possible ways to improve the data quality. We hope this article lays the foundation for future research on this important area.

ACKNOWLEDGMENT

This research was supported in part by The Hong Kong Polytechnic University under grant number A-PA6E.

REFERENCES

Alexander, J.E., & Tate, M.A. (1999). *Web wisdom: how to evaluate and create information quality on the web*. Mahwah, NJ: Lawrence Erlbaum Associates.

Ballou, D., Wang, R., Pazer, H., & Tayi, G. (1998). Modeling information manufacturing systems to determine information product quality. *Management Science, 44*(4), 462-484.

Cappiello, C., Francalanci, C., & Pernici, B. (2004). Data quality assessment from the user's perspective. In *Proceedings of IQIS 2004* (pp. 68-73). Paris, France.

Davis, G.B., & Olson, M.H. (1985). *Management information systems: conceptual foundations, structure, and development*. New York: McGraw Hill Book Company.

Fox, T.L., & Guynes, C.S., Prybutok, V. & Windsor, J. (1999). Maintaining quality in information systems. *The Journal of Computer Information Systems, 40*(1), 76- 80.

Fox, C., Levitin, A., & Redman, T. (1994). The notion of data and its quality dimensions. *Information Processing and Management, 30*(1), 9-19.

Fuld, L.M. (1998). The danger of data slam. *CIO Enterprise Magazine*, September, 28-33.

Gertz, M., Ozsu, M.T., Saake, G., & Sattler, K. (2004). Data quality on the web. *SIGMOD Record, 33*(1), 127-132.

Hawkins, D.T. (1999). What is credible information? *Online, 23*(5), 86-89.

Huang, K., Lee, Y., & Wang R. (1999). *Quality information and knowledge*. Upper Saddle River, NJ: Prentice Hall.

Hub, Y.U., Keller, F.R., Redman, T.C., & Watkins, A.R. (1990). Data quality. *Information and Software Technology, 32*(8), 559-565.

Janicke, L. (1996). *Resource selection and information evaluation* (Tech. Rep.). University of Illinois at Urbana-Champaign.

Kim, Y.J., Kishore, R., & Sanders, G.L. (2005). From DQ to EQ: understanding data quality in the context of e-business systems. *Communications of the ACM, 48*(10), 75-81.

Klein, B.D. (2002). Internet data quality: perceptions of graduate and undergraduate business students. *Journal of Business and Management, 8*(4), 425-432.

Klein B.D. (2001). User perceptions of data quality: Internet and traditional text sources. *The Journal of Computer Information Systems, 41*(4), 9-15.

Lee Y.W., Strong D.M., Kahn B.K., & Wang R.Y. (2002). AIMQ: a methodology for information quality assessment. *Information and Management, 40*, 133-146.

Lemire, E. (1995). Ensuring the integrity of information. *Systems Management, 23*(1), 54-58.

Little, D., & Misra, S. (1994). Auditing for database integrity. *Journal of Systems Management, 45*(8), 6-10.

Muller, H., Leser, U., Freytag, J. (2004). Mining for patterns in contradictory data. In *Proceedings of IQIS 2004*. Paris, France.

Pack, T. (1999). Can you trust Internet information? *Link-up, 16*(6), 24.

Pierce, E.M. (2004). Assessing data quality with control matrices. *Communications of the ACM, 47*(2), 82-86.

Pipino, L.L., Lee, Y.W., & Wang, R.Y. (2002). Data quality assessment. *Communications of the ACM, 45*, 211-218.

Redman, T.C. (1996). Dimensions of data quality. In T.C. Redman (Ed.), *Data quality for the information age* (pp. 245-269). Artech House Inc.

Rieh, S.Y., & Belkin, N.J. (1998). Understanding judgement of information quality and cognitive authority in the WWW. *Journal of the American Society for Information Science, 35*, 279-289.

Shankaranarayan, G., Ziad, M., & Wang R.Y. (2003). Managing data quality in dynamic decision environments. *Journal of Database Management, 14*(4), 14-32.

Solomon, M. D. (2005). It's all about the data. *Information Systems Management, 22*(3), 75-80.

Strong, D.M., Lee, Y.W., & Wang, R.Y. (1997). Data quality in context. *Communications of the ACM, 40*(5), 103-110.

Teo, T.S.H., & Choo, W.Y. (2001). Assessing the impact of using the Internet for competitive intelligence. *Information and Management, 39*, 67-83.

Wand, Y., & Wang, R.Y. (1996). Anchoring data quality dimensions in ontological foundations. *Communications of the ACM, 39*(11), 86-95.

Wang, R.Y., Reddy, M.P., & Kon, H.B. (1995). Toward quality data: An attribute-based approach. *Decision Support Systems, 13*(3-4), 349-372.

Winkler, W.E. (2004). Methods for evaluating and crating data quality. *Information Systems, 29*, 531-550.

Wüthrich B., Cho V., Pun J., & Zhang J. (2000). Data quality in distributed environments. In H. Kargupta & P. Chan (Eds.), *Advances in distributed and parallel knowledge discovery* (pp. 295-316). AAAI Press.

Zmud, R.W. (1978). An empirical investigation of the dimensionality of the concept of information. *Decision Sciences, 9*, 187-195.

KEY TERMS

Data Consumers: Are entities that use and utlize data.

Data Custodians: Are entities that provide and manage resources for processing and storing data.

Data Producers: Are entities that generate data.

Data Quality: Data quality is defined as the ability of a data collection to meet user requirements for his/her decision making on certain tasks.

Chapter XII
"Don't Think but Look"
The Practice of the UDRP Manifests that it is Procedurally Unfair

Konstantinos Komaitis
University of Strathclyde, UK

ABSTRACT

Over the past decade, electronic commerce has expanded and has provided new ways of conducting businesses in a brand new environment. Lately u-commerce seems to be pioneering the field of electronic transactions. Where 'u' stands for ubiquitous, unison, unique and universal, u-commerce offers the opportunity to users to conduct business everywhere and at any given moment in time. The simplicity of u-commerce transactions makes the issue of domain names more relevant than ever before. This chapter examines the procedural unfairness of the Uniform Domain Name Dispute Resolution Policy (UDRP) in an effort to demonstrate that the 'regulatory' framework surrounding domain names does not respect their technological necessity.

INTRODUCTION

The Internet is responsible for a significant wave of change. It introduced new ways of human and business interaction, its email and instant messaging services have dominated and substituted traditional post and other means of communication whilst commercial notions and practices have taken new dimensions. Electronic commerce has provided us with the opportunity to open up to new markets and cultures; it has helped us to exchange goods and services without the need to depend upon national or regional interests; it has allowed us to browse goods in a fast and often a more affordable way. The success of electronic commerce has attracted the attention of governments, which they currently invest money and resources to sustain and develop online transactions, but has also been responsible for technological advancements. The manifestation of these technological innovations can be found in the way commerce is currently translating business transactions.

Mobile commerce (m-commerce) has rejected the necessity of a computer and has allowed users to use their mobile telephony and the Internet to buy and sell goods. And, as if m-commerce was not enough, consumers and business are given the world of u-commerce.

U-commerce, like its predecessor m-commerce, is merely an extension of e-commerce. Where **'U'** stands for **u**biquity, **u**niqueness, **u**niversality and **u**nison, this new form of commerce aims to provide new alternatives for B2C and B2B transactions, develop a more efficient way for conducting business and increase the levels of productivity (Schapp et al, 2001). Watson et al, define u-commerce as *"the use of ubiquitous networks to support personalised and uninterrupted communications and transactions between a firm and its various stakeholders to provide a level of value over, above, and beyond traditional commerce"* (Watson et al., 2002). The four "U" – the main value drivers behind u-commerce - allow user access at any time and from anywhere (ubiquity), provide users with unique identification schemes (uniqueness), determine that mobile devices are compatible with universal standards (universality), and cover the idea that there is *"integrated data across multiple applications so that users have a consistent view on the information-irrespective of the device used"* (Watson, 2000).

The implications of this technological progression provide a new meaning to globalisation and create a chain reaction for consumers and businesses. The ease of purchase and the multitude of options create more competitive markets and provide an incentive for more businesses to acquire an online presence. This online presence is currently materialised through the Domain Name System (DNS), which ensures that entrepreneurs, start-up businesses and established brands will be visible to consumers. Domain names constitute essential features of the Internet and they have established a user-friendly system, which allows the Internet to transform into a global village that indulges the exchange of ideas, cultures, goods, services and information. With 101,214,524 registered domain names and sale revenues rising to $72,132,458, the domain name market has become one of its own.

Domain Names are the alphanumeric text strings to the right of an "@" in an e-mail address or just after the two slashes in a World Wide Web address. By practice, domain names can be mapped to a thirty-two-bid number consisting of four octets (sets of eight binary digits) that specifies a network address and a host ID on a TCP/IP network (White Paper, 1998). They have been called the "human-friendly address of a computer (WIPO, 1999). This potential "friendliness" is the source of many commercial and legal disputes, since businesses have come to realise their domain names as an important identifier, even a brand. These disputes concerning the conflicting rights of trade mark owners and domain name holders are regulated under the umbrella of the Internet Corporations for Assigned Names and Numbers (ICANN) Uniform Domain Name Dispute Resolution Policy (UDRP).

The UDPR is a self-regulated, market-oriented system that falls into the category of Alternative Dispute Resolution (ADR) prototypes and has been successful in resolving domain name disputes in an affordable and fast way. It is using the speed and easiness of the Internet to its advantage transforming the way disputes have been approached by other mechanisms of adjudication. Its creation constituted a direct order from the same White Paper (White Paper, 1998) that opened the Internet to commercial interests and created ICANN and addressed the concerns of the trade mark community concerning issues of abusive domain name registrations and cybersquatting.

The publication of the White Paper gave WIPO the opportunity to become actively involved and instigate the Domain Name Process. Rather than following the fairly modest framework illustrated in the White Paper, WIPO chose to create a system that would ultimately be highly dependent upon the UN body. Pleading the need for speed and noting that the advisory nature of the report should be sent to ICANN for any action, WIPO did not follow the normal procedure to adopt its proposals. Indeed, WIPO altered its normal consultation process, which had as an effect the limitation of the participation of governments and representatives of non-commercial interests (Froomkin, 2002, p.650).

What came out of the consultation process was the suggestion that domain name disputes had reached a *cul de sac*, something, which was also supported by some of the anecdotal evidence presented to WIPO. For example, it was asserted that "typosquatters" – who were immune from the previous dispute resolution mechanism since their registrations were not identical to a trade-marked term – were harming trade mark owners and their brands. The main problem, however, was that of cybersquatting. Cybersquatters were, amongst other things, engaged in the pattern of multiple registrations of domain names which were identical to trademarks. Trademark holders agreed that these cases represented a substantial amount of the problem they were encountering (amongst others trademark owners expressed concerns over warehousing, the practice whereby registrants were registering domain names with the sole purpose of preventing trademark owners from registering them in an attempt to sell them at the highest bidder). Similarly, there was also the problem of "reverse domain name hijacking" (RDNH), where trade mark owners by virtue of their trade mark registrations were intimidating registrants into giving up their domain name registrations. The vast majority of domain name disputes were actually harming the commercial interests of trademark owners, but most of them involved non-commercial uses of domain names (Froomkin, 2002, p.629).

Taking all these on board, and almost on its own, WIPO issued its Final Report on April 30, 1999 (WIPO, 1999). WIPO stated that its design goal was to preserve *"the right to litigate a domain*

name dispute" (WIPO, 1999). Amongst WIPO's most notable proposals – some of which echoed the White Paper – were:

- Using ICANN's influence over the DNS to impose contractual mandatory ODR to all gTLD registrars
- Limiting the scope of the disputes between trademark holders and domain name owners
- A set of rules to be followed in the dispute resolution mechanism
- A set of somewhat confused procedures to administer those dispute resolution processes
- Proposing a special framework for the protection of famous and well-known trademarks
- Not addressing the RDNH problem

After WIPO forwarded its Final Report to ICANN, the corporation began a process to examine whether to adopt it. ICANN rejected the proposal for the protection of famous and well-known marks into the UDRP, but adopted the bulk of WIPO's other proposals, albeit with some amendments (Froomkin et al, 2003). ICANN adopted in principle the UDRP and the accompanying UDRP rules in August 26, 1999, but disagreements over details of the implementing language delayed the final documents until October 24, 1999 (Froomkin, 2002, p.640).

ISSUES OF PROCEDURAL JUSTICE

Within systems of adjudication, especially ones, like the UDRP, that determine legal rights with international application, procedural justice constitutes a pivotal issue. Procedural justice is based on the rationale of availing the disputing parties with participation rights, which are essential for the legitimacy of adjudicatory procedures (Solum, 2002, p.183).

Rawls is one of the proponents of procedural justice and his thesis consists of two main principles. The first one focuses on the fact that each person engaged in an institution or affected by it has an equal right to the most extensive liberty compatible with a like liberty for all. The second one has a negative meaning and acknowledges that inequalities, as defined by the institutional structure or fostered by it, are arbitrary unless it is reasonable to expect that they exist to function to everyone's advantage, and provided that the opportunities that may be furnished are open to all. These principles regulate the distributive aspects of institutions by controlling the assignment of rights and duties throughout the whole social structure, beginning with the formation of a political framework in accordance with which they are then to be applied to legislation. In essence and in principle, distributive justice depends upon finding and formulating a correct social structure in which the fundamental system of rights and duties will be applied (Rawls, 1971, pp.60-75).

These two approaches to justice apply in the first instance to the main institutions of the social system, their arrangements and how they are combined. Such a structure will, therefore, include the political framework and the principal economic and social institutions, which, when combined, define a person's liberties and rights and influence her life prospects, what she may expect to be and her status. In this context, the intuitive idea is that the life prospects of people vary according to their position in society; under this perception, society favours certain individuals over others and these are the basic inequalities that affect life prospects. It is the nature of these inequalities – presumably unavoidable in every society – that these two principles seek to cure (Rawls, 1971, pp.60-75).

Within the socio-legal institution of the UDRP, Rawls' thesis fails to impose a web of external and internal mechanisms with the political and economic realities of trademark law providing an illusionary veil of procedural justice. Where

any adjudication system is meant to protect and ensure the equality of both parties, ICANN's Policy limits the rights of domain name holders and supports inconsistencies in a system that is meant to be uniform.

Limitation of Rights

A key feature of every system of adjudication is to guarantee that the adjudicators and the centres involved in the dispute resolution process are committed to provide incentives to the parties. This attribute is especially identified within the context of arbitration whereby parties are allowed to choose the centre, the arbitrator and the rules that will arbitrate their disputes. The UDRP, which has been modelled upon the arbitral process, lacks this incentive, at least for the domain name holders. Paragraph 4(d) of the Policy states that *"The complainant shall select the Provider from among those approved by ICANN by submitting the complaint to that Provider"* (UDRP, 1999, para. 4(f)). Moreover, in paragraph 1 of the Rules for the UDRP, a Complainant is defined as *"the party initiating a complaint concerning a domain name registration"* (UDRP Rules, 1999, para.1). Within this procedural context, respondents cannot participate as vigorously as complainants, unless they opt for a three member panel and pay half of the fees, which at least will provide them with the opportunity to acquire a more active role within the process. This restriction of legal rights for respondents is sufficient to render ICANN's system as a mechanism designed to motivate only trade mark owners and leave domain name holders inactive in a process that ultimately might affect their legal rights.

Moreover, the identify and the credentials of arbitrators constitute another controversial issue, which explains – up to a certain extent – the way the decisions are being approached. The ICANN accredited centres require their panellists to have expertise in the field of intellectual property law and especially trade mark law. The issue of adjudicators' experience is debatable even within pure arbitral processes and it is asserted that such expertise might potentially create issues of bias and unfairness affecting the outcome of disputes (Thornburg, 2007, p.47). However, within the arbitration system there are internal and external mechanisms at the disposal of the parties, which work to their benefit and are able to 'control' the arbitrators' behaviour (Dinwoodie et al, 2001, p.212). In the UDRP, though, the discretion of the centres to apply their own rules and have their own internal mechanisms allows them to employ panellists according to a set of criteria established individually by each centre. The implication of this discretion, therefore, becomes more considerable in the UDRP than in arbitration for two main reasons: first, since the legal nature of domain names still remains debatable, panellists will be inclined towards trade mark interests for the mere fact that trade marks are acknowledged as valuable property rights; and, second, ICANN's policy does not offer any pragmatic checking functions to its parties.

Nevertheless, even considering that procedural justice can control the issue of bias within the UDRP, a major concern remains because the Policy fails to provide to the parties with any guarantees as to its *modus operandi* and avail them with the opportunity to check the performance of the system. In light of the fact that ICANN's dispute resolution mechanism incorporates elements of an arbitral process as well as those of a ministerial system – the availability of court proceedings and the respect of a predetermined set of rules – one would also anticipate that the mechanism would offer its parties various safeguards. At this stage, it can be suggested that the option of the parties proceeding to court litigation works more as an illusion rather than a sensible alternative. Courts have already asserted that the UDRP cannot create binding precedent upon them and for this reason they have instructed that *de novo* review (Dan Parisi v Netlearning, Inc) would be appropriate for those cases where a UDRP panel has rendered

a previous decision. Because of this absence in internal and external checking mechanisms an alternative should be in place in order to secure the rights of the losing party and *"ensure that the rules produced in the administrative sphere fall within the original legislative mandate and do not violate the rights of individuals or other private interests"* (Lindseth, 1999, p.646).

But, it is the peculiar structure of the UDRP that complicates any potential review process by the courts, considering that they would be willing to proceed to a proper review of this dispute resolution process. The rules of the Policy allow the losing party to initiate court proceedings before a court of 'mutual jurisdiction' (UDRP, Rules, 1999, para.1) – a process that absent to an internal appeals mechanisms has been analogised with an appellate one – albeit not in its traditional sense, which, nonetheless, does not essentially have the same effect as within traditional litigation. The incongruity nature of this process is manifested in the strict ten-day period deadline that the Policy allows the losing party to initiate a court action. Although this rule applies equally for both parties, its practicalities seem to have a negative effect only for respondents. In those cases where the losing party is the complainant, the ten day deadline does not really affect her as much as it would affect the domain name holder, because she was never actually in the possession of the domain name. It is the respondent's status that changes dramatically after the cancellation and/or transfer of the domain name and it is the respondent that needs to adjust in the new state of affairs and seek to protect her rights within a ten-day timeframe. And, even though nothing prevents the respondent from proceeding to court after the ten day period has lapsed, in reality this rule works to her detriment and constitutes a reason for her to loose any incentive to litigate (Dinwoodie et al, 2001, p.204).

In order, however, to appreciate how the strict deadlines impose prohibitions on the legal rights of domain name holders, we need to understand the reality of the Internet. Its commercialisation has created fora that allow new ventures and start-up businesses to develop. Traditional means of commerce and ways of conducting business do not necessarily constitute the norm; entrepreneurial steps can be based solely on online activities and the volume of commercial endeavours based on an online presence increases rapidly. The economics of such initiatives fall outside the scope of this analysis, however, it can be suggested that the Internet has generated a whole new understanding behind commercial interests and this, of course, has a natural effect on many of the businesses' legal status. The ten-day deadline imposed through the UDRP logically works against domain name holders and entrepreneurs and prohibits them from establishing an online presence. Were the UDRP system to allow an internal appeals process and acknowledge the rights of respondents on their domain name registrations, this would definitely provide more incentives to domain name proprietors than requiring them to proceed to time-consuming and expensive court litigation.

In a similar vein, given the ambiguous status of the domain name and trademark interaction, it is still rather debatable whether domain name holders poses the ability or whether it is even advisable to proceed to court litigation. Ownership of a domain name is not necessarily interpreted the same way as ownership of a trademark and this questions the extent of legal rights that domain name holders posses. Michael Froomkin has criticised this legal gap and whether ICANN's Policy is able to provide redress and secure the rights of the respondents (Froomkin, 1999). The fact that the respondent is prohibited from initiating a UDRP action coupled with the unresolved issue of substantive justice in the context of the legal nature of domain names reinforces the limitation of rights that a domain name holder faces under the current status.

Nevertheless, the constructiveness of a uniform rule concerning the effect of traditional litigation is highly controversial especially within the context of the American jurisprudence. The Anticybersquatting Consumer Protection Act (ACPA) in the United States allows the losing party in a domain name dispute to challenge before a federal court the cancellation or transfer of the domain name on the basis that such a sanction was not legitimate under the Lanham Act. To be more precise, the Act's provision states that a court may *"grant injunctive relief to the domain name registrant, including the reactivation of the domain name or transfer of the domain name to the domain name registrant"* (ACPA, 1999 para. 1125d(v)). But, even this affordability of national law can be proven futile, if respondents cannot challenge the decision of a UDRP panel and ask the court to review it on the basis that the decision opposes principles of procedural justice. Within traditional arbitration paradigms, the New York Convention allows the losing party to challenge the arbitral award before national courts (New York Convention, 1958, art.VI). On the contrary, courts are not willing to review UDRP case law and rectify factual or procedural errors that are taking place in the course of disputes (Dinwoodie et al, 2001, p.207).

Furthermore, default cases manifest perfectly the procedural unfairness within the UDRP and the way in which the rights of respondents are repressed. ICANN's dispute resolution mechanism demonstrates a remarkable amount of case law in which domain name holders fail to respond the trademark owners' allegations. Within adjudication systems the participation of the parties is essential and adjudicators should strive towards ensuring the inclusion of all interested actors in the dispute. However, in the case of the UDRP default acts as an indicator of bad faith and the litigation proceeds as normal (UDRP, 1999, Rules, 14(b)). This interpretation causes problems at a level of collective justice, because the UDRP has evolved into a system that operates based on precedent. Even though it can be asserted that the reasons behind the domain name holder's default may hide an element of bad faith, at the same time, they might be for reasons that are more pragmatic, such as the short deadlines or the change of the respondent's address and the subsequent non-update of the domain name holder's information on the WHOIS database (WIPO, 2001, D2001-0901). This approach raises serious issues of legitimacy and transparency within the Policy and questions its ability to conform to long-standing principles of procedural justice.

Issues of Inconsistency

Procedural justice is not only concerned with the equal treatment of the parties during the adjudication process. It goes beyond that and expands to the whole adjudication system ensuring that it is built on solid ground and is able to provide guarantees as to its structure. The manifestation of procedural justice within adjudication mechanisms can, therefore, be seen in the rules that exist and cover issues of jurisdiction and choice of applicable law, internal review mechanisms, such as the existence of an appellate process, as well as the development and influence of encoded informal norms, such as netiquettes. This dual role of procedural justice serves as a 'trustmark' towards the dispute resolution mechanism and armours it with credibility. In the context of ADR where issues of credibility and trust can be proven to be the determinative factor between the success or failure of the mechanism, issues like choice of law and internal review mechanisms are offered to the parties through a matrix of contractual clauses. However, it can safely be argued that ICANN's Policy and its structure fail to adhere to this view of procedural justice.

Within this scope, Dinwoodie and Helfer (Dinwoodie et al, 2001, p.202) suspect that the way the four ICANN-accredited dispute resolution bodies impose their rules on their panellists is unjust. All four centres run under the umbrella of ICANN, are confined by the UDRP and fight the common cause of cybersquatting. It would, therefore, seem reasonable to have uniform rules

and codes of conduct that they would impose upon their panellists. Although impartiality and independence is a pre-requisite within the UDRP, the way the centres view this principle is not consistent and negates the uniformity of the mechanism. WIPO's rules make no mention to the situation where a panellist proves to be impartial (WIPO, 1999, Supplemental Rules, Rule 8); parties have the ability under NAF's rules to challenge the panellist within a tight timeframe (NAF, 2001, Rule 10(d)); and, CPR allows challenges on the basis that the party alleging bias can produce substantial evidence in support of this assertion (CPR, 2002, Supplemental Rules, Rule 9).

This inconsistency, of course, alters the perception of the parties towards the centres and has chaotic implications for the way the dispute resolution providers advertise themselves and attract trade mark owners. At the level of establishing a strong case law, this lack of uniformity may induce the four centres to start competing towards one another. Whether such serious misrepresentation of fairness will incite courts to interfere within the UDRP is unclear, however, it should, at least, invite a proper review of the current system and the practices of the dispute providers. ICANN's uncommitted approach towards its centres leaves room for Rawls' "difference principle" to arise (Rawls, 1971, pp.60-75).

As it has already been asserted, so far courts seem unwilling to review, directly or indirectly, the UDRP and provide some insight as to the level of recognition that UDRP decisions can acquire. It can be argued that the precedent of the *Dan Parisi* case discussing, amongst others, the nature and character of the Policy establishes persuasive power and demonstrates the way courts view ICANN's dispute resolution mechanism and their opposition towards the decisions it produces. At the other end of the spectrum, one might suggest that even this interpretation works as the ultimate review mechanism and can potentially provide guarantees for the system – should courts wish to scrutinise and evaluate the Policy and correct any errors. Considering that courts would be willing to provide a 'quick' fix by reviewing the UDRP, still the way court litigation is offered within the Policy is more of an illusion. The short deadlines and the expenses involved in court litigation work, in most cases, as a catalyst for domain name holders not pursuing the assistance of more traditional means of adjudication; similarly, courts show a certain degree of discomfort, which is more associated with their uneasiness to apply traditional principles of trademark law to domain name disputes.

Assuming, however, that parties do indeed opt for the court option, is the current approach, as instructed by the *Dan Parisi* court, in the position to function as an external body for the evaluation of the UDRP? *De novo* review can potentially be seen as the means that provides answers and clarifies some ambiguities surrounding the complex web of domain name disputes. Traditionally, decisions create precedent and considering that courts guarantee application of procedural justice, then this binding or persuasive nature of the decisions provides a fair amount of security. Within the UDRP body though, *de novo* review fails to provide the same security. Each case is judged on its merits and most courts abstain from commenting whether this form of international 'law-making' is acceptable. It can be argued that their silent approach demonstrates a strong will not to acknowledge ICANN's Policy as the ultimate authority to adjudicate domain name disputes. It also manifests a certain degree of scepticism over how UDRP decisions are reached and how panellists use their discretionary powers when deciding domain name cases. Therefore, the current system is almost disassociated from the dispute resolution mechanisms, even though one is supposed to compliment the other. Where arbitration is involved, for instance, courts abstain because they have acknowledged the finality of arbitral awards (New York Convention, 1958) and interfere only in those cases whereby procedural justice has been misapplied (New York Conven-

tion, 1958, art. V). This state of affairs does not occur within the UDRP and it contributes towards creating two separate sections of domain name case law—one through courts and the other through the Policy—which are often inconsistent with one another.

Under this rationale, it can be envisaged that issues of jurisdiction will play a determinative factor, preventing courts, should they would be willing to actively engage in the UDRP, from proceeding to a proper review of the mechanism. The rules of ICANN's Policy make a strong jurisdictional claim (UDRP, 1999, Rules, para. 15(a)) and allow courts that are located in the same jurisdiction with registrars and registries to adjudicate domain name disputes and indirectly develop expertise in domain name adjudication. Nevertheless, even this provision is futile and can only guarantee short term and limited solutions. Following the White Paper's mandate and ICANN's subsequent obligations to create a more competitive market within the domain name registration system, registries and registrars are multiplying and have come to develop a global market for the registration of online identifiers (Dinwoodie et al, 2001, p.208). The implications of this initiative inevitably create concerns of consistency within the UDRP case law and impose hurdles upon the construction of a unique and coherent set of rules that will allow a proper review of the mechanism by the courts. In any case, each national court is bound by national legislative processes and, to this end, it is doubtful that, under this context, courts will provide any assistance in reassessing the current structure and practices of the UDRP. Currently, it is the Eastern District of Virginia, the place where NSI is located, that acts as the pool for the UDRP case law and for those domain names that end in the .com space.

Dinwoodie and Helfer correctly assert that, although the Eastern District of Virginia, is in the process of forming a consistent case law, still it is rather questionable whether this by itself will provide any meaningful review to the mechanism.

The Eastern District of Virginia mainly deals with disputes that are consequential to domain names ending in .com, due to the fact that NSI is the sole registry of this gTLD and is located in Virginia. However, the 'A' Root has already expanded and it is anticipated that it will expand further to include gTLDs in various endings; this means that more registries and registrars will enter this competitive market and will most likely be located around the world (Dinwoodie et al, 2001, p.208). At the same time, however, how is it feasible for courts to formulate a coherent case law when the permissible scope of the domain name right is not yet established? How is it possible, by applying traditional principles of trade mark law, which vary significantly from jurisdiction to jurisdiction, to devise a set of rules that will be consistent and will penetrate any jurisdictional barriers?

National courts and domestic trade mark legislation will prohibit any attempt to enforce rules that will allow a universal domain name adjudication system to flourish outside the already established UDRP case law (Dinwoodie et al, 2001, p.209). Application of laws and their interpretation by the courts are highly national in nature and do not welcome enforcement of foreign awards apart from exceptional circumstances where the foreign award is consequential to and it derives from an authoritative body, like the decisions that are a direct result of an arbitration process. To this end, the nature of the UDRP does not provide any assistance. Its abstract character coupled with its vague and open-ended principles will negate any interference by courts. Some may view the Policy as an administrative process with no value and effect, whilst others may determine the UDRP to be an arbitral process and, subsequently, apply the principles behind the arbitral model. These irregularities deem any collaboration between the Policy and the courts an impossible task and manifest a certain amount of weakness as well as the Policy's inability to establish itself as an accredited dispute resolution system. The UDRP was meant to assist courts in the same fashion as the arbitral model; it can be suggested that at this level and with its current constitution the Policy creates more problems than cures.

With no potential external review in progress and with no internal checks the UDRP must find another way to determine its parameters and to control its adjudicators. The founding documents of the mechanism exemplify a degree of willingness to create a system for the adjudication of domain names that will adhere, comply and have the legal strength of other international dispute resolution models. At the same time though some other provisions and common practice demonstrate a worrying discretionary power afforded to panellists that will inevitably expand the Policy's initial scope (Dinwoodie et al, 2001, p.225). The strictly national character of trade marks and the need to protect them against abusive registrations of domain names, which are global in nature, could be used as the excuse for the UDRP to create a universal system and provide a model of how domain name disputes should be resolved. This might be plausible but, at the same time, is rather disconcerting considering the fact that ICANN's Policy has failed to address issues that deal with the legal nature and determine the legal rights that derive from ownership of a domain name. Similarly, the UDRP is not the venue whereby these issues should be raised and does not have the authority to create any international legal rules.

The reality is, nevertheless, that, due to lack of alternatives, the UDRP has managed to establish principles that determine the rights and legitimate interests behind domain names. With thousands of disputes being adjudicated thus far the Policy creates a notion of authority over domain names, whilst UDRP panellists are viewed as experts in deciding the conflicting rights between trade marks owners and registrants. Similarly, this wide interpretative scope afforded to panellists (by expanding the subject matter of the UDRP, which is limited to cybersquatting, there is a danger of recognising more rights of an international nature to trade marks) questions the dispute resolution mechanism itself and the authority of the panellists to render decisions and, thus, create a fair judicial system for domain names. The core of ICANN's Policy substantive issues is demonstrated in paragraph 4(a) of the Policy, which lists the circumstances that, if proven by the complainant, a UDRP panel will order transfer or cancellation of the domain name. Taken aside the rather vague principle of the "identical or confusingly similar" nature between the two identifiers [paragraph 4(i)] and the lack of clarification as to the extent of their comparison, as well as the problematic wording of "rights and legitimate interests" of paragraph 4(ii) that the domain name holder should hold, the manifestation of the discretionary power afforded to panellists is mainly found within paragraph 4(iii), where "bad faith registration and use" constitutes the last, albeit crucial, element that will allow a panel to determine the future of a domain name right (Dinwoodie et al, 2001, p.225).

It is especially the third element of paragraph 4(a) that constitutes a great deal of concern as to its interpretative approach by UDRP panellists. Bad faith is already problematic for legal theory, which, in civil law systems in particular, uses its contrast - good faith - as a principle (within civil law jurisdictions good faith is mainly used as a principle in contractual transactions, but it is not limited only to these kinds of legal relationships). And, whilst the principles of good faith are pivotal and their conceptual background is clearly defined by courts and alternative dispute resolution mechanisms (ADR), the concept of bad faith, as proven by its use in the UDRP, cannot be as clearly determined. First of all, we can identify a certain degree of willingness by the drafters of ICANN's Policy to allow panellists to interpret the 'bad faith element' based merely on assumptions than in set rules. To this end, paragraph 4(b) in its opening sentence provides that panels should examine whether one of the illustrative examples of this paragraph is applicable but, at the same time, they state that this list is not exhaustive and panels can "for the purposes... in particular but without limitation ..." determine in their own discretion"... bad faith". (UDRP, 1999, para. 4b) Secondly, the lack of any external checks does not impose any liability upon the panellists should they proceed to interpret bad faith as widely as possible in order to win, on behalf of their centres, the battle within the competitive dispute resolution market.

At this stage, it is worth providing some examples that exemplify the discretionary power that is afforded to the panels regarding the application of the bad faith element. The reason the bad faith element has generated such controversy is due to the fact that this provision is what distinguishes the UDRP from traditional trade mark litigation. Bad faith was added in the Policy with the main aim to target cybersquatters or abusive registrations in particular rather than trade mark infringement or all forms of rights to names. However, as it has already been asserted, the third element of paragraph 4(a) has been responsible for some of the most obvious abuses of procedural justice. The following examples are only illustrative of this abuse:

- **Passive holding:** The most commonly cited case, by far, is Telstra v Nuclear Marshmallows (D2000-0003). This decision established an important precedent, which applies to cases where a respondent registers a domain name and does not use it. For UDRP panels this action equates to bad faith irrespective of whether the mark is well known or not.
- **Knowingly registering a trade mark:** The so-called 'opportunistic bad faith' doctrine asserts that a domain name holder who registers a domain name that is identical or confusingly similar to a trade mark, irrespective of whether the mark in question is famous or not, is by virtue of that fact alone guilty of bad faith registration and use (D2000-0163; D2000-0226; D2000-0277).

No matter the validity of such an approach, this is a very broad dictum and can be seen as negating the two other elements of paragraph 4(a), even though it is very clear that their application is crucial for the outcome of any domain name dispute.

- **False or inaccurate contact details (D2003-0255):** This interpretation of bad faith, albeit logical to an extent, should not create binding precedent in the UDRP case law. If there were a system that could determine the intention of the domain name holder to hide his contact details with the aim to appear invisible to potential complaints then this interpretation would be justifiable. However, such a system does not exist and, thus, once again it proves that panels will go to arms length in order to establish bad faith registration and use.

- **Failing to respond to a trade mark owner's inquiries:** Some panels in their effort to find all three elements of paragraph 4(a) relevant and order the transfer or the cancellation of the domain name have determined that a domain name holder who fails to respond to a trade mark owner's inquiries is in bad faith (D2000-0030).

- **Not contributing any value to the Internet:** This perhaps is the most absurd and wide interpretation of the bad faith factor. According to this approach a respondent may be found in bad faith if *"the Respondent is contributing no value-added to the Internet and the broad community of Internet users will be better served by transferring the domain name to a party with a legitimate use for it"* (D2000-0044).

Last but not least, another pivotal issue in the context of dispute resolution mechanisms is the one concerning the sanctions these systems apply and how these are translated and enforced through decisions. Authors, like Austin, assert that the legal character of any system of adju-

dication is measured against the imposition of sanctions (Austin, 1832, p.36). When it comes to self-regulatory, market-oriented dispute resolution systems the imposition of sanctions has an informal character; their formality depends upon national courts, which possess the ultimate legal authority to recognise and enforce these through the implementation of the decisions that are rendered by dispute resolution mechanisms. To this end, substantial and procedural issues might be challenged by either of the parties, but the interference of courts ensures a degree of guarantee and fairness. The issue becomes diverse when it comes to Internet enforcement. After the ten-day period to challenge a panel decision has lapsed and considering that neither of parties challenges the decision, the ICANN centres instruct the registrar to proceed to the electronic implementation of the decision. The registrar, according to the rules, either transfers or cancels the domain name (UDRP, 1999, Policy, para. 4k).

The issue of sanctions and their appreciation within legal regimes is not only important but also essential for models that are self-regulatory in nature. Because of the vitality to produce decisions that can be recognised by courts, dispute resolution systems, such as Lex Mercatoria (In the Middle Ages, itinerant merchants, engaged in trading activities in many diverse regions in Europe, needed a common ground of law governing and regulating trade and custom that was independent and not influenced by local sovereign law. Lex Mercatoria (law of the merchant) originated from the need to ensure a minimum application of justice in commercial transactions. These laws were developed to resolve disputes that arose between merchants at trade fairs in countries that had substantial and immense differences in their local, feudal, royal and ecclesiastical laws. Generally speaking, merchant customs and laws were not regarded as part of the law of the country where the dispute arose or was adjudicated.), have produced some informal norms, in the form of netiquettes – stricto sensu. The development of these norms is acting as an 'insurance policy' towards the system's credentials, ensuring consistency and the application of justice whilst it also instructs both the parties and the adjudicators that certain actions are not allowed. Especially, restrictions in respect of the discretionary power afforded to the parties and their adjudicators for the best interests of the community is what differentiates a self-regulatory system, which courts will respect, from one that is ill-conceived and courts are not willing to acknowledge (Mangels et al, 1999). As a corollary of this, ensuring that the interests of domain name holders are protected does not constitute a pivotal issue within the UDRP and this is manifested by the way the Policy views and addresses their rights. At this point, reference should be made to the allegations against the Policy for its short deadlines when it comes to submitting a response, the fact that only trade mark owners are able to initiate a dispute, the way panels tread default cases, as well as the 10-day window frame that the losing party has to initiate a court action before ICANN enforces the decision by altering the information on the 'A' Root

We can safely reach the conclusion, therefore, that ICANN's Policy has failed to follow the paradigm set by other dispute resolution archetypes and evolve in a fashion that would allow the mechanisms to produce rules, reach decisions and impose sanctions that are in conformity with principles of substantive and procedural justice. The UDRP has failed to create a model that is neither respected nor acknowledged by national courts.

CONCLUSION

The analysis of the abovementioned ideas has gone beyond the proposition that the UDRP does not comply with principles of procedural justice; rather these analytical propositions have sought to identify the procedural unfairness of the Policy in its practical use. This is in line with the Wittgensteinian theorem behind the 'meaning as use', which suggests *"the meaning of the word is its use in the language"*(Wittgenstein, 1953, PI43). As Wittgenstein teaches us, when investigating meaning, *ergo* the subject matter within a particular community, we must "look and see" the variety of uses to which the word is put (Wittgenstein, 1953, PI66). This brief analysis follows that same rule. Our effort is to investigate the meaning of the procedural unfairness in the context of the UDRP mainly through its use over the past 10 years in order to establish that the ill-drafted rules of ICANN's Policy have the effect of limiting the rights of domain name holders and of creating inconsistencies within a system that is meant to be uniform in nature.

At this stage it can safely be suggested that resolution of the problems surrounding the Policy seem like a chimera. This, of course, is quite worrying considering how the Internet is used in various facets of commerce and the importance of domain names as a driving force behind any such commercial ventures. "Don't think but look!" (Wittgenstein, 1953, PI66) is what Wittgenstein advocates and a close examination of the operation of the Policy allows us to reach the unfortunate result that the UDRP is advancing a system where trade mark owners' rights seem to be secured at the expense of those of domain name holders; it allows us to conclude that this form of ADR lacks any guarantees, it is vague and, at best, practically absurd.

The concept of the Policy and the abusive domain name registrations that it seeks to cure are a noble cause in international dispute adjudication and address various issues that the Internet has generated, such as issues of jurisdiction and choice of law; but, it does so in a manner that creates more problems. This is manifested in the lack of alternatives for those who seem to be treated unfairly within this mechanism and are not provided with any means to become more active. Domain name owners suffer from a system that gives superiority to trade mark rights, fails to provide any incentives to either of the parties, does not have at its disposal internal (an internal appeals process) or external (finality of awards) checks and adjudicates domain name disputes in an inconsistent and unreliable way.

REFERENCES

Anscombe, & Rhees, R. (Ed.) (1953). *Philosophical Investigations*, Wittgenstein, L., Oxford: Blackwell.

Austin, J. (1956). *The province of jurisprudence determined.* Cambridge University Press.

Dinwoodie, G.B., & Helfer, L. (2001). Designing non-national systems: The case of the uniform domain name dispute resolution policy. *William and Mary Law Review, 7*, 141-274.

Froomkin, M.A. (2002). ICANN's uniform dispute resolution policy – Causes and (partial) cures. *Brooklyn Law Review, 67*(3), 608-718.

Froomkin, M.A. (1999). *A commentary on WIPO's management of Internet names and Addresses: intellectual property issues.* Retrieved April 2, 2008, from http://personal.law.miami.edu/~amf/commentary.htm

Froomkin, M.A, & Lemley, A. (2003). ICANN and antitrust. *Illinois Law Review, 1*, 1-76.

Lindseth, P.L. (1999). Democratic legitimacy and the administrative character of supranationalism: The example of the European Community. *Columbia Law Review, 99*, 628.

Mangels, A., & Volckart, O. (1999). Are the roots of the modern Lex Mercatoria really medieval? *Southern Economic Journal*, 65.

Rawls, J. (1971). *A theory of justice.* Oxford: Oxford University Press.

Schapp, S., & Cornelius, R.D. (2001). *U-Commerce, leading the new world of payments* [White paper]. Retrieved April 4, 2008, from http://www.foreshore.net/userfiles/files/Ucommerce%20whitepaper.pdf

Solum, L.B. (2004). Procedural justice. *Southern California Law Review, 78*(1), 181-322.

Thornburgh, E. (2001). Fast, cheap and out of control: Lessons from the ICANN dispute resolution process. *Journal of Small and Emerging Law*, 7.

Watson, R.T. (2000). *U-Commerce: The ultimate.* Retrieved April 4, 2008, from http://www.acm.org/ubiquity/views/r_watson_1.html

Watson, R.T., Pitt, L.F, Berthon, P., & Zinkhan, G.M. (2002). U-Commerce: Extending the university of marketing. *Journal of the Academy of Marketing Science, 30*(4), 329-343.

Conventions and Statutes

Management of Internet Names and Addresses (White Paper), (1998). *63 Fed. Reg.* 31,741

New York Convention, (1958). *Recognition and Enforcement of Arbitral Awards*, United Nations, New York.

Rules of the Uniform Domain Name Dispute Resolution Policy, (UDRP Rules), (1999). Retrieved March 13, 2008, from http://www.icann.org/en/dndr/udrp/rules.htm

Uniform Domain Name Dispute Resolution Policy (UDRP), (1999). Retrieved March 13, 2008, from http://www.icann.org/en/dndr/udrp/policy.htm

WIPO, (1999). *The Management of Internet Names and Addresses: Intellectual Property Issues* – Final Report of the WIPO Internet Domain Name Process.

Case Law

A&F Trademark, Inc. and Abercrombie & Fitch Stores, Inc. v. Gordon Rahschulte, (2001). *WIPO, D2001-0901.*

Banco Inverlat, S.A. v www.inverlat.com, (E.D. Va.2000). *112 F. Supp. 2d*, 521.

Barcelona.com, Inc. v. Excelentisimo Ayuntamiento de Barcelona, (E.D. Va. 2001), *CA-00-1412.*

Caesars World Inc. v Caesars-Palace.com, (E.D. Va. 2000). *112 F. Supp. 2d.*, 502.

Dan Parisi v Netlearning, Inc, (E.D. Va. 2001). *139 F. Supp. 2d.*, 745.

Deutsche Bank AG v. Diego-Arturo, (2000). *WIPO, D2000-0277.*

Educational Testing Service v TOEFL, (2000). *WIPO, D2000-0044.*

Excelentisimo Ayuntamiento de Barcelona v Barcelona.com, Inc., (2000). *WIPO, D2000-0505.*

Lion Nathan Limited v Wallace Waugh, (2000). WIPO, *D2000-0030.*

Telstra v Nuclear Marshmallows, (2000). *WIPO, D2000-0003.*

Parfums Christian Dior v. Javier Garcia Quintas and Christiandior.net, (2000). *WIPO, D2000-0277.*

Verio Inc. v Sunshienehh, (2003). *WIPO, D2003-0255.*

Veuve Clicquot Ponsardin, Maison Fondie en 1772 v. The Polygenix Group Co., (2000). *WIPO, D2000-0226.*

Chapter XIII
South Korea:
Vision of a Ubiquitous Network World

Jounghae Bang
Penn State University Mont Alto, USA

Inyoung Choi
Georgetown University, USA

ABSTRACT

Koreans envision a world in which anyone can access information and the tools to explore it anytime, anywhere. Korea has been one of the leaders in the mobile industry and this chapter explores the past, present and future of mobile technology and markets in Korea. Starting with background and a brief overview of the current situation, this chapter uses the CLIP framework to describe mobile services in Korea. The chapter concludes with a brief discussion of challenges and future strategies.

INTRODUCTION: VISION OF A UBIQUITOUS NETWORK SOCIETY

Koreans are dreaming of and reaching for a ubiquitous network society, or an environment where information and the tools to explore it are "always" available to "everyone" (Reynolds, Kelly, & Jeong, 2005). Along with advancing technology, Koreans' enthusiasm and efforts have brought Korea closer to this vision.

High-speed Internet service has become increasingly popular since May 1998, when it was first introduced to Korea (Jin, 2003). In that year, it was not widely used due to the high monthly fee of US$77. However, by 2001, 13.9 percent of Korea's total population subscribed to high-speed Internet, and by 2002, that number had increased to 19.2 percent, the highest among the member countries of the Organization for Economic Cooperation and Development (OECD) (OECD, 2002). By 2004, more than 75 percent of Korean households were connected to the Internet via high-speed lines, the highest broadband penetration rate by a large margin around the world (Reynolds, Kelly, &

Jeong, 2005). In 2005, Korea maintains some of the cheapest and fastest residential connections at the lowest prices in the world (Jin, 2003; Reynolds, Kelly, & Jeong, 2005).

In addition to leading the world in fixed-line Internet services, Korea has also emerged as a world *mobile* leader (Reynolds, Kelly, & Jeong, 2005). Relative to broadband Internet, mobile service got off to a slow start in 1984 due to the high expectations of customers — low cost and high quality (Jin, 2003). By 1999, however, mobile phone subscribers outnumbered fixed-line phone subscribers (Park, 2000). Korea became one of the first countries in the world to offer IMT-2000 (3G) services and CDMA services (Reynolds, Kelly, & Jeong, 2005). Moreover, Korea's mobile phone manufacturers, Samsung and LG, had the world's second and fifth largest market share in the third quarter of 2004, respectively (Goasduff, 2004).

In this chapter, the past, present and future of mobile technology and markets in Korea will be explored. We will first provide detailed background regarding broadband Internet and mobile markets in Korea. Next, we will describe some successful applications of m-commerce in Korea. After that, we will outline the Korean m-commerce sectors using the CLIP framework. Lastly, we will suggest some key lessons regarding technology, policy and stakeholder strategy.

HISTORICAL OVERVIEW

The Korean mobile market is well known as one of the most advanced in the world and boasts nearly 100 percent coverage across the peninsula. In this section, we will address the evolution of Korean mobile technology and its dynamic market.

According to Reynolds, Kelly, and Jeong (2005), mobile technology in Korea has passed through three distinct phases:

1. **Introduction of analog cellular service in Korea (1984-1994):** In March 1984, the analog mobile phone was introduced and mobile telecommunication services began (Park, 2000). Up until 1991, mobile phone subscribers were no more than 0.37 percent of the total population. The mobile phone was perceived as a luxury product, available only to high-class customers (Lee, 2003).

2. **Strong CDMA era (1995-2000):** Digital CDMA voice services (IS-95A) were launched in 1996 (Park, 2000). By October 2000, Korea had gone through IS-95B (1999) to CDMA2000 1x, which was launched that month (Reynolds, Kelly, & Jeong, 2005). Along with this advance of technology, the mobile phone market expanded noticeably (Lee, 2003), and the penetration rate grew rapidly to more than 50 percent.

3. **Focus on mobile data applications (2001 to date):** As the markets for phones and basic service have become saturated and subscription rates have slowed, focus has shifted to the development of technology that can enable mobile data applications (Reynolds, Kelly, & Jeong, 2005). Since 2002, Koreans have been enjoying third generation, IMT-2000, which has been the cornerstone of the broadband telecommunication and high-speed network (Park, 2000). In May 2002, a nationwide CDMA 2000 1x network was completed and EV-DO mobile data services were launched, and in 2004, services in the IMT-2000 2.1 GHz band and CDMA2000 1x EV-DV services were launched (Park, 2000; Reynolds, Kelly, & Jeong, 2005). WiBro services have been licensed and are ready to commercialize (Reynolds, Kelly, & Jeong, 2005).

As these technologies have evolved, the mobile market has expanded accordingly. Both the number of subscribers and the sales volumes in the mobile market have been growing. Figure 1 shows the trend in: (1) the number of mobile phone subscribers, (2) the number of mobile Internet subscribers and (3) the percentage of mobile phone subscribers who also subscribe to mobile Internet service.

First, the number of mobile *phone* subscribers has been continuously increasing. As shown in Figure 1, the penetration rate was slow during the first several years after mobile phone service started. By August 1999, however, mobile phone subscribers exceeded 20 million, and by 2002, they exceeded 30 million, about 70 percent of the population in South Korea. This number means that almost all citizens except small children and the elderly own a cellular phone. The mobile phone has become the necessary and popular means of communication for people on the move. In September 2002, mobile phone subscribers outnumbered fixed-line phone subscribers (Jin, 2003). Korea was one of the first 15 countries worldwide to make this transition (Reynolds, Kelly, & Jeong, 2005).

Second, mobile *Internet* service launched in 1999 and has become more and more popular, fueled by advanced mobile handsets and devices that are equipped with color LCD and digital cameras and allow for easy mobile Internet access (Jin,

2003). Figure 1 indicates the number of mobile Internet subscribers each year since 2000. In 2000, the number of mobile Internet users was around 16,460,000. By December 2004, the number had reached 35,016,000 (Jin, 2003).

Third, relative to the increase in mobile phone subscribers, the increase in mobile Internet service subscribers is noticeable. The number of mobile Internet subscribers accounted for only 61 percent of total mobile phone users in 2000. However, by 2004, the number of Mobile Internet subscribers was 35,016,000, accounting for 96 percent of mobile phone users.

Along with the increase in the number of mobile service subscribers, the sales volume of mobile Internet service has been continuously increasing (Jin, 2003).

Korean mobile communication service providers saw a drastic increase in the ARPU (Average Revenue per User) for wireless Internet, from 1,104 won at the end of 2000 to 2,261 won in 2001. This increase shows that the number of users and the number of use times in the wireless Internet market are growing explosively (MIC, 2002).

Figure 1. Mobile phone subscribers vs. mobile Internet subscribers

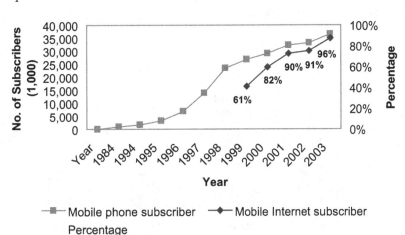

Source: Authors' integration of data from Ministry of Information and Communication, Republic of Korea, 2003; Jin, 2003.

Sales volume increased from 587.4 million won (5.7 percent of total mobile phone service sales) in 2001 to 1,168.4 million won (8.7 percent of total mobile phone service sales) in 2002 (Jin, 2003).

Korea IDC (2003) suggests that ringtones, wallpaper, character downloading, games, adult contents, Location Based Service and the multimedia messaging service have been popular applications among mobile Internet users. As shown in Figure 2, among the applications, LBS is expected to have expanded its market from 124 billion won in 2002 to 850 billion won in 2007. Along with Internet and e-commerce, m-commerce is expected to have expanded its market from 60 billion won in 2002 and 123.1 billion won in 2003 (Jin, 2003) to 2,200 billion won in 2007 (Korea IDC, 2003).

In sum, Korea has been able to develop new technology and to commercialize it. As the Korean mobile market has become saturated, data applications, rather than market penetration, have realized greater importance. The next section describes some successful mobile applications that have become everyday necessities in Korea.

SUCCESSFUL SERVICES IN SOUTH KOREA

For Koreans, a misplaced mobile phone means not only "lost a handset," but also "lost a lot." The "a lot" could include a Web browser, game console, e-wallet, house key, video camera, still camera, MP3 player and organizer, all in one (Reynolds, Kelly, & Jeong, 2005). These various mobile services have been provided successfully and have penetrated so deeply into daily life that Koreans cannot imagine a second without their cell phone in their hand.

Among many stories about successful m-commerce applications, two cases will be presented in this section, and other successful application cases will be briefly addressed in the following CLIP framework section.

In this section, the first case demonstrates how m-banking and m-payment services are provided to individual consumers, and the second case shows how businesses have used mobile services for their advertising campaigns to successfully create new business opportunities. The section concludes with a discussion of barriers to overcome for future growth.

Figure 2. Mobile data service market forecast

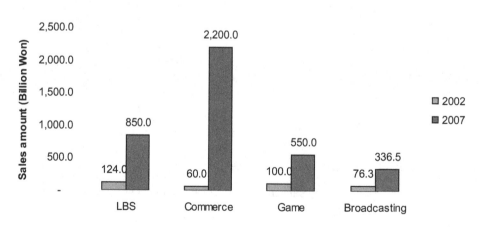

(Source: Korea IDC, 2003)

Case 1: Consumers — SKT *Moneta* (M-Payment and M-Banking)

The following two stories demonstrate how cell phones and PDAs have affected daily life in Korea.

Like many others, Mr. Lee uses his cell phone every single minute. Even when he wants to buy a snack in a convenience store, he checks his cell phone before he pays for it, because he may find a discount promotion code through his phone. When he finds one, he downloads it and shows the bar code to the store clerk. The discount coupon, in the form of a mobile bar code, is scanned and Mr. Lee can utilize the promotions. (Tao Ai Lei, 2002)

Ms. Kim realizes that today the bill for her son's school is due. However, at that very moment, she is mountain climbing with her friends. She is worried because of the high late fee, but she realizes that she has her cell phone, with which she can access a mobile banking service. Via that service, she pays the fee in one minute. (Cheil Economy, 2004, 01-02)

Even though these stories have been simplified, they demonstrate that mobile commerce is no longer in the future; it exists right now. All three mobile operators in Korea offer m-payment and banking services to bring m-commerce into daily life. We will address these services by looking at *Moneta* (m-payment) and *Nemo* (m-banking), both services of SK Telecom (SKT).

1. **Overview of SKT:** SKT is one of the largest mobile operators in Korea. It has 18 million subscribers, with a market share of 54.3 percent in September 2003 (*IT Korea*, 2003). SKT's sales have been increasing dramatically. In the first quarter of 2003, SKT's mobile Internet service sales were

26.5 billion, which was 8 percent higher than same quarter of 2002 and accounted for 13 percent of SKT's total mobile phone revenue (Jin, 2003).

2. **Overall services provided by SKT:** Their services include sweepstakes, online bulletin boards, security/stock information, humor/ gossip and online games under the brand name n.Top (Park, 2000). Additionally, they offer 2G, CDMA 2000 1x and EV-DO services under the brand name June (Jin, 2003). SKT was the first in the world to offer mobile data services over its standard CDMA network (IS-95). In October 2000, it launched its CDMA2000 1x service under the brand name Nate (Reynolds, Kelly, & Jeong, 2005). A prepaid card service called GuideCell, which offers phone-based translation of English, Japanese, Chinese and French, has been also available for tourists and visiting business delegates (Rao, 2000).

3. **SKT's *MONETA* service** (Reynolds, Kelly, & Jeong, 2005; SK Telecom, February, 2002): Since 2002, SKT has consistently introduced new services under the brand name MONETA. For example, the "Mobile Wallet Service" has more than 470,000 terminals around the country. Each terminal, which can be found easily next to a cash register, accepts payments via RFID chips embedded in mobile phones. Users simply wave their phone in front of the Moneta receiver, and the purchase is assigned to the mobile user.

Similarly, mobile phones can be used to pay for public transit: People simply scan their mobile phone over the receiver and the money is debited. This service has over one million subscribers. Refreshments from vending machines is no exception. A cellular handset can be waived in front of a vending machine to pay for drinks or snacks. Tolls can be paid automatically by just putting a mobile phone on the toll sensor (www.

sktelecom.com). Without complicated procedures or approvals, customers can buy and check a lottery ticket through their mobile phone. They simply enter the lottery Website through their cellular phone connection, then download the lottery ticket instantly, and check for winning results.

4. **SKT's NeMo (Network Money) service** (SK Telecom, 2001): This service utilizes multifunctional smart chips to store online banking information securely, and allows users to transfer money through mobile settlement banks in an almost real-time transaction (Reynolds, Kelly, & Jeong, 2005).

5. **Competitors:** "K'merce" service, offered by Korea Telecom Freetel (KFT), has over 500,000 subscribers as of 2005 (Reynolds, Kelly, & Jeong, 2005). In February 2002, KTF launched a mobile payment system and mobile coupon services. Subscribers can download a mobile barcode as a payment interface and receive discounts from various merchants in Korea. In the same year, 657,000 of their 11 million customers signed up for the K'merce initiative, with 13 services including K'merce-stock, K'merce-banking, K'merce-ticketing and K'merce-lottery (Tao Ai Lei, 2002).

LG telecom offers m-commerce transaction and payment services under the brand name "Zoop." LGT is also quickly expanding its services (Reynolds, Kelly, & Jeong, 2005).

6. **Market situation:** Since September 2003, most Korean banks have been providing basic mobile banking services such as money transfer and account inquiry through mobile telecommunication devices like mobile phones or PDAs (Cheil Economy, 2005). Korean mobile users checked their balances and made banking transactions 2.56 million times in December 2003, more than double the 1.1 million times they did so in December 2002 (*Korea Herald*, 2004). The number of mobile banking transactions during December 2004 was reported at 6.28 million, 145.4% greater than in December 2003 (Electronic News, 2005).

As shown in Table 1, the number of Internet banking subscribers in December 2004 was 24.271 million, up 6.7 percent from 2003 (Kim, 2005). Among those subscribers, there were 23 million individual users and 1 million business users. These numbers increased by 6.2 percent and 17.5 percent respectively between 2003 and 2004. Meanwhile, there were 894,000 mobile banking users in 2004, up from 189,000 in 2003. Table 2 indicates the number of transactions via Internet banking and mobile banking services.

Among the mobile banking transactions, there were 5,013,000 inquiries and 1,269,000 money transfers, up from 2003 by 130 percent and 227.6 percent, respectively. Internet banking service accounted for 29.3 percent of total banking services in 2004, a similar percentage to branch usage,

Table 1. Internet banking and mobile banking users

(Unit: 1,000)

		2003	2004
Internet Banking	Individual	21,752	23,094
	Company	1,061	1,177
	Total	22,754	24,271
Mobile Banking		189	894

Source: The Bank of Korea (January 27, 2005)

and 27.6 percent greater than CD/ATM usage (Kim, 2005). Along with the increase in Internet banking usage, the mobile banking services market is expected to reach 1,000,000 subscribers in 2007 (Cheil Economy, 2005). However, the different operating systems offered by each mobile phone carrier cause redundant efforts by content developers. This issue must be resolved for further growth.

Case 2: Businesses — Mobile Advertising

Not only do customers use mobile services successfully; many companies also use mobile services to satisfy customers. As mobile telecommunication technology has evolved, m-advertising has become an increasingly important communication tool in marketing. M-advertising is defined as any paid message sent over the mobile channel medium by a business to encourage specific people to buy products and services and to influence their attitudes, intentions and behaviors (Interactive Mobile Advertising Platform, 2003; Leppaniemi & Karjaluoto, 2004; Lee, 2003).

The increasing use of mobile phones creates an opportunity for mobile advertising agencies. Some companies have established their own subcompanies, while others have invested in shares of mobile advertising companies. Various studies have found that mass and target advertising,

interactive and immediate response, time-based marketing and location-based services are the key features of mobile advertising (Barnes, 2002; IMAP, 2003; Yunos et al., 2003).

Here, starting with an overview of key players in m-advertising in Korea, the m-advertising cases of KTF and SKT are introduced, followed by an overview of the market situation.

1. **Key Players in m-advertising:** Key players have included advertisers, m-advertising companies, media owners, traditional advertising agencies, network operators/carriers, technology providers and customers. Korean m-advertising has been driven mainly by common carriers such as SKT, KTF and LG Telecom.

2. **KTF's advertising campaign**
   a. **Overview of KTF:** KTF has 11.5 million mobile phone subscribers. With its brand Fimm (Park, 2000), KTF has been experiencing a continuous increase in its percentage of annual revenue per unit (ARPU) derived from mobile Internet. Relative to existing 2G or 1X black and white devices and 1X color devices, FIMM 1x and FIMM EV-DO devices have created higher ARPU because consumers can use these color LCD devices to enjoy more content that requires large size

Table 2. Internet and mobile banking transactions

(Unit: 1,000)

		2003	2004
Internet Banking	Inquiry	6,159	7,501
	Transfer	1,055	1,492
	Apply Loan	5.0	2.3
	Total	7,219	8,996
Mobile Banking	Inquiry	2,173	5,013
	Transfer	387	1,269
	Total	2,560	6,281

Source: The Bank of Korea (January 27, 2005)

data transferring, such as real-time broadcasting, movies or music videos (Jin, 2003).

b. **KTF's Campaign for "Anycall Land":** This campaign took place from August 30, 2002 to September 13, 2002, and advertised the launch of "Anycall Land," which is a Website for Anycall (one of the popular cell phones from Samsung) users and prospective users. KTF sent SMS messages to their 15 to 39-year-old customers who used Anycall brand handset devices, such as Anycall X4200, X5900 and X7000 phones. Message content and sending time varied according to the targeted recipients. In total, 56,021 messages were sent and only 250 messages were refused. Total respondents were 24,140, or 43.09 percent of targeted customers. This figure is higher than the click-through ratio for high-speed Internet. The success of this campaign resulted from pinpoint marketing targeted to the individual customers (www.kmobile. co.kr).

3. **AirCROSS and SKT advertising campaign:** AirCROSS, a mobile marketing company previously known as mAdnet, is a pioneer in mobile advertising, and has provided various advertising campaigns for SKT through SMS and cell broadcasting. AirCROSS has had many successful campaigns for companies such as L'Oreal, Coca-Cola, TGIF, Lotte and OB beer (www. aircross.com). One of the successful advertising campaigns was for L'Oreal Korea. L'Oreal Paris launched a new product in Korea and decided to advertise it through mobile messages. AirCross, on behalf of L'Oreal Korea, sent short messages to targeted consumers. This case has been charted in Figure 2.

The target consumers were women, aged 20 to 25, living in Kang-Nam, a relatively rich place in Seoul. Respondents of the text messages visited the TTL store, an SKT retail shop and gave a specific password to receive a free gift. Additionally, they were able to rush to the L'Oreal retail shop and receive free samples of a brand new two-way cake product.

One hundred thousand people responded to the campaign messages. Among them, 28,840 people (28.8 percent) agreed to participate in the event and 21,600 of the participants (74.9 percent) accessed WAP. This campaign aimed to get the L'Oreal brand recognized, to provide consumers with an opportunity to try a new product and to acquire a list of potential customers.

4. **Market situation:** The worldwide mobile advertising market was expected to grow rapidly, from $13 million in 2001 to $17 billion in 2003. This figure is 19.7 percent of total Internet-based advertising (OVUM, 2001).

Jeil Advertising, a major advertising agency in Korea, forecasts that the Korean fixed-line Internet advertising market has been increasing by 45.1 percent per year and will be worth 620 billion won in 2005, up from 140 billion won in 2001 (Lee, 2003). Meanwhile, the mobile advertising market in Korea has been increasing 125.6 percent annually and will be worth 336.7 billion won in 2005. The percentage of mobile advertising out of the total Internet advertising market has also been expanding, from 8.5 percent in 2001 to 35.2 percent in 2005 (Lee, 2003).

The first mobile campaigns were mainly delivered by SMS-based technology. However, with color phones becoming more popular and various representation technologies developing, MMS is expected to become a "killer application" in the mobile advertising market. MMS can deliver color pictures,

Figure 3. M-advertising process of AirCROSS

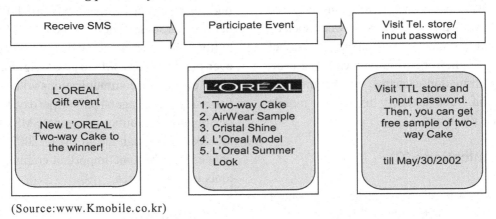

(Source:www.Kmobile.co.kr)

spectacular sound and even moving pictures. This technology, which is complemented by location tracking and customer relationship management (CRM) technology, can enlarge the advertising arena. Additionally, EMS and moving pictures will become prominent means for mobile advertising (Barnes, 2002; IMAP, 2003; Yunos et al., 2003).

5. **Issues:** Mobile advertising is still in its beginning stages. Even though the effectiveness of mobile advertising is widely understood, random advertising transmission can cultivate the perception that mobile advertising is spam. Thus, users should approve advertising message transmission before it actually takes place. Incentives can play an important role in inducing that approval. A survey conducted by Ovum (2000) showed that 70 percent of respondents would accept mobile advertising once an incentive, such as an event invitation, free drink or meal coupon, is offered.

Another barrier for mobile advertising is that advertising agents and advertisers may not realize returns on their investments. This is because revenues from m-advertising are still relatively low, and investment in m-advertising, as well as the numbers of the major agents, is still relatively small. Consequently, the quality of m-advertising content has been low and the market has grown slowly. Once the potential growth becomes more certain, more players will participate in m-advertising, and the market will grow quickly (Yoo, 2001).

Privacy is another hurdle to overcome before mobile advertising can expand. The reason that mobile phone users are reluctant to expose their telephone number is mostly to prevent privacy intrusion and increased spam messages. Since users are exposing their telephone number directly to the content providers, content providers or carriers can easily access the user's personal information and are able to give or sell this information to others. Regulation and policies can ensure privacy protection and thus can induce more users (Yoo, 2001).

VIEWING KOREA'S MOBILE SECTOR IN THE CLIP FRAMEWORK

Korean mobile operators and handset manufacturers, along with the government, envision a society where mobile phones replace keys, wallets, credit cards and remote controls for all the users' appliances (Reynolds, Kelly, & Jeong, 2005). Starting with SKT's *Nate* service, many of these replacement services have become available over the 3G network in Korea, taking one step further toward the ubiquitous network society. M-commerce sectors can be categorized under the CLIP framework: Communication, Locatability, Information exchange and Payment. In this section, each category in Korean mobile services is discussed.

Communications (C)

In South Korea, wireless instant messaging, one of the main services offered by mobile Internet providers, has played an important role in the expansion of communication. Messaging services have evolved from Short Message Service (SMS) to Enhanced Message Service (EMS) to Multimedia Message Service (MMS). SMS is the second most popular service, following voice service, among cell phone services. The increasing use of SMS and instant messaging has created new business opportunities like mobile advertising (as shown in the previous section). Mobile messaging service companies such as Mfreei, Sure.com and Mobitel organize SMS advertising campaigns. Advertisers can directly request mobile advertising through these companies, or can indirectly advertise by partnering with traditional advertising agencies (Ahn, 2003). Furthermore, people can get discounts by presenting coupons they downloaded on cellular phones using SMS from the Websites of affiliated stores or restaurants.

Mobile message services have expanded the range of communication in South Korea. Messages can be sent and received among peers, friends and sweethearts at anytime and anywhere, but recently it has grown to include parents and other elders. Youngsters use SMS to contact their parents who live in other cities and send their regards in that way. It has created a new mobile culture for members of the younger generation, who are called "Thumb Talkers." They spend a large part of their daily life pressing the cellular phone buttons with their thumbs. The speed of button pressing can be as fast as or faster than high speed typing on a PC keyboard. It is hard to believe that some "Thumb Talkers" can press the buttons 300 times per minute (MIC, 2002). Now, even professors use SMS to give assignments and carry out simple communications with students. Currently, an average 64 million per day, 1.9 billion per month and 23 billion per year of SMS messages are floating through the air (MIC, 2002). Mobile phones have become important communication tools in South Korea.

Locatability (L)

The locatability of the mobile phone can be utilized in many ways. A location-based service can immediately locate a user's mobile handset within 10 meters of boundaries using a Global Positioning System (GPS) if the user presses a button on the mobile phone. Customers can use their phones to seek the best and shortest way to a desired destination, and can also be provided all kinds of traffic information through the mobile Internet. They can also get help in an emergency by calling the police on patrol nearby. This service can also help to search for lost children and to protect the elderly.

SKT provides the "Finding Friends" service (SK Telecom, July 2002), which for 80 won per service shows the exact location of a subscriber. Since this service began in 2000, 1.44 million users have subscribed to it. LG telecom has a similar service, which sends the registered requester's location as a text message over certain time intervals.

Location-based services can be combined with other services to generate a synergy effect. These services can complement mobile advertising, which has enjoyed higher rates of response when combined with location-based services. For example, electronic coupons can be sent to people who are hanging around a specific store or store department. Additionally, information on insurance policies can be sent to people who have just arrived at an airport (Ahn, 2003).

According to Ahn (2003), in addition to friend-finding and coupon distribution, telematics has received a lot of attention. Koreans are keenly interested in telematics, or the merger of automobile and mobile communication technologies (Reynolds, Kelly, & Jeong, 2005). Automobiles have become prominent mobile e-service platforms, and telematics has been applied to new services such as remote door locking systems, remote diagnosis and emergency message delivery, in addition to the original positioning and navigation functions. Using Global Positioning System (GPS), navigation services with basic functions like emergency rescue will evolve into dynamic navigation services that will allow users to determine their exact location by providing maps, road guides and information on regions (Ahn, 2003).

Several Korean car manufacturers already have been building telematic systems into their new models (Reynolds, Kelly, & Jeong, 2005). Renault-Samsung has started installing its SM5 telematic technology into its vehicles, while Hyundai Kia has been selling luxury cars such as the Grandeur XG, EF Sonata and Regal with telematics systems preinstalled. These systems have become standard features on mid-range cars in 2005.

In Korea, the telematics market is expected to grow 30 percent every year through 2006. Telematics systems are expected to increase from 4,300,000 in 2000 to 22,130,000 in 2006. The devices market is expected to grow an average of 28.4 percent per year, from 5,310,000 in 2000 to 25,320,000 in 2006. In terms of related services, basic navigation systems have expanded their market from 2,360,000 in 2001 to an expected 4,640,000 in 2006. Although these numbers indicate an average increase of only 14.4 percent per year, dynamic navigation systems, on the other hand, expect a 43.9 percent average increase rate per year, and multifunctional multimedia is

expected to increase 37 percent per year (Ahn, 2003). SKT, KTF and LGT have declared their entry into telematics (Reynolds, Kelly, & Jeong, 2005).

Information (I)

Mobile services can put information about the stock market, personal bank accounts, current events and movies in the palm of your hand. For example, before deciding which movie to see, people can check their PDAs or cell phones first to browse schedules, theater locations and movie lists, and can even purchase tickets for the movies they choose. In a 2002 survey, people who did not use mobile Internet responded that they wanted to use mobile Internet services for travel/traffic information, news searches, information regarding their current location and destination and location information for other people (KRNIC, 2002). The usage rate for information searches via mobile Internet was around 10 percent in 2002, while the usage rate for entertainment such as character, melody downloading and games was 60 percent in 2002. However, information exchange on location, traffic, travel, banking, the stock market and e-books has been increasing while usage for entertainment has been decreasing proportionally (Korea Internet Information Center, 2003).

New applications include enhanced messaging service (EMS) and multimedia messaging service (MMS), which enable users to download images, streaming video and data files. By using the IMT-2000 network, users can enjoy the vivid and clear picture of a DVD player through the cellular phone. Moreover, large volume data such as music videos, cartoon movies and mp3 music files can be sent and received at a high-speed.

Payment (P)

Mobile phones have become new tools for payment. Mobile phones can be used not only to purchase products online or offline, but also to pay for mobile transactions. Moreover, account inquiry and money transfer services are also available through cell phones. The Korean mobile payment market is expected to be 120 billion won in 2007 (see Table 3).

High-speed data networks, such as 2.5 and 3G, with more sophisticated data-enabled wireless devices, have the potential to transform payment. Color screens, greater bandwidth and more compelling content are converging to create an environment where consumers feel more comfortable transacting on the move.

Mobile payment (m-payment) is expected to improve customers' convenience enormously and to expand the online commerce market by providing mobility and accessibility. M-payment, a new payment system, has huge potential to displace a considerable portion of the current payment system (Kim, Yoo, & Oh, 2003).

M-payment can be used not only for online transactions but also for any transaction at a brick-and-mortar retailer. Procedures necessary for m-payment, such as user identity confirmation, delivery of transaction information and transfer of payment itself, are administered either partly online or completely online. M-payment service has been made available in the following ways: (1) adding the payment amount to mobile service bill; (2) buying prepaid m-payment products; and (3) connecting the payment service to the credit card company (Kim, Yoo, & Oh, 2003).

Overall, Korea's mobile industry has been reviewed based on the CLIP framework, and in each category, technology and its applications have been reviewed. In each category of the CLIP framework, it was found that Koreans have been utilizing m-commerce services and technologies. Furthermore, many m-commerce services involve a combination of the C-L-I-P features: communication, locatability, information and payment. Further opportunities for m-commerce services can be generated and developed by investigating the combination of the CLIP features.

ADDITIONAL REFLECTIONS ON SOUTH KOREA'S MOBILE SECTOR

In this section, some additional issues will be discussed, including the role that government can play for fast growth of mobile communication technology, and the social and cultural changes that have resulted from the emergence of this technology. Also, a spin-off of the advanced mobile technology will be addressed.

The Korean government has identified Information Technology, especially mobile telecommunications, as a key strategic industry for the coming decades. In December 1994, the Ministry of Post and Telecommunications (MPT) was expanded in size and administrative function to become the Ministry of Information and Communication (MIC). Newer wireless technologies including Wi-Fi are also spreading as a result of the Korean government's "u-Korea" (or ubiquitous Korea) project (Yang, 2003; Castells et al., 2004).

Table 3. Mobile payment market forecast (2002 ~ 2007)

(Unit: 10 billion won)

Year	2002	2003	2004	2005	2006	2007	GAGR
Mobile payment	230	490	810	1,329	1,798	2,120	55.9%
Mobile data market	1,330	2,260	3,643	4,797	6,024	6,998	39.4%
Ratio	17.3%	21.7%	22.2%	27.7%	29.8%	30.3%	

Source: IDC (2003)

The government's most important contributions have been its liberalization of the market and its encouragement of experimentation with new technologies and services. Currently, the government is also planning "m-government," which aims to allow people to access administrative materials and obtain public services through mobile services (Castells et al., 2004).

The spread of mobile phones has also strengthened traditional networks in South Korea, such as families, friends and co-workers. Yoon's study of "mainstream" high school students in Seoul argues that mobile phones help reinforce the traditional Confucian notion of affinity among teenagers. Therefore, mobile communication keeps them within the existing structures of family, school and peer groups (Yoon, 2003). At the workplace, large conglomerates use mobile technologies to control their distributed workforce, from salespersons to truck drivers. One example is the n-Zone service in use in Samsung Electronics, where workers get automatic forwarding of fixed-line phone calls to their mobile phones when they are away from their desks. To reach their colleagues, they only need to dial the last four digits on their handsets as if they were using traditional wired intra-organizational networks. Samsung Electronics and KTF jointly developed this mobile work phone system. Workers subscribing to n-Zone can call their co-workers and use wireless Internet with no limitation, and the cost is merely $1 per month. While this service is still in an initial stage of development, it is becoming popular among corporations due to its potential to improve work efficiency at low costs (Ha, 2002; Castells et al., 2004).

As shown previously, m-commerce and networks penetrate deep into daily life, everything seems to be linked, and m-commerce services can become more personalized. Even though technology and m-commerce services have moved closer to the vision of a ubiquitous networked society, these services have posed some problems, especially privacy invasion. Since the Internet has become popular, customers have become more concerned about privacy (Krishnamurthy, 2000; Johnson, Bellman, & Lohse, 2002). The number of unwanted text messages and phone calls via mobile phones in South Korea surpasses that of desktop spam mail. Korea Information Security Agency (Kim, 2004) reported that the amount of mobile spam is exponentially growing from 4,864 cases in 2002 to 36,013 in 2003 and 244,151 in the first 10 months in 2004. The unwanted messages cost computer users precious time and effort, and usually carry sexual content, fanning concerns about the influence on youth.

In addition to the messages that are sent, the collection of customer information without customer consent generates concerns. In particular, m-commerce services, which can generate customer location information in real time, can be threatening to customers. Therefore, permission-based marketing will be essential (Ahn, 2003). Sending out commercial messages to, or collecting data about, customers with neither their permission nor the right targeting will turn existing customers against the businesses. Newell (2003) argues that the businesses should let customers manage the relationships, rather than try to manage customers. Thus, mobile Internet and m-commerce offer great potential, but further investigation and careful strategy will be required.

TECHNOLOGICAL AND MANAGERIAL LESSONS FROM KOREA'S MOBILE EXPERIENCE

The Korean mobile Internet market has entered a growth stage, as the total market value of Korean m-commerce is expected to reach over 4 trillion won in 2007 (IDC Korea, 2003). Many mobile applications such as m-payment, m-banking, m-trading and m-advertising have succeeded as described. The main reason for the dramatic growth of mobile commerce in Korea has been the high-speed mobile network infrastructure. Korea already has begun to provide service for

CDMA 2000 1x, CDMA EVDO, 2G network bandwidth and IMT-2000. This telecommunication infrastructure makes it possible to provide various mobile services. Sooner or later, CDMA 1X EVDO service, which has been provided as "June" or "Fimm," will be able to provide the same services as wired Internet. However, several issues still remain unresolved and Lee (2002) has raised some issues for further development.

Network Openness

The mobile network becomes an important technical goal for enlarging the mobile commerce industry. Mobile contents, including mobile portal, gateway and payment systems that were previously dominated by mobile network carriers such as SK Telecom, KTF and LG Telecom, will be provided by mobile content providers as well as Internet content providers. Thus, SK telecom begins to allow content providers to use their mobile network in 2003 (Song, 2004). It is expected that Internet portals like Daum or Yahoo!, mobile information service providers or content providers (CP companies) will enter the network market and compete with existing mobile telecommunication providers. Furthermore, a greater variety of mobile content can be provided to the users. However, network openness has a negative aspect. Some unwanted messages that have been blocked by telecommunication providers may be transferred to mobile phone users, especially to adolescents (Lee, 2002).

Wireless Standardization

For mobile commerce, technology such as platforms, LBS, keypads and so on must be standardized. For example, without a standard application platform, content providers have to develop different versions of content depending on the telecommunication device. The Korea Wireless Internet Standardization Forum and Electronics and the Telecommunications Research Institute

have developed a standard for mobile device interoperation.

This standard, known as "Wireless Internet Platform Interoperability," was developed based on technology acquired from network providers, contents providers and device makers. In May 2002, the Telecommunication Technology Association enacted this standard. Standardization provides great benefits to all stakeholders. For network providers, various contents can be provided and can lead to higher customer satisfaction. Device makers can decrease the time and effort to develop new devices. Furthermore, content providers can spend less time and effort creating mobile content and can supply one format of content to every network provider (Lee, 2002).

Mobile Certification

Payment through mobile telecommunication requires mobile certification for the payer. SKT started the first worldwide mobile public certification service, which was co-developed with Korea Securities Computer Co. in August 2004 (SK Telecom, 2004). It offers public certification only available online through the mobile Internet. This service is expected to strengthen the reliability, usefulness and security of mobile services such as public documentation, insurance contracts and payments. Since mobile certification service will start with the Korea Information Certification Authority, which is a licensed certification authority, the mobile market will grow (Lee, 2002).

Government Support

Positive government commitment to support mobile commerce is required because many technical issues are closely related to governmental policy and strategy. For example, the Korean government has hosted a formal meeting with carriers and banks to discuss standards, and has proliferated mobile commerce by developing public m-payment systems for taxes and other public charges. Additionally, the government has invested a lot of money to support the research and development of mobile Internet telecommunication networks, telecommunication devices, contents and solutions. Its investment amount increased from 2.7 billion won in 2000 to 20 billion won in 2001 (Lee, 2002).

Even though Korea's mobile commerce frontier has been growing by leaps and bounds, many issues remain, such as pricing, contents and policy. To develop more creative and lucrative business models, the cooperation of related stockholders is required.

QUESTIONS FOR DISCUSSION

1. What factors were responsible for South Korea's rapid emergence as a top mobile communications and m-commerce country?
2. "Moneta" and "Nemo" were profiled as two mobile payment and m-commerce services that are already successful in South Korea. What factors account for the success of these? Are such successes transferable to Western mobile telecom markets? Why or why not?
3. What barriers and problems stand in the way of further development of m-commerce in South Korea? What steps do you recommend to overcome these barriers and problems?

REFERENCES

Ahn, J.H. (2003). *Issues of Mobile Business and Tele Communication Technologies*. Seoul, Korea: Seoul National University Electronic Commerce Resource Center.

AirCross Homepage. (2005). Retrieved July 20, 2005, from http://www.aircross.com

Barns, S. J. (2002). Wireless digital advertising: Nature and implications. *International Journal of Advertising, 21*, 399-420.

Castells, M., Fernandez-Ardevol, M., Qiu, J. L., & Sey, A. (2004). *The mobile communication society: A cross-cultural analysis of available evidence on the social uses of wireless communication technology*. University of Southern California Press.

Cheil Economy. (2005). *Digital innovation: Banking service series part 2. Jung, S*. Retrieved January 15, 2005, from http://www.jed.co.kr/SITE/data/html_dir/2005/01/02/200501020039.asp

Electronic News. (2005, Jan 27). Increased Internet banking usage. *Electronic New*. Retrieved from http://www.etnews.co.kr/news/detail.html?id=200501260143

Goasduff, L. (2004). *Gartner reports worldwide mobile phone sales grew 26 percent in the third quarter of 2004*. Retrieved June 10, 2005, from http://www.gartner.com/press_releases/asset_115121_11.html

Ha, J. Y. (2002, Jan 16). Diffusion of the use of cell phones as internal office phones (in Korean). *Joongang Ilbo*.

International Cooperation Agency for Korea IT (2003, Nov). Data bank. *IT Korea Journal, 4*.

Jin, J. Y. (2003). Strategy for Korea mobile market promotion — Based on Chasm theory. *Korea Association for Telecommunication Policies, 15*(13), 2-32.

Johnson, E. J., Bellman, S., & Lohse, G. L. (2002). Defaults, framing and privacy: Why opting in-opting out. *Marketing Letters, 13*(1), 5.

Kim, H. S., Yoo, K.J., & Oh, K.H. (2003). *Trends in mobile payment market and issues in policy*. Korea Information Strategy Development Institute ISSUE REPORT 3-19.

Kim, M. J. (2005, Jan 27). Fast growing mobile banking. *Digital Time*s.

Kim, T-G. (2004). Mobile spam outnumbers desktop's. *The Korea Times.* Retrieved July 20, 2005, from http://times.hankooki.com/lpage/200412/kt2004122116324753460.htm

Kmobile News. (n.d.). Retrieved February 15, 2005, from http://www.kmobile.co.kr

Korea Herald (2004). *Mobile banking transactions doubled in 2003.* Retrieved February 2005, from http://www.koreaherald.co.kr

Korea IDC. (2003). *Korea mobile data service market forecast and analysis 2002-2007*, p. 5.

Korea Internet Information Center. (2003). *Survey on wireless Internet usage.* p. 8.

Korea Network Information Center (KRNIC). (2002). *Survey on the usage of wireless Internet (summary report).* p. 9.

Krishnamurthy, S. (2000). Permission marketing: Turning strangers into friends, and friends into customers. *Journal of Marketing Research, 37*(4), 525.

Lee, S. M. (2002). *Direction of the policy for m-commerce.* Retrieved February 22, 2005, from http://agent.itfind

Lee, Y. J. (2003). *Understanding m-commerce and analyzing its services.* Seoul, Korea: Seoul National University Electronic Commerce Resource Center (ECRC).

Leppaniemi, M., Karjaluoto, H., & Salo, J. (2004). The success factors of mobile advertising value chain. *E-Business Review, (IV)*, 93-97.

Ministry of Information and Communication (MIC). (2002). *IT Korea Guide.* Retrieved June 2005, from http://www.mic.go.kr/eng/res/res_pub_itk_2002_dec.jsp

OECD. (2002). Working party telecommunication and information service policies: Broadband access for business. *OECD.* Retrieved from http://www.olis.oecd.org/olis/2002doc.nsf/43bb6130e5fc1269fa005d004c/a963ab2ca9617affc1256c85005d7190/$FILE/JT00136306.PDF

Ovum. (2000). *Wireless Internet: Opportunity and threat.* London: OVUM.

Ovum. (2001). *OVUM Forecast: Global Mobile Markets 2001-2005.* London: OVUM Ltd.

Park, K-Y. (2000). A study on the competition strategies on m-commerce in Korea. *Global Commerce and Cyber Trade, 3*(1), 25-43.

Rao, L. (2002). *South Korea aims for global leadership in wireless, broadband Internet markets in information age.* Retrieved February 2005, from http://www.inomy.com

Reynolds, T., Kelly, T., & Jeong, J-K. (2005, April 6-8). Ubiquitous network societies: The case of the republic of Korea. *ITU New Initiatives Programme*, Geneva.

SK Telecom. (2001). Retrieved November 5, 2001, from http://www.sktelecom.com/kor/cyberpr/press/1183403_3261.html

SK Telecom. (2002, February). Retrieved February 4, 2002, from http://www.sktelecom.com/kor/cyberpr/press/1183603_3261.html

SK Telecom. (2002, July). Retrieved July 29, 2002, from http://www.sktelecom.com/kor/cyberpr/press/1188252_3261.html

SK Telecom. (2004). Press release dated August 3. Retrieved July 25, 2005, from http://www.sktelecom.com/kor/cyberpr/press/1194806_3261.html

Song, W. J. (2004). *Press release dated February 15.* Retrieved July 25, 2005, from http://www.zdnet.co.kr/news/network/0,39031016,10067682,00.htm

Tao, A.L. (2002). *KTF takes on m-commerce with e-coupons.* Retrieved January 2005, from http://www.asiatele.com/printarticle.cfm?artid=15534

Yang, S. J. (2003, Jan 20). Korea pursuing global leadership in info-tech industry. *The Korea Herald.*

Yoo, J.-K. (2001). *Current status and implication of mobile advertising, information, and communications policy report, 13*(14). Korea Information Strategy Development Institute.

Yoon, K-W. (2003). Retraditionalizing the mobile: Young people's sociality and mobile phone use in Seoul, South Korea. *European Journal of Cultural Studies, 6*(3), 327-343.

Yunos, H. M., Gao, J. Z., & Shim, S. (2003). Wireless advertising's challenges and opportunities. *IEEE Computer, 36*(5), 30-37.

Chapter XIV
Key Issues in Mobile Marketing:
Permission and Acceptance

Stuart J. Barnes
University of East Anglia, UK

Eusebio Scornavacca
Victoria University of Wellington, New Zealand

ABSTRACT

The growth and convergence of wireless telecommunications and ubiquitous networks has created a tremendous potential platform for providing business services. In consumer markets, mobile marketing is likely to be a key growth area. The immediacy, interactivity, and mobility of wireless devices provide a novel platform for marketing. The personal and ubiquitous nature of devices means that interactivity can, ideally, be provided anytime and anywhere. However, as experience has shown, it is important to keep the consumer in mind. Mobile marketing permission and acceptance are core issues that marketers have yet to fully explain or resolve. This chapter provides direction in this area. After briefly discussing some background on mobile marketing, the chapter conceptualises key characteristics for mobile marketing permission and acceptance. The chapter concludes with predictions on the future of mobile marketing and some core areas of further research.

INTRODUCTION

The proliferation of mobile Internet devices is creating an extraordinary opportunity for e-commerce to leverage the benefits of mobility (Chen, 2000; Clarke, 2001; de Haan, 2000; Durlacher Research, 2002; Evans & Wurster, 1997; Kalakota & Robinson, 2002; Siau & Shen, 2003; Yuan & Zhang, 2003). Mobile e-commerce, commonly known as m-commerce, is allowing e-commerce businesses to expand beyond the traditional limitations of the fixed-line personal computer (Barnes, 2002a; Bayne, 2002; Clarke, 2001; Lau, 2003; Siau & Shen, 2003; Sigurdson & Ericsson, 2003). According to a study by Telecom Trends International (2003), global revenues from m-commerce could grow from $6.8 billion in 2003 to over $554 billion in 2008.

Mobile commerce has a unique value proposition of providing easily personalized, local goods and services, ideally, at anytime and anywhere (Durlacher Research, 2002; Newell & Lemon, 2001). Due to current technological limitations, some problems, such as uniform standards, ease of operation, security for transactions, minimum screen size, display type, and the relatively impoverished web sites, are yet to be overcome (Barnes, 2002b; Clarke, 2001).

As each mobile device is typically used by a sole individual, it provides a suitable platform for delivering individual-based target marketing. This potential can improve the development of a range of customer relationship management (CRM) tools and techniques (Seita, Yamamoto, & Ohta, 2002). It is believed that in the near future marketing through the mobile phone will be as common a medium as the newspaper or TV. However, mobile marketing is unlikely to flourish if the industry attempts to apply only basic online marketing paradigms to its use; the medium has some special characteristics that provide quite a different environment for ad delivery, including time sensitivity, interactivity, and advanced personalization. Moreover, a key tenet is likely to be that consumers receive only information and promotions about products and services that they want or need; one of the most important aspects to consider is that wireless users demand packets of hyperpersonalized information, not scaled-down versions of generic information (Barnes, 2002c). Sending millions of messages to unknown users (known as spam) or banner ads condensed to fit small screens (Forrester Research, 2001) are doubtless unlikely to prove ideal modes of ad delivery to a captive mobile audience.

This chapter aims to explore the peculiarities of mobile-oriented marketing, focusing on issues of permission and acceptance, and some of the possible business models. The following two sections provide a basic review of the technological

platform for mobile marketing and an introduction to marketing on the mobile Internet (focusing on advertising), respectively. The fourth section presents a conceptual definition and model for permission on mobile marketing applications, while section five provides a model for mobile marketing acceptance and examines a number of possible scenarios for mobile marketing, based on the previous analysis. Finally, the chapter rounds off with some conclusions, and further research questions, and provides some predictions on the future of wireless marketing.

THE TECHNOLOGICAL PLATFORM FOR MOBILE MARKETING

Kalakota and Robinson (2002) define mobile marketing as the distribution of any kind of message or promotion delivered via a mobile handset that adds value to the customer while enhancing revenue for the firm. It is a comprehensive process that supports each phase of the customer life cycle: acquisition, relationship enhancement, and retention. A variety of technological platforms are available to support mobile marketing. Here we describe briefly some of the principal components. (For a more detailed discussion, see Barnes [2002b, 2002c].) The m-commerce value chain involves three key aspects of technology infrastructure:

- **Mobile transport.** Current networks have limited speeds for data transmission and are largely based on second-generation (2G) technology. These "circuit-switched" networks require the user to dial up for a data connection. The current wave of network investment will see faster, "packet-switched" networks, such as General Packet Radio Service (GPRS), which deliver data directly to handsets, and are, in essence, always connected. In the near future, third-generation

(3G) networks promise yet higher transmission speeds and high-quality multimedia.

- **Mobile services and delivery support.** For marketing purposes, SMS (a text-messaging service) and WAP (a proprietary format for Web pages on small devices) are considered the key platforms in Europe and the United States, with iMode (based on compact hypertext markup language or cHTML) and iAppli (a more sophisticated version of iMode based on Java) taking precedence in Japan (WindWire, 2000). For PDAs, "Webclipping" is often used to format Web output for Palm or Pocket PC devices.

- **Mobile interface and applications.** At the level of the handset and interface, the brand and model of the phone or PDA are the most important part of the purchase decision, with "image" and "personality" being particularly important to young customers (Hart, 2000).

The next section explores the possibilities and experiences of using wireless marketing on these technology platforms.

MARKETING ON THE WIRELESS MEDIUM

The wireless Internet presents an entirely new marketing medium that must address traditional marketing challenges in an unprecedented way (WindWire, 2000). Key industry players in the value chain providing wireless marketing to the consumer are agencies, advertisers, wireless service providers (WSPs), and wireless publishers. For agencies and advertisers, the wireless medium offers advanced targeting and tailoring of messages for more effective one-to-one marketing. For the WSP, the gateway to the wireless Internet (e.g., British Telecom, AT&T, and Telia-Sonera), wireless marketing presents new revenue streams and the possibility of subsidizing access.

Similarly, wireless publishers (e.g., the *Financial Times, New York Times*, and CBS Sportsline), as a natural extension of their wired presence, have the opportunity for additional revenue and subsidizing access to content. At the end of the value chain, there is potential for consumers to experience convenient access and content value, sponsored by advertising (Kalakota & Robinson, 2002; WindWire, 2000).

Like the wired medium, marketing on the wireless medium can be categorized into two basic types: push and pull, which are illustrated in Figure 1. *Push* marketing involves sending or "pushing" advertising messages to consumers, usually via an alert or SMS (short message service) text message. It is currently the biggest market for wireless advertising, driven by the phenomenal usage of SMS—in December 2001, 30 billion SMS messages were sent worldwide (Xu, Teo, & Wang, 2003). An analysis of SMS usage has shown unrivalled access to the 15 to 24 age group—a group that has proved extremely difficult to reach with other media (Puca, 2001).

Pull marketing involves placing advertisements on browsed wireless content, usually promoting free content. Any wireless platform with the capacity for browsing content can be used for pull advertising. WAP and HTML-type platforms are the most widely used. Japan has experienced positive responses to wireless pull marketing, using iMode. Interestingly, wireless marketing in Japan has more consumer appeal than marketing on the conventional Internet. Click-through rates for mobile banner ads during the summer of 2000 averaged 3.6%, whilst those for wireless e-mail on iMode averaged 24.3%. Click-through rates for online banner ads on desktop PCs in Japan often average no more than 0.5 or 0.6% (Nakada, 2001).

Overall, current push services are very much in the lower left-hand quadrant of Figure 1. Until the availability of better hardware, software, and network infrastructure, services will remain basic. With faster, packet-based networks and more

Figure 1. Categorization of wireless marketing—with examples (Barnes, 2002c)

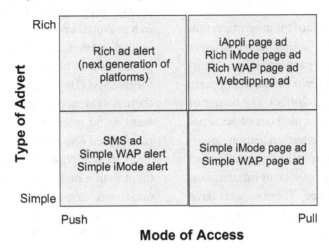

sophisticated devices, protocols and software, richer push-based marketing is likely to emerge, pushing the possibilities into the top left-hand quadrant.

PERMISSION ISSUES FOR MOBILE MARKETING APPLICATIONS

The discussion above has provided some insights about mobile marketing, particularly in terms of the wireless technological platform and basic applications of the medium. However, as yet, we have provided little conceptual discussion. The purpose of this section is to discuss the key variables of mobile marketing and present a conceptual model of permission for applications on this field.

In order for mobile marketing to reach its full potential of personalized information available anytime, anyplace, and on any device, it is necessary to understand the key characteristics of the mobile medium involved. We believe that any mobile marketing application should contemplate the following aspects:

- **Time and Location.** Although two different aspects, we consider them strongly related. An individual's behavior and receptiveness

to advertisement is likely to be influenced by their location, time of day, day of week, week of year, and so on. Individuals may have a routine that takes them to certain places at certain times, which may be pertinent for mobile marketing. If so, marketers can pinpoint location and attempt to provide content at the right time and point of need, which may, for example, influence impulse purchases (Kannan, Chang, & Whinston, 2001). Feedback at the point of usage or purchase is also likely to be valuable in building a picture of time-space consumer behavior.

- **Information.** In particular, data given a context by the user. By itself, data do not contain an intrinsic meaning. It must be manipulated appropriately to become useful. Therefore, information can be defined as the result of data processing, which possesses a meaning for its receiver. Murdick and Munson (1988) point out that quantity of data does not necessarily result in quality of the information. The most important thing is what people and organizations do with the information obtained and its ability of extraction, selection, and presentation of information pertinent to the decision-making process should be considered as a decisive factor.

- **Personalization.** One of the most important aspects to consider is that wireless users demand packets of hyperpersonalized information, not scaled-down versions of generic information (Barnes, 2002c). The nature of the user, in terms of a plethora of personal characteristics such as age, education, socio-economic group, cultural background and so on is likely to be an important influence on how ads are processed. These aspects have already proven to be important influences on Internet use (OECD, 2001), and as indicative evidence has shown above, elements such as user age are proving an important influence on mobile phone usage. The wireless medium has a number of useful means for building customer relationships. Ubiquitous interactivity can give the customer ever more control over what they see, read, and hear. Personalization of content is possible by tracking personal identity and capturing customer data; the ultimate goal is for the user to feel understood and simulating a one-to-one personal relationship. Through relational links of personal preferences, habits, mobile usage, and geographic positioning data the process of tailoring messages to individual consumers can become practical and cost effective.

The combination of the variables mentioned above allows us to understand one of the most important issues in mobile marketing: permission. Godin and Peppers (1999) refer to the traditional way of delivering marketing to customers as "interruption marketing." The authors suggest that instead of interrupting and annoying people with undesired information, companies should develop long-term relationships with customers and create trust through "permission marketing." The concept of permission marketing is based on

approaching customers to ask for their permission to receive different types of communication in a personal and intimate way. It is well known among marketers that asking for a customer's permission is better and easier than asking for forgiveness (Bayne, 2002). In the wireless world, there is evidence to suggest that customers do not want to be interrupted—unless they ask to be interrupted (Newell & Lemon, 2001).

A mobile phone is a more personal environment than a mailbox or an e-mail inbox, and an undesired message has a very negative impact on the consumer (Enpocket, 2003; Godin & Peppers, 1999; Newell & Lemon, 2001). As mobile marketing has a more invasive nature than any other media, much attention must be given to permission issues in order to make the mobile marketing experience pleasant to the users. The information received must be of high value to gain the user's permission. It must produce a win–win situation between user and advertiser.

We understand permission as the dynamic boundary produced by the combination of one's personal preferences, that is, personalization, of time, location, and information. The user should be able to indicate when, where, and what information he/she would like to receive. Here are a couple examples of how mobile marketing can help consumers and businesses:

- You are getting ready to go to the airport and you receive a sponsored message saying that your flight is delayed for 4 hours. Because of this information, instead of spending 4 long and boring hours waiting at an airport lounge, you manage to have an enjoyable dinner with your friends.
- You let your wireless service provider know that you would like to receive during weekdays, from 12 p.m. to 1 p.m., information about the menu specials of all Italian restaurants costing less than $20 and within a 1-mile radius of where you are located.

Now, let us consider the situation if this information was not customer relevant, or time and location sensitive. For example, imagine the following scenario. You are on a business trip, it is 3:30 p.m. and you had to forgo lunch due to an important meeting. Next, your cell phone beeps and you receive an offer of a menu special of an unknown restaurant in your hometown. The value to the recipient of this information is zero; moreover, it is more likely to have a negative impact. Figure 2 helps us visualize the concept of permission on mobile marketing.

The idea of a message being sent directly to an individual's phone is not without legislative concerns. Indeed, all over the world, privacy and consumer rights issues lead to the promotion of "opt-in" schemes. In essence, "opt-in" involves the user agreeing to receive marketing before anything is sent, with the opportunity to change preferences or stop messages at any time. Several current initiatives and industry groups, such as the Mobile Data Association, are helping to build standards of best practice for the mobile data industry (MDA, 2003).

As permission for mobile marketing applications should be dynamic, it is important to be able to identify customer responses to events. Stemming from the technological capabilities of mobile Internet-enabled devices, the measurement of reaction marketing is facilitated. As a consequence, the planning and justification of marketing expenditure becomes more precise. It also will help the identification of which mobile marketing strategies work and which do not. The constant feedback permits marketing strategies to be dynamically adjusted to produce better results for marketers.

ACCEPTANCE OF MOBILE MARKETING

Now we have discussed the technological and conceptual factors surrounding mobile marketing, let us examine the variables that influence customer acceptance. Specifically, this section aims to explore the few studies already accomplished on mobile marketing acceptance and provide a model that summarizes the main variables concerning this issue.

There is no doubt that mobile marketing is still at an embryonic stage. However, several recent studies help us to understand some key factors contributing to the penetration and acceptance of mobile marketing among consumers (Enpocket, 2002a, 2002b; Ericsson, 2000; Godin & Peppers,

Figure 2. Concept of permission for mobile marketing

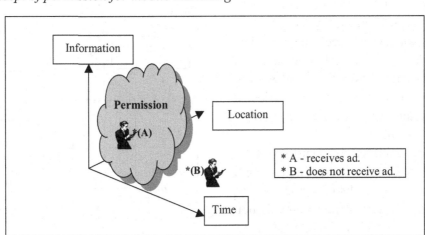

1999; Quios, 2000). The study by Ericsson (2000) had a sample of approximately 5,000 users and 100,000 SMS ad impressions in Sweden; the Quios study (2000) examined 35,000 users and 2.5 million SMS ad impressions in the UK; and the Enpocket study (Enpocket, 2002a, 2002b, 2003) researched over 200 SMS campaigns in the UK, surveying over 5,200 consumers—after they had been exposed to some of the SMS campaigns—from October 2001 to January 2003. The results of the three studies tend to converge, each pointing out that more than 60% of users liked receiving wireless marketing. The reasons cited for the favorable attitudes to mobile marketing include content value, immersive content, ad pertinence, surprise factor, and personal context.

The Enpocket study (2002a, 2002b, 2003) found that consumers read 94% of marketing messages sent to their mobile phones. It is important to point out that all these customers had given permission to receive third-party marketing. Moreover, the viral marketing capability of mobile marketing was identified by the fact that 23% of the customers surveyed by Enpocket showed or forwarded a marketing message to a friend. Another interesting finding is that the average response rate for SMS campaigns (15%) was almost three times higher than regular e-mail campaigns (6.1%). If delivered by a trusted source such as a wireless service provider (WSP) or major m-portal, acceptance of SMS marketing (63%) was considered comparable to that of TV (68%) or radio (65%). Notwithstanding, SMS marketing delivered by another source was far less acceptable—at just 35% of respondents. Similarly, the rejection level of SMS marketing from a WSP or portal was just 9%, while SMS from other sources was rejected by 31% of those surveyed. Telesales was rejected by 81% of respondents.

The indicative evidence about customer trust was further strengthened by other findings from the surveys. For example, 74% of customers indicated that WSPs were the most trusted organisation to control and deliver SMS marketing to their mobile devices. Major brands such as Coca-Cola and McDonald's were preferred by only by 20% of respondents (Enpocket, 2002a). As a result of the close relationship with the user, SMS marketing typically helps to build stronger brand awareness than other medias (Enpocket, 2002b).

It is important to highlight that the statistics presented above are being materialized in the form of profits mainly by mobile marketing and content sponsorship. Some marketers are using the sponsorship revenue model by conveying brand values through association with mobile content that fits the company's product or corporate image (Kalakota & Robinson, 2002). Features such as mobile barcode coupons are allowing a better measurement and understanding of return on investment (ROI) for mobile marketing (12Snap, 2003).

The indicative evidence and discussion above provide strong hints towards three main variables that influence a consumer's acceptance of mobile marketing: user's permission, WSP control, and brand trust. Figure 3 presents a conceptual model for mobile marketing acceptance based on these factors. Note that user permission is weighted in the model (see below).

The model allows us to forecast eight scenarios for mobile marketing acceptance. Table 1

Figure 3. Model for mobile marketing acceptance

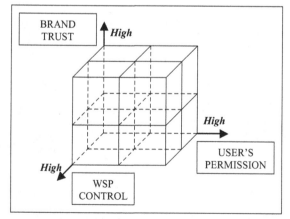

Table 1. Scenarios for mobile marketing acceptance

Scenario	Brand Trust	WSP Control	User's Permission	Acceptance
1	High	High	High	High acceptance
2	Low	High	High	Acceptable
3	High	Low	High	Acceptable
4	High	High	Low	Low acceptance
5	Low	Low	High	Acceptable
6	Low	High	Low	Low acceptance
7	High	Low	Low	Low acceptance
8	Low	Low	Low	Unacceptable

summarizes the different scenarios. An example for scenario 1 would be if a trusted brand such as Coca-Cola sent a marketing message through the user's WSP (e.g., Vodafone) with his/her permission. In this situation, all the variables have a high level and the message should be highly acceptable to the customer. At the opposite end of the spectrum, in scenario 8, an unknown company (brand) sends a message without WSP control and without the user's permission. Here, the probability of rejection is very high.

Scenarios 4 and 5 point out an element that requires further detailed investigation. We believe that the most important variable in this model is "user permission." For example, if Coca-Cola sends a message via an operator to a user who has not granted permission (scenario 4), it should have a lower acceptance than a brand with low trust that sends a message without WSP control to a customer who granted permission. This assumption is supported by the fact that the great majority of the consumers interviewed by Enpocket (2002a) are fearful that SMS marketing will become comparable to e-mail marketing with high levels of unsolicited messages.

The scenarios presented above are based on literature and on secondary data from the three studies previously approached. It would be interesting in the near future to substantiate this conceptual grid with primary data.

WSP control can directly affect how mobile marketing business models are configured. Based on the findings from the above analysis, we present two basic business models in which WSP control is the main differentiator (Figure 4). Figure 4a presents a model where the WSP has full control of the marketing delivery. On the other hand, Figure 4b shows a model where marketers can send messages directly to users without the control of the WSP.

The results of the studies presented by Ericsson (2000), Quios (2000), and Enpocket (2002a, 2002b, 2003) allow us to presume that the model presented by Figure 4a should be more successful than the one in Figure 4b. This assumption can also be supported by the fact that a WSP is usually more highly trusted by the consumers and possesses the technological capabilities to limit the delivery of messages. In addition, consumers interviewed by Enpocket (2002a) expressed a strong preference for the WSPs to become the definitive media owners and permission holders—possibly as a consequence of bad experiences with Internet marketing using nontargeted spam mail.

Figure 4. Possible business models for mobile marketing

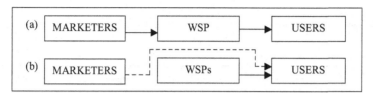

Another issue to be taken into consideration is how WSP control can affect the revenue model for mobile marketing. In Figure 4a, the WSP can easily charge marketers for using its services, but in Figure 4b, this becomes a difficult task.

CONCLUSION

The immediacy, interactivity, and mobility of wireless devices provide a novel platform for marketing. The personal and ubiquitous nature of devices means that interactivity can be provided anytime and anywhere. Marketing efforts are potentially more measurable and traceable. Furthermore, technologies that are aware of the circumstances of the user can provide services in a productive, context-relevant way, deepening customer relationships. The convergence between marketing, CRM, and m-commerce represents a potentially powerful platform for wireless marketing.

Notwithstanding, it is important to keep the consumer in mind; the key to success is the management of and delivery upon user expectations. A key aspect of mobile marketing is likely to be obtaining permission from the users to send information to their mobile devices. Already, the wireless Internet has demonstrated the need for temperance; the wireless Internet is not an emulator of or replacement for the wired Internet, it is merely an additional, complementary channel for services. Further, aside from initial pilot investigations, it is not abundantly clear how consumers will respond to the idea of mobile marketing. Clearly, the issues concerning mobile marketing acceptance need to be further investigated. Alongside, a deeper investigation into business and revenue models is needed; for example, how can companies, marketers, WSPs, and consumers create a win–win environment? In addition, although it is expected that consumers will not tolerate receiving messages without permission, more work is still needed to explain how consumers give permission to receive mobile marketing.

Currently, wireless marketing is embryonic and experimental—the majority of wireless marketing is SMS based (simple push services—lower left-hand quadrant of Figure 1). The next generation of devices and networks will be important in the evolution of wireless marketing; higher bandwidth will allow rich and integrated video, audio and text. In addition, considerable effort is needed in building consumer acceptance, legislation for privacy and data protection, standardizing wireless ads, and creating pricing structures. If these conditions hold, wireless could provide the unprecedented platform for marketing that has been promised. Clearly, it is too early to tell, but future research aimed at examining these fundamental issues will help to further understand the implications of permission-based mobile marketing.

REFERENCES

12Snap. (2003). Mobile barcode coupons—The marketing revolution for marketeers. Retrieved May 18, 2003, from www.12snap.com/uk/help/couponsshort.pdf

Barnes, S.J. (2002a). Under the skin: Short-range embedded wireless technology. *International Journal of Information Management, 22*(3), 165–179.

Barnes, S.J. (2002b). The mobile commerce value chain: Analysis and future developments. *International Journal of Information Management, 22(2)*, 91–108.

Barnes, S.J. (2002c). Wireless digital advertising: Nature and implications. *International Journal of Advertising, 21*(3), 399–420.

Bayne, K.M. (2002). *Marketing without wires: Targeting promotions and advertising to mobile device users.* London: John Wiley & Sons.

Chen, P. (2000). Broadvision delivers new frontier for e-commerce. *M-commerce, October*, 25.

Clarke, I. (2001). Emerging value propositions for m-commerce. *Journal of Business Strategies, 18*(2), 133–148.

de Haan, A. (2000). The Internet goes wireless. *EAI Journal, April*, 62–63.

Durlacher Research. (2002). *Mobile commerce report*. Retrieved July 10, 2002, from www.durlacher.com

Enpocket. (2002a). Consumer preferences for SMS marketing in the UK. Retrieved March 13, 2003, from www.enpocket.co.uk

Enpocket. (2002b). The branding performance in SMS advertising. Retrieved March 13, 2003, from www.enpocket.co.uk

Enpocket. (2003). The response performance of SMS advertising. Retrieved March 13, 2003, from www.enpocket.co.uk

Ericsson. (2000). *Wireless advertising*. Stockholm: Ericsson Ltd.

Evans, P.B., & Wurster, T.S. (1997). Strategy and the new economics of information. *Harvard Business Review, 75*(5), 70–82.

Forrester Research. (2001). Making marketing measurable. Retrieved February 10, 2002, from www.forrester.com

Godin, S., & Peppers, D. (1999). *Permission marketing: Turning strangers into friends, and friends into customers.* New York: Simon & Schuster.

Hart, Peter D. (2000). *The wireless marketplace in 2000*. Washington, DC: Peter D. Hart Research Associates.

Kalakota, R., & Robinson, M. (2002). *M-business: The race to mobility.* New York: McGraw-Hill.

Kannan, P., Chang, A., & Whinston, A. (2001). Wireless commerce: Marketing issues and possibilities. In *Proceedings of the 34th Hawaii International Conference on System Sciences*, Maui, HI.

Lau, A.S.M. (2003). A study on direction of development of business to customer m-commerce. *International Journal of Mobile Communications, 1*(1/2), 167–179.

Mobile Data Association (MDA). (2003). *Mobile Data Association*. Retrieved May 1, 2003, from www.mda-mobiledata.org/

Murdick, R.G., & Munson, J.C. (1988). *Sistemas de Informacion Administrativa*. Mexico: Prentice-Hall Hispano Americana.

Nakada, G. (2001). *I-Mode romps*. Retrieved March 5, 2001, from www2.marketwatch.com/news/

Newell, F., & Lemon, K.N. (2001). *Wireless rules: New marketing strategies for customer relationship management anytime, anywhere.* New York: McGraw-Hill.

NTT DoCoMo. (2003). Sehin Rain-Apu. Retrieved March 13, from http://foma.nttdocomo.co.jp/term/index.html (in Japanese)

Organisation for Economic Co-operation and Development (OEC). (2001). *Understanding the digital divide.* Paris: OECD Publications.

Puca. (2001). Booty call: How marketers can cross into wireless space. Retrieved May 28 2001, from www.puca.ie/puc_0305.html

Quios. (2000). *The efficacy of wireless advertising: Industry overview and case study.* London: Quios Inc./Engage Inc.

Sadeh, M.N. (2002). *M commerce: Technologies, services, and business models.* London: John Wiley & Sons.

Seita, Y., Yamamoto, H., & Ohta, T. (2002). Mobairu wo Riyoushitari Aiaru Taimu Maaketingu ni Kansuru Kenkyu. In *Proceedings of the 8th Symposium of Information Systems for Society,* Tokyo, Japan.

Siau, K., & Shen, Z. (2003). Mobile communications and mobile services. *International Journal of Mobile Communications, 1*(1/2), 3–14.

Sigurdson, J., & Ericsson, P. (2003). New services in 3G—new business models for strumming and video. *International Journal of Mobile Communications, 1*(1/2), 15–34.

Telecom Trends International. (2003). M-commerce poised for rapid growth, says Telecom Trends International. Retrieved October 27, 2003, from www.telecomtrends.net/pages/932188/index.htm

WindWire. (2000). *First-to-wireless: Capabilities and benefits of wireless marketing and advertising based on the first national mobile marketing trial.* Morrisville, NC; WindWire Inc.

Xu, H., Teo, H.H., & Wang, H. (2003,). Foundations of SMS commerce success: Lessons from SMS messaging and co-opetition. In *Proceedings of the 36th Hawaii International Conference on Systems Sciences,* Big Island, HI.

Yuan, Y., & J.J. Zhang (2003). Towards an appropriate business model for m-commerce. *International Journal of Mobile Communications, 1*(1/2), 35–56.

NOTE

An earlier and shorter version of this paper appeared as Barnes, S. J., & Scornavacca, E. (2004). Mobile marketing: The role of permission and acceptance. *International Journal of Mobile Communications, 2*(2), 128–139.

Chapter XV
Accessing Learning Content in a Mobile System:
Does Mobile Mean Always Connected?

Anna Trifonova
University of Trento, Italy

ABSTRACT

This chapter has the aim to point out an important functionality of a ubiquitous mobile system, and more specifically, its application in the learning domain. This functionality is the possibility to access the learning material from mobile devices, like PDAs (personal digital assistants) during their off-line periods and the technique to approach it, called hoarding. The chapter starts with the overview of a concrete mobile learning system—Mobile ELDIT, so as to give a clear idea of when and how this problem appears and why it is important to pay attention to it. Later, a description of the development approaches for both general and concrete solutions are discussed, followed by more detailed description of the important hoarding steps.

INTRODUCTION

The use of mobile devices for educational purposes was explored for the first time quite a long time ago, but the term mobile learning can be more and more often found in the literature of recent years. This is due to the fast advances of the mobile devices industry. On the market a large variety of devices with already reasonably powerful characteristics is available. The prices also allow almost everyone to be in possession of

such a toy. Of course, this leads to the growing desire to use mobile devices more widely in our everyday activities.

At the same time, in the learning domain the research on the use of those mobile devices and technologies for educational purposes is also growing. Learning happens at every time and in every place of our life and the concept of ubiquitous computing overlaps very well the ways we would like to support the learning processes.

As mobile becomes so important, we should consider what makes a mobile learning system different from what we are used to having in an e-learning system, and how we should adapt to the coming changes. One of these differences is the possibility to become disconnected, and in order to allow the user to continue using the system without disturbance, a technique called hoarding might be used. Here we will define what hoarding is, when it will be needed, and how to integrate it into a mobile learning system.

While mobile learning is mainly discussed within universities and research organizations, there are also commercial m-learning products that appear on the market. They include downloadable m-learning modules, online access to learning material especially designed for mobile devices, supportive tools, and complex frameworks for mobile content creation and management. Some examples are given in Table 1 at the end of the chapter.

BACKGROUND

The field of mobile learning is growing with every passing day. New ideas, approaches, and solutions are continuously appearing, involving different mobile devices, different target groups, and having different pedagogical or technology-testing goals.

A review of the literature (Trifonova & Ronchetti, 2003b) shows that there are as many common points researched as there are differences.

Mobile devices, including cell phones, PDAs, and even notebooks, are used for different purposes in different m-learning projects. In certain cases, content is accessed online through the local area network or by using the Internet. In other cases, the devices are used for communication between students and teachers or for cooperation with other students for completing common tasks. Voice or SMS might be used for receiving important educational information, images might be interchanged for sharing experiences, or common spaces might be used for collaborative work. Some of the important research directions are the following:

- The adoption to context, in particular providing location-aware learning
- The pedagogical side of m-learning – new approaches to teaching and studying
- Integration to e-learning and reuse of learning materials
- Usability issues, like facilitation of the input and output
- Provisioning of supportive to learning services
- and so forth

Figure 1. Chapter content

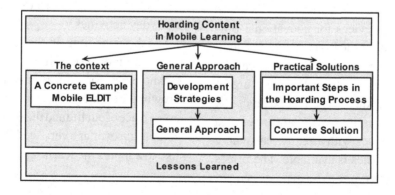

Nevertheless, two things are often overlooked—the support of the user during off-line periods and the possibility to access the study content even if the device is not connected at the moment. The problem appears when the learning material is of large size, especially compared to the available memory of the device, and cannot be fully loaded locally. Generally, the issue is dealt with in two ways: in some cases, the researchers/developers rely that the devices' limitations, like small memory and intermittent connection, will soon disappear. The other alternative often used is that the full content is packed in small predefined modules that fit into the local memory of the device.

Our approach aims to provide a more flexible and adaptable solution. We would like to allow dynamic selection of the "portion" of learning material needed by the current user that should be loaded in the device memory. In order to discuss this problem, we should start from the architecture approaches for building a mobile learning system and the functionalities it includes.

MOBILE ELDIT: A REAL MOBILE LEARNING SYSTEM

The project that will be described here is called Mobile ELDIT. It aims at development of a mobile version of an online language learning system, so that the content of the e-learning platform is available to the mobile users in a ubiquitous way. Here, some details about the system will be given, as this system is the example for the architectural approaches and the working solutions described throughout the following sections. The system should be seen as a proof-of-concept, rather than a model to follow.

Mobile ELDIT (or m-ELDIT) is a mobile version of an existing innovative e-learning platform (Gamper & Knapp, 2003). From the users' point of view, ELDIT consists of two types of data—a searchable dictionary of words, both in German and Italian, and a set of texts, also in German and

Italian, divided thematically into groups. The texts are especially designed for the preparation for the exam in bilingualism that is required in the South Tyrol region in Italy as a precondition for employment in the public sector. The content is prepared in such a way that will allow the user to optimally acquire needed lexical set, work on texts that had appeared on previous exams, and practice with the questions which might be asked for every single text. Though this system is especially suitable for people preparing for the bilingual exams, it can be used also by anyone interested in learning and practicing the Italian and German languages. The user might use the system as a normal electronic dictionary and search for unknown words or might browse the texts for more systematic studying. Currently, in Mobile ELDIT, only one of these two parts is included—the part comprising texts and associated to them words, which allow the users to switch, or at least to shift part of, their methodical study from a PC to a PDA device and to do it "on the go."

Here is a possible scenario of usage of Mobile ELDIT:

Scenario 1: A girl form Germany found nice work in the South Tyrol parts of Italy. In order to keep this work she needs in short time to pass a special exam and acquire a certificate of bilingualism. She starts to prepare herself for the exam by using the especially designed online e-learning system from her desktop PC. For her Christmas holidays she plans to go by train back home to Germany. On the last work day, she synchronizes her PDA with her desktop PC. The next day she gets on the train and, as her travel will be few hours, takes out her PDA device to continue her systematic study. She starts reading an Italian text, which comes next in her study plan, and clicks on *unknown word* to see its meaning. As she is preparing for the exam, she needs to have deep knowledge on every word, different forms, and senses, so she also reads a few examples and other cases of usage of the same word. She also takes a look at the list of words that derive from the chosen one, and later continues reading the text. Continuously, she takes notes on the words she is learning, so that she can re-read them again later. At home she connects the PDA to her PC and some synchronization happens in the background while the device battery charges. On her way back, she continues reading other texts that are needed for her preparation.

This scenario has the goal to give a concrete example for a way to present learning content to the user in a ubiquitous way. It also has to show a few important points that we will discuss further.

1.   How is the learning content presented to a mobile device and to a desktop PC?
2.   What differs in these two cases?
3.   If the content is Web-based, do we always need Internet connection to access it?

In the next section, a description will be given of the architecture that sits behind Mobile ELDIT and the concrete technological solutions to every module.

GENERAL MOBILE LEARNING ARCHITECTURE AND ITS APPLICATION IN PRACTICE

In general, e-learning systems have a wide spectrum of functionalities and responsibilities (Aggarwal, 2000). Maybe the distribution of didactic material stays in first place, but other important functionalities include, but are not limited to, the management of the learning resources, the support of different user roles and thus the identification of users and authorization of their access to the system, and often also the personalization of the learning experience based on the knowledge about the user collected during the system usage or through questionnaires and assessments, the support of collaboration between the participants, and so forth.

Let's imagine another simple scenario where a mobile device is used:

Scenario 2: A user at the university requests an interaction with the mobile learning system from her PDA. The system shows to the user the services which it can provide, and the user selects to request more information about a seminar. The system provides to the user the data about the subject, speaker, and location of the seminar, and asks the user if he is interested. When the user responds positively, the system also creates a reminder, which is triggered depending on what time the user needs to get to the seminar room. Later, the systems give the user directions for how to get to the seminar room. Though in the seminar room no Internet connection is available during the seminar, the user is able to watch the slideshow of the presentation on the PDA display. The student takes notes and later is able to see them from the desktop PC in the library from a standard Web browser.

Confronting the scenario of the first section and the one above with common e-learning functionalities (for details see Trifonova & Ronchetti, 2003a), we reveal three main differences, namely the context, device hardware, and software characteristics and connectivity.

•   **Context:** In the mobile scenario, it is important to obtain the context information that might be dynamically changing and that might influence different behaviour of the user to which the system should react accordingly. By contextual information we mean, for example, the spatial data (i.e., the location in the scenario given previously), other environmental information which might be obtained with special sensors, like surrounding noise level or changes in the available light, availability of resources, like parameters of the infrastructure or the battery condition of the device, and so forth.

- **Device hardware and software characteristics:** The most obvious difference between e-learning and m-learning is the usage of "mobile devices for learning." There is often a discussion about exactly what devices might be considered "mobile devices for learning." Should we stress the size of the device, or underline the fact that the device is mobile (not fixed)? Should laptops be considered "mobile devices for learning?" To be more clear, we define a "mobile device for learning" as *any device that is small, autonomous and unobtrusive enough to be carried in everyday life with the user and that will be used to support the educational processes, teaching or studying*" (Trifonova & Ronchetti, 2003b). Typically compared with a desktop PC, these devices are much smaller; for example, PDAs with a 16 bit colour 240x320 pixels screen. And the screens are not the only hardware difference. Some devices have touch screens instead of keyboard. Other, like mobile phones, do have keyboard, but with a different layout, and in this case the input speed is much more limited. It is visible that the input sometimes could be difficult, but in all cases it is different from the PC. Another very important difference is in the available software, both in sense of existing programs and difference in versions. Even if a mobile version of an application exists, most often it is very limited. For example, most e-learning systems strongly depend on frames to present their content, but the current Internet Explorer version of the Pocket PC has no support for frames.

- **Connectivity:** The connectivity is one of the main prerequisites for any e-learning system. Recently, the high bandwidth requirements are quite strong. Nowadays, there are lots of technological ways to access Internet from a mobile device: WAP, GPRS, UMTS, WiFi, Bluetooth. Though the options grow fast, still very often the bandwidth is comparatively smaller, and the user often gets disconnected, either because the infrastructure is not provided or because the expenses are still high and the user prefers to connect when a cheap connection is again available. We can distinguish disconnected periods that are intentional or not.

Depending on the concrete application that is being created, it is possible that only some of these differences will appear between the desktop and a mobile version of a system. For example, if the mobile devices that will be used are laptops, then the software and hardware characteristics are practically the same as in e-learning. Still, the connectivity is not guaranteed, and the environment of the user might be changing periodically.

To support the described differences, we proposed a general mobile learning architecture (Trifonova & Ronchetti, 2003a) that, if needed, sits on the top of an e-learning system, thus reusing some of the e-learning system functionalities, like, for example, the repository with the study materials, or in other cases the authorization of the user and assigning of proper access rights.

The so-called mobile learning management system (mLMS) consists of three modules that map the three main differences we talked about. The modules are called: (1) "Context Discovery" – the module responsible for finding out the context data, (2) "Mobile Content Management and Presentation Adaptation" – the module where the presented data should be especially adapted to fit the devices limitations (hardware or software), and finally, (3) "Packaging and Synchronization" – the module which should prepare the system for the periods of disconnection, such that the user can study even in those circumstances. The modules should communicate between themselves for optimal performance. The architecture is presented in Figure 2. On the left, you can see the e-learning system and the user with a desktop computer, which receives Web pages, possibly

Figure 2. Mobile learning: General view

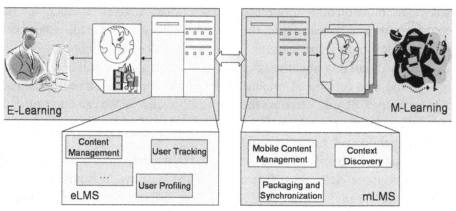

with multimedia content. On the server (see the lower part of the figure) different modules exist (not limited to what is shown on the picture) and interact between themselves. On the right, the mobile user connects to the m-learning system, and receives specially designed pages, the content of which the mobile server might request form the e-learning server. The functionalities of the mLMS modules will be described better with a deeper look at *Scenario 2,* previously described.

Scenario 2 explanation: Considering the previously introduced scenario, here is how it will be supported by the proposed architecture. First, the user request is captured and, in order to proceed, the system needs to know who the user is and what device is being used. This is done automatically by the "Context Discovery" module, which (based on the first request or additional interaction) already holds the information about the user id and the capabilities and limitations of the device (both software and hardware). Based on this data, the system can check the user role (student, teacher, guest, etc.) and access rights in the eLMS to decide what services can be offered at this moment, and propose a list to the user. After the next interaction with the user, the m-learning system requests information about the seminar from the eLMS and triggers the "mobile content management and presentation adaptation" module. Knowing

the capabilities of the device (from the "context Discovery" module), the data is redesigned and returned to the user. Afterward, the user requests a reminder be set up for her. The system needs additional context information, namely the user location, in order to calculate the needed time to get to the seminar room. Once again, the "context discovery" module is triggered to track the user current position. Meanwhile, as the system "knows" that the network is not accessible in the seminar room, it activates the "packaging and synchronization" module. The eLMS might contain a large amount of materials concerning the seminar—the presentation itself, including explanations from the lecturer, related links, additional papers and examples, and so forth. As the system already knows the limitations of the device, the "packaging" module selects (with certain confidence) what part will be more useful and important during the seminar (for example, only the presentation). In order to fit the device memory, the system also "asks" the "presentation adaptation" module to resize the images used. Afterward, the presentation is seamlessly uploaded to the user's PDA and is accessible when needed. During the presentation, user's notes are saved locally on the device, but on next connection to the Internet, synchronization is done and the notes are uploaded to the server in device independent format. The system also saves the interesting and

Figure 3. HTTP request from a mobile device (iPAQ Pocket PC)

```
GET http://science.unitn.it/mELDIT/text.056 HTTP/1.1

Accept: application/vnd.wap.xhtml+xml, application/xhtml+xml;
    profile="http://www.wapforum.org/xhtml", text/vnd.wap.wml, image/vnd.wap.wbmp,
    */*

UA-OS: Windows CE (POCKET PC) - Version 3.0

UA-color: color16

UA-pixels: 240x320

UA-CPU: ARM SA1110

UA-Voice: FALSE

UA-Language: JavaScript

Accept-Encoding: gzip, deflate

User-Agent: Mozilla/2.0 (compatible; MSIE 3.02; Windows CE; PPC; 240x320)

Host: science.unitn.it

Proxy-Connection: Keep-Alive
```

important parts of the presented material together with the notes in the student's personal folder on the server, so that they are accessible later from the desktop PC in the library.

Here is how the modules proposed in this general architecture and described in the above map work to meet the needs of mobile ELDIT, and the solutions that were used in its technical development.

Context Discovery

For the adaptation needs of Mobile ELDIT, the only context information that has to be discovered is the device hardware and software limitation. Knowing the screen size, the browser type and the device's browser support for scripts and frames will allow the "Adaptation" module to create the proper "look" for the Mobile ELDIT pages. As a first step, we chose the easiest way to discover the context—through the device browser's HTTP request that is captured on the server side.

As shown in Figure 3, the HTTP request contains what we needed, that is, what the device is (Windows CE device), what the screen is (240×320), the colour resolution (colour 16),

what the browser is (Mozilla/2.0), and so forth. In other mobile learning systems, or in a more complicated version of Mobile ELDIT, it is possible to use other context discovery methods. There are quite a lot of technological solutions nowadays (for example, the device independence initiative *www.w3.org/2001/di/*). One can imagine also other scenarios where adaptation can be used to show to the user context-dependant (e.g., location-dependant) language learning material, like, for example, the system proposed by Jung (2004). Thus, other methods of context discovery will be also needed, but it is out of the scope of our current work.

Content Adaptation

In order to keep the Mobile ELDIT users' experiences as close to the experiences with the online ELDIT system, we chose to use a browser as an interface to the learning material. Most of the browsers on the mobile devices nowadays still do not support frames, and support only limited versions of script languages. This leads to the need of specific adaptation of the content. The adaptation is also needed because, commonly,

Web pages are designed for screen size at least 800x600, and in most cases are hard to read and navigate from devices with a smaller screen. ELDIT is not an exception. Different adaptation techniques can be used to attack this problem (see Butler, 2001). The adaptation can be server-side, or can be done in a proxy between the server and the client, or can be done on the client side. All of these solutions have their pros and cons.

The data of the ELDIT system consists of XML files, both for the texts and for the word entries. For displaying the data to a desktop PC, on the server side on every user request (on the fly), HTML pages are produced containing frames and Java scripts. The data is mainly text, but the entries are highly interlinked. For the Mobile ELDIT, we have decided to use server-side adaptation, namely XSLT transformations of the XML data on a Cocoon server (for more details, see *http://cocoon.apache.org*). Our decision was pushed by two facts—first, our data was already in XML format, which allowed us to easily create the adaptation rules using XSLT; second, the

adaptation on the server side is a much better solution in the mobile context, as the adaptation process consumes quite a lot of computational power and will not fit well on a mobile device, as the devices are limited in CPU speed, operational memory, and battery.

Figure 4 shows a screenshot of a word entry from the ELDIT system (Figure 4a), displayed in a desktop PC browser. One can see that it is made out of three frames that contain the main information about the selected word in the left-hand frame, and additional information in the right-hand frame. The frame above is dedicated to the searching functionality of the system. In the mobile version, we do not support searching. This decision is because the row data of ELDIT is a much larger amount than the available memory of standard mobile devices. Thus, we are not able to provide the entire dictionary on the device anytime (see next section about packaging and synchronization). It is also impossible to predict what word a user might be searching for. Thus, we have "converted" the screen on the left (4a) into

Figure 4. M-ELDIT content adaptation. 4a (on the left): Browser view of ELDIT word entry with three frames; 4b (right top): m-ELDIT additional information (idiomatic expressions) for a word entry; 4c (right bottom) m-ELDIT basic word entry screen

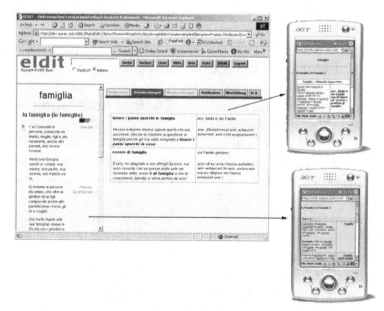

a series of interconnected screens on the mobile device (4b and 4c). When a user wants to see a word entry, first, the main screen is displayed and the user might select to view more detailed information by clicking the links that were added during the XLST transformations on the server.

Packaging and Synchronization

The last functionality in our architecture is called "Packaging and synchronization" and it will be discussed in detail separately in the following section.

HOARDING: WHAT IS IT AND WHY DO WE NEED IT?

In the literature, one can see that quite a lot of years pass, but the supposition that "very soon" every device will always have connection has still not come true. In the fall of 2000, Clark Quinn says:

The vision of mobile computing is that of portable (even wearable) computation: rich interactivity, total connectivity*, and powerful processing. A small device that is* always networked*, allowing easy input through pens and/or speech or even a keyboard when necessary (though it may be something completely different like a chord keyboard), and the ability to see high resolution images and hear quality sound.*

In the above citation, we have italicized few words in order to focus your attention on the key expectations about the future of mobile computing and, as a result, also about m-learning. Though this sooner or later will happen, the current situation is not like we would like it to be. The devices had really become mobile in the sense of light and small for an impressively short period of time and, though there are quite a lot of technological ways to connect to the Internet, through WAP,

GPRS, Wi-Fi, and so forth, still users have long periods of disconnection. These periods might be intentional or not—because of the lack of proper infrastructure or because the connection has high costs. Nevertheless, it is obvious that the vision of ubiquitous learning comprises the importance to give the user the possibility to access the learning materials that he/she wants to study even when the connection is not presented. Moreover, a good situation would be developed in such a way that the user does not bother and does not even understand whether connection exists or not.

To solve the problem described above, there comes to play a technique called hoarding (Trifonova & Ronchetti, 2005). Hoarding in practice is a procedure for automatic selection and caching of the data that the user will need during his off-line periods. Generally, hoarding is needed whenever the full data set of a certain application is bigger than the device's available memory; that is, it is not possible to have all the data on the device all the time. In such a case, it is necessary to select only the most relevant information and to consider how much memory is available. In our mobile learning context the data is the learning material that the user intends to study during the next off-line session. We should emphasis that, in the context of ubiquitous scenario, our interest is in the automation of the process. In other words, we do not want the learner to explicitly say what he/she wants to study, but on the contrary, the system should be able to predict this. The fact that the process is automatic is good for two main reasons. First, we will free the user from tedious operations, and second, often we can not even trust the user in his/her own judgment for his/her knowledge and future needs.

The hoarding process should consist of few steps that we can formalize as follows:

1. **Predict the "starting point":** The algorithm should start by finding the entry point of the current user for the next learning session.

2. **Create a candidate set:** All related documents (objects) should be found and a "can-

didate for caching" set of objects should be created.

3. **Predict the most probable session path:** The algorithm should discover the most probable sequence of LO the user will be following.

4. **Prune the set:** The candidate set should be pruned; that is, the objects that will not be needed by the user should be excluded from the candidate set, thus making it smaller. This should be done on user behaviour observations and domain knowledge.

5. **Find the priority to all objects still in the hoarding set:** When the candidate set is pruned, using all the knowledge available about the user and the current learning domain, every object left in the hoarding set should be assigned a priority value. The priority depends on how important the object is for the next user session, and should be higher if we suppose that there is a higher probability that an object will be used sooner.

6. **Sort the objects, based on their priority:** The hoarding algorithm produces an ordered list of objects.

7. **Cache, starting from the beginning of the list (thus putting in the device cache those objects with bigger priority):** and continue with the ones with smaller weights, until available memory is filled in.

As one can see, the hoarding process and its predictions should be based on the system knowledge about the learner style, preferences, and previous experience. Very useful knowledge can be extracted from the students' previous interactions with the system. These interactions are usually written and saved in log files that can be analyzed. For Mobile ELDIT, such log files are gathered by a local proxy on the mobile device that captures the browsers requests, and is also responsible for the system's cache. Some preprocessing of the log files is needed for doing analysis. The preprocessing is commonly one of the most time and computationally consuming processes, though in our context, this process will most likely be performed on the server, and not when the user is interacting with the online system, and thus it will not be disturbing for the user.

In the context of hoarding, we recognize two groups of characteristics that should be "known" to the system about the user. We schematically call the first "user behaviour," which will be kept in "usage patterns" profiles. The second is "user knowledge," which will be kept in an individual user's profile. The two groups of characteristics will be used differently by the hoarding algorithm. The user behaviour can be described in terms of browsing styles (e.g., consecutive, random, interest driven, etc.), preferred type of educational media (e.g., prefers video to combination of text and pictures), and so forth. Based on the user behaviour, we can group the learners and analyze the similarities and differences between the groups and between the members of the same group. This should help us predict what will be needed; that is, this data will be used to fill in the hoarding set. On the other hand, the user knowledge profile should consist of everything that the system knows about what the user already knows. An example is the system awareness of the user's competence in a certain subject (i.e., beginner, intermediate, advanced) or a list of all the topics already covered by the user previously. In contrast of the user behaviour, the profile of the user knowledge will be used for pruning the entries from the "candidates for hoarding" set; that is, for excluding objects in order to decrease the size of the hoard.

For the Mobile ELDIT application, we tried a few different strategies for hoarding (Trifonova & Ronchetti, 2005), which include the generation of the candidate set, pruning, and prioritizing of the learning objects. First, we discovered that in our scenario the users have often very consecutive browsing behaviour. In other words, when shown a list of texts to be reviewed, the learners almost always read the texts in the order they are listed. This seems to be logical behaviour for students accessing other types of learning materials, where to understand the information presented later in the material there is a prerequisite that they have a good understanding of the information that preceeded it. This consecutive behaviour is a concrete usage pattern that helps to decide the inclusion of material into the candidate hoarding set. Some of the parameters that should be discovered for every user are the depth of the browsing, the number and types of learning objects requested, the time usually spent, and so forth. As far as the pruning is concerned, in the Mobile ELDIT we wanted to test the possibility for fully automatic hoarding, and also the automatic discovery of "user knowledge." A special feature of m-ELDIT is that the learning content is divided into small chunks (texts and connected words) and some of them are repeatedly shown to the user. Because of this fact, we used as a pruning rule the following logic: if the user had the option to review a chunk of the material, but decided not to do it, there is a big probability that the learner knows this chunk and will not need it in the future, and thus it will be pruned next time. Even this simple rule made the hoarding set decrease in size quite fast. However, its simplicity has a negative side also. In certain cases the deduction made with this rule that the user "knows" a certain word is not correct, but the word gets excluded from the hoarding set in the next iteration. This leads to an increased miss rate; that is, the number of unsatisfied user requests. A more sophisticated rule might take into consideration also the time the users spent for reviewing certain content chunks, or the number of times the same chunk was requested.

Possible further improvements in the hoarding might be done by grouping the users by similarity in their behaviour or knowledge. Predictions on what actions will be taken by a user, and thus decisions on what to include or exclude from the

hoard might be taken based on the behaviour or the knowledge of another user that previously had shown very big similarity with the current one. Note that the best similarity measure will differ from one application to another—one case might be the type of reviewed learning material, in another its quantity, in a third the time spent on every portion.

As the learning material and the users of every specific mobile learning system will differ, all these processes, and the decisions taken, will be based often on a big number of parameters that should be defined based on analyzes of the tracking data collected of the specific system. For example, the size of the hoarding set should be a function of the available memory on the mobile device and the size of the learning content chunks. The behaviour of the user might differ based on the learning tasks, and thus things like grouping of the users might be done based on specific classification strategies. Also, the discovering of the user knowledge might be done in various ways—our strategy was automatic discovering, but also other methods are possible, like questionnaires or tests.

Details on the results of the experimentations with hoarding strategies and parameters can be found in Trifonova (2006).

CONCLUSION

Mobile learning seems to be an integral part for the future of learning. And it is a step further on the road from e-learning to ubiquitous learning. Ubiquitous access to learning material supposes that, regardless of whether Internet connection is available or not, the user will have access to the learning material needed at the moment from the device used at the moment. Throughout this chapter it was shown that the technology needed for realizing a ubiquitous learning system, the pieces of the puzzle, are already available. Possibilities are wide and waiting to be explored. Often, ap-

Table 1. Commercial m-learning examples

Downloadable content modules
http://hotlavasoftware.com
Hot Lava Software provides offline course modules for Palm and PocketPC. A number of modules can be downloaded for free, while others are commercial. Some examples are Cisco® mobile learning (example: CCNA® Prep 4-PACK: Networking, TCP/IP, Ethernet), Kids Mobile Learning; (example: 1st Grade Language Arts: Standardized Practice Test), Microsoft mobile learning (example: MCSE Prep Data Networking), COMPTIA A+ mobile learning, English as a Second Language, Business and Sales Skills Mobile Learning, and so forth.
http://www.italyguides.it   Italy Guides provides small audio tourist guides that can be downloaded and listened to with iPod. Information is available for some of the most interesting Italian cities – Rome, Florence, and Venice.
http://www.ipreppress.com   - Merriam-Webster Inc., in collaboration with iPREPpress, offers its learning material on iPod. The commercial 2006 Edition Pocket Dictionary is already available on the site. The 2006 Pocket Thesaurus and the Pocket Atlas are expected soon. Free modules are available also in subjects like the Declaration of Independence (1776), the Constitution of the United States, (1787); the Social Security Act (1935), etc.
Online accessible content
http://en.wapedia.org/
The popular lately Wikipedia provides a cell phone accessible version of its materials.
http://www.alc.co.jp/eow/pocket/
Japan is one of the leading places offering m-learning. Examples are many of the services offered by DoCoMo to i-mode enabled mobile phones. Pocket Eijiro is an English language learning site provided by ALC, where also small multi-choice quizzes can be used to test users' knowledge.
Content creation and management platforms
http://www.axmor.com
AXMOR provides the tools to deliver mobile learning content to PocketPC and Palm devices. The platform consists of .Net-based Web site and Pocket PC part. Content maintenance, user management and reporting of different activities is done online. On the other hand, locally on the mobile device the purchased content is managed and played. The modules are in Macromedia Flash.
http://hotlavasoftware.com
Hot Lava Software, mentioned above, also offers mobile content authoring, publishing, delivery, and tracking for many mobile devices types, including PDAs and cell phones.
http://www.symexuk.com/
Symex offers to teachers a mobile system to facilitate teaching activities, like planning teaching, collecting students data, and managing their results. The system is available for PDAs and can be synchronized by connecting the device to the PC or via the Wi-Fi network.
Other tools
www.macromedia.com
Macromedia provides a Lite version of Flash for creating multimedia movies on mobile devices, including cell phones.
http://www.pocketmobility.com
Different free and commercial tools for mobile education and learning are provided by Pocket Mobility Inc., like Quizzler Maker, to create easily quizzes for any platform. The bundle allows the teacher to collect the average scores in the class, to see which questions were missed the most, and so forth.
http://classinhand.wfu.edu/
DataInHand, created at Wake Forest University, allows from a PDA with wireless connection to control presentations, to receive feedback from classroom answers, and see the distribution of the answers.

plications would be developed in such a way as to utilize the newly appearing fast Internet connections from the mobile device. But when such an option is not possible or is not sufficient, the needed piece of the puzzle is called hoarding.

Hoarding should be based on deep understanding of user behaviour, both specifics of the concrete user and the common patterns in the behaviour of all users of a concrete system. We have shown a possible approach used in a real mobile learning system, which showed us the viability of hoarding in practice. Nevertheless, specific parameters should be extracted in every specific case, as the user behaviour might differ drastically based on the proposed study material and connections between chunks.

ADDITIONAL SOURCES

In Table 1 we give ideas of the existing commercial m-learning tools and systems. We do not intend to give a complete list of available products, but rather examples of available possibilities and starting points for future work. The entries are grouped by provided functionality and are supported with URL and short description.

REFERENCES

Aggarwal, A. (2000). *Web-based learning and teaching technologies: Opportunities and challenges*. Hershey, PA: Idea Group.

Butler, M.H. (2001). *Current technologies for device independence* (HP Labs Tech. Rep. HPL-2001-83).

Gamper J., & Knapp, J. (2003). A data model and its implementation for a Web-based language learning system. In *Proceedings of the Twelfth International World Wide Web Conference (WWW2003)*.

Jung, L. (2004). Context-aware support for computer-supported ubiquitous learning. In *Proceedings of the 2nd IEEE International Workshop on Wireless and Mobile Technologies in Education (WMTE'04)*.

Quinn, C. (2001). *Mobile, wireless, in-your-pocket learning. LiNE Zine: Learning in the new economy*. Retrieved October 16, 2006, from http://www.linezine.com/2.1/features/cqmmwiyp.htm

Trifonova, A., & Ronchetti, M. (2003a, August 30-September 1). A general architecture to support mobility in learning. In *Proceedings of the 4th IEEE International Conference on Advanced Learning Technologies (ICALT 2004 - Crafting Learning within Context)*, Joensuu, Finland.

Trifonova, A., & Ronchetti, M. (2003b, November 7-11). Where is mobile learning going? In *Proceedings of The World Conference on E-learning in Corporate, Government, Healthcare, & Higher Education (E-Learn 2003)*, Phoenix, Arizona.

Trifonova, A., & Ronchetti, M. (2005, June 27- July 2). Hoarding content in an m-learning system. In *Proceedings of the World Conference on Educational Multimedia, Hypermedia and Telecommunications (ED-Media 2005)* (pp. 4786-4794). Montreal, Canada.

Trifonova, A. (2006, March 21). *Towards hoarding content in m-learning context*. PhD thesis, University of Trento, Italy.

This work was previously published in Ubiquitous and Pervasive Knowledge and Learning Management: Semantics, Social Networking and New Media to Their Full Potential, edited by M. Lytras and A. Naeve, pp. 198-215, copyright 2007 by IGI Publishing (an imprint of IGI Global).

Chapter XVI
Leveraging Pervasive and Ubiquitous Service Computing

Zhijun Zhang
University of Phoenix, USA

ABSTRACT

The advancement of technologies to connect people and objects anywhere has provided many opportunities for enterprises. This chapter will review the different wireless networking technologies and mobile devices that have been developed, and discuss how they can help organizations better bridge the gap between their employees or customers and the information they need. The chapter will also discuss the promising application areas and human-computer interaction modes in the pervasive computing world, and propose a service-oriented architecture to better support such applications and interactions.

INTRODUCTION

With the advancement of computing and communications technologies, people do not have to sit in front of Internet-ready computers to enjoy the benefit of information access and processing. Pervasive computing, or ubiquitous computing, refers to the use of wireless and/or mobile devices to provide users access to information or applications while the users are on the go. These mobile devices can be carried by the users, or embedded in the environment. In either case, these devices are connected, most likely through a wireless network, to the Internet or a local area network (LAN).

Mobile technologies come in a large variety and are ever changing. In order to gain the business value of pervasive computing, and at the same time keep the supporting cost under control, it is important to develop an architecture solution. A service-oriented architecture (SOA) would allow an enterprise to easily provision functions to be accessible by certain types of pervasive channels. A service-oriented architecture would also make it possible to quickly integrate data generated by pervasive devices and make them available in the form of an information service.

In this chapter, we will first look at the communication networks and mobile devices that create the various information-access and information-generation touch points in a pervasive computing environment. Then we will discuss the applications and interaction models for pervasive computing. Finally, we will describe a service-oriented architecture that an enterprise can adopt in order to effectively and efficiently support pervasive computing.

MOBILE COMMUNICATION NETWORKS

Mobile communication technologies range from personal area networks (PANs; a range of about 10 meters) and local area networks (a range of about 100 meters) to wide area networks (WANs; a few kilometers). From a network-topology perspective, most networks are based on a client-server model. A few are based on the peer-to-peer model.

Wireless PANs

A wireless personal area network allows the different devices that a person uses around a cubicle, room, or house to be connected wirelessly. Such devices may include the computer, **personal digital assistants (PDAs)**, cell phone, printer, and so forth.

Bluetooth is a global de facto standard for wireless connectivity (Bluetooth SIG, 2005). The technology is named after the 10th-century Danish King Harald, who united Denmark and Norway and traveled extensively.

HomeRF is an early technology for wireless home networking, first marketed in 2000.

The Institute of Electrical Engineers (IEEE) 802.15 wireless-PAN effort (IEEE, 2005a) focuses on the development of common standards for personal area networks or short-distance wireless networks. One technology out of this effort is ZigBee, which is based on the IEEE 802.15.4 standard.

ZigBee is a low-cost, low-power-consumption, wireless communication-standard proposal (ZigBee Alliance, 2005). Formerly known as FireFly, ZigBee is being developed as the streamlined version of HomeRF. A streamlined version would allow most of the functionality with less integration and compatibility issues.

ZigBee's topology allows as many as 250 nodes per network, making the standard ideal for industrial applications. Radio-frequency-based ZigBee is positioned to eventually replace infrared links. To achieve low power consumption, ZigBee designates one of its devices to take on the coordinator role. The coordinator is charged with waking up other devices on the network that are in a sleep mode, moments before packets are sent to them. ZigBee also allows coordinators to talk to one another wirelessly. This will allow for opportunities for wireless sensors to continuously communicate with other sensors and to a centralized system.

For enterprise computing, the wireless PANs are within the corporate firewall. They do not create new requirements for the enterprise architecture to extend access to applications. However, they do require security measures to make sure the device that is receiving information is a rec-

Table 1. Summary of the wireless PANs

Technology	Radio Frequency	Maximum Distance	Data Capacity
Bluetooth	2.4 GHz	10 meters	721 Kbps
HomeRF	2.4 GHz	50 meters	0.4-10 Mbps, depending on distance
ZigBee	2.4 GHz	75 meters	220 Kbps

ognized device. It also creates an opportunity for the computing infrastructure to potentially know where a particular device, and most likely the associated user, is located. How these are handled will be discussed later in the description of the proposed service-oriented architecture.

Wireless LANs

The set of technical specifications for wireless local area networks (WLANs), labeled 802.11 by IEEE, has led to systems that have exploded in popularity, usability, and affordability. Now wireless LAN can be found in many organizations and public places.

With a wireless LAN, a user's device is connected to the network through wireless access points (APs). APs are inexpensive—many are available for less than $100—and will usually work perfectly with little or no manual configuration.

Wireless LANs use a standard, called IEEE 802.11, that provides a framework for manufactures to develop new wireless devices. The first two standards released for wireless LANs were 802.11b and 802.11a. The 802.11b standard was used in most wireless devices in the early adoption of wireless LAN. A new standard, called 802.11g, combines data-transfer rates equal to 802.11a with the range of an 802.11b network (Geier, 2002). It uses access points that are backward compatible with 802.11b devices.

Wireless technology has become so popular that many new devices, especially laptop computers, have built-in wireless LAN capabilities. Windows XP, Mac OS, and Linux operating systems automatically configure wireless settings, and software such as NetStumbler and Boingo provides automatic connections to whatever WLANs they encounter. What is more, community-based groups have furthered neighborhood area networks (NANs) to share wireless Internet access from one building to the next.

Besides 802.11a/b/g technologies that have shipped products, new technologies are emerging, including 802.11h, 802.11i, and 802.1x. The most important developments for wireless security will be contained in the 802.11i and 802.1x specifications. The 802.11i specification addresses encryption (securing the communication channel), whereas 802.1x will address authentication (verifying individual users, devices, and their access levels).

IEEE 802.1x is another authentication protocol, not an encryption protocol. 802.1x by itself does not fix the existing problems with WLAN security that relate to encryption. Therefore, attackers can still easily read network traffic on 802.1x networks. The 802.11i standard will address communication-channel encryption.

In order to increase the throughput of wireless LANs, a technology called Mimo (multiple input-multiple output) has been developed. Mimo allows for transmission rates of more than 100 Mbps, which is much greater than existing wireless LANs. Presently, wireless LANs use a single antenna operating at only one of a limited number of frequencies (channel) that are shared by all users. Mimo technology allows the use of two or more antennas operating on that channel. Normally, this would cause interference degradation of the signal because the radio waves would take different paths—called multipath distortion. However, Mimo uses each of these different paths to convey more information. The Mimo technology corrects for the multipath effects. IEEE is standardizing the technology as IEEE 802.11n.

For an enterprise, wireless LAN technologies allow pervasive information access throughout the campus. Employees with authorized mobile devices such as wireless laptops and PDAs will be able to get online wherever they are on the campus.

Table 2 summarizes the wireless LAN technologies.

Wireless MANs

A wireless metropolitan area network (MAN; also referred to as broadband wireless access, or WiMAX) can wirelessly connect business to

Table 2. Summary of wireless LAN technologies

Technology	Radio Frequency	Maximum Distance	Data Capacity
802.11a	5 GHz	20 meters	54 Mbps
802.11b	2.4 GHz	100 meters	11 Mbps
802.11g	2.4 GHz	100 meters	54 Mbps
802.11i	A security standard for encryption on wireless LANs		
802.11n	Varies	Varies	> 100 Mbps
802.1x	A standard security protocol for user authentication on wireless LANs		

business within the boundary of a city. It is becoming a cost-effective way to meet escalating business demands for rapid Internet connection and integrated data, voice, and video services.

Wireless MANs can extend existing fixed networks and provide more capacity than cable networks or digital subscriber lines (DSLs). One of the most compelling aspects of the wireless MAN technology is that networks can be created quickly by deploying a small number of fixed-base stations on buildings or poles to create high-capacity wireless access systems.

In the wireless MAN area, IEEE has developed the 802.16 standard (IEEE, 2005b), which was published in April 2002, and has the following features.

- It addresses the "first mile-last mile" connection in wireless metropolitan area networks. It focuses on the efficient use of bandwidth between 10 and 66 GHz.
- It enables interoperability among devices so carriers can use products from multiple vendors. This warrants the availability of lower cost equipment.
- It defines mechanisms that provide for differentiated quality of service (QoS) to support the different needs of different applications. The standard accommodates voice, video, and other data transmissions by using appropriate features.

- It supports adaptive modulation, which effectively balances different data rates and link quality. The modulation method may be adjusted almost instantaneously for optimal data transfer. Adaptive modulation allows efficient use of bandwidth and fits a broader customer base.

The WiMAX technical working group has developed a set of system profiles, standards for protocol-implementation conformance, and test suites (http://www.wimaxforum.org).

One particular technology for WiMAX is non line of sight (NLOS) networking (Shrick, 2002). NLOS networks provide high-speed wireless Internet access to residential and office facilities. NLOS uses self-configuring end points that connect to a PC (personal computer). The end point has small attached antennas and can be mounted anywhere without the need to be oriented like satellite antennas. Two major vendors are Navini Networks and Nokia.

With the wireless MAN technology, enterprises can quickly set up a network to provide wireless access to people in a certain area. It is very useful in situations such as an off-site working session or meeting.

Wireless NANs

Wireless neighborhood area networks are community-owned networks that provide wire-

Table 3. Data transmission speed of wireless wide area networks

Technology	Maximum	Initial	Typical
2G: GSM	9.6 Kbps	—	—
2G: CDMA	14.4 Kbps	—	—
2.5G: GPRS	115 Kbps	< 28 Kbps	28-56 Kbps
2.5G: CDMA 1x	144 Kbps	32 Kbps	32-64 Kbps
2.5G: EDGE	384 Kbps	64 Kbps	64-128 Kbps
3G	2 Mbps	< 128 Kbps	128-384 Kbps
4G	20 Mbps	TBD	TBD

less broadband Internet access to users in public areas (Schwartz, 2001). To set up a wireless NAN, community group members lend out access to the Internet by linking wireless LAN connections to high-speed digital subscriber lines or cable modems. These wireless LAN connections create network access points that transmit data for up to a 1-kilometer radius. Anyone possessing a laptop or PDA device equipped with a wireless network card can connect to the Internet via one of these community-established access points.

Wireless NANs have been established in more than 25 cities across the United States. Community-based networks differ from mobile ISPs (Internet service providers) such as Mobile-Star and Wayport that offer subscribers wireless access to the Internet from hotels, airports, and coffee shops. Wireless NANs extend access to consumers in indoor as well as outdoor areas, and the access is typically offered at no charge. For instance, NYC Wireless (http://www.nycwireless. net) provides Internet access to outdoor public areas in New York City. In addition, this organization is negotiating with Amtrak to bring wireless Internet access to Penn Station.

Enterprises could leverage the existing wireless NANs and equip employees with the right devices and security mechanisms in order to use these wireless networks to securely connect to the corporate network.

Wireless WANs

Wireless wide area networks are commonly known as cellular networks. They refer to the wireless networks used by cell phones.

People characterize the evolution of wireless WAN technology by generation. First generation (1G) started in the late 1970s and was characterized by analog systems. The second generation of wireless technology (2G) started in the 1990s. It is characterized by digital systems with multiple standards and is what most people use today. 2.5G and 3G are expected to be widely available 1 to 3 years from now. 4G is being developed in research labs and is expected to launch as early as 2006.

Wireless WAN originally only offered voice channels. Starting from 2G, people have used modems to transmit data information over the voice network. More recent generations offer both voice and data channels on the same cellular network.

One of the major differentiating factors among the wireless generations is the data transmission speed in which the wireless device can communicate with the Internet. The table below is a comparison of the data transmission rates of the 2G, 2.5G, 3G, and 4G technologies (3Gtoday, 2005). Both 2G and 2.5G include different technologies with different data transmission rates. Global Systems for Mobile Communications (GSM) and Code Division Multiple Access (CDMA) are 2G technologies. General Packet Radio Service (GPRS), CDMA 1x, and Enhanced Data for GSM Environment (EDGE) are 2.5G technologies.

In the United States, cellular carriers Verizon and Sprint use CDMA technology. Cingular uses GSM, GPRS, and EDGE technologies. Both Verizon and Sprint have rolled out their CDMA 1x services, which is 2.5G. Cingular has rolled out GRPS service and is starting to roll out EDGE service in selected markets.

Wireless WANs are available wherever cell phones can be used. For now, they are the most pervasive wireless networks. By subscribing to a service plan, an enterprise user's laptop computer or other mobile device can connect to the Internet through the service provider's cellular towers.

Ultrawideband (UWB)

Traditional radio-frequency technologies send and receive information on particular frequencies, usually licensed from the government. Ultrawideband technology sends signals across the entire radio spectrum in a series of rapid bursts.

Ultrawideband wireless technology can transmit data at over 50 Mbps. A handheld device using this technology consumes 0.05 milliwatts of power as compared to hundreds of milliwatts for today's cell phones. Ultrawideband signals appear to be background noise for receivers of other radio signals. Therefore it does not interfere with other radio signals. Ultrawideband is ideal for delivering very high-speed wireless-network data exchange rates (up to 800 Mbps) across relatively short distances (less than 10 meters) with a low-power source.

Another feature of ultrawideband signals is that they can penetrate walls. Therefore, this technology would allow a wireless device to communicate with a receiver in a different room. This feature can also be used to detect buried bodies, people in a building, or metal objects in concrete.

Mesh Radio and Mess Networks

Mesh radio is a wireless network technology that operates in the 28-GHz range of the radio spectrum and provides high-speed, high-bandwidth connectivity to the Internet (Fox, 2001). A mesh radio network consists of antennas connected in a web-like pattern to a fiber-optic backbone. A single antenna attached to the roof of a building could provide Internet access to all of the subscribers residing in the building. Each node on the network has a small, low-power, directional antenna that is capable of routing traffic for other nodes within a 2.8-kilometer radius. In contrast to other wireless networks, mesh radio avoids many of the line-of-sight issues between the base station and each node on the network. Consequently, the configuration of mesh radio reduces the chance of encountering physical obstructions that could impede access to the network.

Mesh radio networks are being developed in two different ways. CALY Networks has developed a system that utilizes the Internet protocol (IP) as its communication mechanism, while Radiant Networks has created a system that communicates using the asynchronous transfer mode (ATM). Providers of mesh radio services include British Telecommunications, TradeWinds Communications (http://www.tnsconnects.com), and Nsight Teleservices (http://www.nsighttel.com).

Features of mesh radio include the following:

- Provides upload and download data rates of up to 25 Mbps
- Supports up to 600 subscribers per square kilometer without degradation of service
- Provides cost-effective access to broadband services in rural communities or urban areas
- Increases network capacity and resilience as the customer base grows

Different from the mesh radio technology, mesh networks enable wireless devices to work as a peer-to-peer network, using the handsets themselves instead of the radio towers to transmit data (Blackwell, 2002). Each handset would be capable of transmitting data at rates from 6 Mbps to 18 Mbps. This technology can be used for a group of users or devices communicating with each other in a peer-to-peer mode without needing an established wireless network. The technology was developed by Mesh Networks Inc., which has been acquired by Motorola.

Sensor Networks

Motes (also called sensor networks or Smart Dusts; Culler & Hong, 2004) are small sensing and communication devices. They can be used as wireless sensors replacing smoke detectors, thermostats, lighting-level controls, personal-entry switches, and so forth. Motes are built using currently available technology and are inexpensive enough to be deployed in mass quantities. Depending on the sensors and the capacity of the power supply, a mote can be as big as 8 cubic centimeters (the size of a matchbox) or as small as one cubic millimeter.

Motes are the result of a joint effort between Defense Advanced Research Projects Agency (DARPA) and the University of California, Berkeley, research labs. Most initial applications are positioned to helping the military for tasks such as surveillance of war zones, the monitoring of transportation, and the detection of missiles and/or biological weapons. Commercial mote sensors are available from Crossbow Technology.

A mote is typically made up of the following:

- A scanner that can scan and measure information on temperature, light intensity, vibrations, velocity, or pressure changes

- A microcontroller that determines tasks performed by the mote and controls power across the mote to conserve energy
- A power supply that can be small solar cells or large off-the-shelf batteries
- TinyOS, an open-source software platform for the motes. TinyOS enables motes to self-organize themselves into wireless network sensors.
- TinyDB, a small database that stores the information on a mote. With the help of TinyOS, the mote can process the data and send filtered information to a receiver.

These motes enable enterprises to constantly collect important information and send the information to the appropriate server for processing so that the appropriate response can be initiated when necessary. The motes become the generator of pervasive information that reflects the status of business processes or environmental conditions.

Pervasive Devices

Pervasive devices come in different forms and shapes. Compared to a networked computer, some pervasive devices, such as landline or cell phones, are more widely available. Other devices are simply more portable and thus can be easily carried around. Yet other devices are embedded in the environment and are able to deliver specialized information. In terms of their functions, some are for accessing the Internet, some are just for entering information while the user is on the go, and others are for storing large amounts of information and can be easily carried around.

Traditional Telephones, Pagers, and Cell Phones

Traditional landline telephone has been the most pervasive communication device around the world. Voice markup languages such as

VoiceXML (voice extensible markup language; Rubio, 2004), together with supporting technologies such as the voice browser and voice gateway, has made the traditional telephone yet another device for connecting the user to the Internet. With speech recognition, users can choose to use touch tone or simply say what they need. Figure 1 shows how a telephone can be used to connect to the Internet.

1.   The user dials the number from any phone (landline or mobile).
2.   The call is routed to the corresponding voice gateway, which maps the phone number to a particular application hosted at the enterprise network.
3.   The voice gateway knows the URL (uniform resource locator) of the application. It uses an HTTP (hypertext transfer protocol) request to fetch the first dialog of the application.
4.   The enterprise Web server and application server return the dialog to the gateway in the form of a VoiceXML document.
5.   The gateway interprets the VoiceXML document, plays the greeting, and asks the user for input. Now the user can use touch tone or speech to provide input. Based on the user input and the application logic as described in the VoiceXML file, the voice gateway decides what dialog to fetch next from the enterprise network.

Pagers allow users to receive alerts with a limited amount of text. With two-way pagers, users can also reply with a text message.

With cell phones (not smart phones), besides the same communication capabilities of a landline telephone, most users can use short-message service (SMS) to send and receive text messages. This is good for near-real-time conversational communications.

Smart Phones, Wireless PDAs, and Blackberry Devices

Smart phones are cells phones that have both voice and data capabilities. Such a cell phone comes with a mini Web browser and thus can be used to access Internet content. However, since the smart phones typically have rather small screens, they can only access pages specifically designed for small screens and coded in a special markup language such as Wireless Markup Language (WML). Some smart phones are equipped with a computing platform such as the Java Virtual Machine that can run applications written in J2ME (Java 2 Micro Edition).

Wireless PDAs typically have larger screens than cell phones and can directly access HTML (hypertext markup language) pages. Some wireless PDAs can also be used to make phone calls, and are referred to as PDA phones. Since many people prefer to carry only one of such mobile device around, there is a competition between

Figure 1. Voice gateway connects the phone network with the data network

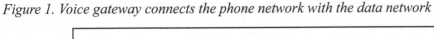

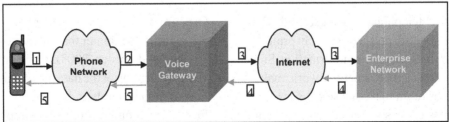

PDA phones and smart phones, a war in which the smart phones seem to be winning.

ViewSonic (http://www.viewsonic.com) made a super-sized PDA, called the ViewPad, that offers a regular 800x600-pixel screen. The ViewPad can be a very useful mobile device when regular screen size is a necessity while light weight and zero-boot-up time are also desired.

Blackberry devices made by Research in Motion (http://www.rim.com) has been a big success for enterprise users as they provide a very convenient way for reading and typing e-mails while being away from the office.

Laptop or Tablet PCs with Wireless Access

When size and weight are not inhibitive, mobile users may choose to carry a laptop or tablet PC while on the go. These mobile PCs use wireless cards to connect to either a wireless LAN or wireless WAN. Many such laptops now have built-in wireless LAN cards, and have slots for users to insert a wireless WAN card such as the AirCard made by Sierra Wireless (http://www. sierrawireless.com). An enterprise also needs to be prepared to provide support to mobile users in order to help them connect to the Internet through Wi-Fi hot spots (Hamblen, 2005).

Wireless LAN is often available at a corporation campus, or at public hot spots such as many airports and Starbucks Cafés. Wireless WAN is available wherever cellular service is available for the specific provider that the wireless card is registered with.

IP Phones

IP phones are telephones that use a TCP/IP (transmission-control protocol/Internet protocol) network for transmitting voice information. Since IP phones are attached to the data network, makers of such devices often make the screens larger so that the phones can also be used to access data.

What makes IP phones pervasive devices is that a user who is away from his or her own desk can come to any IP phone on the same corporate network, log in to the phone, and make the phone work as his or her own phone. The reason is for this is that an IP phone is identified on the network by an IP address. The mapping between a telephone number and an IP address can be easily changed to make the phone "belong" to a different user.

In terms of the information-access capability, Cisco (http://www.cisco.com) makes IP phones that can access information encoded in a special XML format. Example applications on the phone include retrieving stock quotes, flight departure and arrival information, news, and so forth.

Pingtel (http://www.pingtel.com) developed a phone that runs a Java Virtual Machine. This makes the phone almost as powerful as a computer.

Mitel (http://www.mitel.com) made an IP phone that allows a user to dock a PDA. With this capability, users can go to any such IP phone, dock their PDA into the phone, and immediately have their address books on the PDA available to the telephone. Users can also have their personal preferences transferred from the PDA to the phone and start to use the phone the way they prefer. In addition, users can benefit from new applications on the PDA, such as portable voice mail and dialing by the address book.

The Mitel IP phone seamlessly blends the wired and wireless world for the user so that they are no longer dealing with two separate communication tools. It also provides users with location transparency within the network.

Orbs (Ambient Devices)

Orbs are simple devices that convey information at a glance in a manner that is easy to observe and comprehend (Feder, 2003). Orbs only present a visual indication of the data, not detailed information or actual numbers. Orbs come in different forms. One common orb is a simple globe that changes color and intensity. Other forms include the following:

- Wall panels that adjust color or blink
- Pens, watch bezels, and fobs that change color
- Water tubes that vary the bubble rate
- Pinwheels that change speed

Orbs operate via wireless pager networks under the command of a server. This server gathers pertinent information from sources, including the Web, condenses it to a simple value, and periodically sends the information to the orbs.

Orbs are currently available from several retailers. The wireless service costs about $5 per month per device. Ambient Devices (http://www.ambientdevices.com) sells orbs and provides the communications service.

The information displayed by orbs is configurable. There are currently available data feeds for stock-market movement and weather forecasts.

Input Technologies: Dictation, Anoto Pen, and Projection Keyboard

Two natural ways for mobile users to input information are speech and handwriting.

Speech input can be at two levels: question-and-answer vs. dictation. Question-and-answer speech input is useful for entering structured information where the answers can be predefined using a grammar. Dictation technology allows users to speak freely and tries to recognize what the user has said. Diction technology typically requires a training phase to tune the speech recognizer to each particular speaker in order to achieve high recognition accuracy. Leading dictation products are Dragon NaturallySpeaking from ScanSoft (http://www.scansoft.com) and ViaVoice from IBM (http://www.ibm.com).

The Swedish company Anoto (http://www.anoto.com) invented a technology for pen-based input (McCarthy, 2000). It consists of a digital pen that feels like a regular ballpoint pen, a special

paper with patterns of dots printed on it, and a wireless technology such as Bluetooth that sends handwritten information stored in the pen to a computer. As the user writes, the pen not only records what has been written, but also the order in which the user writes it. Anoto has partnered with companies such as Logitech (http://www.logitech.com) and Nokia (http://www.nokia.com) to bring this technology to end users.

For users who want to use a keyboard without carrying one, Canesta (http://www.canesta.com) developed the projection keyboard, in which the image of a keyboard is projected on a surface. By typing on the projection keyboard, information is entered into the associated PDA device.

Application Scenarios

From an enterprise's perspective, the following applications areas are where pervasive computing brings business value.

- Allow employees to stay in touch with phone calls, voice mail, e-mail, and so forth while being away from the office.
- Give employees access to information or transactions via mobile devices while on the road.
- Provide employees with access to the corporate network from anywhere on the Internet (i.e., remote access).
- Send location-based information to employees and customers.
- Monitor device status, perimeter security, and so forth using a wireless sensor network.

COMMUNICATION: UNIFIED COMMUNICATION AND INSTANT COMMUNICATION

With cell phones and pagers, it is not very hard to keep mobile users in touch. But some pervasive communication technologies have reached a higher level. Let us look at two such technologies:

unified communication and instant communication.

Unified communications refers to technologies that allow users access to all their phone calls, voice mails, e-mails, faxes, and instant messages as long as they have access to either a phone or a computer. With a computer, a software phone allows the user to make or receive phone calls. Voice-mail messages can be forwarded to the e-mail box as audio files and played on the computer. Fax can be delivered to the e-mail box as images. With a phone, a user can listen to e-mail messages that the system would read using the text-to-speech technology. A user can request a fax to be forwarded to a nearby fax machine.

Unified communications services are offered by most traditional telecommunications technology providers such as Cisco, Avaya, and Nortel.

Instant communication refers to the ability of reaching someone instantly via a wearable communication device. Vocera (http://www.vocera. com) offers a system that uses 802.11b wireless local area networks to allow mobile users to instantly communicate with one another. Each user only needs to have a small wearable device to stay connected. To reach someone, the user would only need to speak a name, a job role, a group, or a location to the system, and the system will take care of the rest. By combining a small wearable device and the speech-recognition capability, Vocera offers a highly usable solution for mobile communication within an organization.

The functions and features of Vocera include the following:

- Instant communication via a small wearable device and speech commands
- Hands-free communication. Except for pressing the button to start and stop a conversation, a user's hands are free during the communication.
- Flexibility in how to specify the recipients. A user can use a name, role, group, or location to tell the system whom to contact.

- The option of having a conversation or leaving a message, for both one-to-one and group communications
- Call controls such as call transfer, blocking, or screening
- Outside calling through the private branch exchange (PBX). The Vocera server can be connected to the PBX to allow users of Vocera to contact people outside the organization.

The Vocera technology has been well received in organizations such as hospitals where users' hands are often busy when they need to communicate with others.

Mobile Access to Information and Applications

Organizations can benefit significantly by allowing mobile access to information and applications. Here are a few examples.

Sales-Force Automation

Salespeople are often on the road. It is important for them to have access to critical business information anywhere at anytime. Pervasive access to information increases their productivity by using their downtime during travel to review information about clients and prospects, about the new products and services they are going to sell, or to recap what has just happened during a sales event when everything is still fresh in their memory. Being able to use smart phones or wireless PDAs to conduct these activities is much more convenient for salespeople as opposed to having to carry a laptop PC.

Dashboard or Project-Portfolio Management

For busy executives, it is very valuable for them to be able to keep up to date on the dashboard while they are away from the office and to take actions when necessary. It is also very helpful for them to be able to look at the portfolio of projects they are watching, update information they have just received during a meeting or conversation, and take notes or actions about a specific project.

Facility Management and Other On-Site Service Applications

Mobile access to information can significantly boost the productivity of on-site service people such as facility- or PC-support staff. With mobile access, they can retrieve ticket information on the spot, update the ticket as soon as they are done with the work, and get the next work order without having to come back to the office. Mobile access also reduces the amount of bookkeeping, which requires a lot of manual intervention, and thus reduces the chance of human errors.

Remote Access to Corporate Network

Allowing employees access to the corporate network from anywhere on the Internet could certainly bring convenience to employees and boost productivity. There are two primary fashions of allowing remote access.

One approach is through a technology called virtual private network, or VPN. This typically requires the user to carry a laptop offered by the employer. Once the user is connected to the Internet, a secure connection (called a VPN tunnel) is established between the laptop and the corporate network after both user and device are authenticated. Then the user will have access to all the information and applications just as if the user were in the office.

The other approach does not require the user to carry a corporate laptop. It simply requires that the user has access to a Web browser. In this case, for security reasons, two-factor authentication is often employed, in which the user not only needs

to provide a user ID and password, but also something else, such as the security code generated by a hard token. With this approach, an enterprise can choose which applications to make available for remote access. Terminal service technology offered by Citrix (http://www.citrix.com) can be used to offer browser-based remote access to applications, both Web based and desktop based.

Location-Based Services

A special type of pervasive application is location-based service. With wireless LANs, when a mobile user is in the vicinity of an access point, location-specific information can be delivered to the user's mobile device. With wireless WANs, a user's location can be determined by the cellular tower(s) that the user's handset is communicating with, or by the GPS (Global Positioning System) receiver the user is using. Location-based services include pushing information about local businesses, sending promotions to the user's device based on the user's profile and preferences, and showing meeting agendas and meeting material if the user is on the meeting attendee list for the room at the time.

If location needs to be accurately determined, an ultrasonic location system called the bat system can be used. This 3-D location system uses low power and wireless technology that is relatively inexpensive. An ultrasonic location system is based on the principle of *trilateration*: position finding by the measurement of distances. A short pulse of ultrasound is emitted from a transmitter or bat that is attached to a person or object to be located. On the ceiling are receivers mounted at known points. These receivers can measure the pulse and length of travel.

An ultrasonic location system is composed of three main components.

- **Bats:** Small ultrasonic transmitters worn by an individual or on an object to be located

- **Receivers:** Ultrasonic signal detectors mounted in the ceiling
- **Central controller:** Coordinator of the bats and receivers

To locate a bat, the central controller will send the bat's ID via a 433-MHz bidirectional radio signal. The bat will detect its ID through the embedded receiver and transmit an ultrasonic signal containing a 48-bit code to the receiver in the ceiling. The central controller will measure the elapsed time that it took for the pulse to reach the receiver. The system developed at the AT&T Cambridge facility can provide an accuracy of 3 centimeters.

Overall, location-based services are still in research mode. Once the technology becomes mature and "killer apps" are identified, there could be an explosive adoption.

User-Interaction Models

In the context of pervasive computing, it is usually inconvenient, if not impossible, for the user to enter text using a regular keyboard. Sometimes, it is also inconvenient for the user to read text. Therefore, other input and output mechanisms have to be employed.

Nontraditional input mechanisms include speech recognition, gesture, touch screen, eye gazing, software keyboard, and projection keyboard. Among these, a combination of speech-recognition and pen-based touch-screen input is most natural for most situations. This is also what PDAs and tablet PCs typically offer.

Nontraditional output mechanisms include converting text to speech and using sound, blinking, and vibration to convey information (as in ambient computing described earlier in this chapter).

Multimodal interaction allows a user to choose among different modes of input and output. For mobile users, speech is typically the most conve-

nient way for input, while visual means may still be the most powerful way of seeing the output (especially when the output includes pictures or diagrams).

Kirusa (http://www.kirusa.com) has developed technologies to support multiple levels of multi-modal interaction. SMS multimodality allows users to ask a question in voice and have the answers delivered to their mobile devices in the form of an SMS message. Sequential multimodality allows users to use the interaction mode deemed most appropriate for each step of the process. Simultaneous multimodality lets users combine different input and output modes at the same time. For example, for driving directions, a user can say "I need directions from here to there," while pointing to the start and end points.

Both IBM and Microsoft have developed technologies that will support multimodal interaction. IBM's solution is based on the XHTML+VoiceXML (or simply X+V) specification. Microsoft's solution is based on the speech application language tags (SALT) specification, which defines speech input and output tags that can be inserted into traditional Web pages using XHTML.

Besides deciding on what interaction mode to support, much effort is needed to apply user-centered design in order to deliver a good use experience for mobile users (Holtzblatt, 2005).

A Service-Oriented Architecture to Support Pervasive Computing

For an enterprise to leverage pervasive computing, instead of deploying various point solutions, the better way is to build an architecture that is well positioned to support pervasive devices and usage. In order to provide mobile users with maximum access to enterprise information and applications with customized interaction methods and work flow, and at the same time minimize the extra cost in supporting pervasive access, a service-oriented architecture should be established.

Figure 2. *A service-oriented architecture that supports pervasive computing*

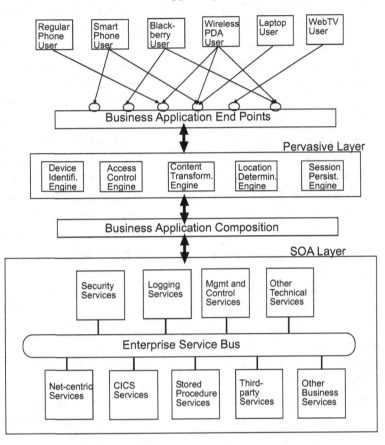

The following picture shows a service-oriented architecture that supports pervasive computing. Let us look at this architecture from the top to the bottom.

- Users access applications from different devices. Some devices, such as the regular telephone, have only the voice channel. Some, such as the Blackberry devices, only have the visual display. Others may have both voice and visual channels. The size of the visual display ranges from 1 inch for cell phones, several inches for the PDA and Blackberry, and 15 or more inches for laptops.
- The user devices may be on different network connections, ranging from wireless LAN and wireless WAN to telephone networks.
- Users access applications through the applications' end points. This could be a URL, a phone number, or a start screen stored on the end user's device.
- The pervasive layer sits between the application end points and the SOA layer to provide services to specifically support the mobile users.
  - The device identification engine uses a unique ID to identify the device the user is using. This requires the augmentation of some of the communication protocols to include a universally unique ID (such as the radio frequency identifier, or RFID) of the device that is initiating the request. With this ID, the system

can uniquely identify the device and thus have knowledge of its capabilities, the associated user, and so forth. The ID information is also passed to the security service in the SOA layer to help decide whether the user is authorized to access the application.

○ The access-control engine uses information about the device and the communication channel it is coming from to determine the best way to communicate with the device: voice only, visual only, SMS, or some type of multimodal interaction.

○ Based on the desired interaction mode with the user, the content-transformation engine either calls the appropriate version of the application or dynamically transforms the information into the appropriate markup language: HTML, WML, VoiceXML, X+V, and so forth, using the eXtensible Stylesheet Language transformation (XSLT) technology.

○ The location-determination service uses mechanisms built into the networks to determine the geographic location of the user, and then decides whether the information should be tailored based on the location and whether additional location-based information should be pushed to the user.

○ The session-persistence engine uses the device ID and user-identity information to keep the user in the same session while the user is roaming from one network to another, or from disconnected mode to connected mode again during a short period of time. For smart-client applications, where data may be temporarily stored on the device when connection is lost, the session-persistence layer would also take care of synchronizing the data on the device with data on the server.

• The business-application composition layer uses information received from the pervasive layer to determine how to integrate the business services together to best fit the need of this mobile user.

• The SOA layer provides the business services and technical services that are integrated together through the enterprise service bus. The business services can be built using Net-centric technologies such as Java or Microsoft .NET, or they can be built based on existing legacy business functions such as customer information control system (CICS) transaction and stored procedures. They can also be based on business functions built using third-party tools or existing in-house business modules developed in C or C++, COBOL, and so forth.

After the establishment of such an architecture (which can be gradually built across multiple projects), when building an application that supports pervasive access, business services are either reused or built. When an existing business service is reused, the project team needs to go through the service's specification to verify that the service will work well with the pervasive layer to support all the pervasive channels that the application is going to support. If not, the first thing the project team should try to modify is the pervasive layer. If the issue really lays in the fact that the business service is not a "pure" service, that is, the service is tied to access methods, then the service needs to be either modified or wrapped in order to support the new requirements. When such a modification occurs, the service needs to be made backward compatible, and existing applications that use the service need to be regression tested. Eventually, the service definition needs to be modified to reflect the changes.

With this architecture, when a new pervasive access channel appears, or there is a change in an existing channel, then the only thing that needs to be modified is the pervasive channel. All business services can remain the same.

FUTURE DIRECTIONS

Moving forward, there needs to be much research and development work on building a system infrastructure that can use different sources of information to judge where the user is, and what devices and interaction modes are available to the user during a pervasive session. This will enable smarter location-based information push to better serve the user.

A related research topic is how to smoothly transition an interaction to a new device and interaction mode as the user changes locations and devices. Some initial work on this subject, referred to as seamless mobility, is being conducted at IBM and other organizations.

Another area that deserves much attention is the proactive delivery of information that users will need based on their profiles and information such as activities on their calendars or to-do lists. This relates to previous research efforts on intelligent personal assistants with integration into the pervasive computing environment.

REFERENCES

3Gtoday. (2005). Retrieved November 5, 2005, from http://www.3gtoday.com

Blackwell, G. (2002, January 25). Mesh networks: Disruptive technology? *Wi-Fi Planet*. Retrieved October 25, 2005, from http://www.wi-fiplanet. com/columns/article.php/961951

Bluetooth SIG. (2005). *The official Bluetooth wireless info site*. Retrieved November 3, 2005, from http://www.bluetooth.com

Culler, D. E., & Hong, W. (Eds.). (2004). Wireless sensor networks. *Communications of the ACM, 47*(6), 30-57.

Feder, B. (2003, June 10). Glass that glows and gives stock information. *New York Times*, P.C1.

Fox, B. (2001, November 21). "Mesh radio" can deliver super-fast Internet for all. *New Scientist*. Retrieved November 15, 2005, from http://www.newscientist.com/news/news.jsp?id=ns99991593

Geier, J. (2002, April 15). Making the choice: 802.11a or 802.11g. *Wi-Fi Planet*. Retrieved October 16, 2005, from http://www.wi-fiplanet.com/tutorials/article.php/1009431

Hamblen, M. (2005). Wi-Fi fails to connect with mobile users. ComputerWorld, *39*(37), 1, 69.

Henderson, T. (2003, February 3). Vocera communication system: Boldly talking over the wireless LAN. *NetworkWorld*. Retrieved November 12, 2005, from http://www.networkworld.com/reviews/2003/0203rev.html

Holtzblatt, K. (Ed.). (2005). Designing for the mobile device: Experiences, challenges, and methods. *Communications of the ACM, 48*(7), 32-66.

IEEE. (2005a). *IEEE 802.15 Working Groups for WPAN*. Retrieved November 7, 2005, from http://www.ieee802.org/15/

IEEE. (2005b). *The IEEE 802.16 Working Group on Broadband Wireless Access Standards*. Retrieved November 22, 2005, from http://www.wirelessman.org

McCarthy, K. (2000, April 7). Anoto pen will change the world. *The Register*. Retrieved September 14, 2005, from http://www.theregister.co.uk/2000/04/07/anoto_pen_will_change/

Rubio, D. (2004, October 20). VoiceXML promised voice-to-Web convergence. *NewsForge*. Retrieved November 23, 2005, from http://www.newsforge.com/article.pl?sid=04/10/15/1738253

Schrick, B. (2002). Wireless broadband in a box. *IEEE Spectrum*. Retrieved November 19, 2005, from http://www.spectrum.ieee.org/WEBONLY/publicfeature/jun02/wire.html

Schwartz, E. (2001, September 26). Free wireless networking movement gathers speed. *InfoWorld.* Retrieved December 5, 2005, from http://www.infoworld.com/articles/hn/xml/01/09/26/010926 hnfreewireless.xml

ZigBee Alliance. (2005). Retrieved November 11, 2005, from http://www.zigbee.org/en/index.asp

Chapter XVII
Trust Models for Ubiquitous Mobile Systems

Mike Burmester
Florida State University, USA

ABSTRACT

This chapter introduces the notion of trust as a means to establish security in ubiquitous mobile network systems. It argues that trust is an essential requirement to enable security in any open network environments, and in particular, in wireless ad hoc environments where there is no network topology. In such environments, communication can only be achieved via routes that have to be trusted. In general it may be hard, or even impossible, to establish, recall, and maintain trust relationships. It is therefore important to understand the limitations of such environments and to find mechanisms that may support trust either explicitly or implicitly. We consider several models that can be used to enable trust in such environments, based on economic, insurance, information flow, and evolutionary paradigms.

INTRODUCTION

Wireless mobile networks are a paradigm for mobile communication in which wireless nodes do not rely on any underlying static network infrastructure for services such as packet routing, name resolution, node authentication, or distribution of computational resources. The communication medium is broadcast. Nodes in range communicate in a direct peer-to-peer manner, while nodes out of range establish routing paths dynamically through other nodes where possible. The recent rise in popularity of mobile wireless devices and technological developments have made possible the deployment of wireless mobile networks for several applications. Examples include emergency deployments, disaster recovery, search-and-rescue missions, sensor networks, military (battlefield) operations, and more recently e-commerce. Since the network nodes are mobile, the network topology frequently changes: Communication links are established or broken as nodes move in and out of range, and the network may get partitioned with the connectivity restricted to the partitions. As a result it may be much harder (or even impossible) to establish trust associations.

The trend in trust management is to view trust implicitly through delegation of privilege via certificates. Certificates can be chain-linked (linking à priori trust relationships) and used to propagate and distribute trust over insecure media, without the danger of being manipulated.

In this chapter, we give an overview of several models that can be used to support trust in mobile networks, based on economic, insurance, information flow, and evolutionary paradigms.

TRUST IN WIRELESS MOBILE NETWORKS

We consider environments in which there may be no fixed underlying network infrastructure, such as static base stations, for services such as packet routing, name resolution, node authentication, or the distribution of computational resources. In such environments, recalling and maintaining trust relationships is particularly challenging. Mobile systems share many of the complexities of fixed infrastructure systems. For example, nodes may have (Burmester & Yasinsac, 2004):

1. No prior relationship or common peers
2. No shared proprietary software
3. Different transmission, memory and processing capabilities
4. Different mobility characteristics
5. Different lifetime properties

Defining Trust

Trust is a highly abstract concept and it is unlikely that any simple definition can comprehensively capture all the subtleties of its essence. Informally we may define trust as a behavioral expectation of one party toward another. There are two perspectives in this definition, one in which a party *awards* trust to another (Alice trusts that Bob's

public key is PK(Bob)), the other in which a party *gains* trust from another (Alice has convinced Bob that her public key is PK(Alice)).

Representing Trust: Certificates vs. Tokens

In any stateful trust model, trust must be represented by some type of persistent structure. Certificates are the de facto standard for representing trust relationships that are protected by cryptography. Certificates are portable and bind a cryptographic key (a digital string) to an entity, thus guaranteeing the authenticity of actions performed by that entity. Trust tokens are another structure that can be used to represent trust in a more direct way, analogous to the relation between checks and cash. Checks guarantee payment by tying the purchaser to some identifying information (like a certificate), while the value of cash is self-contained.

Trusted Third Parties

A trusted third party (TTP) can facilitate significantly the establishment of trust in mobile environments. For example, if two parties *A* and *B* who do not know each other have a trust relationship with a third party *T*, then *T* can be an effective intermediary for transactions between *A* and *B*. However in general, wireless mobile networks may not have any infrastructure components that are typically used as TTPs. In such cases, TTPs have to be elected or assigned by using an appropriate election or assignment protocol.

MODELS FOR TRUST IN WIRELESS MOBILE ENVIRONMENTS

Trust is *context* driven (e.g., A may trust *B* for event *x*, but not for event *y*). Trust may also be qualitative rather than Boolean (e.g., A may trust *B* more than *C*). Finally, trust relationships may be fixed or dynamic. Dynamic trust relationships are most appropriate for the requirements of mobile environments.

Models for dynamic trust must support establishing, changing, and permanently revoking trust between parties, and must also consider network environment issues. In the following sections we shall consider several models that can be used to support trust in wireless mobile networks (Burmester & Yasinsac, 2004).

A Mathematical Model for Trust: The Trust Graph

We may represent the trust in a network by a directed graph, the *trust graph*, whose links (A, B) correspond to the explicit trust that node A has in node B. Such links are indicated by A $\Rightarrow$ B. The implicit trust that a node X has in another node Y is then represented by a trust path from X to Y:

$$X = X_0 \Rightarrow X_1 \Rightarrow X_2 \ldots \Rightarrow X_{n-1} \Rightarrow X_n = Y$$

in which node X awards trust to node Y via a chain of intermediary nodes X_i, where X_i awards trust explicitly to the next node X_{i+1} in the chain. Such trust may be supported by certificates. For example, node X_i may certify (digitally sign) that key $PK(X_{i+1})$ is the public key of node X_{i+1}. A chain of certificates can then be used for implicit certification. This is essentially the trust model for the X509 PKI authentication infrastructure (ISO/IEC 9594-8, 1995). This particular trust infrastructure is hierarchical, with trust centrally managed (by a Root Certifying Authority, which is also a single-point-of-failure). PGP (Zimmermann, 1995) uses a web of trust in which trust is distributed "horizontally." See Burmester and Desmedt (2004) for a discussion on security issues of hierarchical vs. horizontal infrastructures.

In the basic trust graph model, trust is transitive but not necessarily reflexive. That is, even though A may award trust to B, B may not award trust to A. However, trust is binary: A $\Rightarrow$ B is either true or false. Therefore, there is a natural trust metric which is one unit for explicit trust. This is also the trust of a trust path that links A to B. In this model the trust that A awards to B is represented by the trust flow of A, B, which is also the connectivity of A, B. This model is appropriate for Byzantine faults environments in which the adversary can corrupt a bounded number of nodes, and trust has to be based on à priori beliefs, and not statistical profiles.

A Model Based on a Weighted Trust Graph

There are several other ways to define trust. For a stochastic model based on statistical profiling, we can define the explicit trust that A awards to (or has in) B as the probability with which A trusts B, based on, say, a history of good behavior by B. See the next section for a discussion on trust based on observed behavior. In this model we have a weighted trust graph in which each link A $\Rightarrow$ B is assigned a weight $t \in [0,1]$, which corresponds to the (explicit) trust that A has in B. If $\pi_1, \pi_2, \ldots, \pi_n$ are (all) the trust paths that link X to Y, then the implicit trust that X has in Y can be computed as follows (Burmester, Douligeris, & Kotzanikolaou, 2006):

$$\sum_{\pi i} \prod_{tk \in \pi i} tk - \sum_{\pi i \neq \pi j} \prod_{tk \in \pi i \cup \pi j} tk + \ldots + (-1)^{n+1} \prod_{tk \in \pi 1 \cup \ldots \cup \pi n} tk$$

For example, if there are three disjoint paths from X to Y with trust weights (t_1, t_2), (t_3, t_4), (t_5, t_6) respectively, then the implicit trust that X has in Y is:

$$t_1 t_2 + t_3 t_4 + t_5 t_6 - t_1 t_2 t_3 t_4 - t_3 t_4 t_5 t_6 + t_1 t_2 t_3 t_4 t_5 t_6$$

One can extend this model to allow for a dynamic model in which trust is regularly updated, by using a trust-ranking algorithm similar to that used by Web search engines (e.g., PageRank of Google [PageRank, 1997]).

A Model Based on Observed Behavior

A natural way to acquire trust is through direct observation. At its most fundamental level, trust is a decision, subject to emotions and intuition. In this scenario, personal observation is preferred to second-hand methods because of hints, nuances, and feelings that can be garnered. Though feelings are not considered in computer trust systems, there are advantages in doing so. Not all actions give insight into trustworthiness. The challenge is to translate such observations into trust decisions.

A challenge to trust management systems is that trust relationships need to be constructed *before* they are exercised. There are four basic categories of activity that affect trust (Burmester & Yasinsac, 2004):

1. Trust earning actions over time
2. Trust earning actions by count
3. Trust earning actions by magnitude
4. Trust defeating actions

Combinations of the first three allow cautious parties to grant trust frugally. Untrustworthy parties will be challenged to conduct a sufficient quality and quantity of trustworthy actions to gain trust. On the other hand, observation of malicious, reckless, or otherwise unpredictable actions allows reduction or revocation of awarded trust.

A Model Based on the Internet Paradigm

The economic opportunity provided by the Internet has driven rapid establishment of many new trust models. Companies like eBay, Amazon, and Priceline conduct all of their business with customers with whom they have no personal relationship or interaction with. Early work on supporting trust models was from a business perspective (Pardue, 2000). Some work has been done more recently to identify models that support cryptographic protection of trust relationships. In Zhong, Chen, and Yang (2003), a token-based trust model is proposed in which parties accumulate trust, transaction-by-transaction. For trust-earning actions, parties are awarded tokens that can be retained and later presented to reflect the earned trust. If no additional trust information is gathered, tokens may be revoked or restricted. This novel approach to trust acquisition has many properties that are well-suited to mobile networks. Tokens can be created, awarded, and verified via distributed algorithms, allowing a global aspect to trust decisions. Conversely, if the trust algorithm is well understood, parties that desire to perform malicious acts can become sleepers, behaving perfectly until they acquire sufficient trust to allow successful mischief.

Transitive Trust

Transitivity is in many respects a natural attribute of trust and is encountered in some of the most used security systems (Steiner, Neuman, & Schiller, 1988; Zhong et al., 2003). With transitive trust models, trust must be explicit (i.e., parties must know that if they place their trust in one party, then they are automatically placing their trust in other potentially unknown parties as well). For example, if Alice trusts Bob and Bob trusts Carol, then Alice must trust Carol. Such models make strong trust requirements on intermediaries or third parties. Unfortunately, there are inherent dangers in models with transitive trust (Christianson & Harbison, 1997).

A Model Based on Trust Classes

Trust may be considered as a two party relationship or there may be environments where nodes take on *class* trust properties, as in the Bell-LaPadula model (Bell & LaPadula, 1973). One way to form trust management functionality is to establish a trust promotion system. For example, consider a simple trust environment in which nodes can be categorized into the following five trust classes (from most to least trusted): *Highly trusted, Trusted, Unknown, Untrusted, Highly untrusted.* We can then establish a set of rules for promoting and demoting members between groups. These rules will be identified by the desired promotion rule. If promotion is not allowed for highly untrusted parties, then no rule is established for this class. The model may be further extended by designating a subset of the class of most trusted nodes as *promoters*. Promoters are responsible for determining if requestors meet the promotion requirements as designated in the promotion rules and in taking action to effect the justified group movement. While promotion is requested directly, demotion must be requested second hand.

A Financial Model

Trust can also be *contractually* secured. In this case, a Trusted Third Party guarantees the trust. As with secured loans, if the guaranteed trust is violated, the guarantor will deliver the promised security to the offended party. Secured trust is a pure form of transitive trust. It is unique in that its trust graph tree has height one and trust is secured by a contractually agreed value. As with secured financial interactions, the secured value may take many forms, including the following: a *co-signed trust certificate, a trust insurance policy, a trust bond and a trust collateral.*

These correspond to security mechanisms of the financial world. For a co-signed certificate, the co-signing party would have credentials that exceed those of the target and would assume liability for any adverse events that occur as a result of a trust breech. The insurance policy model is similar, except that the security is provided by a well recognized organization that promises benefits to the executor of the policy. The last two models are similar in that the trust target provides the value that secures the trust. The value can be

monetary, property, or other items or issues of suitable value to the source.

CONCLUSION

We have considered several models that can be used to manage the trust in mobile wireless environments. These models are highly distributed and address many of the trust management properties that are needed to secure mobile environments.

ACKNOWLEDGMENT

This material is based on work supported in part by the National Science Foundation under grant number NSF 0209092 and in part by the U.S. Army Research Laboratory and the Army Research Office under grant DAAD19-02-1-0235.

REFERENCES

Bell, D. E., & LaPadula, L. (1973). Secure computer systems: Mathematical foundations and model, *MITRE Corp.* M74-244, Bedford, MA.

Burmester, M., & Desmedt, Y. (2004). Is hierarchical public-key certification the next target for hackers? *Communications of the ACM, 47*(8), 68-74.

Burmester, M., & Yasinsac, A. (2004). Trust infrastructures for wireless mobile networks. *WSAES Transactions on Telecommunications* (pp. 377-381).

Burmester, M., Douligeris, C., & Kotzanikolaou, P. (2006). Security in mobile ad hoc networks. In C. Douligeris & D. Serpanos (Eds.), *Network security: Current status and future directions.* Piscataway, NJ: IEEE Press.

Christianson, B., & Harbison, W. S. (1997). Why isn't trust transitive? In *Proceedings of the 4th International Workshop on Security Protocols* (LNCS 1189, pp. 171-176).

ISO/IEC 9594-8. (1995). Information technology, Open Systems Interconnection. *The Directory: Overview of concepts, models, and services. International Organization for Standardization.* Geneva, Switzerland.

PageRank. (1997). Google. Retrieved from http://www.google.com/technology/

Pardue, H. (2000). A trust-based model of consumer-to-consumer online auctions. *The Arrowhead Journal of Business, 1*(1), 69-77.

Steiner, J., Neuman, C., & Schiller, J. I. (1988). Kerberos and authentication service for open network systems. In *Proceedings of USENIX*, Dallas, TX.

Zhong, S., Chen, J., & Yang, R. (2003). Sprite: A simple, cheat-proof, credit-based system for mobile ad hoc networks. In *Proceedings of INFOCOM 2003*.

Zimmermann, P. (1995). *The official PGP user's guide.* Cambridge, MA: MIT Press.

This work was previously published in Secure E-Government Web Services, edited by A. Mitrakas, P. Hengeveld, D. Polemi, and J. Gamper, pp. 63-70, copyright 2007 by IGI Publishing (an imprint of IGI Global).

Chapter XVIII
Evolving Information Ecologies:
The Appropriation of New Media in Organizations

Hanne Westh Nicolajsen
Technical University of Denmark, Denmark

Jørgen P. Bansler
Technical University of Denmark, Denmark

ABSTRACT

This chapter examines how people in organizations appropriate new computer-based media, that is, how they adopt, reconfigure, and integrate advanced communication technologies such as groupware or desktop conferencing systems into their work practice. The chapter presents and analyzes findings from an in-depth field study of the adoption and use of a Web-based groupware application—a "virtual workspace"—in a large multinational firm. The analysis focuses, in particular, on the fact that people in modern organizations have plenty of media at their disposal and often combine old and new media to accomplish their work tasks. Furthermore, it highlights the crucial role of organizational communication genres in shaping how people adopt and use new media. The authors argue that understanding and facilitating the process of appropriation is the key to the successful introduction of new media in organizations.

INTRODUCTION

This chapter provides an account of how people in organizations adopt new computer-mediated communication (CMC) technologies and incorporate them into their working practices. It focuses specifically on how people fit the new media together with their existing communication technologies, creating a configuration of media that matches their communication needs. The current proliferation of new computer-based media such as chat, SMS, instant messaging, desktop conferencing, virtual workspaces, and MOO-based meeting technologies (see, e.g., Yoshioka, Yates,

& Orlikowski, 2002) exacerbates the challenges associated with establishing and maintaining appropriate configurations of media in the workplace. Although the potential for developing very effective patterns of media use is high, given the large number of diverse technologies to choose from, there is also a significant risk that the outcome will be messy and inefficient.

It is well documented that established organizational communication genres influence how individuals and groups adopt and use new CMC technologies (Crowston & Williams, 2000; Orlikowski & Yates, 1994; Yates, Orlikowski, & Okamura, 1999). Genres, as conventions for social interaction, both shape and are shaped by organizational members' communicative practices. When new communication media are introduced in the organization, existing genres provide people with a resource that they can draw on in their efforts to incorporate the new technology into their daily work practice. In doing so, they not only reproduce but also redefine their existing repertoire of genres.

We address these issues based on an analysis of a longitudinal field study of the adoption and use of a Web-based groupware application in a large multinational company. The analysis employs insights and concepts from two strands of research on electronic communication in organizations. The first strand is concerned with understanding the "affordances" (i.e., the distinctive communicative properties, see the next section) of different communication technologies and how these affordances affect the process, content, or outcome of communication (see, e.g., Whittaker, 2003, for an overview). The second strand comprises an emergent body of work on organizational communication genres (e.g., Grimshaw, 2003; Yates & Orlikowski, 1992; Yates et al., 1999). This research explores the complex interrelations between media and genres and sheds light on how genres evolve over time as new technologies are introduced.

THEORETICAL BACKGROUND

Technology appropriation is the process by which people in organizations adopt, reconfigure, and integrate new technologies into their work practice (Dourish, 2003). This involves not only adapting or "customizing" the technology to suit local needs and requirements, but also devising appropriate ways of using the technology for one's own, particular purposes. As Dourish (2003) points out, understanding how people appropriate new CMC technologies is a "key problem" for both researchers and practitioners, "since it is critical to the success of technology deployment" (p. 465).

Attempts to introduce new CMC technologies in organizations often fail because managers and technologists underestimate the time and effort it takes successfully to appropriate and incorporate a new communication medium into the existing "information ecology," that is, the system of people, practices, genres, and information and communication technologies in the local environment. Appropriation is difficult to achieve because information ecologies are diverse, continually evolving, and "marked by strong interrelationships and dependencies among [the] different parts" (Nardi & O'Day, 1999, p. 51). For instance, communication media, genre repertoires (that is, the set of genres in use within a community [Orlikowski & Yates, 1994]), and local work practices are interrelated and fit together in complex and subtle ways.

Change in an ecology is systemic and difficult to predict (Nardi & O'Day, 1999). Changing one element sometimes can have self-reinforcing effects that can be felt throughout the whole system, but in other instances, if the changes are incompatible with the rest of the system, they may disappear without a trace. For instance, studies have shown that, when a new electronic medium is introduced in an organization, it sometimes transforms the entire organization and the ways in which work is conducted (see, e.g., Sproull & Kiesler, 1991), whereas in other cases it may have only marginal impact or fail completely, because people stick to their old familiar media and habitual modes of communication (see, e.g., Ciborra, 1996; Mark, 2002).

The ecology metaphor draws attention to the fact that no communication medium exists in the workplace in isolation. When introduced in an organization, a new communication medium must "compete" with existing media, either displacing one or more existing technologies (such as telephone and fax have done to the telegraph) or fitting into a niche that can ensure its "survival" alongside the existing media. In other words, potential users must perceive the new technology as reliable and useful, and they must be both willing and able to adjust their work practices and communication patterns to exploit the new opportunities afforded by the technology.

Despite its practical importance, there has not been much research into how new media are appropriated in organizations and the process is not yet well understood. The fundamental goal of research in computer-mediated communication "has been to explain the relationship between the affordances of different mediated technologies and the communication that results from using those technologies" (Whittaker, 2003, p. 244), rather than to understand how people in real work settings combine different media and use them in complementary ways to accomplish their tasks. Although CMC research has used a variety of methods (e.g., interviews, surveys, and ethnographic studies), the bulk of the available data on the use of electronic media comes from "laboratory studies where users are given predefined technologies, tasks, and instructions" (Whittaker, 2003, p. 248). These studies leave out important aspects of "real life" media use in organizations—for instance, how people use different media in combination with each other or how communication genres and conventions of use develop when the technology is used by a community for extended periods of time.

In the following, we expand upon the concepts of *affordances* and *organizational communication genres* and use them to explain important aspects of technology appropriation.

Technology Affordances

Most advanced CMC technologies are flexible, generic media, which can support a wide variety of possible communication patterns. However, despite their inherent flexibility and open-endedness, these electronic media have a constraining as well as enabling materiality. For example, e-mail and chat convey only text (linguistic information), whereas videoconferencing provides a combination of speech (linguistic information) and images (visual information).

In other words, different CMC technologies possess different affordances[1] (Hutchby, 2001a), that is, they offer different possibilities for action, and these affordances "constrain both the possible meanings and the possible uses of the technologies" (p. 447):

... affordances are functional and relational aspects which frame, while not determining, the possibilities for agentic action in relation to an object. In this way technologies can be understood as artefacts which may be both shaped by and shaping of the practices of human use in interaction with, around and through them. (Hutchby, 2001a, p. 444)

As Hutchby points out, the affordances of a technological artifact are not just functional but also relational aspects of its materiality. Affordances are *functional* in the sense that they facilitate certain actions: for instance, using a calculator to compute a number or using a fax to communicate across distance. However, affordances may differ from person to person and from context to context, and in that sense they are *relational*. For instance, a PC with a compiler has the affordance of programmability, but only if you are a skilled programmer and know the appropriate programming language (and only if you have access to appropriate input-output devices, a stable power supply, and so on). Similarly, an advanced, digital camera has different affordances for a novice and a professional photographer.

The full range of affordances of any technology cannot be perceived immediately, for two reasons. First, as just mentioned, the affordances depend on the user and the context. The possibilities that a technology affords, therefore, will only be revealed through actual use and, in many cases, only after extended periods of time in which people gain hands-on experience with the technology and learn how to utilize it. Second, the affordances may change over time as the context evolves and users develop their competence and skills. The technology's affordances exist regardless of whether people exploit them or not, but they only become manifest when people act in terms of them.

Although—in their effort to accommodate certain imagined communicative purposes and use patterns—designers deliberately design specific features into the technology, they are unable to control, or even fully grasp, the entire range of the technology's communicative affordances (Hutchby, 2001b). The result is that designers are often taken aback by the way people "tamper with" their designs and make use of them for quite novel and unintended purposes.

Conventions and Genres

Social conventions are essential for governing communication and guiding the use of communication media. There are, for instance, widespread social conventions about the use of one medium rather than another for specific purposes (e.g., you do not send your condolences to a bereaved person by e-mail or SMS).

When a new communication medium is introduced in an organization, people need to develop appropriate conventions for when and how to use

it. As Mark (2002) recently has pointed out, people cannot just be given a new CMC technology (e.g., a groupware system) and "be expected to optimally use it without some common agreements on the means of operation" (p. 351). Rather, conventions must evolve to regulate behavior so as to provide a "*modus vivendi* for making interactions proceed smoothly" (p. 351)—and if such conventions fail to develop, the technology will fail too.

In the context of computer-mediated communication, *genres* constitute a particularly important type of conventions. Organizational communication genres—such as the business letter, meeting minutes, or project plan—are social conventions that both structure and are structured by people's communicative practices. Genres are important because they help people make sense of interactions and guide them both in how to communicate and how to interpret the communicative actions of others.

Orlikowski and Yates (1994) have defined genres as "distinctive type[s] of communicative action, characterized by a socially recognized communicative purpose and common aspects of form" (p. 543). Genres—like technology affordances—both enable and constrain action without determining it:

A genre established within a particular community serves as an institutionalized template for social interaction—an organizing structure—that influences the ongoing communicative action of members through their use of it within and across their community. Genres as organizing structures shape, but do not determine, how community members engage in everyday interaction. (Yates & Orlikowski, 2002, p. 15)

Genres are produced, reproduced, or changed through the everyday communicative practices of people. That is, even though genres structure the communicative actions, they are not fixed, unchangeable. On the contrary, when engaging in communication and enacting established genres, people sometimes advertently or inadvertently challenge and modify elements of existing genre rules (Yates & Orlikowski, 1992). These modifications may be triggered by social or technological changes in the organizational context, for instance, by the introduction of a new electronic communication medium, which possesses new affordances and thus offers new opportunities for action. For example, Crowston and Williams (2000) have shown that the World Wide Web has led to the emergence of new genres that exploit the features of hypermedia linking provided by the Web technology.

What typically happens when a new communication medium is introduced in an organization is that people draw on existing genres in their efforts to make sense of the medium and to figure out how to use it (Orlikowski & Yates, 1994; Yates & Orlikowski, 1992; Yates et al., 1999). In many instances, and especially in the beginning, they simply reproduce familiar genres in the new medium, adapting them slightly to fit the technology, but without substantially departing from the existing genre rules. However, over time, as people learn more about the new technology's affordances and introduce more significant changes and modifications to the established genre rules, new genres may emerge.

Yates et al. (1999) suggest that these "processes of genre structuring are ongoing, and do not just occur at the initial implementation of the new medium" (p. 96). They distinguish between implicit and explicit genre structuring. *Implicit structuring* comprises the unreflective and unintentional shaping of genres and communicative practices,

which take place through people's mundane, day-to-day interactions, for example, when familiar genres inadvertently spread from one medium or community to another. Two types of implicit structuring can be identified, namely migration and variation (see Table 1). Migration is the transfer of established genres from one medium or community to another, while variation denotes a change in existing genres that emerges tacitly from use of the technology over time. *Explicit structuring* applies when individuals or groups deliberately try to either reinforce or change established patterns of communication, for example, by adapting existing genres to the new medium. Explicit structuring includes planned replication, planned modification, and opportunistic modification (see Table 1). Planned replication aims to reproduce existing genres within a new medium with minimal changes. In contrast, planned modification aims to alter the genres rules, for instance, by changing the purpose and the intended audience or readership. The last type, opportunistic modification, "involves purposeful changes introduced in response to some unexpected occurrence, condition, or request" (p. 98), for instance as a result of prior actions intended to either replicate or modify existing genres.

It is, however, important to stress that communication genres are social conventions and that they therefore cannot be designed like technologies can. One may attempt to influence the communicative practices of a community in various ways, for example, by codifying genre rules or by sanctioning "inappropriate" behavior, but one can never control the outcome.

Table 1. Processes of genres structuring (based on Yates et al., 1999)

	Implicit structuring	**Explicit structuring**
Reproduction of genre rules	Migration	Planned replication
Change of genre rules	Variation	Planned modification Opportunistic modification

FIELD STUDY

Organizational Setting

In the field study, we examined how people in a large multinational corporation appropriated a novel CMC application intended to support the company's globally dispersed product development groups. Medica (a pseudonym) is a highly successful pharmaceutical company, which manufactures a range of pharmaceutical products and provides a host of services. Medica's headquarters are situated in Northern Europe, but the corporation has production facilities, research centers, and sales offices in more than 60 countries around the world.

Product development projects in Medica are complex, large-scale, long-term endeavors. A typical project lasts 9-10 years and involves up to 500 people from many different functional areas within the company. Most of the activities take place at sites in Northern Europe, but clinical trials are conducted in the U.S., Singapore, Japan, and a number of other countries worldwide. The fact that a growing number of Medica's new medicinal drugs are developed in close collaboration with external partners in other parts of the world adds to the distributed and complex nature of these projects. The development process itself is highly structured and regulated by the health authorities in various countries, particularly the U.S. Food and Drug Administration (FDA). Getting a new drug approved by the health authorities entails standardized deliverables, following strict procedures, and detailed documentation, which involves high levels of confidentiality (see, e.g., the Hoffman LaRoche pharmaceutical case in Ciborra, 1996).

The development projects in Medica are organized in the following way: Work is carried out by a number of interdependent teams responsible for different parts of the development process such as clinical testing, registration, manufacturing, and marketing. Together, the managers of these teams form the so-called "core group" of the project. A full-time project director, responsible for meeting pre-established goals of cost, schedule, and functionality imposed by senior management, heads the core group. Each project director has a project assistant who acts as his or her "right hand". The project director (and his or her assistant) usually follows a project from beginning to end, while most other participants only work on the project for shorter periods of time and, in most cases, they work on several projects simultaneously. All project directors and project assistants are located at company headquarters, in the Project Management Unit (PMU). Most project members hold a university degree at master or PhD level, but their knowledge about IT and their experience with electronic media varies significantly.

Although formal as well as informal face-to-face meetings are central to communication within the projects, the dispersed nature of the organization means that project members also rely heavily on a variety of communication technologies to facilitate various modes of collaborative work. These include familiar technologies such as mail, telephone, and fax, as well as more advanced technologies like FTP, shared LAN (local area network) drives, e-mail, videoconferencing, and electronic calendars.

The CMC technology, *ProjectWeb*, which we studied, is a Web-based application of the virtual workspace type (similar to BSCW from GMD in Germany, see bscw.fit.fraunhofer.de, or Lotus® Quickplace® from IBM, see www.lotus.com), offering facilities for sharing documents, exchanging files, publishing information, event notifications, group management, and so forth. The purpose of the system was to improve communication and collaboration among participants in the drug development projects across organizational boundaries and geographical distance.

We followed the introduction and use of ProjectWeb in three projects, of which two were joint ventures that involved close collaboration with external partners in the U.S. and Europe. The three projects were chosen because they were considered to be examples of "successful implementation" by the head of the project management unit (PMU), and not because they were considered to be typical in some sense or representative of ProjectWeb use in Medica.

Data Collection and Analysis

Our investigation of Medica's use of ProjectWeb was part of a larger longitudinal field study of computer-mediated communication in the company (see, e.g., Bansler & Havn 2006; Strand 2006). Data collection started in 1999 and continued until the end of 2002.

Consistent with the focus of our research, we followed an interpretive case study approach of the constructivist type (Guba & Lincoln, 1994; Walsham, 1993). This implies that "the investigator and the object of investigation are assumed to be interactively linked so that the 'findings' are *literally created* as the investigation proceeds" (Guba & Lincoln, 1994, p. 111). The interpretive-constructivist approach is particularly appropriate for understanding human thought and action in natural organizational settings (Klein & Myers, 1999), and it allowed us to gain detailed insights into the processes related to the introduction, appropriation, and use of the technology. Moreover, this approach is also useful for discovering new insights when little is known about a phenomenon. It allows for casting a new light on complex processes whose structure, dimensions, and character are yet to be completely understood (Myers, 1997).

Data were collected in four phases, separated by periods in which we analyzed the data and interpreted our findings in the light of relevant literature. This iterative process of investigation, analysis, and interpretation, which allowed insights from one phase to inform data collection in the next, helped us focus our fieldwork, and improve the overall quality of our findings (Klein & Myers, 1999).

We have used several data sources and modes of inquiry (for triangulation). The primary data source was semi-structured and open-ended interviews, but we also examined archival data and participated in a number of formal and informal meetings with developers and users of the technology. We conducted more than 30 interviews with managers and employees in Medica. Interviewees included project directors, project assistants, members of the core management group, members of the various working groups (e.g., medical writers, production engineers, lawyers, and marketing people), as well as the designers and programmers of ProjectWeb. The interviews lasted between ½ hour and 2 hours, and all interviews were recorded and transcribed.

We analyzed the interviews, our field notes, and the archival data in an iterative manner; a process "not unlike putting the pieces of a puzzle together, except that the pieces are not all given but have to be partially fashioned and adjusted to each other" (Klein & Myers, 1999, p. 79). As already mentioned, we sought to place our findings in the context of relevant literature, and, in interpreting our data, we continually referred to relevant bodies of research on technology appropriation, genres, and computer-mediated communication.

FINDINGS

In the following, we will provide some examples that illustrate how people in Medica's product development projects have appropriated ProjectWeb and incorporated the new medium in their work practices. First, however, we will briefly describe communication practices in the development projects prior to the introduction of ProjectWeb.

As mentioned earlier, the development projects are very complex work arrangements involving people from many different parts of the organization and with work teams spread across different countries. Already before the advent of ProjectWeb, project members had for some time employed a wide range of communication technologies to coordinate work and communicate with co-workers at a distance. *Face-to-face meetings* played a prominent role and regularly took place both within and across working groups. As the geographic distribution of project members increased, face-to-face meetings became less frequent but were still given high priority. Face-to-face meetings were often supplemented with periodic *videoconferences* to reduce travel costs. *Shared LAN (local area network) drives* were commonly used for sharing documents and large data files in co-located work teams, and were typically configured to meet the specific local requirements. *E-mail* was widely used for disseminating information and distributing documents (as attachments), both within small, local groups as well as in vast international networks of people connected by *list servers*. E-mail was, of course, also used extensively for person-to-person communication, not only between distant co-workers, but also between co-located project members, for instance, when people were not available for synchronous communication. *FTP (file transfer protocol)* were often used for long distance exchange of large data files, for example, between engineering teams in headquarters and production units in China or Japan, because it was considered the simplest and most secure way to exchange files over the Internet.

In other words, project members used a whole array of different communication media, depending on the communicative purpose and content as well as the number and location of the communicating partners. They took advantage of the fact that different technologies possess different communicative affordances, and they often used several technologies in combination (e.g., e-mail and LAN drives or face-to-face meetings and videoconferences).

When ProjectWeb was introduced into this "information ecology", it triggered people to reconsider their old technologies and prompted them to experiment with new ways of communi-

cating. Over time, this brought about significant changes in established genres and communication patterns. In the following, we present four examples that shed light on different aspects of this development.

Example 1: Distributing Documents

The first example illustrates the *planned replication* of genres to take advantage of the affordances of the new medium, that is, the deliberate and predetermined reproduction of well-established genres with minimal modifications of purpose and form.

The earliest and most widespread use of ProjectWeb in Medica was for disseminating documents of all kinds to relatively large, distributed groups of people. People found it particularly well suited for this purpose because it combined global geographical and organizational reach with a "user friendly" graphical interface and a central document repository or archive. One project assistant simply described it as the "ideal communication tool":

ProjectWeb is the greatest revolution since the e-mail. You can communicate in a much better way. It's more graphical, and you have a kind of library that includes all the information. It is possible that the exact same information already has been sent as an attachment to a mail—a monthly report etc.—but it's a lot easier to find, when it's all in one spot, instead of one having to search through old mails.2 (Project Assistant, Project #1)

When it comes to disseminating many documents to many people in many different locations, the affordances of ProjectWeb were superior to both e-mail and shared LAN drives. The geographical scope of LAN drives is, per definition, very limited; and the drawback of distributing documents by means of e-mail (as attachments) is that the burden of organizing and storing the documents for (potential) future use is placed on the individual receiver.

The so-called "Project Development Plan" (PDP) provides a good example of an important document that was much easier to distribute and manage with the use of ProjectWeb. The PDP is an overall project plan that includes milestones and decision points, and it is a document for managing, planning, and coordinating work across the different groups in the project. This document must be available to all project members throughout a project's lifetime, and the company requires that it be updated regularly (at least once or twice a year). Thus, the PDP is a very voluminous document, and before ProjectWeb, it was printed in hard copies, assembled in binders, and distributed by mail.

Of course, this was extremely time-consuming, expensive and cumbersome, so it is not surprising that the PDP was one of the first documents to be transferred to ProjectWeb and distributed over the net:

As one of the first things, I have chosen to upload our PDP, which we compile once a year, on ProjectWeb. There are a lot of appendices, which are updated continually. When we had to send out paper copies... We would have just sent out a copy and then we'd get a new update. It was so irritating. But now it is on ProjectWeb, and everyone can find the latest version of the PDP, with all the necessary appendices. (Project Assistant, Project #3)

Using ProjectWeb to disseminate the document was not just much easier, faster, and cheaper, it also had the additional advantage that people could be absolutely sure that they always had access to the latest version of the document. This was not the case with the old paper-based procedure.

The transfer, or remediation (Bolter & Grusin, 1996), of the PDP from paper to ProjectWeb neither changed the document's purpose, content, nor its intended readership.

Example 2: Distributing Meeting Minutes

This is an example of *planned modification* of genres, that is, the deliberate and pre-planned effort to modify genres rules. It shows that initiatives to transfer existing, communication genres to a new medium may lead to rethinking certain aspects of the genres such as the communicative purpose, the content, and the target group. Furthermore, it illustrates how two communication technologies (ProjectWeb and e-mail) can be combined to solve a specific task.

In two of the projects (#1 and #2), the project director decided to start publishing the minutes from core group meetings on ProjectWeb instead of distributing them as e-mail attachments. This apparently quite straightforward and inconsequential move prompted a fundamental reconsideration of the purpose of the minutes. Before ProjectWeb, the minutes were only distributed to the participants in the meeting (and possibly a few others, typically project members with a particular interest in the topics discussed). However, when the minutes were published on ProjectWeb, they immediately became available to all project members.3

In the first project, the project director chose to publish all core group meeting minutes on ProjectWeb without any limitations or restrictions. This marked a fundamental break with the former practice of keeping these minutes confidential. The change was motivated by a desire to keep project members better informed and more up to date:

I would rather risk disclosing proprietary knowledge than have people being unable to maneuver. (Project Director, Project #1)

The underlying assumption was that a higher level of communication and information sharing throughout the project would motivate people to do their best and provide a better foundation for coordination and decision making in the project:

It is a question of people management rather than project management, because once you get people on board, you can motivate them, and get them all to pull in the same direction, well, ya, then work becomes the least of it. (Project Assistant, Project #1)

Interestingly, not all project members agreed with management. They did not embrace the idea of totally open communication but found that it was in the company's interest to impose some limits on the flow of information. In particular, they were unwilling to share freely information with employees outside the company's headquarters in Northern Europe:

Maybe it's best that not all employees know everything, particularly in the subsidiaries where mobility is greater. It's not sensible that an employee that perhaps has worked for a competitor is given access to our ProjectWeb only, then, ironically to return to his or her former employer. (Scientific Manager, Core Group Member, Project #1)

In Project #2, the project director opted for a more cautious approach than the director of Project #1. She decided to publish the core group minutes on ProjectWeb and thus make them publicly available, but at the same time, she decided to change the content of the minutes so that they did not contain information perceived as too confidential or sensitive:

At a core group meeting we can discuss things that are strictly internal, but then we don't record it in the minutes. If there are instances, and there have been a few, where we need some kind of minutes, then we ask the project assistant to send it out as a separate mail. (Working Group Leader, Packaging, Project #2)

In other words, the project director and her assistant created a new "sanitized" version of the minutes suitable for open publication and

continued to circulate confidential information within the core group by e-mail.

In both projects, the new practice of putting the minutes from core group meetings on ProjectWeb and, in that way, making them "public" altered, or maybe rather augmented, their communicative purpose. The original purpose was to coordinate work in the core group by keeping track of key decisions, tasks, and responsibilities. In addition to this, the purpose of publishing the minutes on ProjectWeb was to keep all project members well informed and raise their general awareness of project priorities.

Many project members found the open publication of meeting minutes—not only from the core group, but also from various other working groups—to be extremely useful because it improved communication and coordination within the project as a whole. A person responsible for the development of packaging for new products told us, for instance, that she regularly checked the minutes from the logistics group, because its decisions might have an impact on her own work.

I often look at the minutes from the logistic group's meetings to see if there is anything new in them, because it is important to packaging. (Working Group Leader, Packaging, Project #2)

While a new communication technology like ProjectWeb creates new opportunities for improving communication, it may also create new problems or difficulties to be dealt with. For instance, a general drawback associated with using ProjectWeb to disseminate minutes and other types of documents was that people had to "pull down" the files themselves, instead of receiving an e-mail in their inbox with the file attached. As a consequence, if people did not regularly check ProjectWeb, then they might be quite unaware of recent developments in the core group. To counter this and ensure that people actually received important documents, the project assistants sometimes used e-mail to prompt others that a new document had been added to ProjectWeb:

I wouldn't say that ProjectWeb in itself works perfectly, not if we don't combine it with e-mails. E-mail is something that everyone has at hand all the time. People just have to be prompted with an e-mail. (Project Assistant, Project #1)

When to send out e-mail notifications and to whom was, however, a difficult question. If e-mails were sent too often or addressed to the wrong group of people, then they would be considered a nuisance—a kind of spam—rather than helpful reminders. People in Medica already thought that they received way too much e-mail, so they were not very tolerant of e-mail found to be irrelevant or trivial:

I don't know if you have a feel for the way things work here; what a typical workday is like. But if I'm gone for a day, there'll be more than 50 e-mails in my in-box, and the work of just reading them, copying them, deleting them—because they can't stay there forever—is enormous. It takes me half a day, if I've been away for just one day. There's been an explosion [of e-mails]. (Medical Writer, Project #3)

When uploading minutes from core group meetings, the project assistant in Project #1 tried to find a workable solution to this dilemma by sending e-mail notifications to core group members only, although the minutes might also be relevant to others (as discussed earlier).

Example 3: Publishing News, Personal Stories, and Background Information

The third example also illustrates the *planned modification* of genres. In this case, however, the purposeful adaptation of genres is associated with elements of *migration* and *variation,* that is, the

unreflective and emergent reproduction/adaptation of genres that arise tacitly from the situated use of technology over time.

After having used ProjectWeb for some time, the management team in two of the projects (#1 and #2) began to rethink their whole approach to communication and information sharing. They realized that ProjectWeb could be used not only to disseminate "hard facts" and other work-related information (such as the PDP or meeting minutes). It could also be used to create a common identity or sense of belonging among project members by publishing background information, personal stories, pictures from important social events, and so forth.

The project assistant from Project #1, for instance, explained that she wanted ProjectWeb to be a living forum that inspired people and encouraged them to work hard to make the project a success:

We really want it to be a living forum, so people know that we regularly update the site and that it's worthwhile visiting it. They should have it as a "favorite" [bookmark], which they check every day to see if "there is something new." (...) News, it could be case stories. They're very good. A case is when a doctor contacts Medica and says, "we've used this product and it really helped." We send it out in the organization, and everyone cheers. (Project Assistant, Project #1)

First, she simply took existing documents, photos, PowerPoint slides, and so forth, and put them on the Web, but later she started asking people to write news items, case stories, background papers, and personal histories specifically for ProjectWeb. She became fascinated by the notion of "organizational storytelling", and how stories can be used to motivate people and create shared feelings of identity:

I recently got a hold of this book. It's called "Organizational Storytelling." Exactly. How one goes

about building the employees' sense of identity.
(Project Assistant, Project #1)

As an example, she referred to the story about the Gamma product (a pseudonym): how a single, heroic researcher—despite the skepticism of her colleagues and the reluctance of her superiors—believed so much in her idea that she succeeded in overcoming all obstacles and creating a new miraculous drug, which turned out to be a very lucrative business:

Because there is a story behind this gamma-product, and it is actually a researcher that has fought it through. (...) Because it was actually her, her alone—that is the interesting part, when you have a product that can be associated with one person. One thing is, you have a company that develops and introduces a product, but when there is only one person behind it all. It's such a unique story that isn't, so that ya, we shouldn't miss a chance at... at focusing on it. (Project Assistant, Project #1)

Many project members told us that they valued these more personal news, stories, and pictures, and that they helped create team spirit and a sense of belonging within the project:

It can also be announcements that so-and-so has just had a baby or things like that. It's neat. I think that Peter [project director] and Laura [project assistant] are good at it [striking a balance]. I mean you get the human dimension without letting it overshadow everything. At the moment, there's a picture of John [a colleague] in a kilt, from an event in Scotland, and I think it's funny to upload pictures like that. It is not something you spend lots of time on, you look at the pictures, laugh a little, and then you go on [with your work]. (Working Group Leader, Project #2)

What these examples show is that ProjectWeb, over time, triggered the gradual development of

a variety of new organizational communication genres such as the *case story*, the *private news item*, the *humorous picture,* and the *historical background article.* Although all of these context-specific, local genres resemble more general and familiar communication genres known from, for example, corporate newsletters, business magazines, and the press, they exploited many of the unique affordances of ProjectWeb as a medium of communication, for example, the broad scope and the ability to publish not only text but also graphics and pictures in a nice and inviting way.

Example 4: Co-Authoring Documents

The last example has been included to demonstrate that people often find new uses for a technology, which its designers had not originally intended or thought of. It is an example of *opportunistic modification,* that is, the purposeful, but not predefined adaptation of existing genres in response to some unexpected problem or opportunity. Moreover, it provides another illustration of how different technologies with complementary affordances (ProjectWeb, LAN drives, and e-mail) can be used in concert.

Although ProjectWeb was not designed to support close collaboration, such as the co-authoring of documents (it did not, for instance, include facilities for version control or for locking documents), after a while people were using it for exactly this purpose—despite its shortcomings.

It happened in Projects #2 and #3, which were carried out as joint ventures together with external partners in the U.S. and Europe. In these projects, the usual ways of distributing and sharing documents—via shared LAN drives or as e-mail attachments—within the working groups for various reasons did not work very well. The geographical distance made the use of common LAN drives impossible; limits to the size of e-mails (including attachments) were often imposed by the different e-mail systems; and company policy with regard to the protection of business information made using e-mail attachments cumbersome because Medica required that all outgoing e-mails had to be encrypted, if they contained confidential information.

It turned out that ProjectWeb provided a workable solution to the problem of co-authoring documents across distance and organizational boundaries. It had global reach, and it was perceived as much easier to use than encrypted e-mail:

But it is also because we at Medica have had it hammered into our heads how dangerous it is to send documents by e-mail. It [the project Web site] is a much safer place to exchange documents than is throwing them in a fax or sending them around by e-mail. And we don't fill our mailboxes either, or get the nasty messages about taking up too much space, because we've put it on the Web instead. We're very happy with it. I think it is really well suited. And we don't have to cryptograph and pack it and send passwords all over the place, so it works really well. (Project Assistant, Project #2)

It was, however, still far from a perfect solution, and in some respects, it was actually inferior to LAN drives and e-mail. For instance, people had to keep track of different document versions themselves, and they had to take care not to work simultaneously on the same document so as to avoid accidentally overwriting each other's work.

Furthermore, some project members found ProjectWeb rather awkward to work with compared to the shared LAN drives because it was not possible to work directly "on" the documents in the workspace. To work on a document in ProjectWeb, it had to be downloaded to a PC first, and when completed, it had to be uploaded again. This procedure also precluded using common multi-user services in the Windows® environment, such as locking documents, which were available when working on a shared LAN drive:

It's difficult working in ProjectWeb, I think, in the sense that you have to download it [the document], work with it and, then, you have to save it under a different name and upload it again. And then it is not very user-friendly. I think it should be like a file-server that is just there and you work on it, and when you say save, then it's saved up there. And if others go in and work on it at the same time, then there should be some standard rules so that it is read only. That's how it should be. (Working Group Leader, Marketing, Project #2)

When using ProjectWeb to support co-authoring, people often used e-mail to coordinate work, for example, by notifying others that a new version of a document had been uploaded, soliciting comments to a draft, giving feedback to the author, or negotiating the next step in the preparation of the document:

It's a place where documents are uploaded. You use e-mails to notify others that it's on ProjectWeb and where it's located. Bring it home, look at it, upload it again and give a comment, and, then, we'll take it down again. It's a replacement for the working directory [on the shared LAN drive]. (Working Group Leader, Engineering, Project #2)

In some cases, people also combined ProjectWeb with shared LAN drives to exploit the unique advantages of each technology. Typically, people in the same office or department used their shared LAN drive in the beginning of the writing process, when producing the first drafts or versions of a document. But as soon as the document reached a more final state, ready to be shared with others, it was uploaded to ProjectWeb and made broadly available to project members. In one of the projects, for instance, minutes from local working group meetings were first discussed internally via the LAN drive and later published on ProjectWeb:

Typically, I take our minutes, once they have been approved, and put them out on ProjectWeb. In some way, we have a mirror of these folders [on the LAN drive] on ProjectWeb. (Working Group Leader, Engineering, Project #2)

Taken together, these four examples illustrate how people often mix and match different communication technologies to meet their needs. The examples also show that the introduction of a new communication technology does not mean that people stop using their old tools. Instead, they seek to integrate the new medium in their work practices, combining it with the existing technologies and taking advantage of the unique affordances of each technology. In this process, they redefine not only the role and meaning of existing technologies, but also of communication patterns, genres, and work practices.

DISCUSSION

The primary concern of this chapter is to explore the appropriation process for new media in organizations—the processes by which new communication technologies are adopted and incorporated in people's work practice. Our study is premised on the assumption that introducing a new communication medium in an organization involves a mutual adaptation of the technology and work practice, a co-evolution of social and technical aspects of work within a specific locality. This is what we metaphorically refer to as an *information ecology*. The ecology metaphor draws attention to several key aspects of technology use in organizations: (1) there are strong interrelationships and dependencies among different technologies and work practices; (2) there are different kinds of technological resources and people with different kinds of skills and knowledge, which work together in complementary ways; (3) work practices and technologies constantly (co-)evolve; and (4) these practices and

technologies are grounded in local settings and evolve in response to specific material and social circumstances (Nardi & O'Day, 1999).

The analysis of the case confirms that the use of communication technologies in organizations has a strong systemic quality and is highly situated. We found that people in Medica had a wide variety of different communication technologies at their disposal and that they—as part of their everyday work—routinely used many different kinds of media for a host of purposes. They took advantage of the different affordances, which the different media possess, and used the media in complementary ways, dependent on their objective and the specific circumstances of the tasks at hand.

The introduction of the virtual workspace technology, ProjectWeb, led to complex and often unexpected changes in the established patterns of media use and communicative behavior. The introduction of ProjectWeb did not simply result in the substitution of the old (e.g., e-mail) with the new. On the contrary, people continued to use all of their "old" media, but they found a niche for the new technology, combining it with their existing communication technologies. This usually entailed a redefinition of the existing technologies and their role in the organization's communication. In some projects, for instance, the role of e-mail changed substantially. Prior to the introduction of ProjectWeb, project members used e-mail attachments to distribute all sorts of documents, but with ProjectWeb, people uploaded the documents to a virtual workspace and used e-mail to notify others that the documents were available for downloading.

These changes in the prevailing media use and organizational communication patterns did not happen overnight. Rather, they emerged slowly over time, as people became more familiar with the new technology and learned about its affordances. Thus, our findings confirm Nardi and O'Day's (1999) proposition that organizations are "filled with people who learn and adapt and create" and that information ecologies continually evolve "as new ideas, tools, activities, and forms of expertise arise in them" (p. 52):

Even when tools remain fixed for a time, the craft of using tools with expertise and creativity continues to evolve. The social and technical aspects of an environment coevolve. People's activities and tools adjust and are adjusted in relation to each other, always attempting and never quite achieving a perfect fit. (Nardi & O'Day, 1999, p. 53)

In many cases, and especially in the beginning, the use of the virtual workspace was based on remediation of existing organizational communication genres, that is, on transferring and adapting familiar genres to the new medium. This is a relatively straightforward and very common way to begin using a new communication technology (see, e.g., Crowston & Williams, 2000; Hutchby, 2001b; Yates et al., 1999). However, along with the apparent recreation of the familiar genres, users gained experience with the communicative affordances of the new medium and novel patterns of communicative behavior evolved. This, in turn, set the stage for further evolution of genres and practices.

As Hutchby (2001b) points out, the appropriation and use of new media "both rely upon and transform basic communicative patterns" (p. 3). That is, while the technology itself may be fixed (at least for some time), it is difficult to control or even predict how the actual use of the medium will evolve in a given organizational context. This is, according to Hutchby (2001b), because "in an important sense, the affordances of an artefact are 'found' by its users in the course of their attempts to use it for various ends" (p. 123). The emerging use of ProjectWeb to facilitate co-authoring provides a good example. Although ProjectWeb was never designed with this purpose in mind, users soon figured out that they could support co-authoring and other collaborative work processes by combining ProjectWeb with the use of LAN drives and e-mail notifications.

The reproduction and adaptation of communication genres in Medica was always the result of a complex interplay of planned, improvised, and tacit structuring processes; and we found that, in general, it was very difficult to distinguish clearly between the different forms of structuring, that is, migration, variation, planned replication, planned modification, and opportunistic modification. Although these concepts have great analytical and theoretical value, they are difficult to separate from one another empirically. They overlap with gradual transition from one course of action to another.

IMPLICATIONS FOR RESEARCH AND PRACTICE

People in contemporary organizations have a multitude of communication media at their disposal and routinely pick and choose among them to achieve their tasks. Consequently, we have argued that understanding the appropriation of new media in today's organizations must include an understanding of how people mix and match different communication technologies and adapt existing communication genres to accommodate their communication needs.

Prior empirical studies of the introduction of new computer-based media in organizations have shown that appropriation and sustained use of these technologies is often difficult to achieve for a number of reasons. Ciborra (1996) found that groupware systems often fail because they are rejected or bypassed by users who prefer more familiar technologies, which are considered to be more reliable and easy to use. In a study of videoconferencing, Mark, Grudin, and Poltrock (1999) found that people had difficulties with setting up and operating the technology, and that their inexperience with the technology resulted in communication failures and interaction problems. Ngwenyama (1998), in a study of groupware implementation, discovered that the new technology had numerous unintended organizational consequences, which complicated the adoption process. A study of the introduction of video telephony by Kraut, Rice, Cool, and Fish (1998) demonstrated that social norms influence adoption and are just as important in determining success or failure as the objective utility of the technology. Finally, Mark (2002) has emphasized that new media may fall through because people fail to develop appropriate conventions of use (i.e., agreements on how to use the technology and for what purposes).

While these studies have demonstrated that the introduction of new media in organizations is a highly complex, contested, and uncertain process, they have not examined the interaction among different communication technologies and genres—that is, how people incorporate new media into their communicative practices by adapting current genres and creating working configurations or assemblages of media with complementary affordances. The present study of ProjectWeb suggests that this interaction is an important aspect of computer-mediated communication in contemporary organizational life, and that people are both willing and able to use a range of different media to accomplish their tasks. Therefore, as researchers we need to concentrate on the—often novel and ingenious—ways in which people *combine* several media to meet their communication needs, rather than focus on how the affordances of *individual* media affect communication behaviors. A better understanding of this process requires longitudinal field studies of how people, in practice, appropriate new media and mix them to form practical and useful configurations.

The complex, dynamic, and often highly problematic nature of the appropriation process raises an important practical question: How can we facilitate the introduction and appropriation of new media in organizations? There are no simple, straightforward, and general strategies for how to do so, but one obvious starting point would be to acknowledge that the appropriation of new media requires substantial time and effort. Too often, managers and technologists seriously underestimate the attention, support, and resources it takes to successfully introduce new communication technologies in an organization.

The appropriation of a new medium involves a mutual adaptation of technology and organization. Advanced computer-based communication technologies, such as groupware or desktop conferencing systems, are generic, general-purpose media that must be customized to the local context of use. And local work practices, communication patterns, conventions, and genres must be adapted to take advantage of the new technological opportunities. The users of the technology must necessarily play a key role in this process because they have an intimate knowledge of the local needs and circumstances, and they are the ones who are required to change their behavior and adjust to the new technology.

However, the enrollment of users and their active participation in the mutual adaptation of technology and organization requires three things. First, they must be given the necessary time to take part in the process. Second, they must be allowed to "play around" and experiment with the new technology to explore its affordances and discover its potential uses. Third, they must be provided with ongoing support and resources, for example, in terms of training and access to technical expertise. This can be organized, for instance, by creating a new position as gardener (Nardi & O'Day, 1999) or mediator (Orlikowski, Yates, Okamura, & Fujimoto, 1995), responsible for customizing the technology and helping users. Several studies have indicated that such gardeners or mediators can have an important function by assisting users and enabling them to integrate the new technology in their work practice (Bansler & Havn, 2006; Gantt & Nardi, 1992; Henriksen, Nicolajsen, & Pors, 2002; Orlikowski et al., 1995).

ACKNOWLEDGMENT

We are grateful to the employees of Medica who participated in this research. We also thank Erling Havn, Dixi L. Strand (earlier Henriksen) and Jens K. Pors for their assistance in the fieldwork. This study was supported in part by a grant from the Danish Research Councils (grant no. 99-00-092).

REFERENCES

Bansler, J., & Havn, E. (2006). Sensemaking in technology-use mediation: Adapting groupware technology in organizations. *Computer Supported Cooperative Work, 15*, 55-91.

Bolter, J. D., & Grusin, R. (1996). Remediation. *Configurations, 3*, 311-358.

Ciborra, C. U. (1996). What does groupware mean for the organizations hosting it? In C. U. Ciborra (Ed.), *Groupware & teamwork* (pp. 1-19). New York: Wiley.

Crowston, K., & Williams, M. (2000). Reproduced and emergent genres of communication on the World Wide Web. *Information Society, 16*(3), 201-215.

Dourish, P. (2003). The appropriation of interactive technologies: Some lessons from placeless documents. *Computer Supported Cooperative Work, 12*, 465-490.

Gantt, M., & Nardi, B. A. (1992). Gardeners and gurus: Patterns of cooperation among CAD users. In *Proceedings of CHI'92*, Monterey, CA, June 3-7 (pp. 107-117). New York: ACM Press.

Gibson, J. J. (1977). The theory of affordances. In R. E. Shaw, & J. Bransford (Eds.), *Perceiving, acting, and knowing* (pp. 67-82). Hillsdale, NJ: Lawrence Erlbaum Associates.

Gibson, J. J. (1979). *The ecological approach to perception*. London: Houghton Mifflin.

Grimshaw, A. D. (2003). Genres, registers, and contexts of discourse. In A. C. Graesser, M. A. Gernsbacher, & S. R. Goldman (Eds.), *Handbook of discourse processes* (pp. 25-82). Mahwah, NJ: Lawrence Erlbaum.

Guba, E. G., & Lincoln, Y. S. (1994). Competing paradigms in qualitative research. In N. K. Denzin, & Y. S. Lincoln (Eds.), *Handbook of qualitative research* (pp. 105-116). Thousand Oaks, CA: Sage Publications.

Henriksen, D., Nicolajsen, H. W., & Pors, J. K. (2002). Towards variation or uniformity? Comparing technology-use mediations of Web-based groupware. In S. Wrycza (Ed.), *Proceedings of the 10th European Conference on Information Systems*, Gdansk, Poland, June 6-8 (pp. 1174-1184). Poland: University of Gdansk.

Hutchby, I. (2001a). Technologies, texts and affordances, *Sociology, 35*(2), 441-456.

Hutchby, I. (2001b). *Conversation and technology*. Cambridge: Polity Press.

Klein, H. K., & Myers, M. D. (1999). A set of principles for conducting and evaluating interpretive field studies in information systems. *MIS Quarterly, 23*(1), 67-94.

Kraut, R. E., Rice, R. E., Cool, C., & Fish, R. S. (1998). Varieties of social influence: The role of utility and norms in the success of a new communication medium. *Organization Science, 9*(4), 437-453.

Mark, G. (2002). Conventions and commitments in distributed CSCW groups. *Computer Supported Cooperative Work, 11*, 349-387.

Mark, G., Grudin, J., & Poltrock, S. E. (1999). Meeting at the desktop: An empirical study of virtually collocated teams. In S. Bødker, M. Kyng, & K. Schmidt (Eds.), *Proceedings of the 6th European Conference on Computer Supported Cooperative Work*, Copenhagen, Denmark, September 12-16 (pp. 159-178). Dordrecht: Kluwer Academic Publishers.

Myers, M. D. (1997). Qualitative research in information systems. *MISQ Discovery*. Retrieved March 2, 2006, from http://www.qual.auckland.ac.nz/

Nardi, B. A., & O'Day, V. L. (1999). *Information ecologies*. Cambridge, MA: MIT Press.

Ngwenyama, O. K. (1998). Groupware, social action, and organizational emergence: On the process dynamics of computer mediated distributed work. *Accounting, Management and Information Technologies, 8*, 127-146.

Nicolajsen, H. W., & Scheepers, R. (2002). Configuring Web-based support for dispersed project groups. In T. Terano, & M. D. Myers (Eds.), *Proceedings of the 6th Pacific Asia Conference on Information Systems*, Tokyo, Japan, September 2-4 (pp. 81-95). Tokyo: Japan Society for Management Information.

Norman, D. (1988). *The psychology of everyday things*. New York: Basic Books.

Norman, D. (2005). *Affordances and design*. Retrieved November 23, 2005, from http://www.jnd.org/dn.mss/affordances_and_desi.html

Orlikowski, W. J., & Yates, J. (1994). Genre repertoire: The structuring of communicative practices in organizations. *Administrative Science Quarterly, 39*, 541-574.

Orlikowski, W. J., Yates, J., Okamura, K., & Fujimoto, M. (1995). Shaping electronic communication: The metastructuring of technology in the context of use. *Organization Science, 6*(4), 423-444.

Sproull, L., & Kiesler, S. (1991). *Connections – New ways of working in the networked organization*. Cambridge, MA: MIT Press.

Strand, D. L. (2007). Incompleteness and unpredictability of networked communications in use. In S. B. Heilesen, & S. S. Jensen (Eds.), *Designing for networked communications: Strategies and*

development (pp. 26-51). Hershey: Idea Group Publishing.

Walsham, G. (1993). Interpretive case studies in IS research: Nature and method. *European Journal of Information Systems, 4*(2), 74-81.

Whittaker, S. (2003). Theories and methods in mediated communication. In A. C. Graesser, M. A. Gernsbacher, & S. R. Goldman (Eds.), *Handbook of discourse processes* (pp. 243-286). Mahwah, NJ: Lawrence Erlbaum.

Yates, J., & Orlikowski, W. J. (1992). Genres of organizational communication: A structurational approach to studying communication and media. *The Academy of Management Review, 17*(2), 299-326.

Yates, J., & Orlikowski, W. J. (2002). Genre systems: Structuring interaction through communicative norms. *The Journal of Business Communication, 39*(1), 13-35.

Yates, J., Orlikowski, W. J., & Okamura, K. (1999). Explicit and implicit structuring of genres in electronic communication: Reinforcement and change of social interaction. *Organization Science, 10*(1), 83-103.

Yoshioka, T., Yates, J.-A., & Orlikowski, W. (2002). Community-based interpretive schemes: Exploring the use of cyber meetings within a global organization. In *35th Annual Hawaii International Conference on System Sciences, (HICSS'02) – Volume 8*, Hawaii, January 7-10 (pp. 271-280). IEEE Computer Society Press.

ENDNOTES

[1]   The term affordance is widely used within the fields of computer-mediated communication, industrial design, human-computer interaction, and CSCW and "has taken on a life far beyond the original meaning" (Nor-

man, 2005). However, our use of the term is based on the work of the British sociologist Ian Hutchby (2001a, 2001b) and differs from the common use in HCI and CSCW in that it is much closer to the original definition. The American psychologist James J. Gibson (1977, 1979) invented the concept of affordance to refer to the possibilities for action, which objects in the world offer to different species (humans or animals). "The affordances of the environment are what it offers the animal, what it provides or furnishes, either for good or ill" (Gibson, 1979, p. 127). According to Gibson, these affordances are objectively measurable and exist independently of the individual's ability to recognize them. Within HCI and other

design-oriented fields, the term has taken on a new meaning and denotes *perceived* affordance as opposed to real or objective affordance. For instance, Donald Norman (1988), in his influential book *The Psychology of Everyday Things,* uses the term to describe the properties of a designed object (e.g., a door handle) that indicate how that object can be used.

2   All quotes have been translated into English by the authors.

3   In principle, it was possible to restrict access to selected documents in ProjectWeb, but the management team, in this case, decided against making use of this option. For more information, see Nicolajsen and Scheepers (2002).

This work was previously published in Designing for Networked Communications: Strategies and Development, edited by S. Heilessen and S. Jensen, pp. 1-25, copyright 2007 by IGI Publishing (an imprint of IGI Global).

Compilation of References

12Snap. (2003). Mobile barcode coupons—The marketing revolution for marketeers. Retrieved May 18, 2003, from www.12snap.com/uk/help/couponsshort.pdf

3Gtoday. (2005). Retrieved November 5, 2005, from http://www.3gtoday.com

A&F Trademark, Inc. and Abercrombie & Fitch Stores, Inc. v. Gordon Rahschulte, (2001). *WIPO, D2001-0901.*

Abdul-Gader, A.H., & Kozar, K.A. (1995). The impact of computer alienation on information technology investment decisions: an exploratory cross-national analysis. *MIS Quarterly, 19*(4), 535-559.

Abowd, G. D., & Mynatt, E. D. (2000). Charting past, present and future research in ubiquitous computing. *ACM Transactions on Computer-Human Interaction, 7*(1), 29-58.

Abowd, G. D., Mynatt, E. D., & Rodden, T. (2002). The human experience – reaching for Weiser's vivion. *Pervasive Computing,* January-March, 48-57.

Abowd, G.D. et al (1997). Cyberguide: A mobile context-aware tour guide. *ACCM Wireless Networks, 3,* 421-433.

Abowd, G.D., & Salber, D. (1998). *The design and use of a generic context server* (Technical Report GIT-GVU-98-32). Georgia Institute of Technology.

Adam, D.A., Nelson, R.R., & Todd, P.A. (1992). Perceived usefulness, ease of use, and usage of information technology, a replication. *MIS Quarterly, 16,* 227-250.

Adelstein, F., Gupta, S.K.S., Richard III, G.G., & Schwiebert, L. (2005). *Context-aware computing, fundamentals of mobile and Pervasive Computing* (pp. 91-92). New Delhi: Tata McGraw-Hill Publishing Company.

Afuah, A., & Tucci, C. (2001). *Internet business models and strategies.* New York: McGraw-Hill Companies, Inc.

Agarwal, R., & Prasad, J. (1998). A conceptual and operational definition of personal innovativeness in the domain of information technology. *Information Systems Research, 9*(2), 204-215.

Aggarwal, A. (2000). *Web-based learning and teaching technologies: Opportunities and challenges.* Hershey, PA: Idea Group.

Ahearne, M., Jelinek, R., & Rapp, A. (2005). Moving beyond the direct effect of SFA adoption on salesperson performance: Training and support as key moderating factors. *Journal of Personal Selling and Sales Management, 34*(4), 379-388.

Ahn, J.H. (2003). *Issues of Mobile Business and Tele Communication Technologies.* Seoul, Korea: Seoul National University Electronic Commerce Resource Center.

Ahuja, M.K., & Thatcher, J. (2005). Moving beyond intentions and toward the theory of trying: effects of work environment and gender on post-adoption information technology use. *MIS Quarterly, 29*(3), 427-459.

AirCross Homepage. (2005). Retrieved July 20, 2005, from http://www.aircross.com

Ajzen, I. (1991). The theory of planned behavior. *Organizational Behavior and Human Decision Processes, 50*(2), 179-211.

Ajzen, I., & Fishbein, M. (1980). *Understanding attitudes and predicting social behavior.* Englewood Cliffs, NJ: Prentice-Hall.

Åkesson, M. & Ihlström-Eriksson, C. (2007). The vision of ubiquitous media services: how close are we? In M.J. Smith & G. Salvendy (Eds.) *Human Interfaces, Part II, HCII 2007.* Heidelberg: Springer-Verlag Berlin. (LNCS 4558 pp. 222-232).

Akkiraju, R., & Goodwin R. (2004). Semantic matching in UDDI, external matching in UDDI. In *Proceedings of IEEE International Conference on Web Services (ICWS),* July 2004, San Diego, USA

Alexander, J.E., & Tate, M.A. (1999). *Web wisdom: how to evaluate and create information quality on the web.* Mahwah, NJ: Lawrence Erlbaum Associates.

Allee, V. (2000). Reconfigurating the value network. *Journal of Business Strategy, 21*(4).

Alter, S. (1999). The Siamese twin problem: a central issue ignored by dimensions of information system effectiveness. *Communications of AIS, 2*(20), 40-55.

Amit, R., & Zott, C. (2001). Value creation in e-business. *Strategic Management Journal, 22,* 493-520.

Anand, K. S., & Aron, R. (2003). Group-buying on the Web: a comparison of price-discovery mechanisms. *Management Science, 49*(11), 1546-1562.

Anscombe, & Rhees, R. (Ed.) (1953). *Philosophical Investigations,* Wittgenstein, L., Oxford: Blackwell.

Anthony, D., Kotz, D., & Henderson, T. (2007). Privacy in location –Aware computing environments. *IEEE-Pervasive Computing Mobile and Ubiquitous Systems, 6*(4), 64.

Austin, J. (1956). *The province of jurisprudence determined.* Cambridge University Press.

Avlonitis, G., & Panagopoulos, N.G. (2005). Antecedents and consequences of CRM technology acceptance in the sales force. *Industrial Marketing Management, 34*(4), 355-368.

Bagozzi, R. P., & Yi, Y. (1988). On the evaluation of structural equation models. *Journal of the Academy of Marketing Science, 16*(1), 74-94.

Bagozzi, R.P., Davis, F.D., & Warshaw, P.R. (1992). Development and test of a theory of technological learning and usage. *Human Relations, 45*(7), 660-686.

Ballou, D., Wang, R., Pazer, H., & Tayi, G. (1998). Modeling information manufacturing systems to determine information product quality. *Management Science, 44*(4), 462-484.

Banco Inverlat, S.A. v www.inverlat.com, (E.D. Va.2000). *112 F. Supp. 2d,* 521.

Bansler, J., & Havn, E. (2006). Sensemaking in technology-use mediation: Adapting groupware technology in organizations. *Computer Supported Cooperative Work,* 15, 55-91.

Barcelona.com, Inc. v. Excelentisimo Ayuntamiento de Barcelona, (E.D. Va. 2001), *CA-00-1412.*

Barnes, S.J. (2002). Under the skin: Short-range embedded wireless technology. *International Journal of Information Management, 22*(3), 165–179.

Barnes, S.J. (2002). The mobile commerce value chain: Analysis and future developments. *International Journal of Information Management, 22(2),* 91–108.

Barnes, S.J. (2002). Wireless digital advertising: Nature and implications. *International Journal of Advertising, 21*(3), 399–420.

Bayne, K.M. (2002). *Marketing without wires: Targeting promotions and advertising to mobile device users.* London: John Wiley & Sons.

Bell, D. E., & LaPadula, L. (1973). Secure computer systems: Mathematical foundations and model, *MITRE Corp.* M74-244, Bedford, MA.

Bell, G., & Dourish, P. (2007). Yesterday's tomorrows: notes on ubiquitous computing's dominant vision. *Personal and Ubiquitous Computing, 11(*2), 133-143.

Benbasat, I. Dexter, A.S. & Todd, P. (1986). The influence of color and graphical information presentation in a managerial decision simulation. *Human-Computer Interaction, 2*(1), 65-92.

Benbasat, I., & Dexter, A.S. (1986). An investigation of the effectiveness of color and graphical presentation under varying time constraints, *MIS Quarterly, 10*(1), 59-84.

BenMoussa, C. (in press). A barrier-based model for justifying new ICT support: Focusing on mobile support. In *Proceedings of 7th International Conference on Mobile Business.* Barcelona, Spain. July 7-8, 2008.

Bentler, P.M. (1990). Comparative fit indexes in structural models. *Psychological Bulletin, 107* (2), 238-46.

Bessen, J. (1999). *Real Options and the Adoption of New Technologies.* On-line working paper at http://www.researchoninnovation.org/online.htm#realopt

Bikhchandi, S., Hirschleifer, D., & Welch, I. (1992). A Theory of Fads, Fashion, Custom and Cultural Change as Informational Cascades. *Journal of Political Economy, 100*(5), 992-1026.

Birkinshaw, J., & Gibson, C. (2004). Building Ambidexterity into an Organization. *Sloan Management Review, 45*(4), 47–55.

Black, N.J., Lockett, A., Winklhofer, H., & Ennew, C. (2001). The adoption of Internet financial services: a qualitative study. *International Journal of Retail & Distribution Management, 29* (8/9), 390-398.

Blackwell, G. (2002, January 25). Mesh networks: Disruptive technology? *Wi-Fi Planet.* Retrieved October 25, 2005, from http://www.wi-fiplanet.com/columns/article.php/961951

Bluetooth SIG. (2005). *The official Bluetooth wireless info site.* Retrieved November 3, 2005, from http://www.bluetooth.com

Bolter, J. D., & Grusin, R. (1996). Remediation. *Configurations, 3*, 311-358.

Booth D., Haas H., McCabe F., Newcomer E., Champion M., Ferris C., & Orchard D. (2004). *Web services architecture.* Retrieved February 2004, from http://www.w3.org/TR/ws-arch

Bordini, R.H., & Hübner, J.F. (2007). *Jason Project Homepage.* Retrieved from http://jason.sourceforge.net/

Bourdeau de Fontenay, A., & Kim, D. (2007). Interview with President and CEO of SK Communications. *Communications & Strategies, 65,* 1st quarter, 119-124.

Bovey, J.D., Chen, X. & Brown, P.J. (1997, October). Context-aware applications: From the laboratory to the marketplace. *IEEE Personal Communications.*

Boyd, G., & Moersfelder, M. (2007). Global business in the metaverse: money laundering and securities fraud. The SciTech Lawyer, 3(3), Winter.

Braudel, F. (1979). *Civilisation matérielle, économique et capitalisme XV-XVIII siécle-les structures du quotidian: le possible et l'impossible.* Librairie Géneral Francaise.

Brown, M., & Cudeck, R. (1993). Alternative ways of assessing model fit. In K.A. Bollen and J.S. Long (Eds.), *Testing structural equation models* (pp. 136-162). Newbury Park, CA: Sage.

Brown, S.A. & Venkatesh, V. (2005). Model of adoption of technology in households: a baseline model test and extension incorporating household life cycle. *MIS Quarterly, 29*(3), 399-426.

Brown, S.J., Goetzmann, W.N., & Park, J.M. (2000). Hedge funds and the Asian currency crisis. *Journal of Portfolio Management, 26*(4), 95-101.

Buehrer, R. E., Senecal, S., Bolman E.P. (2005). Sales force technology usage—Reasons, barriers, and support: An exploratory investigation. *Industrial Marketing Management, 34*(4), 389-398.

Burkhardt, J. Henn, H., Hepper, S., Klaus Computing, & Schack, T. (2005). *Device technology, pervasive computing* (pp. 57). New Delhi: Pearson Education

Burmester, M., & Desmedt, Y. (2004). Is hierarchical public-key certification the next target for hackers? *Communications of the ACM, 47*(8), 68-74.

Burmester, M., & Yasinsac, A. (2004). Trust infrastructures for wireless mobile networks. *WSAES Transactions on Telecommunications* (pp. 377-381).

Burmester, M., Douligeris, C., & Kotzanikolaou, P. (2006). Security in mobile ad hoc networks. In C. Douligeris & D. Serpanos (Eds.), *Network security: Current status and future directions.* Piscataway, NJ: IEEE Press.

Butler, M.H. (2001). *Current technologies for device independence* (HP Labs Tech. Rep. HPL-2001-83).

Cadway, R. P. (2001). *New daytrading rules.* Retrieved from, http://www.princetondaytrading.com/newsletter-princeton/NL-9-31-2001.html

Caesars World Inc. v Caesars-Palace.com, (E.D. Va. 2000). *112 F. Supp. 2d.*, 502.

Cappiello, C., Francalanci, C., & Pernici, B. (2004). Data quality assessment from the user's perspective. In *Proceedings of IQIS 2004* (pp. 68-73). Paris, France.

Castells, M., Fernandez-Ardevol, M., Qiu, J. L., & Sey, A. (2004). *The mobile communication society: A cross-cultural analysis of available evidence on the social uses of wireless communication technology.* University of Southern California Press.

Chan, Y., & Lou, H. 2002. Distance learning technology adoption: a motivation perspective. *The Journal of Computer Information Systems, 42*(2), 38-43.

Chari, V., & Hopenhayn, H. (1991). Vintage human capital, growth and the diffusion of new technology. *Journal of Political Economy, 99*(6),1142-1165.

Cheil Economy. (2005). *Digital innovation: Banking service series part 2. Jung, S.* Retrieved January 15, 2005, from http://www.jed.co.kr/SITE/data/html_dir/2005/01/02/200501020039.asp

Chen, P. (2000). Broadvision delivers new frontier for e-commerce. *M-commerce, October,* 25.

Cheng.G , & Kotz, D. (2000). *A survey of context aware computing research* (TR 2000-381). Hanover, NH: Dartmouth Computer Science Technical Report.

Chesbrough, H., & Rosenbloom R. (2002). The role of the business model in capturing value from innovation: Evidence from Xerox Corporation's technology spin-off companies. *Industrial and Corporate Change, 11*(3), 529-555.

Chimera, R, & Shneiderman, B. (1993). *Sparks on innovation in human computer interaction.* NJ: Ablex.

Chin, W., & Gopal, A. (1995). Adoption intention in GSS: relative importance of beliefs. *Data Base, 26*(2), 42- 63.

Chircu, A., & Kauffman, R. (2000). Reintermediation Strategies in Business-to-Business Electronic Commerce. *International Journal of Electronic Commerce, 4*(4), 7-42.

Chiu, C.M., Hsu, M.H., Sun, S.Y., Lin, T.C., & Sun, P.C. (2004). Usability, quality, value and e-learning continuance decisions. *Computers and Education.*

Cho, V. (2006). A study of the roles of trusts and risks in information-oriented online legal services using an integrated model. *Information & Management, 43,* 502-520.

Christianson, B., & Harbison, W. S. (1997). Why isn't trust transitive? In *Proceedings of the 4th International Workshop on Security Protocols* (LNCS 1189, pp. 171-176).

Chung, D. (2005). Something for nothing: Understanding purchasing behaviors in social virtual environments. *CyberPsychology & Behavior, 8*(6), 538 -554.

Ciborra, C. U. (1996). What does groupware mean for the organizations hosting it? In C. U. Ciborra (Ed.), *Groupware & teamwork* (pp. 1-19). New York: Wiley.

Clarke, I. (2001). Emerging value propositions for m-commerce. *Journal of Business Strategies, 18*(2), 133–148.

Colvin, J., Tobler, N., & Anderson, J. A. (2004). Productivity and multi-screen displays. *Rocky Mountain Comm. Review 2*(1), 31-53.

Cougaar Project (2007). *Cougaar: Cognitive Agent Architecture*. Retrieved from http://cougaar.org/

Cowles, D.L., Kiecker, P., & Little, M.W. (2002). Using key informant insights as a foundation for e-retailing theory development. *Journal of Business Research, 55,* 629-636.

Crowston, K., & Williams, M. (2000). Reproduced and emergent genres of communication on the World Wide Web. *Information Society, 16*(3), 201-215.

Culler, D. E., & Hong, W. (Eds.). (2004). Wireless sensor networks. *Communications of the ACM, 47*(6), 30-57.

Czerwinski, M., Smith, G., Regan, T., Meyers, B., Robertson, G., & Starkweather, G. (2003). Toward characterizing the productivity benefits of very large displays. In *Proceedings of INTERACT 2003* (pp. 9-16). IOS Press.

Daft, R., & Lengel, R.H. (1986). Organizational information requirements, media richness and structural design. *Management Science, 32*(5), 554-571.

Dahlbom, B., & Ljungberg, F. (1998). Mobile Informatics. *Scandinavian Journal of Information Systems, 10*(1,2), 227-234.

Dan Parisi v Netlearning, Inc, (E.D. Va. 2001). *139 F. Supp. 2d.,* 745.

Davies, J., Studer, R., & Warren, P. (2006). *Semantic Web technologies: Trends and research in ontology-based systems.* West Sussex: Wiley Publishing, John Wiley & Sons

Davis, F.D. (1989). Perceived usefulness, perceived ease of use, and user acceptance of information technology. *MIS Quarterly,13*(3), 319-340.

Davis, F.D., Bagozzi, R.P., & Warshaw, P.R. (1989). User acceptance of computer technology: A comparison of two theoretical models. *Management Science, 35,* 982-1003.

Davis, F.D., Bagozzi, R.P., &. Warshaw, P.R. (1992). Extrinsic and intrinsic motivation to use computers in the workplace. *Journal of Applied Social Psychology, 22,* 1111-1132.

Davis, G.B., & Olson, M.H. (1985). *Management information systems: conceptual foundations, structure, and development.* New York: McGraw Hill Book Company.

De Furio, I., & Frattini, G. (2006). A semantic enabled service provisioning architecture. In *Proceedings of the 6th Business Agents and the Semantic Web (BASeWEB) Workshop,* Hakodate, Japan, May 2006.

de Haan, A. (2000). The Internet goes wireless. *EAI Journal, April,* 62–63.

Dennis, A.R., Wixom, B.H., & Vandenberg, R.J. (2001). Understanding fit and appropriation effects in group support systems via meta-analysis. *MIS Quarterly, 25*(2), 167-193.

Deutsche Bank AG v. Diego-Arturo, (2000). *WIPO, D2000-0277.*

Dey, A., & Abowld, G. (2000). *Towards a better understanding of context and context-awareness.* Paper presented at the CHI 2000 Workshop on the What, Who, Where, When, Why and How of Context-Awareness.

Dey, A.K. (2000). *Providing architectural support for building context-aware applications.* Doctoral Thesis, College of Computing, Georgia Institute of Technology.

Dey, A.K. (2001). Understanding and using context. *Personal and Ubiquitous Computing Journal, 5*(1), 4-7.

Dey, A.K., Abowd, G.D., & Salber, D. (1999). The context toolkit: Aiding the development of context-enabled applications. In *Proceedings of CHI'99* (pp.434-441).

Dinwoodie, G.B., & Helfer, L. (2001). Designing non-national systems: The case of the uniform domain name dispute resolution policy. *William and Mary Law Review, 7,* 141-274.

Dogac, A., Kabak, Y., & Laleci, G. (2004). Enriching ebXML registries with OWL ontologies for efficient service discovery. In *Proceedings of RIDE'04,* Boston, March 2004.

Dogac, A., Laleci, G. B., Kabak, Y., & Cingil, I. (2002). Exploiting Web service semantics: Taxonomies vs. ontologies. *IEEE Data Engineering Bulletin, 25*(4).

Doraszelski, U. (2004). Innovations, improvements, and the optimal adoption of new technologies. *Journal of Economic Dynamics & Control, 28,* 146–1480.

Dourish, P. (2003). The appropriation of interactive technologies: Some lessons from placeless documents. *Computer Supported Cooperative Work, 12,* 465-490.

Duke, A., & Richardson, M. (2006). A semantic service-oriented architecture for the telecommunications industry. In J. Davies, R. Studer, & P. Warren (Eds.), *Semantic Web technologies: Trends and research in ontology-based systems.* John Wiley & Sons.

Dulaney, K. (1996, October). The automated sales force. *American Demographics*, 56-63.

Duri, S. et al (2001). An approach to providing a seamless end user experience for location-aware applications. In *Proceedings of the 1st International Workshop on Mobile Commerce* (pp. 20-25).

Durlacher Research. (2002). *Mobile commerce report.* Retrieved July 10, 2002, from www.durlacher.com

EbXML. (2005). OASIS ebXML RegRep Standard. Available at http://docs.oasis-open.org/regrep/v3.0/regrep-3.0-os.zip

Edelson, P.J. (2001). *E-learning in the USA: The Storm after the storm.* Paper presented at the Annual Conference of the University Association for Continuing Education, Glasgow, Scotland April 9-11.

Educational Testing Service v TOEFL, (2000). *WIPO, D2000-0044.*

Electronic News. (2005, Jan 27). Increased Internet banking usage. *Electronic New.* Retrieved from http://www.etnews.co.kr/news/detail.html?id=200501260143

Ellis-Chadwick, F., McHardy, P., & Wiesnhofer, H. (2000). Online Customer Relationships in the European Financial Services Sector: A Cross – Country Investigation. *Journal of Financial Services Marketing,* (June, 6/4), 333-345.

Engel, R.L., & Barnes, M.L. (2000). Sales force automation usage, effectiveness and cost-benefit in Germany, England and United States. *Journal of Business and Industrial Marketing, 15*(4), 216-241.

Enpocket. (2002). Consumer preferences for SMS marketing in the UK. Retrieved March 13, 2003, from www.enpocket.co.uk

Enpocket. (2002). The branding performance in SMS advertising. Retrieved March 13, 2003, from www.enpocket.co.uk

Enpocket. (2003). The response performance of SMS advertising. Retrieved March 13, 2003, from www.enpocket.co.uk

Erffmeyer R.C., & Johnson, D.A. (2001). An exploratory study of sales forces automation practices: Expectations and realities. *Journal of Personal Selling and Sales Management, 21*(2), 167-175.

Ericsson. (2000). *Wireless advertising.* Stockholm: Ericsson Ltd.

ESSI. (2007). The European semantic systems initiative site. Retrieved June 2007, from http://www.essi-cluster.org/

Etezadi-Amoli J, & Farhoomand AF. (1996). A structural model of end user computing satisfaction and user performance. *Information and Management, 30,* 65-73.

Evans, P.B., & Wurster, T.S. (1997). Strategy and the new economics of information. *Harvard Business Review, 75*(5), 70–82.

Excelentisimo Ayuntamiento de Barcelona v Barcelona.com, Inc., (2000). *WIPO, D2000-0505.*

Fano, A., & Gershman, A. (2002). The future of business services in the age of ubiquitous computing. *Communications of the ACM, 45*(12), 83-87.

Featherman, M., & Fuller, M. (2003). Applying TAM to E-services adoption: The moderating role of perceived risk. In *Proceedings of the 36th Hawaii International Conference on System Sciences (HICSS'03),* 191.

Feder, B. (2003, June 10). Glass that glows and gives stock information. *New York Times*, P.C1.

Fetscherin, M., & Lattemann, C. (2007). *User acceptance of virtual worlds: an explorative study about second life.* June 2007. Report prepared by SL Research Team.

Forman, D., Nyatanga, L., & Rich, T. (2002). E-learning and educational diversity. *Nurse Education Today, 22,* 76-82.

Fornell, C., & Larcker, D.F. (1981). Evaluating structural equation models with unobservable and measurement error. *Journal of Marketing Research, 18,* 39-50.

Forrester Research. (2001). Making marketing measurable. Retrieved February 10, 2002, from www.forrester. com

Fox, B. (2001, November 21). "Mesh radio" can deliver super-fast Internet for all. *New Scientist.* Retrieved November 15, 2005, from http://www.newscientist.com/news/news.jsp?id=ns99991593

Fox, C., Levitin, A., & Redman, T. (1994). The notion of data and its quality dimensions. *Information Processing and Management, 30*(1), 9-19.

Fox, J. (2008). Retrieved from, http://www.nber.org/digest/oct98/w6427.html

Fox, T.L., & Guynes, C.S., Prybutok, V. & Windsor, J. (1999). Maintaining quality in information systems. *The Journal of Computer Information Systems, 40*(1), 76- 80.

Fram, E. (2002). E-Commerce Survivors: Finding Value amid Broken Dreams. *Business Horizons,* Jul. /Aug., (pp. 15-20).

Franke, N., von Hippel, E., & Schreier, M. (2006). Finding commercially attractive user innovations: A test of lead-user theory. *Journal of Product Innovation Management, 23*(4), 301-315.

Frankel, M. (1955). Obsolescence and technological change in a maturing economy. *American Economic Review, 45*(3), 296-319.

Froomkin, M.A, & Lemley, A. (2003). ICANN and antitrust. *Illinois Law Review, 1,* 1-76.

Froomkin, M.A. (1999). *A commentary on WIPO's management of Internet names and Addresses: intellectual property issues.* Retrieved April 2, 2008, from http://personal.law.miami.edu/~amf/commentary.htm

Froomkin, M.A. (2002). ICANN's uniform dispute resolution policy – Causes and (partial) cures. *Brooklyn Law Review, 67*(3), 608-718.

Fuld, L.M. (1998). The danger of data slam. *CIO Enterprise Magazine,* September, 28-33.

Galanxhi-Janaqi, H., & Nah, F. (2004). U-Commerce: Emerging Trends and Research Issues. *Industrial Management and Data Systems, 104*(9), 744-755.

Gallaugher, J. (2002, July). E-Commerce and the Undulating Distribution Channel. *Communications of the ACM, 45*(7), 89-95.

Gallivan, M.J. (2001). Organizational adoption and assimilation of complex technological innovations: Development and application of a new framework. *Database for Advances in Information Systems, 32*(3), 51-86.

Gamper J., & Knapp, J. (2003). A data model and its implementation for a Web-based language learning system. In *Proceedings of the Twelfth International World Wide Web Conference (WWW2003).*

Gantt, M., & Nardi, B. A. (1992). Gardeners and gurus: Patterns of cooperation among CAD users. In *Proceedings of CHI'92,* Monterey, CA, June 3-7 (pp. 107-117). New York: ACM Press.

Gebauer, J., & Shaw, M.J. (2004). Success factors and impacts of mobile business applications: Results from a mobile e-procurement study. *International Journal of Electronic Commerce, 8*(3), 19-41.

Gefen, D., & Straub, D.W. (2000). The relative importance of perceived ease of use in IS adoption: a study of e-commerce adoption. *Journal of the Association of Information Systems, 1*(8), 1-28.

Geier, J. (2002, April 15). Making the choice: 802.11a or 802.11g. *Wi-Fi Planet.* Retrieved October 16, 2005, from http://www.wi-fiplanet.com/tutorials/article.php/1009431

Gertz, M., Ozsu, M.T., Saake, G., & Sattler, K. (2004). Data quality on the web. *SIGMOD Record, 33*(1), 127-132.

Gibson, J. J. (1977). The theory of affordances. In R. E. Shaw, & J. Bransford (Eds.), *Perceiving, acting, and knowing* (pp. 67-82). Hillsdale, NJ: Lawrence Erlbaum Associates.

Gibson, J. J. (1979). *The ecological approach to perception.* London: Houghton Mifflin.

Gilbert. (2004, July). No strings attached. *Sales and Marketing Management*, 22-27.

Gisolfi, D. (2001). *Web services architect, Part 2: Models for dynamic e-business.* Retrieved January 2007, from http://www-128.ibm.com/developerworks/webservices/library/ws-arc2.html

Giussani, B. (2001) .*The intimate utility, roam making sense of the wireless Internet* (pp.12-24). London: Random House Business Books.

Goasduff, L. (2004). *Gartner reports worldwide mobile phone sales grew 26 percent in the third quarter of 2004.* Retrieved June 10, 2005, from http://www.gartner.com/press_releases/asset_115121_11.html

Godin, S., & Peppers, D. (1999). *Permission marketing: Turning strangers into friends, and friends into customers.* New York: Simon & Schuster.

Gohmann S.F., Guan, J., Barker, R.M., & Faulds, D.J (2005). Perceptions of sales force automation: Difference between sales force and management. *Industrial Marketing Management, 34*(4), 337-343.

Goodhue, D.L., & Thompson, R.L (1995). Task technology fit and individual performance. *MIS Quarterly, 19*(2), 213-236

Gort, M., & Klepper. S. (1982). Time paths in the diffusion of product innovations. *The Economic Journal, 92*(3), 630-653.

Grimshaw, A. D. (2003). Genres, registers, and contexts of discourse. In A. C. Graesser, M. A. Gernsbacher, & S. R. Goldman (Eds.), *Handbook of discourse processes* (pp. 25-82). Mahwah, NJ: Lawrence Erlbaum.

Guba, E. G., & Lincoln, Y. S. (1994). Competing paradigms in qualitative research. In N. K. Denzin, & Y. S. Lincoln (Eds.), *Handbook of qualitative research* (pp. 105-116). Thousand Oaks, CA: Sage Publications.

Ha, J. Y. (2002, Jan 16). Diffusion of the use of cell phones as internal office phones (in Korean). *Joongang Ilbo.*

Hair, J.F., Anderson, R.E., Tatham, R.L., & Black W.C. (1998). *Multivariate data analysis.* NJ: Prentice Hall.

Hamblen, M. (2005). Wi-Fi fails to connect with mobile users. ComputerWorld, *39*(37), 1, 69.

Han, S. (2005, April). Understanding user adoption of mobile technology: focusing on physicians in Finland (Doctoral Dissertation). *TUCS Dissertations, 59.*

Hart, Peter D. (2000). *The wireless marketplace in 2000.* Washington, DC: Peter D. Hart Research Associates.

Hawkins, D.T. (1999). What is credible information? *Online, 23*(5), 86-89.

Hay, A. Hodgkinson, M., Peltier, J.W., & Drago, W.A. (2004). Interaction and virtual learning, *Strategic Change, 13*(4), 193-204.

Hedman, J., & Kalling, T. (2003). The business model concept: theoretical underpinnings and empirical illustrations. *European Journal of Information Systems, 12*, 49-59.

Henderson, T. (2003, February 3). Vocera communication system: Boldly talking over the wireless LAN. *NetworkWorld.* Retrieved November 12, 2005, from http://www.networkworld.com/reviews/2003/0203rev.html

Henkel, J. & von Hippel, E. (2005). Welfare implications of user innovation. *Journal of Technology Transfer, 30*(1/2), 73-87.

Henriksen, D., Nicolajsen, H. W., & Pors, J. K. (2002). Towards variation or uniformity? Comparing technology-use mediations of Web-based groupware. In S. Wrycza (Ed.), *Proceedings of the 10th European Conference on Information Systems,* Gdansk, Poland, June 6-8 (pp. 1174-1184). Poland: University of Gdansk.

Heß, A., Johnston, E., & Kushmerick, N. (2004). ASSAM: A tool for semi-automatically annotating Semantic Web Services. In *Lecture Notes in Computer Science 3rd International Semantic Web Conference (ISWC 2004)*. Springer-Verlag.

Hitachi Group. (2007). *Autonomous Mobility Support Project, Ubiquitous Location Information System Prototype Demonstration*. Retrieved from http://www.film.hitachi.jp/en/movie/movie562.html

Hoffman, D.L., & Novak, T.P. (1996). Marketing in hypermedia computer-mediated environments. *Journal of Marketing, 60*(3), 50-117.

Holmquist, L. E. (2004). User-driven innovation in the future applications lab. In *Proceedings of the International Conference for Human-Computer Interaction (CHI2004)* (pp. 1091-1092). Vienna, Austria.

Holtzblatt, K. (Ed.). (2005). Designing for the mobile device: Experiences, challenges, and methods. *Communications of the ACM, 48*(7), 32-66.

Honeycutt, E.D. (2005). Technology Improves sales Performance-doesn't it? *Industrial Marketing Management, 34*(4), 301-304.

Hsu, C., & Lu, H. (2007). Consumer behavior in online game communities: A motivational factor perspective. *Computers in Human Behavior 23*, 1642-1659.

Hsu, C.L., & Lu, H.P. (2004). Why do people play online games? An extended tam with social influences and flow experience. *Information & Management, 41*(7), 853-868.

Huang, K., Lee, Y., & Wang R. (1999). *Quality information and knowledge*. Upper Saddle River, NJ: Prentice Hall.

Hub, Y.U., Keller, F.R., Redman, T.C., & Watkins, A.R. (1990). Data quality. *Information and Software Technology, 32*(8), 559-565.

Hutchby, I. (2001). Technologies, texts and affordances, *Sociology, 35*(2), 441-456.

Hutchby, I. (2001). *Conversation and technology*. Cambridge: Polity Press.

IBM Research Labs. (2007). *Aglets*. Retrieved from http://www.trl.ibm.com/aglets

IEEE. (2005). *IEEE 802.15 Working Groups for WPAN*. Retrieved November 7, 2005, from http://www.ieee802.org/15/

IEEE. (2005). *The IEEE 802.16 Working Group on Broadband Wireless Access Standards*. Retrieved November 22, 2005, from http://www.wirelessman.org

Igbaria, M., Guimaraes, T., & Davis, G.B. (1995). Testing the determinants of microcomputer usage via a structural equation model. *Journal of Management Information Systems, 11*, 87- 114.

Igbaria, M., Zinatelli, N., Cragg, P., & Cavaye, A. (1997). Personal computing acceptance factors in small firms: a structural equation model. *MIS Quarterly, 21*(3), 279-305.

Igbarria, M. (1993). User acceptance of microcomputer technology: An empirical test. *Omega, 21*(1), 73-91.

Im, Y., & Lee, O. (2004). Pedagogical implications of online discussion for preservice teacher training. *Journal of Research on Technology in Education, 36*(2), 155-170.

Ingram, T.N., LaForge, R.W., & Leigh, T.W. (2002). Selling in the new millennium: A joint agenda. *Industrial Marketing Management, 31*(7), 559-567.

International Cooperation Agency for Korea IT (2003, Nov). Data bank. *IT Korea Journal, 4*.

Intrachooto, S. (2004). Lead users concept in building design: its applicability to member selection in technologically innovative projects. *The TQM Magazine, 16*(5), 359-368.

ISO/IEC 9594-8. (1995). Information technology, Open Systems Interconnection. *The Directory: Overview of concepts, models, and services. International Organization for Standardization*. Geneva, Switzerland.

Ito, T., Ochi, H., & Shintani, T. (2002). A group buy protocol based on coalition formation for agent-mediated e-commerce. *International Journal of Computer & Information Science, 3*(1).

Jackson, C.M., Chow, S., & Leitch, R.A. (1997). Toward an understanding of the behavioural intentions to use an information system, *Decision Science, 28*, 357-389.

Jallat, F., & Capek, M. (2001 Mar/Apr.). Disintermediation in Question: New Economy, New Networks, New Middleman, *Business Horizons*, (pp. 55-60).

Janicke, L. (1996). *Resource selection and information evaluation* (Tech. Rep.). University of Illinois at Urbana-Champaign.

Jeon, N., Leem, C., Kim, M., & Shin, H. (2007). A taxonomy of ubiquitous computing applications. *Wireless Personal Communications, 43*(4), 1229-1239.

Jin, J. Y. (2003). Strategy for Korea mobile market promotion — Based on Chasm theory. *Korea Association for Telecommunication Policies, 15*(13), 2-32.

Jini Implementation Community (2007). *Apache River Project*. Retrieved from http://incubator.apache.org/river/

Johnson, E. J., Bellman, S., & Lohse, G. L. (2002). Defaults, framing and privacy: Why opting in-opting out. *Marketing Letters, 13*(1), 5.

Jones, E., Sundaram, S., & Chin, W. (2002). Factors leading to sales force automation use: A longitudinal analysis. *Journal of Personal Selling and Sales Management, 22*, 145-156.

Joreskog, K. G., & Sorbom, D. (1996). *LISREL 8: Users reference guide*. Chicago: Scientific Software International.

Joseph, J., & Fellenstein, C. (2004). *Introduction to grid computing* (pp. 12-13). New Delhi: Pearson Education.

Jovanovic, B., & Lach, S. (1989). Entry, exit and diffusion with learning by doing. *American Economic Review, 79*(4), 690-699.

Jovanovic, B., & MacDonald, G. (1994). Competitive Diffusion. *Journal of Political Economy, 102*(1), 24-52.

Jung, L. (2004). Context-aware support for computer-supported ubiquitous learning. In *Proceedings of the 2nd IEEE International Workshop on Wireless and Mobile Technologies in Education (WMTE'04)*.

Jung, T., Youn, H., & McClung, S. (2007). Motivations and self-presentation strategies on Korean-based Cyworld weblog format personal homepages. *Cyberpsychology & Behavior, 10*(1), 24-31.

Junglas, I. A. (2003). *U-Commerce: An experimental investigation of ubiquity and uniqueness*. Doctoral Dissertation, University of Georgia.

Junglas, I. A., & Watson, R.T. (2003, Dec. 14-17). *U-Commerce: A conceptual extension of e- and m-commerce*. Paper presented at International Conference on Information Systems, Seattle, WA.

Kalakota, R., & Robinson, M. (2002). *M-business: The race to mobility*. New York: McGraw-Hill.

Kannan, P., Chang, A., & Whinston, A. (2001). Wireless commerce: Marketing issues and possibilities. In *Proceedings of the 34th Hawaii International Conference on System Sciences*, Maui, HI.

Karahanna, E., & Straub, D.W. (1999). The Psychological origins of perceived usefulness and ease-of-use. *Information & Management, 35*, 237-250.

Keen, P., & Mackintosh, R. (2001). *The freedom economy: gaining the m-commerce edge in the era of the wireless Internet*. Berkeley, CA: Osborne/Mcgraw-Hill.

Keil, M., Beranek, P.M., & Konsynski, B.R. (1995). Usefulness and ease of use: field study evidence regarding task considerations. *Decision Support Systems, 13*(1), 75-91.

Kelly, K. (2006). We are the Web 2.0. *Wired*. August, 2006.

Kiang, M., & Chi, R. (2001). A Framework for Analyzing the Potential Benefits of Internet Marketing. *Journal of Electronic Commerce Research, 4*(2), 157-163.

Kim, H. S., Yoo, K.J., & Oh, K.H. (2003). *Trends in mobile payment market and issues in policy*. Korea Information Strategy Development Institute ISSUE REPORT 3-19.

Kim, M. J. (2005, Jan 27). Fast growing mobile banking. *Digital Time*s.

Kim, T-G. (2004). Mobile spam outnumbers desktop's. *The Korea Times*. Retrieved July 20, 2005, from http://times.hankooki.com/lpage/200412/kt2004122116324753460.htm

Kim, Y.J., Kishore, R., & Sanders, G.L. (2005). From DQ to EQ: understanding data quality in the context of e-business systems. *Communications of the ACM, 48*(10), 75-81.

Klein B.D. (2001). User perceptions of data quality: Internet and traditional text sources. *The Journal of Computer Information Systems, 41*(4), 9-15.

Klein, B.D. (2002). Internet data quality: perceptions of graduate and undergraduate business students. *Journal of Business and Management, 8*(4), 425-432.

Klein, H. K., & Myers, M. D. (1999). A set of principles for conducting and evaluating interpretive field studies in information systems. *MIS Quarterly, 23*(1), 67-94.

Kmobile News. (n.d.). Retrieved February 15, 2005, from http://www.kmobile.co.kr

Koetzle, L. (2004). *IT spends follows organizational structure*. Retrieved from, http://www.forrester.com/

Kolari, J. et al (2004, June). The Kontti Project—Context-aware services for mobile users. *VTT Publications, 539*, 167-170.

Komulainen, H., Mainela, T., Sinisalo, J., Tähtinen J., & Ulkuniemi P. (2006). Business model scenarios in mobile advertising. *International Journal of Internet Marketing and Advertising, 3*(3), 254-270.

Korea Herald (2004). *Mobile banking transactions doubled in 2003*. Retrieved February 2005, from http://www.koreaherald.co.kr

Korea IDC. (2003). *Korea mobile data service market forecast and analysis 2002-2007*, p. 5.

Korea Internet Information Center. (2003). *Survey on wireless Internet usage*. p. 8.

Korea Network Information Center (KRNIC). (2002). *Survey on the usage of wireless Internet (summary report)*. p. 9.

Kothandaraman, P., & Wilson, D. T. (2001). The future of competition: Value-creating networks. *Industrial Marketing Management, 30*, 379-389.

Kraemer, K.L., Danziger, J.N., Dunkle, D.E., & King, J.L. (1993). The usefulness of computer-based information to public managers. *MIS Quarterly, 17*, 129-148.

Kraut, R. E., Rice, R. E., Cool, C., & Fish, R. S. (1998). Varieties of social influence: The role of utility and norms in the success of a new communication medium. *Organization Science, 9*(4), 437-453.

Krikke, J. (2005). T-engine: Japan's ubiquitous computing architecture is ready for prime time. *IEEE Pervasive Computing* .

Krishnamurthy, S. (2000). Permission marketing: Turning strangers into friends, and friends into customers. *Journal of Marketing Research, 37*(4), 525.

Kristoffersen, S., & Ljungberg, F. (1998). Representing modalities in mobile computing. In *Proceedings of Interactive applications of Mobile Computing*.

Lau, A.S.M. (2003). A study on direction of development of business to customer m-commerce. *International Journal of Mobile Communications, 1*(1/2), 167–179.

Le Peuple, J., & Scane, R. (2003). *User interface design*. United Kingdom: Crucial.

Lederer, A.L., Maupin, D.J., Sena, M.P., & Zhuang, Y. (2000). The Technology Acceptance Model and the World Wide Web. *Decision Support Systems, 29*, 269-282.

Lee Y.W., Strong D.M., Kahn B.K., & Wang R.Y. (2002). AIMQ: a methodology for information quality assessment. *Information and Management, 40*, 133-146.

Lee, J., & Lee, S. (2005). Developing business models in ubiquitous era: exploring contradictions in demand and supply perspectives. In *Computational science and its applications – ICCSA 2005*. Heidelberg: Springer Berlin. (LNCS 3483 pp. 96-102).

Lee, S. M. (2002). *Direction of the policy for m-commerce.* Retrieved February 22, 2005, from http://agent.itfind

Lee, Y. J. (2003). *Understanding m-commerce and analyzing its services.* Seoul, Korea: Seoul National University Electronic Commerce Resource Center (ECRC).

Lemire, E. (1995). Ensuring the integrity of information. *Systems Management, 23*(1), 54-58.

Leppaniemi, M., Karjaluoto, H., & Salo, J. (2004). The success factors of mobile advertising value chain. *E-Business Review,* (IV), 93-97.

Li, C., Chawla, S., Rajan, U., & Sycara, K. P. (2004). Mechanism design for coalition formation and cost sharing in group-buying markets. *Electronic Commerce Research and Applications, 3*(4), 341-354.

Liang, T.P. (1987). User interface design for decision support systems: A self-adaptive approach. *Information & Management, 12,* 181-193.

Liebermann, Y., Stashevsky, S. (2002). Perceived risks as barriers to Internet and e-commerce usage. *Qualitative Market Research, 5*(4), 291-300.

Lilien, G. L., Morrison, P. D., Searls, K., Sonnack, M., & von Hippel, E. (2002). Performance assessment of the lead user idea-generation process for the new product development. *Management Science, 48*(8), 1042-1059.

Lim, K.H., & Benbasat, I. (2000). The effects of multimedia on perceived equivocality and perceived usefulness of information systems. *MIS Quarterly, 24*(3), 449-471.

Lin, H. & Lu, I. (2000). Toward an understanding of the behavioral intention to use a Web site. *International Journal of Information Management, 20,* 197-208.

Lin, H. (2007). The role of online and offline features in sustaining virtual communities. *Internet Research, 17*(2), 119-138.

Lindseth, P.L. (1999). Democratic legitimacy and the administrative character of supranationalism: The example of the European Community. *Columbia Law Review, 99,* 628.

Lion Nathan Limited v Wallace Waugh, (2000). WIPO, *D2000-0030.*

Little, D., & Misra, S. (1994). Auditing for database integrity. *Journal of Systems Management, 45*(8), 6-10.

Liu, C., Marchewka, J., Lu, J., Yu, C. (2005). Beyond concern: a privacy-trust-behavioral intention model of electronic commerce. *Information & Management, 41*(2), 289-304.

Lucas, H. C., & Spitler, V. K. (2000). Implementation in a world of workstations and networks. *Information and Management, 38*(2), 119-128

Lukowicz, P., Timm-Giel, A., Lawo, M., & Herzog, O. (2007). Wearable computing. *IEEE-Pervasive Computing Mobile and Ubiquitous Systems, 6*(4).

Lumpkin, G.T., & Dess, G.G. (1996). Clarifying the entrepreneurial orientation construct and linking it to performance. *Academy of Management Review, 21*(1), 135-172.

Lüthje, C., & Herstatt, C. (2004). The lead user method: an outline of empirical findings and issues for future research. *R&D Management, 34*(5), 553-658.

Lyytinen, K. & Yoo, Y. (2002). Issues and challenges in ubiquitous computing. *Communications of the ACM, 45*(12), 62-65.

Lyytinen, K., & Y. Yoo (2002). The next wave of nomadic computing: A research agenda for information systems research. *Information Systems Research, 13*(4), 377-388.

Madsen, S.R. (2004). Academic service learning in human resource management education. *Journal of Education for Business,* 328-332.

Mahmoud, Q. (2005). *Service-oriented architecture (SOA) and Web services: The road to enterprise application integration (EAI).* Technical Articles, Sun Development Network. Retrieved October 19, 2005, from http://java.sun.com/developer/technicalArticles/WebServices/soa/

Management of Internet Names and Addresses (White Paper), (1998). *63 Fed. Reg.* 31,741

Mangels, A., & Volckart, O. (1999). Are the roots of the modern Lex Mercatoria really medieval? *Southern Economic Journal*, 65.

Mark, G. (2002). Conventions and commitments in distributed CSCW groups. *Computer Supported Cooperative Work*, 11, 349-387.

Mark, G., Grudin, J., & Poltrock, S. E. (1999). Meeting at the desktop: An empirical study of virtually collocated teams. In S. Bødker, M. Kyng, & K. Schmidt (Eds.), *Proceedings of the 6th European Conference on Computer Supported Cooperative Work*, Copenhagen, Denmark, September 12-16 (pp. 159-178). Dordrecht: Kluwer Academic Publishers.

Martin, D., Burstein, M., Hobbs, J., Lassila, O., McDermott, D., McIlraith, S., et al. (2004). *OWL-S: Semantic markup for Web services, version 1.1.* Available at http://www.daml.org/services/owl-s/1.1/overview/

Mathieson, K. & Chin, W.C. (2001). Extending the technology acceptance model: the influence of perceived user resources. *The Data Base for Advances in Information Systems*, 32(3), 86-113.

Matthyssens, P., Vandenbempt, K., & Berghman, L. (2006). Value innovation in business markets: breaking the industry recipe. *Industrial Marketing Management*, 35, 751-761.

McCarthy, K. (2000, April 7). Anoto pen will change the world. *The Register*. Retrieved September 14, 2005, from http://www.theregister.co.uk/2000/04/07/anoto_pen_will_change/

McKnight, D.H., Choudhury, V., & Kacma, C. (2002). Developing and validating trust measures for e-commerce: An integrative typology. *Information Systems Research*, 13(3), 334-359.

Miller, A.I. (2002). *Einstein, Picasso: Space, Time, and the Beauty That Causes Havoc.* New York, Basic Books.

Miller, T.W., & King, F.B. (2003). Distance education: pedagogy and best practices in the new millennium. *International Journal of Leadership in Education*, 6(3), 283-297.

Ministry of Information and Communication (MIC). (2002). *IT Korea Guide.* Retrieved June 2005, from http://www.mic.go.kr/eng/res/res_pub_itk_2002_dec.jsp

Miyazaki, A.D., & Fernandez, A. (2001). Consumer perceptions of privacy and security risks for online shopping. *The Journal of Consumer Affairs*, 35(1), 27-44.

Mobile Data Association (MDA). (2003). *Mobile Data Association.* Retrieved May 1, 2003, from www.mda-mobiledata.org/

Möller, K., Rajala, A., & Svahn, S. (2005). Strategic business nets – their type and management. *Journal of Business Research*, 58, 1274-1284.

Moore, G. C., & Benbasat, I. (1991). Development of an instrument to measure the perceptions of adopting an information technology innovation. *Information Systems Research* 2(3), 192-222.

Moreno, A., Valls, A., & Viejo, A. (2003). *Using JADE-LEAP to implement agents in mobile devices.* Retrieved from http://jade.tilab.com/papers/EXP/02Moreno.pdf

Morris, M.G., & Venkatesh, V. (2000). Age differences in technology adoption decisions: implications for a changing work force. *Personnel Psychology*, 53(2), 375-403.

Morris, M.G., Venkatesh, V., & Ackerman, P.L. (2005). Gender and age differences in employee decision about new technology: An extension to the theory of planned behavior. *IEEE Transactions on Engineering Management*, 52(1), 69-84.

Morrison, P. D., Roberts, J. H. & von Hippel, E. (2000). Determinants of user innovation and innovation sharing in a local market. *Management Science*, 46(12), 1513-1527.

Morrison, P. H, Roberts, J. H., & Midgley, D. F. (2004). The nature of lead users and measurement of leading edge status. *Research Policy*, 33(2), 351-362.

Muller, H., Leser, U., Freytag, J. (2004). Mining for patterns in contradictory data. In *Proceedings of IQIS 2004*. Paris, France.

Murdick, R.G., & Munson, J.C. (1988). *Sistemas de Informacion Administrativa*. Mexico: Prentice-Hall Hispano Americana.

Myers, M.D. (1997). Qualitative research in information systems. *MISQ Discovery*. Retrieved March 2, 2006, from http://www.qual.auckland.ac.nz/

Nakada, G. (2001). *I-Mode romps*. Retrieved March 5, 2001, from www2.marketwatch.com/news/

Nardi, B. A., & O'Day, V. L. (1999). *Information ecologies*. Cambridge, MA: MIT Press.

New York Convention, (1958). *Recognition and Enforcement of Arbitral Awards*, United Nations, New York.

Newell, F., & Lemon, K.N. (2001). *Wireless rules: New marketing strategies for customer relationship management anytime, anywhere*. New York: McGraw-Hill.

Ngwenyama, O. K. (1998). Groupware, social action, and organizational emergence: On the process dynamics of computer mediated distributed work. *Accounting, Management and Information Technologies, 8*, 127-146.

Nicolajsen, H. W., & Scheepers, R. (2002). Configuring Web-based support for dispersed project groups. In T. Terano, & M. D. Myers (Eds.), *Proceedings of the 6th Pacific Asia Conference on Information Systems,* Tokyo, Japan, September 2-4 (pp. 81-95). Tokyo: Japan Society for Management Information.

Nielsen C., & Sondergaard, A. (2000). Designing for mobility: an integrative approach supporting multiple technologies. In *Proceedings of Nordic CHI 2000*. Royal Institute of Technology, Stockholm, Sweden.

Norman, D. (1988). *The psychology of everyday things*. New York: Basic Books.

Norman, D. (2005). *Affordances and design*. Retrieved November 23, 2005, from http://www.jnd.org/dn.mss/affordances_and_desi.html

NTT DoCoMo. (2003). Sehin Rain-Apu. Retrieved March 13, from http://foma.nttdocomo.co.jp/term/index.html (in Japanese)

O'Reilly, C.A. III., & Tushman, M.L. (2004, April). The ambidextrous organization. *Harvard Business Review*, (pp. 74-81).

O'Reilly, T. (2006). *What is Web 2.0: Design patterns and business models for the next generation of software*. O'Reilly Website, 30th September 2005. O'Reilly Media Inc. Available online at: http://www.oreillynet.com/pub/a/oreilly/tim/news/2005/09/30/what-is-Web-20.html [Accessed Jan. 17, 07].

OASIS. (2007). The OASIS semantic execution environment TC site. Retrieved June 2007, from http://www.oasis-open.org/committees/tc_home.php?wg_abbrev=semantic-ex

OECD. (2002). Working party telecommunication and information service policies: Broad-band access for business. *OECD*. Retrieved from http://www.olis.oecd.org/olis/2002doc.nsf/43bb6130e5fc1269fa005d004c/a963ab2ca9617affc1256c85005d7190/$FILE/JT00136306.PDF

Olson, E. L. & Bakke, G. (2001) Implementing the lead user method in a high technology firm: A longitudinal study of intentions versus actions. *Journal of Product Innovation Management, 18*(6), 388-395.

Ong, C.S., & Lai, J.Y. (2004). Gender differences in perceptions and relationships among dominants of e-learning acceptance, *Computers in Human Behavior*.

Organisation for Economic Co-operation and Development (OEC). (2001). *Understanding the digital divide*. Paris: OECD Publications.

Orlikowski, W. J., & Yates, J. (1994). Genre repertoire: The structuring of communicative practices in organizations. *Administrative Science Quarterly, 39*, 541-574.

Orlikowski, W. J., Yates, J., Okamura, K., & Fujimoto, M. (1995). Shaping electronic communication: The metastructuring of technology in the context of use. *Organization Science, 6*(4), 423-444.

Ovum. (2000). *Wireless Internet: Opportunity and threat.* London: OVUM.

Ovum. (2001). *OVUM Forecast: Global Mobile Markets 2001-2005.* London: OVUM Ltd.

Pack, T. (1999). Can you trust Internet information? *Link-up, 16*(6), 24.

PageRank. (1997). Google. Retrieved from http://www.google.com/technology/

Pardue, H. (2000). A trust-based model of consumer-to-consumer online auctions. *The Arrowhead Journal of Business, 1*(1), 69-77.

Parente, S. 1994. Technology adoption, learning by doing and economic growth. *Journal of Economic Theory, 63*(2): 346-369.

Parfums Christian Dior v. Javier Garcia Quintas and Christiandior.net, (2000). *WIPO, D2000-0277.*

Parikh, M. & Verma, S. (2002). Utilizing internet technologies to support learning: an empirical analysis. *International Journal of Information Management, 22,* 27-46.

Park, K-Y. (2000). A study on the competition strategies on m-commerce in Korea. *Global Commerce and Cyber Trade, 3*(1), 25-43.

Patton, S. (2001). The truth about CRM. *CIO Magazine, 14,* 16-23.

Pavlou, P.A. (2003). Consumer acceptance of electronic commerce: integrating trust and risk with the technology acceptance model. *International Journal of Electronic Commerce, 7*(3), 69-103.

Pavlou, P.A. & Gefen, D. (2004). Building effective online marketplaces with institution-based trust. *Information Systems Research, 15*(1), 37-59.

Perttunen, M., & Riekki, J. (2005). *Introducing context-aware features into everyday mobile applications.* LoCA 2005. (LNCS 3479 pp. 316-327)

Pfeiffer Consulting (2005). *The 30-inch Apple Cinema HD Display. Productivity Benchmark.* Retrieved from, http://www.pfeifferreport.com/Cin_Disp30_Bench_Rep.pdf

Piccoli, G., Ahmad, R., & Ives, B. (2001). Web-based virtual learning environments: a research framework and a preliminary assessment of effectiveness in basic IT skills training. *MIS Quarterly, 25*(4), 401-426.

Pierce, E.M. (2004). Assessing data quality with control matrices. *Communications of the ACM, 47*(2), 82-86.

Pipino, L.L., Lee, Y.W., & Wang, R.Y. (2002). Data quality assessment. *Communications of the ACM, 45,* 211-218.

Prahalad, C. K. & Ramaswamy, V. (2004). Co-creating unique value with customers. *Strategy & Leadership, 32*(3), 4-9.

Prahalad, C. K., & Ramaswamy, V. (2004). Co-creation experiences: the next practice in value creation. *Journal of Interactive Marketing, 18*(3), 5-14.

Puca. (2001). Booty call: How marketers can cross into wireless space. Retrieved May 28 2001, from www.puca.ie/puc_0305.html

Quinn, C. (2001). *Mobile, wireless, in-your-pocket learning. LiNE Zine: Learning in the new economy.* Retrieved October 16, 2006, from http://www.linezine.com/2.1/features/cqmmwiyp.htm

Quios. (2000). *The efficacy of wireless advertising: Industry overview and case study.* London: Quios Inc./Engage Inc.

Rajasekaran, P., Miller, J., Verma, K., & Sheth, A. (2004). Enhancing web services description and discovery to facilitate composition. In *Proceedings of SWSWPC2004: International Workshop on Semantic Web Services and Web Process Composition.* Retrieved from, http://lsdis.cs.uga.edu/lib/download/swswpc04.pdf

Rajkamal (2007). *Mobile communications, mobile computing* (pp. 26-27). New Delhi: Oxford University Press.

Ramírez, R. (1999). Value co-production: Intellectual origins and implications for practice and research. *Strategic Management Journal, 20,* 49-65.

Rangarajan, D., Jones, E., & Chin, W. (2005). Impact of sales force automation on technology-related stress, effort, and technology usage among salespeople. *Industrial Marketing Management, 34*(4), 345-354.

Rao, L. (2002). *South Korea aims for global leadership in wireless, broadband Internet markets in information age.* Retrieved February 2005, from http://www.inomy.com

Raskino, M. (2005, April 1). *Bigger and better display will boost productivity at last.* (Report G00126172). Gartner Research.

Rawls, J. (1971). *A theory of justice.* Oxford: Oxford University Press.

Redman, T.C. (1996). Dimensions of data quality. In T.C. Redman (Ed.), *Data quality for the information age* (pp. 245-269). Artech House Inc.

Reuters, A. (2007). Hi-end Second Life profit growth stalls. Feb 8, 2007. *Second Life news center.* http://secondlife.reuters.com/stories/2007/02/08/hi-end-second-life-profit-growth-stalls

Reynolds, T., Kelly, T., & Jeong, J-K. (2005, April 6-8). Ubiquitous network societies: The case of the republic of Korea. *ITU New Initiatives Programme*, Geneva.

Rha, J-Y, & Widdows, R. (2002) The Internet and the consumer: countervailing power revisited. *Prometheus, 20*(2), 107-118.

Rieh, S.Y., & Belkin, N.J. (1998). Understanding judgement of information quality and cognitive authority in the WWW. *Journal of the American Society for Information Science, 35,* 279-289.

Rigby, D.K., Reichheld, F.F., & Schefter, P. (2002). Avoid the four perils of CRM. *Harvard Business Review, 80*(2), 101-108.

Rivers, L.M., & Dart, J. (1999). The acquisition and use of sales force automation by mid-sized manufacturers. *Journal of Personal Selling & Sales Management, 19*(2), 59-73.

Robertson, G., Czerwinski, M., Baudisch, P., Meters, B., Robbins, D., Smith, G., & Tan, D. (2005). The large-display user experience. *IEEE Computer Graphics and Applications: A Special issue on Large Displays, 25*(4), 44-51.

Robinson, L., Jr., Marshallb, G.W., Stamps, M.B. (2005). An empirical investigation of technology acceptance in a field sales force setting. *Industrial Marketing Management, 34*(4), 407-415

Rogers, E. (1995). *Diffusion of innovation (4ᵗʰ ed.).* New York: The Free Press.

Roman, D., Keller, U., & Lausen, H. (2004). *Web service modeling ontology - Standard (WSMO - Standard), version 0.2.* Available at http://www.wsmo.org/2004/d2/v1.0

Roussos, George (2006). *Ubiquitous and pervasive commerce: New frontiers for electronic business.* London: Springer.

Rubio, D. (2004, October 20). VoiceXML promised voice-to-Web convergence. *NewsForge.* Retrieved November 23, 2005, from http://www.newsforge.com/article.pl?sid=04/10/15/1738253

Rules of the Uniform Domain Name Dispute Resolution Policy, (UDRP Rules), (1999). Retrieved March 13, 2008, from http://www.icann.org/en/dndr/udrp/rules.htm

Sadeh, M.N. (2002). *M commerce: Technologies, services, and business models.* London: John Wiley & Sons.

Salam, A.F., & Stevens, J. R. (2006). *Semantic Web technologies and E-Business: Toward the integrated virtual organization and business process automation.* Hershey, PA: Idea Group Publishing.

Salter, W. 1969. *Productivity and Technical Change,* Cambridge: Cambridge University Press.

Sarker, S., & Wells, J.D. (2003). Understanding mobile handheld device use and adoption. *Communications of the ACM, 46*(12), 35-40.

Schapp, S., & Cornelius, R.D. (2001). *U-Commerce, leading the new world of payments* [White paper]. Retrieved April 4, 2008, from http://www.foreshore.net/userfiles/files/Ucommerce%20whitepaper.pdf

Schilit, B., Adams, N., & Want, R. (1994). *Context-aware computing applications.* Paper presented at Workshop on Mobile Computing Systems and Applications, Santa Cruz, CA, U.S.

Schiller, J. (2004). *Telecommunication systems, mobile communications* (pp. 7-8). New Delhi: Pearson Education

Schillewaert, N., Ahearnw, M., Frambach, R.T., & Moenaert, R.K. (2005). The adoption of information technology in the sales force. *Industrial Marketing Management, 34,* 323-336

Schmidt, A., & Laerhoven, K.V. (2001, August). How to build smart appliances? *IEEE Personal Communications,* 66-71.

Schreier, M. & Prügl, R. (2006). *Extending lead user theory: antecedents and consequences of consumers' lead userness.* Working paper. Vienna University of Economics and Business Administration.

Schrick, B. (2002). Wireless broadband in a box. *IEEE Spectrum.* Retrieved November 19, 2005, from http://www.spectrum.ieee.org/WEBONLY/publicfeature/jun02/wire.html

Schwartz, E. (2001, September 26). Free wireless networking movement gathers speed. *InfoWorld.* Retrieved December 5, 2005, from http://www.infoworld.com/articles/hn/xml/01/09/26/010926hnfreewireless.xml

Seita, Y., Yamamoto, H., & Ohta, T. (2002). Mobairu wo Riyoushitari Aiaru Taimu Maaketingu ni Kansuru Kenkyu. In *Proceedings of the 8th Symposium of Information Systems for Society*, Tokyo, Japan.

Selim, H.M. (2003). An empirical investigation of student acceptance of course websites. *Computer and Education, 40,* 343-360.

Shankaranarayan, G., Ziad, M., & Wang R.Y. (2003). Managing data quality in dynamic decision environments. *Journal of Database Management, 14*(4), 14-32.

Sharma, V. (2007, December). Case study – Meru Taxis driven by technology. *Information Technology,* 54-55.

Sharp, R., & Rehman, K. (2005). The 2005 UbiApp Workshop: What makes good application-led research? *Pervasive Computing, 4*(3), 79-82.

Sheasley, W.D., 2000, Taking an Options Approach to New Technology Development, *Research Technology Management,* 43 (6): 37-43(7)

Shehory, O., & Kraus, S. (1996) Formation of overlapping coalitions for precedence-ordered task-execution among autonomous agents. In *Proceedings of the 2nd International Conference on Multiagent Systems.*

Shilit, B.N. (1995). *A context-aware system architecture for mobile distributed computing.* Ph.D. thesis, Dept of Computer Science, Columbia University.

Shilit, B.N., Adams, N., & Roywant (1994). Context-aware computing applications. In *Proceedings of the Workshop on Mobile Computing Systems and Applications.* IEEE.

Shin, B., & Lee, H.G. (2005). Ubiquitous computing-driven business models: A case of SK Telecom's financial services. *Electronic Markets, 15*(1), 4-12.

Shin, D. (2007). User acceptance of mobile Internet: Implication for convergence technologies. *Interacting with Computers, 19*(4), 45-59.

Siau, K., & Shen, Z. (2003). Mobile communications and mobile services. *International Journal of Mobile Communications, 1*(1/2), 3–14.

Sigurdson, J., & Ericsson, P. (2003). New services in 3G—new business models for strumming and video. *International Journal of Mobile Communications, 1*(1/2), 15–34.

Sivashanmugam, K., Verma, K., Sheth, A. P., & Miller, J. A. (2003). Adding semantics to Web services standards. In *Proceedings of The 2003 International Conference on Web Services (ICWS'03)* (pp. 395-401).

SK Telecom. (2001). Retrieved November 5, 2001, from http://www.sktelecom.com/kor/cyberpr/press/1183403_3261.html

SK Telecom. (2002, February). Retrieved February 4, 2002, from http://www.sktelecom.com/kor/cyberpr/press/1183603_3261.html

SK Telecom. (2002, July). Retrieved July 29, 2002, from http://www.sktelecom.com/kor/cyberpr/press/1188252_3261.html

SK Telecom. (2004). Press release dated August 3. Retrieved July 25, 2005, from http://www.sktelecom.com/kor/cyberpr/press/1194806_3261.html

Solomon, M. D. (2005). It's all about the data. *Information Systems Management, 22*(3), 75-80.

Solum, L.B. (2004). Procedural justice. *Southern California Law Review, 78*(1), 181-322.

Song, J., & Kim, Y. (2006). Social influence process in the acceptance of a virtual community. *Information System Frontier, 8*, 241-252.

Song, W. J. (2004). *Press release dated February 15.* Retrieved July 25, 2005, from http://www.zdnet.co.kr/news/network/0,39031016,10067682,00.htm

Speier, C., & Venkatesh, V. (2002). The hidden Minefields in the adoption of sales force automation technologies. *Journal of Marketing, 66*(3), 98-111

Sproull, L., & Kiesler, S. (1991). *Connections – New ways of working in the networked organization.* Cambridge, MA: MIT Press.

Steiner, J., Neuman, C., & Schiller, J. I. (1988). Kerberos and authentication service for open network systems. In *Proceedings of USENIX*, Dallas, TX.

Stevens, G.R. and McElhill, F. 2000, A qualitative study and model of the use of e-mail in organizations, *Electronic Networking Applications and Policy*, 10 (4): 271-283.

Strand, D. L. (2007). Incompleteness and unpredictability of networked communications in use. In S. B. Heilesen, & S. S. Jensen (Eds.), *Designing for networked communications: Strategies and development* (pp. 26-51). Hershey: Idea Group Publishing.

Strong, D.M., Lee, Y.W., & Wang, R.Y. (1997). Data quality in context. *Communications of the ACM, 40*(5), 103-110.

Struss, J., El-Ansary, A. and Frost, R. 2003, *E-Marketing*, 3rd edition, Prentice Hall, New Jersey.

Sun Microsystems. (2007). *Jini™ Technology Surrogate Home.* Retrieved from https://surrogate.dev.java.net/

Szajna, B. (1996). Empirical evaluation of the revised technology acceptance model. *Management Science, 42*(1), 85-92.

Talukder, A.K. & Yavagal, R.R. (2005). *Introduction, mobile computing* (pp. 7-8). New Delhi: Tata McGraw Hill.

Tao, A.L. (2002). *KTF takes on m-commerce with e-coupons.* Retrieved January 2005, from http://www.asiatele.com/printarticle.cfm?artid=15534

Tarasewich, P. (2003). Designing mobile commerce applications. *Communications of the ACM, 46*(12), 57-60.

Taylor S., & Todd, P. (1995). Understanding information technology usage: a test of competing models. *Information Systems Research, 6*(2), 144-176.

Telecom Italia Labs (TiLab) (2007). *Jade: Java Agent Development Framework.* Retrieved from http://jade.tilab.com/

Telecom Trends International. (2003). M-commerce poised for rapid growth, says Telecom Trends International. Retrieved October 27, 2003, from www.telecomtrends.net/pages/932188/index.htm

Telstra v Nuclear Marshmallows, (2000). *WIPO, D2000-0003.*

Teo, T.S.H., & Choo, W.Y. (2001). Assessing the impact of using the Internet for competitive intelligence. *Information and Management, 39*, 67-83.

Thatcher, J., & George, J. (2004). Commitment, trust, and social involvement: An exploratory study of antecedents to Web shopper loyalty. *Journal of Organizational Computing and Electronic Commerce, 14*(4), 243-268.

The Economist (2006). Living a second life: Virtual economy. *The Economist,* 28 April, 2006.

Thong, J.Y.L., Hong, W., & Tam, K.Y. (2002). Understanding user acceptance of digital libraries: what are the roles of interface characteristics, organizational context, and individual differences? *International Journal of Human-Computer Studies, 57*, 215-242.

Thornburgh, E. (2001). Fast, cheap and out of control: Lessons from the ICANN dispute resolution process. *Journal of Small and Emerging Law, 7.*

Timmers, P. (1998). Business models for electronic markets. *Electronic Markets, 8*(2), 3-8.

Trifonova, A. (2006, March 21). *Towards hoarding content in m-learning context.* PhD thesis, University of Trento, Italy.

Trifonova, A., & Ronchetti, M. (2003, August 30-September 1). A general architecture to support mobility in learning. In *Proceedings of the 4th IEEE International Conference on Advanced Learning Technologies (ICALT 2004 - Crafting Learning within Context),* Joensuu, Finland.

Trifonova, A., & Ronchetti, M. (2003, November 7-11). Where is mobile learning going? In *Proceedings of The World Conference on E-learning in Corporate, Government, Healthcare, & Higher Education (E-Learn 2003),* Phoenix, Arizona.

Trifonova, A., & Ronchetti, M. (2005, June 27- July 2). Hoarding content in an m-learning system. In *Proceedings of the World Conference on Educational Multimedia, Hypermedia and Telecommunications (ED-Media 2005)* (pp. 4786-4794). Montreal, Canada.

Tsai, H.-R., & Chen, T. (2008). Online collaborative stock control and selling among e-retailers. *Lecture Notes in Computer Science, 4947,* 613-620.

Tsvetovat, M., Sycara, K., Chen, Y., & Ying, J. (2000). Customer coalitions in the electronic marketplace. In *Proceedings of the 3rd Workshop on Agent Mediated Electronic Commerce.*

Turban, E., Aaronson, J., & Liang, T.P. (2006). *Electronic commerce, decision support systems and intelligent systems* (pp. 744-745). New Delhi: Prentice Hall of India Pvt Ltd.

UDDI Version 3.0.2. (2004). OASIS standard. Available at http://www.oasis-open.org/committees/uddi-spec/doc/tcspecs.htm#uddiv3.

Uniform Domain Name Dispute Resolution Policy (UDRP), (1999). Retrieved March 13, 2008, from http://www.icann.org/en/dndr/udrp/policy.htm

Urban, G.L. & von Hippel, E. (1988). Lead user analyses for the development of new industrial products. *Management Science, 34*(5), 569-582.

Venkatesh, V. (2000). Determinants of perceived ease of use: integrating control, intrinsic motivation, and emotion into the technology acceptance model. *Information Systems Research, 11*(4), 342-366.

Venkatesh, V., & Davis, F.D. (1996). A model of the antecedents of perceived ease of use: development and test. *Decision Sciences, 27*(3), 451-481.

Venkatesh, V., & Davis, F.D. (2000). A theoretical extension of the technology acceptance model: four longitudinal field studies. *Management Science, 46*(2), 186-204.

Venkatesh, V., & Morris, M.G. (2000). Why don't men ever stop to ask for directions? Gender, social influence, and their role in technology acceptance and usage behavior. *MIS Quarterly, 24*(1), 115-139.

Venkatesh, V., Morris, M.G., & Davis, F.D. (2003). User acceptance of information technology: toward unified view. *MIS Quarterly, 27*(3), 425-478

Venkatraman, N. (1989). The concept of fit in strategy research: Towards verbal and statistical correspondence. *Academy of Management Review, 14*(3), 423-444

Verio Inc. v Sunshienehh, (2003). *WIPO, D2003-0255.*

Veuve Clicquot Ponsardin, Maison Fondie en 1772 v. The Polygenix Group Co., (2000). *WIPO, D2000-0226.*

Vikram, J.G. with Ishikawa, C. (2007). *The T-Engine tomorrow happening today* (pp. 75-76). New Delhi. Information Technology.

Viswanathan, S. 2000. Competition across Channels: Do Electronic Markets Complement or Cannibalize Traditional Retailers? *Proceeding of International Conference on Information Systems,* 513-519.

von Hippel, E. (1986). Lead users: a source of novel product concepts. *Management Science, 32*(7), 691-705.

von Hippel, E. (1989). New product ideas from 'lead users'. *Research Technology Management, 32*(3), 24-27.

Walsham, G. (1993). Interpretive case studies in IS research: Nature and method. *European Journal of Information Systems, 4*(2), 74-81.

Walter, A., Ritter, T., & Gemünden, H.G. (2001). Value creation in buyer-seller relationships: Theoretical considerations and empirical results from a supplier's perspective. *Industrial Marketing Management, 30*, 365-377.

Wand, Y., & Wang, R.Y. (1996). Anchoring data quality dimensions in ontological foundations. *Communications of the ACM, 39*(11), 86-95.

Wang, R.Y., Reddy, M.P., & Kon, H.B. (1995). Toward quality data: An attribute-based approach. *Decision Support Systems, 13*(3-4), 349-372.

Wang, Y.S. (2003). Assessment of learner satisfaction with asynchronous electronic learning systems. *Information & Management, 41*, 75-86.

Want, R., Hopper, A., Falcao, V., & Gibbons, J. (1992, January). The active badge location system. *ACM Transactions on Information Systems, 10*, 91-102.

Watson, R. T., Pitt, L. F., Berthon, P. and Zinkhan, G. M. 2002. U-Commerce: Extending the Universe of Marketing, *Journal of the Academy of Marketing Science,* 30(4): 329-343.

Watson, R.T. (2000). U-Commerce: The ultimate. *Ubiquity: An ACM Magazine.* Retrieved from, http://www.acm.org/ubiquity/views/r_watson_1.html

Watson, R.T., Pitt, L.F, Berthon, P., & Zinkhan, G.M. (2002). U-Commerce: Extending the university of marketing. *Journal of the Academy of Marketing Science, 30*(4), 329-343.

Weill, P. & Vitale, M. (2001). *Place to space: migrating to e-business models.* Boston: Harvard Business School Press.

Weiser, M. (1991). The computer for the 21st century. *Scientific American, 265*(3), 94-104.

Werthner, H., Hepp, M., Fensel, D., & Dorn, J. (2006). Semantically-enabled service-oriented architectures: A catalyst for smart business networks. In *Proceedings of the Smart Business Networks Initiative Discovery Session*, June 14-16, Rotterdam, The Netherlands

Whittaker, S. (2003). Theories and methods in mediated communication. In A. C. Graesser, M. A. Gernsbacher, & S. R. Goldman (Eds.), *Handbook of discourse processes* (pp. 243-286). Mahwah, NJ: Lawrence Erlbaum.

Widmier, S. M., Jackson, D.W., & McCabe, D.B. (2002). Infusing technology into personal selling. *Journal of Personal Selling and Sales Management, 22*(3), 189-198.

Wilson, J. (2006). 3G to Web 2.0? Can mobile telephony become an architecture of participation? *Convergence, 12*(2), 229-242.

WindWire. (2000). *First-to-wireless: Capabilities and benefits of wireless marketing and advertising based on the first national mobile marketing trial.* Morrisville, NC; WindWire Inc.

Winkler, W.E. (2004). Methods for evaluating and crating data quality. *Information Systems, 29*, 531-550.

WIPO, (1999). *The Management of Internet Names and Addresses: Intellectual Property Issues* – Final Report of the WIPO Internet Domain Name Process.

Wu, J. & Liu, D. (2007). The effects of trust and enjoyment on intention to play online games. *Journal of Electronic Commerce Research, 8*(2), 128-140.

Wüthrich B., Cho V., Pun J., & Zhang J. (2000). Data quality in distributed environments. In H. Kargupta & P. Chan (Eds.), *Advances in distributed and parallel knowledge discovery* (pp. 295-316). AAAI Press.

Xu, H., Teo, H.H., & Wang, H. (2003). Foundations of SMS commerce success: Lessons from SMS messaging and co-opetition. In *Proceedings of the 36th Hawaii International Conference on Systems Sciences*, Big Island, HI.

Xu, Y., Yen, D.C., Lin, B., & Chou, D.C. (2002). Adopting customer relationship management technology. *Industrial Management and Data Systems, 102*(8), 442-452.

Yamamoto, J., & Sycara, K. (2001). A stable and efficient buyer coalition formation scheme for e-marketplaces. In *Proceedings of International Conference on Autonomous Agents*, Canada.

Yamazaki, K. (2004). Research directions of ubiquitous services. In *Proceedings of the 2004 International Symposium on Applications and the Internet (SAINT'04)*.

Yang, S. J. (2003, Jan 20). Korea pursuing global leadership in info-tech industry. *The Korea Herald*.

Yap, A., & Synn, W. (2008). Evolution of online financial trading systems: E-service innovations in the brokerage sector. In A. Scupola (Ed.), *Cases on Managing E-services*. Hershey, PA: IGI Global.

Yates, J., & Orlikowski, W. J. (1992). Genres of organizational communication: A structurational approach to studying communication and media. *The Academy of Management Review, 17*(2), 299-326.

Yates, J., & Orlikowski, W. J. (2002). Genre systems: Structuring interaction through communicative norms. *The Journal of Business Communication, 39*(1), 13-35.

Yates, J., Orlikowski, W. J., & Okamura, K. (1999). Explicit and implicit structuring of genres in electronic communication: Reinforcement and change of social interaction. *Organization Science, 10*(1), 83-103.

Yoo, J.-K. (2001). *Current status and implication of mobile advertising, information, and communications policy report, 13*(14). Korea Information Strategy Development Institute.

Yoon, K-W. (2003). Retraditionalizing the mobile: Young people's sociality and mobile phone use in Seoul, South Korea. *European Journal of Cultural Studies, 6*(3), 327-343.

Yoshioka, T., Yates, J.-A., & Orlikowski, W. (2002). Community-based interpretive schemes: Exploring the use of cyber meetings within a global organization. In *35th Annual Hawaii International Conference on System Sciences, (HICSS'02) – Volume 8,* Hawaii, January 7-10 (pp. 271-280). IEEE Computer Society Press.

Yuan, S.-T., & Lin, Y.-H. (2004). Credit based group negotiation for aggregate sell/buy in e-markets. *Electronic Commerce Research and Applications, 3,* 74-94.

Yuan, Y., & J.J. Zhang (2003). Towards an appropriate business model for m-commerce. *International Journal of Mobile Communications, 1*(1/2), 35–56.

Yunos, H. M., Gao, J. Z., & Shim, S. (2003). Wireless advertising's challenges and opportunities. *IEEE Computer, 36*(5), 30-37.

Zhang, D.Q., Pung, H.K., & Gu, T. (2005). A service-oriented middleware for building context-aware services. *Journal of Network and Computer Applications, 28*(1), 1-18.

Zhong, S., Chen, J., & Yang, R. (2003). Sprite: A simple, cheat-proof, credit-based system for mobile ad hoc networks. In *Proceedings of INFOCOM 2003*.

ZigBee Alliance. (2005). Retrieved November 11, 2005, from http://www.zigbee.org/en/index.asp

Zigurs, I., & Buckland, B. K. (1995). A theory of task-technology fit and group support systems effectiveness. *MIS Quarterly, 22*(3), 313-334.

Zigurs, I., Buckland, B.K., Connoly, J.R., & Wilson, E.V. (1998). A test of task technology fit theory for group support systems. *The Database for Advances in Information Systems, 30*(3-4), 34-50.

Zimmermann, P. (1995). *The official PGP user's guide.* Cambridge, MA: MIT Press.

Zmud, R. (1983). The effectiveness of external information channels in facilitating innovation within software development groups. *MIS Quarterly, 7*(2), 43-58.

Zmud, R.W. (1978). An empirical investigation of the dimensionality of the concept of information. *Decision Sciences, 9,* 187-195.

Zwass, V. (2003). Electronic commerce and organizational innovation: aspects and opportunities. *International Journal of Electronic Commerce, 7*(3), 7-37.

Zwass, V. 1996. Electronic Commerce: Structures and Issues, *International Journal of Electronic Commerce*, (1)1, 3-23.

Zwick, R., Weg, E., & Rapoport, A. (2000) Invariance failure under subgame perfectness in sequential bargaining. *Journal of Economic Psychology, 21*(5), 517-544.

About the Contributors

Humphry Hung is a visiting fellow of the Department of Management and Marketing of the Hong Kong Polytechnic University. He has more than 20 years' practical experience in training and development. His research interests include mobile marketing, creativity and innovation management, and entrepreneurship. Dr. Hung has published in several international refereed journals and conference proceedings.

Y. H. Wong is an associate professor of the Department of Management and Marketing of the Hong Kong Polytechnic University. His research interest is in the fields of ubiquitous marketing, relationship management and customer services. He has more than 12 years' practical experience in Marketing. His publications include a book, *Guanxi: Relationship Marketing in a Chinese Context* and refereed journal articles.

Vincent Cho is specialized on data mining, stock index forecasting, database marketing, yield management and e-commerce infrastructure and strategy. His research papers are published on various international journals including *Information & Management, Journal of Computer Information Systems, Expert Systems, Knowledge and Information Systems, Journal of Computational Intelligence in Finance, Journal of Hospitality and Tourism Research, International Journal of Hospitality Management, International Journal of Tourism Research, Annals of Tourism Research*. Before joining the university, he had several years of experience in systems development in some prestige international consulting firms. He is also interested in consultancy works.

* * *

Jounghae Bang is a doctoral candidate in the marketing area of the College of Business Administration at University of Rhode Island (URI), USA. Her research bridges the areas of marketing and MIS. Her research interests are customer relationship management, relationship marketing, online marketing, data mining and e-commerce. Luxury branding and service marketing are also included in her interests. She was involved in several IS projects as an IT consultant at Deloitte Consulting in Korea and as a researcher in Ewha Center for Informatization Strategy (ECIS) at Ewha Woman's University in Korea. She holds a MA in management information systems and a BA in business administration from Ewha Womans University in Korea.

Jørgen P. Bansler is an associate professor in the Center for Information and Communication Technologies at the Technical University of Denmark. His research interests include computer-mediated communication, computer-supported collaborative work, information systems design, and organizational implementation and use of IT. His current research focuses on the use of information and communication technology in health care. Jørgen Bansler holds a PhD in computer science from the University of Copenhagen, Denmark.

Stuart J. Barnes is chair and professor of management at the University of East Anglia, UK. Stuart has been teaching and researching in the information systems field for over a decade. His academic background includes a first class degree in economics from University College London and a PhD in business administration from Manchester Business School. He has published three books and more than seventy articles including those in journals such as *Communications of the ACM*, the *International Journal of Electronic Commerce*, the *e-Service Journal*, *Electronic Markets*, and the *Journal of Electronic Commerce Research*. Two more books are in progress for 2005.

Chihab BenMoussa is a senior researcher at the Institute for Advanced Management Systems Research (IAMSR). He received his MBA from AlAkhawyn University, Morocco and his PhD in information systems from Åbo Akademi University, Finland. Prior to joining IAMSR and its doctoral program, he was a senior consultant at PricewaterhouseCoopers. He combines research skills with real-world experience to identify growth and innovation opportunities where information and communication technologies could create a competitive edge for companies. His current research focuses on mobile business, knowledge management and information systems audit.

Mike Burmester is a professor at Florida State University since 2000. Earlier, he was at Royal Holloway, London University. He got his BSc from Athens University and PhD from Rome University. His research interests include privacy, anonymity, network security and watermarking and he has numerous publications in these areas. He is a member of the International Association for Cryptological Research and a fellow of the Institute of Mathematics and Applications.

Federico Ceccarini received the Laurea degree in mathematics and application at the "Federico II" University of Naples. He was with the R&D Centre for Information and Communications Technologies of Sema Group, and since 2007, he has been a research engineer in the Telecom VAS and Media Unit, of Engineering.IT. His research interests include mobile applications and services, human-computer interaction, and affective computing. At present he is involved in WiSe Research Project and was author of several papers.

Toly Chen received the BS degree, the MS degree, and the PhD degree at industrial engineering from National Tsin Hua University. He is now an associate professor in the Department of Industrial Engineering and Systems Management of Feng Chia University, an IEEE member, and an IIE senior member. He has publications in journals such as *Computers and Industrial Engineering*, *Fuzzy Sets and Systems*, *International Journal of Advanced Manufacturing Technology*, *European Journal of Operational Research*, *Journal of Intelligent Manufacturing*, *Neurocomputing*, *Intelligent Data Analysis*, *International Journal of Innovative Computing*, *Information and Control*, and *Applied Soft Computing*. He is also on the editorial boards of *Open Operational Research Journal*, and *Open Statistics and Probability Journal*.

Inyoung Choi is a postdoctoral research fellow at the Imaging Science and Information Systems Research Center at Georgetown University. Her research interests include information strategy planning (ISP), strategic use of information technology (SUIT), and knowledge management. She has over 10 years of experience in an information technology strategy development, system implementation planning and evaluation including four years of experience as IT consultant at Ernst and Young Consulting. Dr. Choi received her PhD from Ewha Womans University in management information systems.

Giovanni Frattini received his Laurea degree in physics from University of Naples. He has worked for several companies with different roles. From 2000 his focus is on new solutions for telecommunication value added services (VAS). He has covered different roles: among the others delivery unit manager and enterprise architecture champion. Currently he is working as chief architect coordinating several research and operational projects. As researcher is main focus is currently on multimodal mobile services and SOA architectures for Telecommunication.

Ivano De Furio received the Laurea degree in electronic engineering at the "Federico II" University of Naples. He was with the R&D Centre for Information and Communications Technologies of Bull HN Information Systems, and since 2000, he has been a research engineer in the Telecom VAS and Media Unit, of Engineering.IT. His research interests include artificial intelligence, rule systems for business agents, semantic web service approaches and architectures. He has been involved in several research projects, such as HiVDS, SERVICEWARE and WISE and was author of several papers. In March 2007, Ivano De Furio received degree cum laude in computer science engineering.

Vishal Jain was a Master student of Dr. Jon Quah.

Timo Koivumäki is research professor of mobile business applications at VTT Technical Research Centre of Finland and at University of Oulu. His research interests include consumer behavior in e-commerce, m-commerce and ubi environments, user-driven open innovation, e-business, m-business, mobile marketing, digital economy, information goods and sports marketing. He is the associate director of OASIS research lab in the University of Oulu. Prof. Koivumäki has published e.g. in *Electronic Markets, NetNomics, International Journal of Mobile Communications, Behaviour and Information Technology*, and *International Journal of Information Technology and Management*.

Konstantinos Komaitis, PhD, is currently a lecturer at the University of Strathclyde in Glasgow, UK. His main areas of research are Internet governance and intellectual property. Dr. Komaitis is involved in a project on multistakeholder participation and in September 2009 he will be publishing his book on domain name regulation, investigating in particular the legal nature of domain names and their relationship with trademarks.

Kaisa Koskela is a doctoral student at the Marketing Department of the University of Oulu. Her main research interests lie in user involvement in new technology-intensive product and service development and especially in the lead user approach.

Yu-Cheng Lin received the PhD degree in industrial engineering from National Tsin Hua University. He is currently an assistant professor of the Department of Industrial Engineering and Management of the Overseas Chinese Institute of Technology.

Hanne Westh Nicolajsen is an assistant professor in the Center for Information and Communication Technologies at the Technical University of Denmark. Her research interests include organizational implementation and use of IT, knowledge management, and computer-mediated communication. Her current research focus is on the use of information and communication technology for innovation in the service sector. Hanne Nicolajsen holds a PhD from the Technical University of Denmark.

Teea Palo is a doctoral student at the Marketing Department of the University of Oulu. Her main research interests lie in strategic nets and their business models especially in the field of new technology-based services, such as ubiquitous services.

Jon T.S. Quah is currently a faculty staff with the School of Electrical and Electronic Engineering, Nanyang Technological University. Dr. Quah lectures in both undergrad as well as graduate courses such as software development methodology, software quality assurance and project management, object-oriented system analysis and design, and software engineering. His research interests include financial market modeling using neural network, software reliability, and Internet related topics such as e-commerce and e-learning. Other than academic services, Dr. Quah has undertaken joint projects with major companies in banking and airline industries, as well as statutory boards of the government body. Prior to his academic pursuits, Dr. Quah was a director of a local company dealing with industrial chemicals.

N. Raghavendra Rao is a professor at SSN School of Management & Computer Applications, Chennai, India. Dr. Rao has a Master's degree in commerce from Osmania University and a PhD in finance from the University of Poona. He has also three post graduate diplomas in the areas of financial management, portfolio management and tax laws from the University of Madras. He has a rare distinction of having experience in the combined areas of information technology and business applications. His rich experience in industry is matched with a parallel academic experience in management & IT in business schools. He has over two decades of experience in the development of application software related to manufacturing, service oriented organizations, financial institutions and business enterprises. He contributes chapters for books. He presents papers related to information technology and knowledge management at national and international conferences. he contributes articles on information technology to main stream news papers and journals. His area of research interest is mobile computing, space technology and knowledge management.

Luigi Romano received his Laurea degree in physics from University of Naples in 1996. In 1997 he attended the pre-doctoral school in communication systems at the Swiss Federal Institute of Technology Lausanne (EPFL). From 1997 on he was engaged in different roles for several telecommunication operators and in 2000 he started working in the system integration area of Sema Group. In the 2003 he was involved in a research project, in Atos Origin Italia, attempting to ground mobile value added services in innovative architectures. He followed other research projects related to multimodal systems and artificial intelligence and he is currently involved in a project aiming to explore the potential of semantic grid computing in e-government applications for Engineering.IT.

Roberto Russo was born in 1974, degree in computer science at Federico II University of Naples. Since 1999 he has been working for Engineering.IT (ex Atos Origin with different roles. Currently he is team leader of several projects; his research interests include human-computer interaction, mobile application and architectures. He has been involved in several research projects such as SERVICEWARE and WISE and was author of several papers.

Eusebio Scornavacca is lecturer of electronic commerce at the School of Information Management, Victoria University of Wellington, New Zealand. Before moving to Wellington, Eusebio spent two years as a researcher at Yokohama National University, Japan. He has published and presented more than thirty articles in conferences and academic journals. Eusebio is on the editorial board of the *International Journal of Mobile Communications* and the *International Journal of Electronic Finance*. His current research interests mobile business, electronic business, e-surveys, and IS teaching methods.

Dong Hee Shin is an assistant professor of the computer and information sciences, Towson University, USA. Dr. Shin was previously an assistant professor at the College of Information Sciences and Technology, Penn State University (2004-2008). Dr. Shin earned his PhD and Master degrees in information sciences and technology from Syracuse University. Dr. Shin focuses on human-computer interaction and technology management in organization, market, and policy contexts. Dr. Shin was the vice chair of the 2006 International Conference on Telecommunication Systems. His project was funded by the Korea Communications Commission. Dr. Shin has published 32 articles in international journals and presented at 30 conferences. Dr. Shin was nominated for an Information Management and Technology Interdisciplinary Fellowship at the Syracuse University in 2005 and received an Outstanding Researcher Award at the Penn State University in 2007.

Jaana Tähtinen is professor of marketing at the University of Oulu, Finland. Her main research interests include dissolution and dynamics of business relationships, mobile advertising, and value creation in business networks. She has published e.g. in the *European Journal of Marketing, Industrial Marketing Management, International Journal of Service Industry Management, and Marketing Theory*. She has also co-edited a special issue on relationship dissolution in *Journal of Marketing Management* and is one of the founders of biannual Nordic Workshop on Relationship Dynamics (from 2000).

Anna Trifonova has graduated at New Bulgarian University (Sofia, Bulgaria) in 1999. Her specialty was information systems and technologies - applications in business and office. She finished her PhD at the International Graduate School of Information and Communication Technologies at the University of Trento, Italy in March 2006. Her research topic was "Mobile Learning: Wireless and Mobile Technologies in Education". Her scientific interests and publications to that time are mainly in the mobile learning domain, and starting from year 2003 she has more than 15 articles in international peer-reviewed conferences and workshops on this topic.

Horng-Ren Tsai received the PhD degree at electrical engineering from National Taiwan University of Science and Technology. He is currently an associate professor of the Department of Information Technology at Lingtung University.

Yi-Chi Wang received the PhD degree in industrial engineering from Mississippi State University. He is currently an assistant professor of the Department of Industrial Engineering and Systems Management of Feng Chia University.

Alexander Y. Yap is an associate professor of information systems at Elon University, North Carolina. He holds a PhD degree in information systems from Copenhagen Business School (Denmark), an MBA in international management from Exeter University (UK), and a Master's in development economics from Williams College (USA). He won the prestigious 'ICIS Best Paper Award' in Helsinki, Finland. His research papers have been published in the *Journal of Global Information Management*, the *Journal of E-Commerce Research, Journal of Electronic Markets*, and the *Journal of Enterprise Information Systems*, among others. He has also published in prestigious IS conferences, which include the ICIS, ECIS, and ACM.

Zhijun Zhang received his bachelor's degree in computer science from Peking University, Beijing, China, in 1990. He developed computer software for three years before starting his graduate study at the University of Maryland, where he conducted research in software engineering and human-computer interaction. He received his PhD degree in computer science from the University of Maryland in 1999. Besides teaching at University of Phoenix, Dr. Zhang was a technology researcher at a large financial service company, focusing on emerging mobile technologies and their impact on human-computer interaction. He is now an enterprise architect for the same company, working on service-oriented architecture and other strategic architecture initiatives.

Index